T0374797

THE I TATTI
RENAISSANCE LIBRARY

James Hankins, General Editor

SALUTATI

POLITICAL WRITINGS

ITRL 64

THE I TATTI RENAISSANCE LIBRARY

James Hankins, General Editor
Shane Butler, Associate Editor
Martin Davies, Associate Editor
Leah Whittington, Associate Editor
Ornella Rossi, Assistant Editor

Editorial Board

Michael J. B. Allen
Francesco Bausi
Brian P. Copenhaver
Vincenzo Fera
Julia Haig Gaisser
Walther Ludwig
Nicholas Mann
Silvia Rizzo

Advisory Committee

Lino Pertile, Chairman

Robert Black	Massimo Miglio
Michele Ciliberto	John Monfasani
Caroline Elam	John O'Malley
Arthur Field	Marianne Pade
Anthony Grafton	David Quint
Hanna Gray	Christine Smith
Ralph Hexter	Rita Sturlese
Craig Kallendorf	Francesco Tateo
Jill Kraye	Mirko Tavoni
Marc Laureys	Carlo Vecce
Francesco Lo Monaco	Ronald Witt
David Marsh	Jan Ziolkowski

COLUCCIO SALUTATI
✦ ✦ ✦
POLITICAL WRITINGS

EDITED BY

STEFANO U. BALDASSARRI

TRANSLATED BY

ROLF BAGEMIHL

THE I TATTI RENAISSANCE LIBRARY
HARVARD UNIVERSITY PRESS
CAMBRIDGE, MASSACHUSETTS
LONDON, ENGLAND
2014

Copyright © 2014 by the President and Fellows of Harvard College
All rights reserved
Printed in the United States of America

Series design by Dean Bornstein

Library of Congress Cataloging-in-Publication Data

Salutati, Coluccio, 1331–1406.
[Works. Selections. English. 2014]
Political writings / Coluccio Salutati ; edited by Stefano U. Baldassarri ;
translated by Rolf Bagemihl.
pages cm. — (The I Tatti Renaissance library)
English translation on the recto with original Latin text on the verso.
Includes bibliographical references and index.
ISBN 978-0-674-72867-7 (alkaline paper) 1. Salutati, Coluccio, 1331–1406 —
Political and social views. 2. Salutati, Coluccio, 1331–1406 —
Correspondence. 3. Florence (Italy) — Politics and government —
To 1421 — Sources. 4. Political science — Italy — History — To 1500 —
Sources. 5. Despotism — Early works to 1800. 6. Statesmen — Italy —
Florence — Correspondence. I. Baldassarri, Stefano Ugo. II. Bagemihl,
Rolf. III. Salutati, Coluccio, 1331–1406. De tyranno. English. IV. Title.
DG737.24.S26A25 2014
320.01 — dc23   2014011725

Contents

ॐ§§ॐ

Introduction

꽃ৄৢ

Scholars of Italian humanism tend to depict Coluccio Salutati as a Janus-like figure, a man at a crossroads, an author on the threshold of a new era that he himself has significantly contributed to usher in while retaining some no-less-significant features of the age about to disappear. There is solid evidence to justify this view of Salutati, as shown in the next pages, discussing his writings collected in the present anthology. Yet a widespread consequence of such an approach—especially when brought to extremes without contextualizing this humanist's figure—is that modern readers (even the most knowledgeable) are often disappointed by Salutati's work, finding it both inconsistent and below their high expectations. In regard to what is tempting to call the "demon" of consistency, one of the dogmas of literary criticism today, suffice it to say that if this were the main criterion for judging authors we should dismiss, among others, Plato, Cicero, Dante, and Tolstoy for lack of coherence either between their various works or between theory and practice. Speaking, instead, of high expectations (another sort of contemporary "fundamentalism," though this time one that trespasses by far the boundaries of literary criticism), the twentieth century has furnished many examples of scholars projecting their own desires and political agendas onto the subjects they studied. A well-known case is Hans Baron's distorted (and yet highly influential) view of the wars that Florence fought against Milan between the end of the fourteenth and the first half of the fifteenth centuries.[1] Interestingly, this very conflict constitutes the background to Salutati's *De tyranno*, many of his state letters, and his long reply to Loschi's invective against the Florentines, all of which are edited and translated in this volume. Putting aside our own ideological velleities, let us then try to contextualize briefly

the writings chosen for this anthology and provide, first of all, some basic information on Salutati's life and major works.[2]

Like most chancellors of Florence in the late Middle Ages and the early Renaissance, Coluccio Salutati (1331–1406) was born in the *contado* (as Florentine territory was then called), in Stignano, a hamlet close to the border with Lucca. His family was of rather humble condition,[3] and his father, Piero, was a notary by profession. Since the latter served Taddeo de' Pepoli, lord of Bologna, it was there that Salutati was raised and educated, studying rhetoric with Piero da Moglio (a disciple of Petrarch) first and being trained in the *ars notaria* later, just as his father was before him.[4] His early career led him to serve for several years as notary, chancellor, and secretary in various places (his hometown first, then Todi, and finally the papal curia). He later became *Segretario delle Riformagioni* (legislative secretary) of Lucca in 1370, before being appointed Chancellor of Florence in 1375, a post that he kept until his death, in May 1406. The chancellorship of this city was conferred on him just two months before the so-called "War of the Eight Saints" (1375–78) broke out between Florence and the Church.[5] This crisis — caused by the menacing expansion of the papal state in central Italy that the Avignon popes had set as a condition for their return to Rome — forced Salutati to pen a series of "missives," or official state letters, on behalf of the Signoria, as the Florentines strove to resist the pontiff's enactment of the doctrine known as *plenitudo potestatis*. It was precisely on the grounds of this controversial doctrine upholding the Church's political (and, consequently, military) power that the pope tried to defend ecclesiastical prerogatives in central Italy and even extend them through his French prelates and the use of mercenary forces. Despite Florence's eventual defeat by the papacy, Salutati's fiery epistles — which make up part of the first documents in this anthology[6] — earned the chancellor immediate fame. To a large extent, this was a consequence of the effectiveness of his letters.[7] In

the first stages of the war, Florence's main strategy was to stir rebellion among the cities subject to the papacy. Also thanks to Salutati's passionate missives, between late 1375 and February 1376 the following cities, whose councils had all been influenced by the Florentine chancellor's reiterated calls to overthrow papal rule, successfully revolted against the pontiff: Città di Castello, Perugia, Gubbio, Todi, Urbino, Forlì, and, finally, such key centers as Bologna and Ascoli. Conversely, the Church's response to a situation mostly caused by the Florentine government (of which Salutati was a high-ranking official) was both rapid and harsh: in March 1376 Gregory XI issued an interdict against Florence, and two years later, shortly before dying, he even started a trial for heresy against Salutati himself.[8]

It is worth stressing that the content of Florence's missives was dictated to the chancellor by the highest local authorities (the priors of the Florentine guilds and commune); as such, the missives cannot be taken at face value as unquestionable evidence of Salutati's personal political convictions.[9] Their similarities with the humanist's private letters—which several scholars have duly remarked[10]—and, at the same time, the inevitable discrepancies will both be discussed later in relation to his treatise on tyranny. For the time being, instead, it is appropriate to emphasize that the missives penned by Salutati immediately stood out for their innovative rhetoric, the display of classical culture, and their ability to shape a new image of the city (largely based on the connection of Florence's republican present to its ancient Roman heritage), which would prove to be a sharp, effective, and flexible tool of propaganda for decades to come.[11] This is shown by their wide circulation and use as literary models all over the Italian peninsula and beyond. Even the Milanese, that is the Florentines' main political enemies at the turn of the century, proved sensitive to the rhetorical allure of Salutati's missives.[12] The reasons for such a "success" have been convincingly explained as follows by David Peterson in

an essay on the War of the Eight Saints: "As the propagandist of Florence's strategy to guarantee its own security by republicanizing central Italy, Salutati developed an anthropology of liberty that made its Roman genealogy accessible to all Italians in an ideology that was, at the same time, new and distinctively Florentine."[13]

Accomplishing such a deed was far from simple or predictable in the mid-1370s. Guelf Florence was then fighting—as just shown—against the pope, that is, its traditional ally and overlord. The Florentines' major accusation was that the Holy Father (at the time still residing in Avignon) was plotting to subdue all of Italy through the corrupt French legates whom he had put in charge of physically protecting the clergy as well as their rights and possessions in Italy. It is to them that Salutati alludes in his official letters with epithets such as "Gallic vultures," "barbarian and foreign peoples," "defamers," and the like.[14] Hence the Florentines—who in Salutati's missives always style themselves, in keeping with an age-old tradition, as "the most devout sons of the Church"—felt compelled to reply (in a war that, as often noted, was mostly fought on paper) to defend not only their own liberty but that of the whole peninsula as well, taking on the role of standard-bearers of Italian liberty against all forms of tyranny. In so doing, Salutati shaped a language, devised a set of images, and articulated a kind of ideology that would prove most congenial to Florentine propaganda until at least the mid-fifteenth century, when the role increasingly played by the Medici family on the local scene would demand a significant shift in the city's political discourse at all levels.[15]

We can best perceive this momentous change through the accounts of the origins of Florence that local humanists would put forth in the course of the Quattrocento. In this respect, too, Salutati set a crucial precedent by proposing a version that would immediately be taken up and exploited in full by his most distinguished disciple, Leonardo Bruni.[16] Within this anthology, the

main passage on this topic is to be found in Salutati's reply to Loschi's *Invective against the Florentines* (1401). Salutati authored this text — whose full title in English translation here reads *Reply to a Malevolent Detractor Who Has Written Vexingly Against the Renowned City of Florence*[17] — in the first half of 1403, less than a year after his city had won the war against Milan, thanks to Giangaleazzo Visconti's sudden death, in September 1402. Rebutting Loschi's accusation that the Florentines boasted their Roman origins without providing any evidence, Salutati launches into a passionate account to prove that the city was in fact founded under the Roman republic, thus before Caesar and Augustus put the senate under their own control. He does so in a highly innovative fashion, by relying not only on literary sources (some of which, like Pliny the Elder and Ptolemy, had never been used to this purpose before) but on archaeology and philology as well. In these few yet fundamental paragraphs of the *Contra maledicum et obiurgatorem*,[18] Salutati deploys his knowledge of classical literature (above all Sallust and, even more significantly from an ideological point of view, Cicero) to demonstrate that Florence must have been established by the Romans (more precisely, by veterans of Sulla's army) right after the so-called Social War, which means around 88 BCE. Not only do utterly reliable literary sources support this, Salutati writes, but even the archaeological remains — he adds — that are still to be seen in the city to this day (all of which can clearly be recognized as Roman in style) attest to it without a shadow of a doubt.

This Roman republican heritage still informs the whole city and its inhabitants, as Salutati repeatedly claims in his reply to the Visconti secretary. This historical claim serves as a response to the latter's accusations that the Florentines are plotting — contrary to their obfuscatory propaganda — to subdue all of Italy, while posing as its defenders. To be sure, the Ciceronian aura permeating the text is not to be taken as a literary stratagem only. First of all, though determined — as already noted — not to attribute the *Invec-*

tiva in Florentinos to his one-time disciple and sincere admirer Loschi,[19] Salutati is bent just the same on outdoing his opponent
from a cultural point of view. His abundant use of Cicero (both as
a source and as a rhetorical model) comes through as an important
scholarly and political statement at one and the same time. On the
one hand, Salutati is eager to prove himself superior to his opponent by means of frequent and well-chosen quotations from both
Latin and Greek authors.[20] In this respect, considerable attention
should be given to his use of such unusual sources for the time as
Plutarch and Ptolemy.[21] As is well known, in 1396 Salutati had
been instrumental in convincing the erudite Byzantine teacher
Manuel Chrysoloras to come to Florence and accept the first chair
in Greek language and literature at any modern university in
Western Europe. A year later Chrysoloras started teaching in the
Florentine Studium (a post he kept until 1399), with the hand-
some yearly salary of three hundred gold florins. The outstanding
sum was generously paid for by Palla Strozzi, who would eventually make a name for himself as a successful banker and refined
art patron, apart from being one of Chrysoloras's Florentine students. Whether Palla (whom Giovanni Rucellai, his son-in-law,
later praised as one of the ethical and cultural role models of fifteenth-century Florence)[22] was already a member of Salutati's humanist circle at the time — if not a friend — alongside figures like
Jacopo Angeli da Scarperia, Poggio Bracciolini, Leonardo Bruni,
and Pier Paolo Vergerio has not yet been proven, but it seems
most likely. Chrysoloras's three-year stay in the city turned out to
be seminal for the rebirth of Greek in Latin Europe.[23] For the
purpose at hand, it is worth noting that Salutati owes to his disciples (in all likelihood Bruni and Jacopo Angeli) and their studies
with Chrysoloras the little knowledge of Greek that he displays in
Contra maledicum et obiurgatorem. It is also probable that in that text
Salutati coins the adjective "Plutarchean," just as a few years before
he had invented a similar literary epithet ("Dantean") in *De fato et*

fortuna.[24] On the other hand, Salutati's intense use of Cicero (including technical works like the *De inventione*, as emphasized here in the notes to the text) to confute his Milanese opponent reveals how the chancellor was striving to prove republican freedom (and, therefore, Florentine culture) superior to tyranny in all respects, both practical and theoretical.

This takes us back to the first paragraph above and to its apparent dilemma. How is it possible that Salutati—who is duly regarded as the inventor of Florentine republican propaganda in the late Trecento—authored a text like *De tyranno*, in which he defends his beloved and admired fellow citizen Dante Alighieri for putting Caesar's murderers (Brutus and Cassius) in the lowest hell, with none other than Judas? Like his treatise *De saeculo et religione* (dating from 1381–82), on the contemplative versus the active life, or *De fato et fortuna* (1396), on the role of Divine Providence in man's life and history,[25] *De tyranno* has elicited a host of varied and yet in most cases disappointed responses by readers of Salutati. Even as keen a scholar of this humanist as Ronald Witt could not but express his dissatisfaction with what he called "this puzzling little tract" in his first essay on it.[26] Another famous expert on Italian humanism, the aforementioned Hans Baron, referred to *De tyranno* as "a problematical book," and his description has remained to this day a sort of derogatory tag attached to it.[27] And yet, as shown by Daniela De Rosa and, to a lesser extent, by Witt himself many years after his first article cited above, *De tyranno* does have a greater amount of consistency than critics usually acknowledge.[28] Once again, it is a matter of paying attention to Salutati's other works as well as to their respective literary genres and never losing sight of their original background, both political and cultural. For obvious reasons, this short introduction is not the right place for a detailed analysis of either *De tyranno* or the many different readings of it that scholars have offered from the early twentieth century (when the first critical editions and extended studies

of his text appeared)[29] to the present. Rather, a summary of the contents is given, and, above all, it is shown how — though forced — Salutati's defense of Dante's choice to punish Cassius and Brutus in the worst way possible for killing Caesar is not as inconsistent with his previous writings as some scholars hold.

Salutati wrote *De tyranno* in the summer of 1400 to answer two questions he had been asked by a law student in Padua, Antonio of Aquila, most likely a disciple of the famous jurist Francesco Zabarella, a friend of the chancellor of Florence.[30] One of the two questions is what we find in the penultimate paragraph (§7) of the fifth and last chapter, just before the closing remarks. Here Salutati mentions Antonio's desire to know whether he regarded Antenor and Aeneas as traitors to Troy, as some believed, or not. Since this topic is quickly discussed in what may be deemed no more than a short appendix to the text, it is quite clear that Salutati's main interest in writing *De tyranno* lies elsewhere; it has to do with the topic extensively debated in the preceding chapters and sections of the book. It can thus be surmised that Antonio's other (and probably first) question to Salutati in a now lost letter ran something like this: Were Cassius and Brutus traitors to Rome for murdering Caesar? Antonio may then have also asked Salutati, as a sequel to this query, whether Dante was right in punishing Caesar's assassins in Canto 34 of *Inferno* alongside Judas. To any Florentine, however, and in particular to such a fond lover of Dante's poetry as Salutati,[31] this last issue could not be avoided and called for an explanation. The treatise's structure can be summarized as follows, basically translating the titles accompanying each section: 1) Preface to Antonio of Aquila, 2) How to define a tyrant, 3) Is tyrannicide justifiable?, 4) Was Caesar a tyrant?, 5) Was Caesar justly murdered by Brutus and Cassius?, 6) Was Dante right in placing Brutus and Cassius in hell for murdering Caesar? Salutati's answer to the question concerning Antenor and Aeneas is inserted, as said above, in this last chapter.

As anticipated, most modern readers of De tyranno have been taken aback by Salutati's condemnation of Brutus and Cassius, on the ground that Caesar was not a tyrant. In fact, Salutati holds, Caesar was loved by the majority of the Romans, as attested by the honors that the common people paid to him at his funeral. True enough, Caesar did win the war against Pompey, but the latter did not appear any less violent than his opponent; they both craved power and would have done anything to attain it, as is typical not just of military conflicts but — above all — of civil wars, which are known to be the most ferocious. Besides, Caesar acted in a most clement way after coming to power, a quality acknowledged by all sources, including his former enemy Cicero. More important still to an assessment of De tyranno, Salutati adopts an Augustinian interpretation of history not unlike Dante's to assert that Caesar's victory was willed by God as part of a preordained divine plan. The latter was aimed at pacifying the whole world in view of Christ's coming; and such an accomplishment demanded the creation of as vast a monarchy as possible, which turned out to be the Roman Empire. Cassius and Brutus's unfortunate fate was, then, decreed by God himself as the fitting punishment for their crime. Consequently, Dante is right in consigning Caesar's assassins to the lowest pit of hell in his "divine poem."

As mentioned, Hans Baron has been one of the most disappointed readers of De tyranno. Discussing this text in his famous Crisis, he speaks of a reversal of Salutati's previous anti-Caesarean spirit, as expressed, for instance, in his public and private letters. In Baron's eyes such a turnabout is so profound to even raise doubts about Salutati's republicanism at the time, as if in old age he had gone through an astounding ideological change.[32] Witt and De Rosa have provided a convincing refutation of Baron's reading of De tyranno. Both, although in various ways and with different emphasis, have highlighted a number of key features that are worth summarizing here. First, as also noted by Robert Black, we

cannot expect Salutati to show the same consistency in treating such matters as we would expect of a political philosopher.[33] His political statements were inevitably dictated by the needs of the Florentine state at precise moments; seen from this perspective, rhetorical ability (almost synonymous with flexibility, to use a contemporary catchword) mattered more than coherence. This is also true of *De tyranno*, a text written in 1400, when Florence — once again at war with the duke of Milan, as it had been almost continuously since 1390 — was trying to have Emperor Wenceslaus (Giangaleazzo Visconti's most influential ally) deposed and replaced with Robert of Bavaria. Eventually the Florentines succeeded at this and even convinced the newly elected emperor — not without disbursing a considerable sum — to come to their help in Italy fighting against the Milanese. A rebuttal of Cicero's well-known condemnation of Caesar for his authoritarian aims, which Salutati himself had adopted again and again in his missives and elsewhere, was necessary to defend Dante's reading of that period of Roman history. Understandably, such a move demanded that Salutati carry out a reassessment — at least partially — of the respective merits of monarchy, on the one hand, and of republican freedom, on the other. Such reevaluation of monarchy as we find in *De tyranno*, however, is not altogether inconsistent with the chancellor's previous writings. In this treatise he resorts to a medieval commonplace to assert that, theoretically speaking, a one-man rule (provided such man is righteous) is better than any other political system, as it most resembles God's rule over the universe. In practice, however, it often happens that kings are not just and therefore deserve to be overthrown by the very people they should govern. Salutati then resorts to another point that had already been exploited by previous medieval thinkers (and that Savonarola, too, adopted in his late fifteenth-century treatise on the Florentine government).[34] Like Ptolemy of Lucca, Salutati argues that not all communities are fit to be ruled by a monarch; some are

actually better off with a popular government, because such is the kind of system that their nature demands.[35] Florence is precisely such a place, but that does not contradict what Salutati has stated before about monarchies being theoretically closer to the divine model than republics.

Scholars, as previously noted, have always emphasized the combination of traditional and innovative features in Salutati's thoughts and writings. Some speak of an affinity between this humanist and scholasticism, as shown by the very books he owned and quotes from in many of his texts. The same—let it be said in passing—is true of many other humanists, but this should not surprise us. Such secularizing views as Bruni's or Valla's turn out to be exceptions more than the rule, if we read this kind of literature while keeping our ideological expectations or prejudices in check. In the case of *De tyranno*, however, a few aspects should be mentioned in brief. First of all, if Salutati's view of Caesar seems controversial and ambiguous, it should be kept in mind—as Witt himself warned in one of his studies—that the very figure of Caesar was particularly ambivalent throughout the Middle Ages.[36] Authors would, for instance, chastise his authoritarian goals while praising his outstanding clemency or extol his military prowess while condemning his reckless political conduct. At that time, no less than today, Caesar aroused interest and stirred debate exactly by being such a strong and controversial figure.

Similar nuances must be taken into account when talking about medieval political theories. Even supporters of the empire would grant that the emperor was at the top of a hierarchy that included—without effacing local peculiarities and age-old rights— kingdoms, provinces, and cities. The latter, because of their size, could certainly be run (and were in fact more efficiently run) by a republican government. Also, Saint Augustine (one of Salutati's favorite Fathers of the Church) taught that whereas some Roman emperors shamed themselves by indulging the most wicked vices,

the establishment of the empire per se had been necessary to the diffusion of the Christian faith, both because it brought peace to the world when Jesus was born and also because, after the emperors had embraced the only true religion, it could prove a most beneficial instrument for the salvation of human souls. It was not the empire in and of itself, therefore, that deserved to be condemned but only its misuse by vicious rulers. It was from Saint Augustine, again, as well as from the histories of Orosius, Augustine's disciple, and from Dante's worldview that Salutati derived — especially toward the end of his life, from the last decade of the fourteenth century onward — a providential reading of history. In Salutati's eyes, Divine Providence intervened in human affairs so as to carry out a preordained plan that could not be understood at first, but only seen in its true perspective much later. This view of history is first best expressed by the aging chancellor in his *De fato et fortuna*, a text that represents an important ideological stage that contributed to his writing a treatise like *De tyranno*. It is in *De fato et fortuna*, for instance, that we find the following passage on God's intervention in the Roman civil war, which pitted Octavian and Mark Antony against Caesar's murderers:

> But with the Divine Will deciding that at the coming of the true king, His Son, the world would be under one prince of princes and, since the disposition of God was the power behind worldly affairs — about which our Dante says: "Your wisdom has no means of countering her; she foresees, judges, and pursues her reign, no less god than the gods who reign elsewhere" — I say this disposition of God ordained all matters of the civil war toward the goal of a future monarchy, so that by chance and beyond the intention of the actors those things occurred that led to the end of the senatorial regime.[37]

As noted above, and as was convincingly argued by Witt, Dante's influence on Salutati grew considerably toward the end of

the chancellor's life. The passage above is a mark of this. Significantly, it was especially excerpts from Dante's masterpiece on such topics as Divine Providence and Fortune that the aged humanist quoted and translated into Latin as his admiration for the Florentine poet increased.[38] More important still, Salutati wrote *De tyranno* mostly to defend Dante from the accusation of having unjustly put Brutus and Cassius on a par with Judas. This is probably the only thing on which we can find some sort of scholarly consensus regarding the treatise.[39] Evidence that Salutati's stance on this matter was not easy to defend—above all in the eyes of his own humanist disciples, whose attitude, as one would expect, was more daring on a number of cultural and political issues— is offered above all by Bruni's well-known *Dialogi ad Petrum Paulum Histrum*.[40] Much ink has been spilled on this two-book composition by Salutati's most famous pupil. Some scholars have even gone as far as to claim that Bruni sneers at the late master by exposing the embarrassing inconsistencies (once again!) in his thought. I believe, instead, that not only Bruni but virtually all scholars of the time felt deep and sincere admiration for Salutati.[41] Evidence of this is offered by his house in Piazza de' Peruzzi, close to the Santa Croce basilica in Florence, which became the main Italian center of humanist studies from the late Trecento until his death, in May 1406. This was a house, let it be said in passing, that Salutati never bought but preferred to rent for many years instead, as he spent almost his entire patrimony to buy books, so that by the end of his life he owned some six hundred manuscripts—an astonishing figure for the time, and one which made his private library one of the richest in all of Europe. His private correspondence, too, proves that he had come to replace Petrarch and Boccaccio as the leading scholar and the cultural reference point for the Italian peninsula. It is also worth noting that his epistles imitate the two Florentine "crowns" just mentioned—above all Petrarch—by their being, quite often, veritable short essays on

major philosophical, literary, moral, and political topics. The latter, understandably enough, are usually discussed along the same lines as the official missives. And yet discrepancies may be noted in this realm too, as differences are inevitably dictated by—or at least linked to—important events in the author's life.

It need not surprise us, then, that Salutati's formulaic borrowings from Cicero's correspondence, as well as his ideological similarities with him, become more noticeable right after his accidental rediscovery in 1392 of the Roman orator's *Epistulae ad familiares*.[42] Likewise, echoes from Dante's works, especially the *Divine Comedy*, are more frequent in the chancellor's late private epistles, especially after two nearly simultaneous events: the death of his second wife, Piera, and his writing of *De fato et fortuna* in 1396. Understandably, with time his attitude became more indulgent toward the limitations of human nature, and the mature Salutati became less insistent on the absolute fulfillment of the highest standards of virtue. His reading of the famous anecdote about Brutus the Elder putting his own sons to death for conspiring against the Roman state is just one of several examples that can be drawn from the chancellor's private correspondence. While initially regarding Brutus's decision as an unparalleled example of love for one's own country, he later saw more than a tinge of vainglory in it, suspecting that love of fame must have dictated this memorable deed by the man he nevertheless considered the greatest Roman hero of all times.[43] What does remain constant—as evidenced by all of his works, including the voluminous and unfinished *De laboribus Herculis*—is Salutati's intellectual curiosity. Suffice it to recall once again, for brevity's sake, his enthusiastic interest in Greek language and literature when he was almost seventy (certainly a venerable age for that time, enough to be deemed *longaevus*, to echo the title of a humanist treatise on this topic).[44] Remarkable too are his experiments with accents in Italian, again in old age, experiments inspired by the smattering of Greek he had picked up from Chry-

soloras and his students, his short yet pioneering treatise on punctuation, the significant contribution that he made to the development of humanistic script, and the unremitting research on the allegorical meanings of Hercules's myths, which he gathered in *De laboribus Herculis*.[45]

Not surprisingly, this last work, too, has caused scholars some embarrassment, as it reveals Salutati's lifelong affinities with traditional (that is medieval) scholarly methods such as allegorism, thematic compilation, and the hermeneutical approach known as "the four senses of Scripture." As often happens, secularizing and anachronistic expectations come into play. Speaking of Quattrocento Florentine humanists, the same affinities can be noticed in Manetti, Ficino, and Poliziano, just to name a few. Again, Salutati's protégé Leonardo Bruni, often regarded as the bellwether of the humanist flock, should be seen as the exception, not the norm. The typical method of these humanists in political propaganda (as well as the connected realm of myth-making) was to deploy an eclectic patchwork of sources and strategies, which inevitably seem forced or incoherent to modern ears. From among the writings collected in the present anthology, characteristic samples of this method can be found in Salutati's missives as well as in his *Contra maledicum et obiurgatorem*. Since the former have been collected here mostly following a typological criterion, that is, to offer samples of the various kinds of official epistles the Florentine chancellor was expected to compose at the time, the latter is briefly concentrated on here, though reference is made to the missives whenever their political content ties in with the *Contra maledicum et obiurgatorem*.

Salutati authored his reply to Loschi's invective against Florence, as noted above, a few months after the conflict between the Duchy of Milan and the Tuscan republic had come to an end, thanks to Giangaleazzo Visconti's death, on 3 September 1402. This text of Salutati's is his last contribution to the long series of wars, on paper and on the battlefield, between the two cities that

lasted almost constantly for about twelve years. As a chancellor he had already intervened with a considerable number of missives; an excellent example would be the so-called *Letter to the Italians* in spring 1390, which he wrote immediately after the outbreak of the first conflict with Milan.[46] In *Contra maledicum et obiurgatorem*, too, we find together statements and stances that could be deemed inconsistent at first sight, although they become more than justifiable once properly contextualized. Such is the case, for instance, with Salutati's adherence to Giovanni Villani's myth of the Carolingian rebuilding of Florence almost nine centuries after its Roman foundation. After expounding his novel account of the republican origins of Florence in the opening paragraphs of this text, based on archaeological and philological evidence, Salutati does not refrain from subscribing to the legend of Charlemagne's reconstruction of the city (§158), which had been first put down in writing by Villani in the early Trecento.[47] That is why, in another passage from this text (§109), he refers to the French as "our fathers," as he does in virtually all the missives that he addressed to their royal house on behalf of the Florentine government. See, for instance, the letter he sent to Charles VI on 28 September 1391,[48] in the midst of the first war against Giangaleazzo Visconti. In it Salutati proclaims Florence's age-old loyalty to the kings of France and to the Church, as the city's traditional Guelfism demanded, and stresses this double alliance, remembering once again how "Charlemagne, founder of the royal lineage, gave this city new life and endowed it with many privileges, after the rapacious conquests and cruel destruction by Totila."[49] A few years later, as is well known, Bruni would debunk this Carolingian myth, in his *History of the Florentine People*.[50] In Salutati's time, however, the pressing political and military circumstances demanded a different stance. In the state letters addressed to the king of France and to the pope asking for support during the three almost consecutive wars Florence fought against Milan, Salutati constantly celebrates

the city's fidelity to the Church together with its strong and centuries-old connection to the French crown. Fighting against the Visconti—he repeatedly asserts in the missives, turning it into a slogan—is key to the freedom of all Italy.[51] More than that, resisting Milanese assaults is for the Florentines tantamount to continuing their traditional, unwavering fight on the side of the Church against the German emperors and their vicious Ghibelline supporters in the peninsula.[52] The atmosphere is now very different from that which prevailed during the "War against the Eight Saints," previously discussed. The chancellor does not hesitate to ingratiate the city with the pope—whom his republic is calling upon for help against Milan—with phrases like the following:

> God our Lord, who disposes of all things in this lower world, has bound so closely together the State of the Church and the welfare of our liberty and of the Florentine people, that neither can we be prosperous without the State of the Church's prosperity, nor can the well-being of the Church last for long if we are in difficulties.[53]

The same concepts, images, and rhetorical formulas—in regard to both the French royal house and the papacy—punctuate Salutati's *Contra maledicum et obiurgatorem*. This is not surprising, of course, since the text against Loschi is Salutati's last contribution—acting this time as a private individual—to Florence's war of propaganda against Milan. As Salutati himself writes in the opening section of the work and in the accompanying letter to his younger friend and colleague Pietro Turchi, secretary to Carlo Malatesta (lord of Rimini),[54] he has sufficient reasons to consider himself the most fit of all Florentines to rebut the accusations moved against their city; he is now almost seventy-three and has spent the greatest part of his life in the service of Florence. Who else then should stand up in defense of the country (this sort of "ideal mother, to which we must feel ourselves, beyond all our

other efforts, eternally in debt," as he tells Turchi, echoing Cicero's precepts)[55] that some vile, anonymous Milanese has slandered once again? Not surprisingly, his passionate rebuttal of Loschi's short invective easily grows to become a veritable and exhaustive panegyric of Florence, comprising all those features (literature, economics, art and architecture, politics, and so on) that Bruni would include — although in a more concise and classicizing way — just a year later, in his *Laudatio florentinae urbis*.[56] Even less surprising is that, as noted above, after this thorough reply to Loschi, Salutati resolved never to answer Milanese propaganda on issues that, after Giangaleazzo's death, were being rapidly replaced by new political scenarios and new challenges. After all, Salutati's lifelong loyalty to the Florentine republic is one thing about which no one could ever accuse him of being inconsistent.

Finally, I wish to express my deepest gratitude to two friends and colleagues whose assistance has proved invaluable to me ever since I started editing humanist texts some twenty years ago: Giuliano Tanturli and James Hankins. Without their experienced support, this volume would never have been conceived, let alone completed.

Stefano U. Baldassarri
Florence, July 28, 2012

NOTES

1. For a recent assessment of the so-called "Baron thesis," see M. Jurdjevic, "Hedgehogs and Foxes: The Present and Future of Renaissance Intellectual History," *Past and Present* 195 (2007): 241–68.

2. Four recent and important volumes on Salutati are worth mentioning as significant contributions that shed new light on this humanist: *Coluccio Salutati e l'invenzione dell'Umanesimo. Firenze, Biblioteca Medicea Laurenziana, 2 novembre 2008 — 30 gennaio 2009*, ed. T. De Robertis, G. Tanturli, and S. Zamponi (Florence: Mandragora, 2008), a catalog of a major exhibition of manuscripts and documents connected with Salutati, hereafter cited as

Catalogo; Coluccio Salutati e Firenze. Ideologia e formazione dello Stato. Firenze, Archivio di Stato 9 ottobre — 14 marzo 2009, ed. R. Cardini and P. Viti (Florence: Pagliai, 2008); *Coluccio Salutati e l'invenzione dell'Umanesimo. Atti del convegno internazionale di studi (Firenze, 29–31 ottobre 2008)*, ed. C. Bianca (Rome: Edizioni di storia e letteratura, 2010); and *Coluccio Salutati cancelliere e politico. Atti del Convegno internazionale del Comitato nazionale delle celebrazioni del VI centenario della morte di Coluccio Salutati, Firenze-Prato, 9–12 dicembre 2008*, ed. R. Cardini and P. Viti (Florence: Polistampa, 2012).

3. On 26 November 1400, Salutati was finally granted Florentine citizenship, as a reward for his unremitting efforts in the service of the republic. The privilege also applied to all his male descendants. The classic study of the humanist chancellors of Florence in the Quattrocento remains E. Garin, "I cancellieri umanisti della Repubblica fiorentina da Coluccio Salutati a Bartolomeo Scala," *Rivista storica italiana* 71 (1959): 185–208, republished in his *La cultura filosofica del Rinascimento italiano* (Florence: Sansoni, 1961), pp. 3–37, with new appendices. See also R. Black, "The Political Thought of the Florentine Chancellors," *The Historical Journal* 29 (1986): 991–1003, reprinted in Black's *Studies in Renaissance Humanism and Politics* (Farnham, Surrey: Ashgate Variorum, 2011), item 14.

4. On Salutati's studies with Pietro da Moglio, see R. G. Witt, *"In the Footsteps of the Ancients": The Origins of Humanism from Lovato to Bruni* (Leiden: Brill, 2000), pp. 292–94. Also known as "Peter the Rhetorician," Pietro da Moglio was instrumental in putting young Salutati in touch with Petrarch. On Salutati's admiration for Petrarch and his successful efforts to save such texts of his as *Secretum* and *Africa* from potential oblivion, see now M. Pellegrini, *Religione e umanesimo nel primo Rinascimento da Petrarca ad Alberti* (Florence: Le Lettere, 2012), pp. 72–83.

5. The war was named after a committee of eight members — later called "Otto Santi" (Eight Saints), to acknowledge their excellent work in the service of the state — that the Florentine government appointed in July 1375 to take fiscal measures in view of the conflict with the papacy. A survey of these events and the way they are treated by Florentine humanists from Salutati onward is D. S. Peterson, "The War of the Eight Saints in Florentine Memory and Oblivion," in *Society and Individual in Renaissance Florence*, ed. W. J. Connell (Berkeley: University of California

Press, 2002), pp. 173–214. See also the section by F. Sznura entitled *La guerra tra Firenze e papa Gregorio XI* in *Coluccio Salutati e Firenze*, pp. 89–92.

6. See below, Letters 1–3, pp. 2–29.

7. In this respect it is worth recalling that the papal chancery tried in vain, at least on one occasion, to imitate the innovative style of Salutati's official letters so as to strike back at Florence soon after the war began. See Witt, *"In the Footsteps of the Ancients,"* p. 302, note 21.

8. On these papal sanctions, see Peterson, "The War of the Eight Saints," pp. 177–90; Sznura, *La guerra*, pp. 90–91; and the section by De Rosa entitled *Coluccio Salutati notaio e cancelliere* in *Catalogo*, pp. 35–38.

9. This should always be kept in mind, lest we run the risk of reading Salutati's state letters as his own unsolicited political reflections. Such an oversight may lead to interpreting them as though they were excerpts from Petrarch's epistolary collections or Montaigne's *Essays*. See P. Herde, "Politik und Rhetorik in Florenz am Vorabend der Renaissance," *Archiv für Kulturgeschichte* 47 (1965): 141–220, esp. 159; H. Langkabel, *Die Staatsbriefe Coluccio Salutatis. Untersuchungen zum Frühhumanismus in der Florentiner Staatskanzlei und Auswahledition* (Cologne-Vienna: Böhlau, 1981), p. 79; R. Black, "The Political Thought," pp. 992–93.

10. Remarks on the substantial agreement between Salutati's official and private letters can be found in A. Petrucci, *Coluccio Salutati* (Rome: Istituto della Enciclopedia Italiana, 1972); R. G. Witt, *Coluccio Salutati and his Public Letters* (Geneva: Droz, 1976), and idem, *Hercules at the Crossroads. The Life, Works, and Thought of Coluccio Salutati* (Durham, NC: Duke University Press, 1983). More specifically, see D. De Rosa, *Coluccio Salutati. Il cancelliere e il pensatore politico* (Florence: La Nuova Italia, 1980), pp. 75–85.

11. For an account of the stylistic innovations introduced by Salutati in his missives, see Witt, *"In the Footsteps,"* pp. 302–3. Witt also points out a crucial feature that many modern scholars of humanist literature often forget: Salutati's official letters were designed to be read aloud. Among other things, this explains the frequent use of devices such as verbal reiteration or tricolons, with an effect that students of Italian humanism sometimes condemn as repetitious or long-winded. In fact, such devices

helped audiences that included many hearers with little or no Latin to follow and understand better.

12. As attested by Giangaleazzo Visconti's well-known saying that a single letter by Salutati was worth a thousand horsemen. On this adage and the variations on it that circulated in early fifteenth-century Italy, see Witt, "*In the Footsteps*," p. 302, note 30. A more tangible and reliable way of assessing Salutati's impact on Milanese culture is to note the wide circulation of his works in Lombardy and their use as models in various literary genres. These works include, alongside Salutati's official letters, his famous *Declamatio Lucretiae*, a rhetorical showpiece. See C. M. Monti, "Salutati visto dal Nord: la prospettiva dei cancellieri e maestri viscontei," in *Coluccio Salutati e l'invenzione dell'umanesimo*, pp. 193–223. See also the articles on Salutati's letters (both private and official) and the *Declamatio Lucretiae* in *Catalogo*, pp. 127–36 and 191–94, respectively.

13. Peterson, "The War of the Eight Saints," p. 190.

14. These expressions punctuate Letters 1–3, pp. 2–29, below.

15. On the importance of the innovative propaganda orchestrated by Salutati, especially in regard to Florence's Guelf past, see R. G. Witt, "A Note on Guelfism in Late Medieval Florence," *Nuova Rivista Storica* 53.1 (1969): 134–45. See also idem, *Hercules*, pp. 111–46.

16. For an overview of such theories as expounded in the fifteenth century by Salutati to Poliziano, see *Images of Quattrocento Florence. Selected Writings in Literature, History and Art*, ed. S. U. Baldassarri and A. Saiber (New Haven-London: Yale University Press, 2000), pp. 3–36. I have discussed this topic at length in the following articles: "A Tale of Two Cities: Accounts of the Origins of Fiesole and Florence from the Anonymous *Chronica* to Leonardo Bruni," *Studi Rinascimentali* 5 (2007): 29–56; "Like Fathers like Sons: Theories on the Origins of the City in Late Medieval Florence," *Modern Language Notes* 124.1 (2009): 23–44; and "Le città possibili: arte e filologia nel dibattito sull'origine di Firenze da Giovanni Villani a Leonardo Bruni," *Letteratura e Arte* 9 (2011): 23–41 (conference proceedings of "*Proxima Studia*": *Arte e letteratura a Firenze (1300–1600). Convegno internazionale di studi (Palazzo Rucellai, 21–22 ottobre 2008)*, ed. S. U. Baldassarri). From the rich bibliography cited there, see

in particular, R. G. Witt, "Salutati and the Origins of Florence," *Il pensiero politico* 2.2 (1969): 161–72, and C. Vasoli, "Coluccio Salutati e la storia," in *Atti del convegno su Coluccio Salutati: Buggiano Castello, giugno 1980* (Buggiano: Comune di Buggiano, 1980), pp. 27–46: esp. 36–41.

17. As I have shown in the section on this text in *Catalogo*, pp. 171–73, the complete Latin title is *Contra maledicum et obiurgatorem qui multa pungenter adversus inclitam civitatem Florentiae scripsit*, which here and elsewhere I abbreviate as *Contra maledicum et obiurgatorem*. On the correct form of the title and its possible Petrarchan model, see also my recent book *La vipera e il giglio. Lo scontro tra Milano e Firenze nelle invettive di Antonio Loschi e Coluccio Salutati* (Rome: Aracne, 2012), p. 17, and 55 note 1. Formulas such as *Responsiva in Luschum* or *Invectiva in Luschum* are not only unattested in the manuscript tradition but go against Salutati's clear statement at the outset of his text (§3) and in the accompanying letter (§§2–4), where he writes that, for various reasons, he cannot ascribe the *Invectiva in Florentinos* to Loschi. Salutati's authorial role, purpose, and context, and the extensive space devoted to dissecting Loschi's text line by line, all distinguish the *Reply* from an important predecessor, Petrarch's *Invective against a Detractor of Italy* (in Petrarch, *Invectives*, tr. D. Marsh, ITRL 11 [Cambridge, MA.: Harvard University Press, 2003], pp. 364–475).

18. See §§22–32, pp. 200–213, below, and the related endnotes.

19. On the Loschi-Salutati relationship before the *Invectiva in Florentinos* and the response to it were written (that is, 1401 and 1403, respectively), see Baldassarri, *Umanesimo e traduzione da Petrarca a Manetti* (Cassino: Pubblicazioni dell'Università di Cassino, 2003), pp. 65–72, and the bibliography reported in *La vipera e il giglio*, note 31 on pp. 58–59. See also the entry by G. Barbero in *Catalogo*, pp. 95–97.

20. It may be added that if Salutati really thought Loschi—contrary to his statements in both *Contra maledicum et obiurgatorem* and the accompanying letter—to be the author of the invective against the Florentines, his display of Ciceronian culture would also be aimed at outdoing the very scholar who in the 1390s had written the *Inquisitio artis in orationibus Ciceronis*. This treatise was at the time the best-known humanist com-

mentary on Cicero's speeches. On it see the bibliography listed in *La vipera e il giglio*, note 19 on pp. 56–57.

21. On Salutati's pioneering interest in Plutarch, see pp. 80–92 in *Catalogo*, and the vast bibliography mentioned there by G. Tanturli and D. Speranzi. Regarding Salutati's use of Plutarch in his *Contra maledicum et obiurgatorem*, see *La vipera e il giglio*, pp. 41 and 48.

22. See Giovanni Rucellai's survey of early fifteenth-century Florentine society (dating from 1457) in a passage from his *Zibaldone quaresimale* translated in *Images of Quattrocento Florence*, p. 74: "This age has also had four notable citizens who deserve to be remembered. The first one is Palla di Nofri Strozzi, who possessed all seven of the things necessary for a man's happiness: a worthy homeland, noble and distinguished ancestors, a good knowledge of Greek and Latin, refinement, physical beauty, a good household, and honestly earned wealth." The other three Florentines mentioned by Rucellai are Cosimo de' Medici (whose granddaughter Nannina would marry Rucellai's son Bernardo in 1466), Leonardo Bruni, and Filippo Brunelleschi (ibid., p. 74).

23. As shown by a number of volumes and essays, from the classic work of G. Cammelli, *I dotti bizantini e le origini dell'umanesimo. I. Manuele Crisolora* (Florence: Vallecchi, 1941), to *Manuele Crisolora e il ritorno del greco in Occidente. Atti del convegno internazionale (Napoli, 26–29 giugno 1997)*, ed. R. Maisano and A. Rollo (Naples: Istituto Universitario Orientale, 2002), and *I Decembrio e la tradizione della "Repubblica" di Platone tra Medioevo e Rinascimento*, ed. M. Vegetti and P. Pissavino (Naples: Biblioplis, 2005). For further bibliography on this topic, see pp. 84–87 by D. Speranzi in *Catalogo*.

24. I first pointed out this possibility in my essay "Prime ricerche per un'edizione critica della *Invectiva in Antonium Luscum*," *Medioevo e Rinascimento* 22 (2008): 105–29. See ibid., p. 128. See also *La vipera e il giglio*, p. 41.

25. On these two works of Salutati's, see now the entries by C. Caby and C. Bianca, respectively, in *Catalogo*, pp. 137–39 and 142–45, both providing exhaustive bibliography.

26. See R. G. Witt, "The *De Tyranno* and Coluccio Salutati's view of Politics and Roman History," *Nuova rivista storica* 53.3–4 (1969): 434–74. The opening paragraph reads: "A student of the political ideas of Coluccio Salutati cannot be blamed for wishing that one of the humanist's tracts, the *De tyranno*, had been proven spurious or that it could be counted among the 'lost' works of the author." There follows, on the same page, his definition of *De tyranno* as "this puzzling little tract." Some twenty years later Witt reworked this same essay—developing, as we shall see, a more nuanced and balanced approach to the treatise—which became chapter 14 ("Politics, History, and the Sanctity of Medieval Traditions") in his *Hercules*, pp. 368–91.

27. See H. Baron, *The Crisis of the Early Italian Renaissance. Civic Humanism and Republican Liberty in an Age of Classicism and Tyranny. Revised one-volume edition with an epilogue* (Princeton, NJ: Princeton University Press, 1966), p. 165: "What makes *De Tyranno* a problematical book, and has caused modern scholars to advance the most contradictory appraisals of it, is the astounding lack of a normal and natural osmosis between its intellectual intention and the political exigencies of the moment in which it was composed." For Baron's analysis of the *De tyranno*, see his *Crisis*, pp. 146–66; see also the entry on this text by D. Quaglioni in *Catalogo*, pp. 165–67.

28. Some of the inconsistencies perceived by modern critics are the result of anachronistic understandings of Salutati's political terminology, as is shown by J. Hankins, "Coluccio Salutati e Leonardo Bruni," in *Il contributo italiano alla storia del pensiero. Ottava Appendice: Filosofia* (Rome: Istituto della Enciclopedia Italiana, 2012), pp. 85–94. On this view, Salutati's commitment to republican government and liberty is compatible with monarchical forms of the republic. On the history of the term *respublica* more generally, see J. Hankins, "Exclusivist Republicanism and the Non-Monarchical Republic," *Political Theory* 38.4 (2010): 452–82.

29. I refer to A. von Martin, *Coluccio Salutatis Traktat* Vom Tyrannen. *Eine kulturgeschichtliche Untersuchung nebst Textedition* (Berlin-Leipzig: Rothschild, 1913), and Salutati, *Tractatus de Tyranno*, ed. F. Ercole (Berlin-Leipzig: Rothschild, 1914). E. Emerton, *Humanism and Tyranny. Studies in the Italian Trecento* (Cambridge, MA: Harvard University Press, 1925),

commented as follows on the almost simultaneous appearance of von
Martin and Ercole's books on the same topic by the same publishing
house: "It is a somewhat curious fact, certainly interesting and perhaps
significant, that there should have appeared in Germany on the very eve
of the World War two editions of an early Renaissance treatise the purpose of which was to define the word *tyrant* and to defend the conception
of the benevolent despot." Emerton's introduction to his English translation of *De tyranno* (see ibid, pp. 25–69, followed by the translation on
70–116) is interspersed with reflections on contemporary politics and
references to Mussolini. Emerson would certainly have been interested to
find out (had he not died in 1935) that Ercole, a staunch supporter of the
fascist regime, reedited Salutati's *De tyranno*, although without any philological apparatus and some misprints in the text, but providing it with an
Italian translation, shortly before Mussolini's downfall: see Salutati, *Il
trattato* De tyranno *e lettere scelte*, ed. F. Ercole (Bologna: Zanichelli, 1942).

30. He is possibly to be identified with Antonius Vinitti de Pereto, later
minister general of the Franciscan Order (1405–8 and 1415–20); see the
Note on the Text, below.

31. Salutati's admiration for Dante increased as he grew older, as is convincingly shown by Witt, *Hercules*, esp. pp. 313–15 and 368–86. Eventually,
Salutati came to consider the Florentine "divine poet" (as he usually
called him) not only as an outstanding literary genius but as a most wise
philosopher and even a role model, owing to both his scholarly accomplishments and his Christian virtues.

32. See Baron, *The Crisis*, pp. 146–66.

33. See Black, "The Political Thought," p. 994: "Salutati's political ideas
can never be fully understood or reconciled as a coherent political philosophy [. . .]; Salutati may have been a political thinker but he was not
a political philosopher." A similar remark is in Witt, *Coluccio Salutati and
his Public Letters*, p. 80: "Not a political philosopher, concerned as he was
with problems of political theory only incidentally, Coluccio Salutati
seems never to have examined thoroughly his view of politics."

34. See the abridged English translation of this text in *Images of Quattrocento Florence*, pp. 252–65. On page 254 (Book 1, chapter 3 of Savona-

rola's treatise), for instance, one reads: "There can be no doubt, if one pays close attention to what I have said, that if the Florentine people were to tolerate the rule of a single monarch, this man would be a wise, just and good prince, not a tyrant. Once we examine the opinions and the ideas of erudite philosophers and theologians, however, we shall see that the Florentines, because of their nature, are not suited for this form of government. The rule of a prince—they argue—is fitting for people who are servile by nature, lacking in either courage or intelligence or both."

35. For the political thought of Ptolemy of Lucca, see James M. Blythe, *The Worldview and Thought of Tolomeo Fiadoni (Ptolemy of Lucca)* (Turnhout: Brepols, 2009).

36. See Witt, "The *De tyranno*," pp. 443–48. See also idem, *Hercules*, pp. 369–75.

37. I quote from Witt's English translation of this passage in his "*In the Footsteps*," p. 333. For the original Latin text, see C. Bianca's critical edition of *De fato et fortuna* (Florence: Olschki, 1985), 3.12, pp. 201–2. The citation from Dante is *Inferno* 7.85–87.

38. On Salutati's translations of verses from Dante's *Divine Comedy* into Latin hexameters, see Baldassarri, *Umanesimo e traduzione*, pp. 61–91 (chapter 2: "Coluccio Salutati dantista e traduttore"), and F. Bausi, "Coluccio traduttore," *Medioevo e Rinascimento* 22 (2008): 33–58.

39. In addition to the bibliography already mentioned, see F. Ercole, "Coluccio Salutati e il supplizio dantesco di Bruto e Cassio," *Bullettino della Società Dantesca Italiana*, n.s., 21 (1914): 127–34; R. Ruini, "Bruto e Cassio in *Inf.* XXXIV 55–69 e la riflessione politica fiorentina quattrocentesca," *Studi (e testi) italiani* 4 (1999): 145–78; and F. Mazzoni, "Filologia dantesca all'ombra di Salutati," *Studi Danteschi* 70 (2005): 193–236. Ruini's essay has been republished in idem, *Quattrocento fiorentino e dintorni. Saggi di letteratura italiana* (Rome: Phasar, 2007), pp. 9–36.

40. See my critical edition of this text (Florence: Olschki, 1993), esp. 4–12 of the introductory essay and the first of the two dialogues (pp. 235–59). For bibliography on this work of Bruni's, see ibid., pp. 283–90.

41. On Salutati's reputation during his life and well into the fifteenth century, see the entries in *Catalogo*, pp. 55–113 (i.e., the sections entitled *Le biografie, Le relazioni*, and *La memoria*).

42. On this see pp. 251–59 in *Catalogo* by A. Daneloni and S. Zamponi, with bibliography.

43. On his different reaction, over the years, to this well-known episode of Roman history, see De Rosa, *Coluccio Salutati*, pp. 139–40.

44. I refer to Giannozzo Manetti's 1440 collection of biographies entitled *De illustribus longaevis* (*On Famous Men of Great Age*), which includes Salutati himself. Some fifteen years later Manetti reworked this short biography of Salutati for the sixth book of his *Adversus Iudaeos et gentes*. See the excerpts edited and translated in G. Manetti, *Biographical Writings*, ed. and tr. S. U. Baldassarri and R. Bagemihl, ITRL 9 (Cambridge, MA: Harvard University Press, 2003), pp. 114–15 and 148–51, respectively. See also the entry by M. Marchiaro in *Catalogo*, pp. 60–62, with updated bibliography. It may be said in passing that Manetti's two biographical sketches of Salutati in these works are excellent examples, though brief, of how fifteenth-century humanists praised the combination of political, scholarly, and civic tasks. After listing all of Salutati's works in the *Adversus Iudaeos et gentes*, Manetti writes: "To the great glory of his name, it is known that he wrote all this despite the pressure of numerous public and private cares, for he was at once the chancellor of the Florentine people — in which office he served for some thirty years — and a hard-working father who carefully raised ten children" (Manetti, *Biographical Writings*, p. 151).

45. On Salutati's *Ratio punctandi*, see the essay by G. Tanturli in *Catalogo*, pp. 203–4 and the related manuscript description by S. Zamponi on 205–6. As I point out in *La vipera e il giglio*, pp. 41–42, and 62 note 46, Ms. O (Oxford, All Souls College 94) of *Contra maledicum et obiurgatorem* furnishes a precious example of Salutati's punctuation practice. For Salutati's paleographic and codicological interests, the classic study is B. L. Ullman, *The Origin and Development of Humanistic Script* (Rome: Edizioni di storia e letteratura, 1960), in particular chapter 1 ("Background and Inspiration: Coluccio Salutati," on pp. 11–19), and idem, *The Humanism of*

Coluccio Salutati (Padua: Antenore, 1963), pp. 263–80 (chapter II: "Coluccio's Books and their Scribes"). For a reassessment of Ullman's view, however, see the final section in *Catalogo*, pp. 345–63, by T. De Robertis and S. Zamponi, entitled *Libri e copisti di Coluccio Salutati: un consuntivo,* esp. pp. 347–51. This last essay is very helpful also in regard to Salutati's library. Finally, on *De laboribus Herculis,* see the entry by C. M. Monti in *Catalogo,* pp. 117–22, with bibliography.

46. See Letter 5 below, pp. 34–47, dated Florence, 25 May 1390. As repeatedly pointed out in the endnotes to the English translation of *Contra maledicum et obiurgatorem,* this letter shares much in common with Salutati's reply to Loschi—in terms of both content and rhetoric—despite the twelve years and more separating the two texts.

47. On this legend see the studies mentioned above in note 16. In particular, for Salutati's use of it, see P. Gilli, "Coluccio Salutati, chancellier de Florence, et la France," *Bibliothèque d'Humanisme et Renaissance* 55.3 (1993): 479–501, and idem, *Au miroir de l'humanisme. Les représentations de la France dans la culture savante italienne à la fin du Moyen Âge* (Rome: École Française de Rome, 1997), pp. 283–98.

48. The letter is edited and translated below, pp. 46–53, as Letter 6 in this collection.

49. See below, p. 53 (§6).

50. See L. Bruni, *History of the Florentine People,* ed. and trans. J. Hankins, vol. 1, ITRL 3 (Cambridge, MA: Harvard University Press, 2001), pp. 96–97, corresponding to Book 1, chapter 77.

51. Salutati reiterates this point in his official letters to Florence's allies also after Giangaleazzo's death; see, for instance, Letter 9 to Francesco Novello, lord of Padua (dated 17 December 1403), on pp. 60–63, below.

52. See, for instance, Letters 7 and 8 to Boniface IX (dated 13 September 1397, and 30 June 1402, respectively) below, pp. 54–61. Both missives were written while Florence was at war with Milan. The second is particularly dramatic, as Salutati wrote it right after Bologna fell to Milan, and Florence seemed about to be surrounded by the Visconti troops.

53. I quote from Letter 7 to Boniface IX (§1), for which see below, p. 55.

54. On Turchi see *La vipera e il giglio*, ad indicem.

55. See the first paragraph in Salutati's letter to Turchi, p. 169, below.

56. For a close comparison between Salutati's *Contra maledicum et obiurga-torem* and Bruni's *Laudatio*, see *La vipera e il giglio*, pp. 46–54. I previously highlighted some significant similarities between these two works in the notes to my critical edition of L. Bruni, *Laudatio florentinae urbis* (Florence: SISMEL-Edizioni del Galluzzo, 2000).

POLITICAL WRITINGS

EPISTULAE

: I :

Romanis

1 Magnifici domini, fratres nostri carissimi. Deus benignissimus cuncta disponens et sub immutabilis iustitiae ordine—nobis incognito—res mortalium administrans, miseratus humilem Italiam ingemiscere sub iugo abominabilis servitutis, suscitavit spiritum populorum et erexit oppressos contra foedissimam tyrannidem barbarorum. Et, ut videtis, undique pari voto excita demum Ausonia libertatem fremit, libertatem ferro viribusque procurat.

2 Quibus nos requirentibus in tam praeclaro proposito ac tam favorabili causa nostra subsidia non negamus. Quae cuncta vobis, tamquam publicae libertatis auctoribus ac patribus, credimus ad iocunditatem accedere, cum cognoscantur ad maiestatem Romani populi et vestrum naturale propositum pertinere.

3 Hic enim libertatis amor olim Romanum populum contra regiam tyrannidem impulit et ad abrogandum imperium decemvirum illam ob compressionem Lucretiae, istud ob damnationem Virginiae, concitavit. Haec libertas Horatium Coclitem solum contra infestos hostes ruituro obiecit in ponte. Haec Mucium sine spe salutis in Porsennam immisit et propriae manus incendio stupendum regi omnique posteritati praebuit admirandum. Haec duos Decios sponte devotae morti et gladiis hostium consecravit.

SELECTED STATE LETTERS

: I :

To the Romans

Magnificent lords, dearest brothers of ours. God most loving, who   1
disposes all, and who administers the vicissitudes of mortals under
an unchanging order of justice inscrutable to us, moved to pity at
seeing Italy groan under the yoke of a hateful enslavement, has
reawakened the courage of its peoples and has raised up the oppressed against the tremendous tyranny of the barbarians. And as
you see, in all places, stirred by a single desire, Italy finally desires
liberty, and takes care of liberty with the sword and with her
strength.

To those who beseech us in so noble a purpose and so worthy a   2
cause we do not deny our help. All of which we believe should
delight you, as protectors and fathers of public liberty, since all
these things are known to agree with the majesty of the Roman
people and your natural intentions.

In fact this same love of liberty once incited the Roman people   3
against royal tyranny and led them to abolish monarchy and the
rule of the decemvirs, the former on account of the rape of Lucretia and the latter on account of the injustice suffered by Virginia.
This same liberty brought about Horatius Cocles's single-handed
opposition to an enemy threat on a bridge that was about to collapse. It led Mucius [Scaevola], with no hope of survival, before
Porsenna, to sacrifice his own hand in the flames, a gesture that
astonished the king and won the admiration of posterity. It led the
two Decii to elect a noble death, run through by enemy swords.[1]

Et ut singulos mortales vestrae civitatis ingentia lumina dimittamus, haec sola fecit ut Romanus populus—rerum dominus, victor gentium—innumerabilibus victoriis totum orbem, sanguinem etiam effundendo, peragraverit. Ob quod, fratres carissimi, cum omnes ad libertatem naturaliter incenduntur, vos soli ex debito hereditario, quodam iure, obligamini ad studia libertatis.

4   Quid erat aspicere nobilem Italiam, cui iuris est ceteris nationibus imperare, tam saeva pessumdari servitute? Quid erat videre hanc barbariem, praedae et sanguini Latinorum saevae crudelitatis nixibus inhiantem, per miserum Latium desaevire? Quocirca insurgite et vos, inclitum nedum Italiae caput sed totius orbis domitor populus, contra tantam tyrannidem fovete populos, expellite abominationem de Italiae finibus et libertatem cupientes protegite et, si quos vel ignavia vel iugum fortius ac durius sub servitute continet, excitate.

5   Haec sunt opera vere Romanorum. Nolite pati per iniuriam hos Gallicos voratores vestrae Italiae tam crudeliter imminere. Nec sinceritatem vestram seducant blanditiae clericorum, quos scimus vos privatim et publice ambire suggerereque vobis quod placeat et velitis statum ecclesiae sustinere, offerentes papam curiam Romanam in Italiam translaturum et in magno verborum lenocinio vobis quendam optabilem urbis statum ex adventu curiae designantes.

6   Denique haec omnia huc redeunt, hoc concludunt: facite, Romani, quod Italia serviat, opprimatur et conculcetur et hi Gallici dominentur. An potest vobis aliquod proponi lucrum aliquidve pretium deputari quod praeponendum sit Italicae libertati? Quid plura? An potest levitati barbarae aliquid credi aut de gente

And without mentioning each of the many instances that have given luster to your city, it was that same liberty, and nothing else, that caused the Roman people—master of all creation and victor over its peoples[2]—thanks to their countless victories and even the shedding of their blood, to spread over the entire orb. Therefore, dearest brothers, although all peoples all are stirred by a natural love of liberty, only you are truly bound by a kind of hereditary stipulation, by a kind of law, to love liberty.

What a sight to behold noble Italy—she whose right it is to   4 rule over other nations—subjected to such cruel enslavement! What a sight to behold barbarians, ever lusting to seize upon the possessions and persons of the Latins, running wild over Latium![3] Rise up, then, and you who are not only the noble capital of Italy but the people that rules the entire world, give courage to its peoples against this tyranny, chase out of Italian borders this disgrace, protect all who yearn for liberty, and if any should hesitate due to ignorance or the yoke of a particularly heavy and pressing tyranny, wake them!

These are truly Roman endeavors. Do not permit these Gallic   5 vultures so cruelly and unjustly to threaten your Italy. Neither let your innocent minds be seduced by the ruses of the clerics; we know that openly and in secret they plot and they seek to convince you to favor them and to sustain the State of the Church, with the promise that the pope will restore the Roman curia to Italy, describing with much verbal pandering the high standing that the city would acquire from the curia's return.

In the end, all this comes down to one thing. The point is this: 6 O Romans, your actions are causing Italy to be enslaved, oppressed and ruled over, and making these Gauls your masters. But can there possibly be any gain or reward preferable to the liberty of Italy? In short, could one possibly trust in the flighty barbarians or

instabili certum aliquid opinari? Pridem Urbanus quanta spe per-
petui incolatus reduxit curiam? Et quam subito—seu naturali vitio
et levitate seu satietate Italiae seu Galliarum suarum desiderio—
hoc tam constans propositum commutavit? Addite quod summum pontificem trahebat in Italiam sola civitas Perusina, quam—
cum omnibus Tusciae urbibus videatur excellere—sedem sibi
continuam praeparabat; et si quid humano commercio fieri poterat
cum hac gente sperari, totum a vobis erat, si recte respicitis, abfu-
turum.

7   Nunc autem, desperatis rebus, offerunt quod facturi non erant.
Et ideo, fratres carissimi, considerate ipsorum facta, non verba:
non illos enim vestra utilitas sed dominandi cupido in Italiam evo-
cabat. Nolite decipi in nectare verborum sed, prout diximus, Italiam vestram—quam compte progenitores vestri universo orbi,
multa impensa sanguinis, praefecerunt—saltem nolite pati barbaris et exteris gentibus subiacere. Dicite nunc, immo repetite ex
publico consulto illud incliti Catonis dictum: 'Nolumus tam liberi
esse quam cum liberis vivere.'

Data Florentiae die quarta Ianuarii xiiii *Indictione.*

Nos autem commune nostrum omnemque nostram militarem potentiam ad beneplacita vestra paratam offerimus in vestri nominis
gloriam transmissuri.

expect something stable from the fickleness of an unstable people? Did not Pope Urban[4] some time ago bring back the curia with the great hope that it would remain forever? And did he not change straightaway — it matters little whether because of natural weakness, or inconstancy, or boredom with Italy, or nostalgia for his Gauls — this plan of his that was so fixed and permanent? Moreover, it was the city of Perugia alone that drew the pope into Italy, and it was that city — seemingly the best of all cities of Tuscia[5] — which he readied in order to make it his permanent residence. Even if anything of human value is to be gained by commerce with this people, you, if you think on it, would stand to gain nothing at all.

Now that they find themselves in desperate straits, they make 7 promises that they would not have made then. For this reason, dearest brothers, look well to their actions and not their words: what drew them to Italy was not your well-being but lust for dominion.[6] Don't be deceived by sweet words; but, as we said, at least don't allow Italy — which your forebears in so orderly a way made to be mistress of the world at great expense of blood — to become subject to barbarian and foreign peoples. Say now — still better confirm with an official decree — the words of the celebrated Cato: "We want not so much to be free as to live among free men."[7]

Florence, January 4, [1376], thirteenth indiction.

Our commune and all our military forces stand ready to do your will: we offer to send them for the glory of your name.

: II :

Collegio cardinalium

1 Reverendissimi in Christo patres et domini. Ingenti cordis amari-
tudine et displicentia summa percepimus tantum maledicorum
conspirationem contra nos, ecclesiae devotissimos filios, valuisse
quod sanctissimi patris clementiam in fervorem et aestum grandis
iracundiae converterunt. 'Qui cum sapientes sint ut faciant mala,
bene quidem facere non noverunt, acuerunt in nos linguas quasi
serpentes,' et quasi 'gladius in labiis eorum' super nos mala locuti
sunt; fingentes apud apostolicam maiestatem de nobis abomi-
nationes multas et narrationem texentes iniquitatum induxerunt
benignissimum patrem, ut in turbatione magna de nobis terribili-
ter dicat: 'Dabo eos in furorem universis regnis terrae' et 'adducam
super eos gentes de longinquo, gentem robustam, gentem antiquam, gentem cuius ignorabunt linguam nec intelligent quid lo-
quatur.' 'Et comedet segetes eorum et panem ipsorum, devorabit
filios eorum et filias, opprimet gregem suum et armenta sua, comedet vineam suam et ficum suam, conteret et urbes munitas suas,
in quibus habent fiduciam, gladio.'

2 Nec mirum: suaserunt enim illi in maliloquio suo nos multas
plurium ecclesiarum terras per violentiam invasisse, cum tamen
inauditum sit cunctis saeculis quod affirmant, adeo ut numquam
tot retro temporibus super hoc contra nos quicquam fuerit exposi-
tum per querelam. Suggesserunt etiam nos contra ecclesiasticam
libertatem multa enormia patravisse, condidisse leges in clericos,
inquisitoris hereticae pravitatis officium impedisse, diripuisse
bona clericorum, sacerdotes publico affecisse supplicio, coegisse

: II :

To the College of Cardinals

Most reverend fathers in Christ and lords: With great bitterness   1
of heart and high displeasure we have discovered that the great
conspiracy of slander against us, most devout children of Holy
Church, has been able to turn the clemency of the Most Holy
Father into a passionate outburst of great anger. "As they are
learned in doing evil, but know not how to do good, they have
sharpened their tongues against us like serpents," and, as if they
had "a sword betwixt their lips," they have defamed us.[8] Concocting innumerable misdeeds on our part and weaving a tale of iniquities to His Majesty the Pontiff, they have induced that most
benign of pontiffs, in a state of high agitation, to utter terrifying
threats against us: "I will render them fearful to all the realms of
the earth" and "I will send against them peoples from afar, a people
strong and ancient, a people whose tongues they will not know
and whose words they will not understand."[9] "And he will eat their
meals and their bread, he will devour their sons and daughters, he
will destroy his flock and his herds, he will eat of his vineyards
and figs, he will raze to the ground his fortified cities, in which
they trust, with his sword."[10]

No wonder: with lies they have managed to convince him that   2
we have made an armed invasion of the landed property of numerous churches, although everything they allege is unheard of; for
centuries past no such complaint has ever been laid against us.
They further insinuate that we have committed many horrendous
crimes against ecclesiastical liberty: that we have instituted laws
against the clergy, that we have hindered the Inquisition of Heretical Depravity, that we have seized the property of the clergy,
subjected priests to civil punishments, that we have forced the

9

religiosos confessionum revelare secreta et ex huiusmodi testimonio furem quendam exposuisse suspendio, in christos Domini manus temerarias iniecisse, fovere tyrannos et in praviloquio sacrilegas linguas contra beatissimum summum pontificem extendisse, violasse ligas quas cum ecclesia Romana contraximus et denique nos terras ecclesiae in rebellionem asserunt deduxisse. Quicquid in Italia ecclesiae Romanae contigit detrimenti, ignavia vel culpa illorum officialium 'quorum oculi et cor ad avaritiam et ad sanguinem innocentem effundendum et ad cursum mali operis' intendebant, Florentinorum machinationibus imputantes.

3   In quibus, nisi conscientiae nos hortaretur integritas et nisi humanitas patris sanctissimi spem praeberet nique sacratissimi vestri coetus favores et assistentiam speraremus, iam liceret dicere: 'Maius est peccatum nostrum quam ut veniam mereamur.' Sed haec omnia, cum per nuntios nostros purganda et excusanda censuerimus viva voce, ne haec epistula longius protrahatur, quamquam ea diluere facillime valeremus, sine responsione praesentium seriem dimittemus et ad vestri candidatus sacrum concilium recurrentes humili devotione et devota humilitate suppliciter deprecamur quatenus, utcumque res sint et utcumque in nos aemulorum factionem praevalere contigerit, dignemini favores vestros nobis, devotissimis ecclesiae filiis, exhibere.

4   Non recordetur, vobis faventibus, Christi vicarius solum iniquitatum quas de nobis aemuli confinxerunt, sed animadvertat secumque recogitet quem poterit populum invenire—nedum intra fines Italiae sed in totius orbis ambitu—qui continuatis affectibus et devotione inconcussa pro honore et statu sanctae matris ecclesiae tantum bello paceque gesserit quantum populus Florentinus. Nos in Henricos, Fredericum, Manfredum, Conradinum, Lodovicum et alios persecutores ecclesiae, magno nostro periculo magnaque nostri cruoris impensa, pro ecclesiae salute surreximus. Nos plurium populorum et principum, quos nominare consulte nolumus

religious to reveal the secrets of the confessional and used such testimony to hang a certain thief, that we have laid rough hands on the anointed of the Lord, that we have favored tyrants, that we have defamed with sacrilegious tongue the most blessed Supreme Pontiff, that we have violated agreements signed with the Roman Church, and finally, that we have fomented rebellion in the lands of the Church. Whatever damage is done to the Roman Church in Italy they charge to the baseness or the guilt of those officials whose "eyes and heart seeking gain, are ready to shed innocent blood and to do evil,"[11] ascribing it to the machinations of the Florentines.

Were it not for our clear conscience, the kindness of the most holy pope, and our hope for your college's favor and support, it might now be legitimate to say: "Our sin is greater than may be pardoned."[12] But we have decided to refute and explain these things in person through our ambassadors, and we omit to treat the issues one by one in the present response, easy as that would be, in order not to lengthen this letter. Turning to your holy college in humble devotion and devoted humility, regardless of how matters stand and whatever preponderant influence our enemies may have, we pray that you will deign to show favor to us, who are most devout sons of the Church. 3

May the vicar of Christ, with your help, remember not only our iniquities (fabricated by our enemies) but also consider and reflect whether any other people—in this peninsula or indeed the whole world—has labored for the honor and standing of Holy Mother Church with such unflagging love and unbroken devotion, in peace and in war, as the Florentine people has. We have stood up to the Henries, to Frederick, Manfred, Conradin, Louis and other enemies of the Church,[13] at great peril to ourselves and loss of blood, for the safety of the Church. Fighting on behalf of the Church we have occasioned the hatred and opposition of countless 4

ne cicatricantia vulnera detegentes illorum animos accendamus, indignationem et inimicitias pro ecclesia dimicando contraximus.

5   Recenseant maliloquaces isti, si possunt, aliquos bellicos ecclesiae Romanae successus in quibus Florentinorum subsidia non fuerint. Referant etiam, si sine mendacio valent, ubi fuerit umquam eadem ecclesia bello per vim armorum oppressa in quo non reperiatur Florentinorum exercitus superatus, ut iam pudere debeat illos (quamvis obstinate nobis infensos) toties de ecclesia bene meritum populum ante tribunal apostolici throni in maliloquio suo tam hostiliter offendisse.

6   Sed putabant illi se tot et tanta in nostram perniciem cogitasse tamque verisimiliter quaecumque nobis obiciunt persuasisse 'quod non esset qui misereretur nostri ne qui contristaretur propter nos aut qui iret ad rogandum pro innocentia nostra.' Attamen decepti estis in cogitationibus vestris et dissipata sunt consilia vestra. Ecce sacer ordo cardinalium 'novabit pro nobis novale et spinas quas saevistis' evellet et memor beneficiorum nostrorum sanabit vulnera nostra et obtundet adversiones vestras, quibus nos perdere voluistis.

7   Quod, o benignissimi patres, nolite negligere sed pro devotissimo populo favores vestros apponite. Nolite pati hanc christianissimam civitatem tantae severitatis sententia vulnerari. Scitis enim, oculatissimi domini, Florentinos totum terrarum orbem implesse, ut nulla sit civitas, nullum oppidum, quantumcumque in remotissimis partibus situatum, in quod non venerit nostrorum civium incolatus, ut iam non sola Florentina civitas tali sententia sed simul universus orbis, si quis bene respiciat, feriatur. Cavete, o terrarum caelestis et prorsus divine senatus, ne talis sententia, si illam forte contigerit fulminari, plus videatur habere saevitiae quam rectitudinis et iustitiae continere. Nam cum notissimum sit

peoples and rulers, whose names I omit in order not to enrage them or open old wounds.

May these defamers recount, if they can, any successes in war 5 the Roman Church has had in which Florence did not lend her support. And let them tell us, if they can do so without lying, of any instance at all in which the Church was defeated in war without Florence also suffering defeat. They should be ashamed by now, bitter enemies though they are, for giving in their numerous defamatory speeches before the tribunal of the Holy See such hateful offense to a people that has deserved so well of the Church.

They were convinced that they had contrived things to our dis- 6 favor of such a kind and number, and that they had persuaded [the pope] of their accusations against us with such verisimilitude that "there is no longer anyone who will have mercy on us, feel sorry on our account, or speak out in favor of our innocence."[14] Yet nevertheless you are mistaken, and your plans are proven useless. Behold: the sacred order of cardinals will "till for us an unbroken field, and the thorns you have sown"[15] will be removed; remembering our contributions, it will heal our wounds and repulse the attacks by which you meant to ruin us.

May you not neglect to do so, O most benevolent fathers, but 7 may you rather show favor to a very devout people. Do not permit this most Christian city to be injured, sentenced to so severe a punishment. You well know, being the most well informed of men, that the Florentines are distributed through all the earth, such that there is no city or village, however remote, to which there has not come a settlement of our fellow citizens. Therefore, the consequences of such a sentence would be felt not by Florence alone but by the entire world. Take care, O celestial and truly divine senate on earth, that such a sentence, if it should happen to strike us down from on high, may not appear to possess more the spirit of savage anger than of rectitude and justice. For since it is very well

Florentinum populum semper Romanae ecclesiae devotissimum fuisse cultorem, non sic de facili poterit cunctis audientibus contrarium persuaderi.

8   'Dispergetne et lacerabit pastor bonus gregem pascuae suae?' Perdetne Christi vicarius innocentes et etiam si forsan praesupponatur multorum iniquitas, quae tamen inveniri non poterit, perdetne iustum cum impio? Absit a domino nostro, qui Dei vices repraesentat in terris, ut non parcat pro iustorum meritis etiam multitudini, si forsan exstiterit, impiorum. An posset ipse idem sibimet salva conscientia persuadere quod non sint in medio tantae civitatis plus quam quinquaginta, etsi non iusti, saltem odientes malum, timentes Deum vel ad minus omnium quae fecisse credimur innocentes et — quod certissimum est — infiniti status ecclesiae devotissimi zelatores? Parcebat Dominus quinque civitatibus propter decem iustos et tamen unum repertum Dei cultorem et iustum in medio tot urbium salvum esse decrevit. An vicarius eius non parcet uni civitati propter multos aut innocentes cum iniquis eadem sententia permiscebit? Dabitne oves suas sparsas per universum orbem unius sententiae fulmine quasi servos in praedam? Attendite, patres, quod non novit vulgus ex qualitate delicti sed ex atrocitate poenae ponderare sententias, ut non possit tanta culpa praecedere quae non relinquat severius iudicium in multitudinis animo minus iustum.

9   Ite igitur, patres optimi, et ut 'Dominus noster corripiat nos' — si quid forsan errasse dicamur, cuius tamen oppositum discusso negotio reperietur — 'non in furore suo, ne forsan ad nihilum redigamur, sed in benigno iudicio' dignemini persuadere. 'Si enim iniquitatem maledicentium observaverit, quis sustinebit?.'

known that the Florentine People are completely devoted to the Roman Church, it will not be easy to convince all those who hear it of the contrary.

"Does the Good Shepherd disperse and ravage the sheep of his 8
own flock?"[16] Will the Vicar of Christ damn the innocent and, even if the iniquity of many may be presumed — though this is something that cannot be discovered — will he damn the righteous along with the impious?[17] May it never come to pass that our lord, who represents God on earth, fail to spare the crowd of the impious, if such happens to be the case, for the merits of the righteous! Can he truly be certain in all conscience that so large a city holds not more than fifty persons who, if not righteous, at least hate evil, fear God, or at all events are innocent of the things we are believed to have done and (what is certain) are devoted lovers of the Church? God spared five cities because of ten righteous men in them and decreed that the one worshipper of God and just man who could be found in the midst of so many citizens was to be saved.[18] And now his vicar will not spare a city on account of many [just men]? Will he mix the innocent in with the guilty under a single sentence of condemnation? Will he perhaps by the thunderbolt of a single sentence give up his sheep, scattered about the world, as slaves for booty? Be aware, O fathers, that the common people do not know how to judge sentences from the character of the crime but only from the severity of the punishment meted out, so that a great fault which does not leave behind a more severe judgment could not take precedence in the mind of the populace over a less just judgment.

If perhaps we may be said to have erred in some respect — al- 9
though close examination will show the opposite — well, come then, excellent fathers, may you deign to persuade [the pope], and "let our Lord correct us, not in his anger, lest perhaps we be reduced to nothing, but with benevolent judgment." "For if he shows respect for the injustice of detractors, who shall be able to bear it?"

'Effundat indignationem suam super gentes quae non cognoverunt
eum, super provincias quae nomen Domini non invocaverunt,' et
hanc devotissimam civitatem non in grandis irae suae aestuatione
perdat sed in sua humanitate conservet et, si forte opinione sua ab
habitu solitae devotionis credimur deviasse, non in iudicii nos ter-
ribilitate percutiat, sed nobis in suae clementiae benignitate remit-
tat.

Data Florentiae die VIII *mensis Martii* XIIII *Indictione* MCCCLXXV.

: III :

Regi Francorum

1 Serenissime atque invictissime princeps. Nuper in litteris quas ad
maiestatem vestram destinavit nostra devotio — quibus excusationem inter alia legitimam faciebamus de litteris quas dudum ad
Romanos transmisimus, quas audiveramus in manus vestrae celsitudinis pervenisse — inspiratione quadam divina praediximus epis-
tulas illas aut corruptis exemplaribus aut iniqua interpretatione
trahi ad iniuriam Gallicorum.

2 Sicut enim tunc testati sumus, gloriosissime princeps, nos nihil
in Francorum contumeliam scripsisse cognovimus, sed illis, quos
in Italia praefecerat ecclesiae praesulatus, detraxisse — exigentibus
ipsorum demeritis — ingenue confitemur. Et per quandam copiam
quam vidimus de parte epistulae super hoc ad maiestatem vestram
per summum pontificem destinatae manifeste percepimus aut in
manus suae sanctitatis has litteras pervenisse corruptas aut ad
vestram sublimitatem mutatis pluribus vocabulis fuisse transmis-
sas. Ubicumque autem vitiatae fuerint, hoc plane constat nobis

"Release your anger on peoples you have not known, on provinces that have not called upon the name of the Lord,"[19] and let him not condemn this devoutest of cities in the boiling over of his great rage but let him preserve it with his kindness and humanity. If perchance he thinks that we have strayed from our customary devotion, let us not be struck down by his terrible justice but let him forgive us in the benevolence of his clemency.

Florence, March 8, 1376,[20] fourteenth indiction.

: III :

To the King of the Franks[21]

Most serene and invincible prince. In our recent letter sent with   1
devotion to your majesty — in which among other things we gave a
legitimate defense of the letter sent not long previously to the Romans, which we knew had reached the hands of your highness —
by a kind of divine inspiration we predicted that the said document would be construed as unjust to the Gauls, whether because
of errors that had crept into the text or because of a misleading
interpretation.

As we declared on that occasion, most glorious prince, we are   2
certain that we wrote nothing offensive with regard to the Franks,
but we confessed in all sincerity that, driven to it by their misdeeds, we disparaged those whom the papal chair had named as
heads of the Church in Italy. Thanks to a copy we have obtained
of part of the letter about the matter sent to your majesty by the
supreme pontiff, we are able to determine beyond all doubt that
the document either reached His Holiness in a corrupt form or
else was transmitted to your highness with many words altered.

illarum litterarum continentiam permutatam; duobus enim in locis solum hoc vocabulo 'Gallici' sumus usi, ubi videlicet dicitur:
'Nolite pati per iniuriam hos Gallicos voratores vestrae Italiae tam
crudeliter imminere,' in quibus verbis quis non manifeste videat
nos nihil de gente sed solum de his qui dominabantur per Italiam
cogitasse? Et paulo post, ubi diximus: 'Italia serviat, opprimatur et
conculcetur et hi Gallici dominentur,' in quo loco etiam apparet
nos idem sensisse quod proxime confitemur. Alibi autem per totam epistulam aut 'barbaris' aut 'avenis' aut 'externis' aut 'exteris' usi
sumus et sic ubi 'Gallici' reperiatur, hoc per nos insertum fuisse
planissime diffitemur.

3   Et quoniam quasdam glossulas vidimus quibus praefatae litterae ad contumeliam inflectuntur, cum tamen sciamus tres fore
Gallias, prout in principio commentariorum belli Gallici testatur
Iulius Caesar, et Franciam sciamus unius Galliae quotam fore particulam, potentia tamen et nobilitate cunctis Galliis excellentem,
quam iniquum est hoc ascribi specialiter ad Francos, quorum nullus in Italia praesidebat! Cur non magis, quod secundum intentio-
nem nostram fuit, Lemovicenses, qui in partibus istis dominabantur, volunt intelligi? Si hoc dixerint, non negabimus sed sine
controversia expositionem istam affirmabimus fore veram. Deinde
quod beatissimus pater nobis et usurarum voraginem et aliud detestabile crimen obiciat, patienter et humiliter tamquam a Christi
vicario toleramus; credimus tamen sanctitatem suam aemulorum
nostrorum calliditatibus informatam putare se vera dicere, cum
tamen propter paucorum infamiam sit iniquum tantum populum
condemnari.

For it is evident to us that in those passages where the text is corrupt the content is always distorted. Indeed we had used the term "Gauls" in only two places, namely, one when it is said "Do not unjustly allow these Gallic vultures to threaten your Italy with such cruelty," and here who does not plainly see that we referred, not to the people as a whole, but to those individuals who were lording it over Italy up and down the peninsula? And soon after, when we said: "that Italy be enslaved, oppressed and crushed underfoot and that these Gauls be the masters,"[22] once again it is obvious that our thought was the same as above. In the remainder of the letter, instead, we adopted terms such as "barbarians," "foreigners," "outsiders," "strangers;" hence in the other cases where "Gauls" is found we utterly deny that this was the word we wrote.

Now we have seen some short glosses in which the said letter is 3 twisted into an insult. But we know that Gaul has three parts, as Julius Caesar states at the start of his commentary on the Gallic Wars,[23] and we know that France is but one portion of one part of Gaul, though it is the noblest and most powerful part. Is it not then unjust to associate this term [Gauls] of ours with the Franks, not one of whom was ruling in Italy? Why don't they rather want one to understand by this term the Limousins, as we intended, who were lording it over these regions? If this was what they had said we would not deny it; on the contrary we would affirm that this was incontestably the correct reading. That the Most Holy Father should accuse us of being a sinkhole of usury and another foul crime[24] are criticisms we bear with patience and humility, as coming from the vicar of Christ; we continue to believe that His Holiness has been affected by the wiles of our enemies and believes he is speaking the truth, although it would be unjust to condemn a great people on account of the infamous behavior of a few.

4   Demum, gloriosissime princeps, quid fuit dicere quod ad sedem apostolicam nullam reverentiam habeamus ex eo, quod sine additamento 'bonae memoriae' simpliciter dicerimus 'Urbanus,' cum veteri more ac etiam temporum nostrorum consuetudine nunc illud, nunc istud sine differentia faciamus, cum ipse idem etiam summus pontifex, sine alia circumlocutione, dicere soleat 'apostolorum Petri et Pauli,' quasi hoc 'felicis recordationis,' 'bonae memoriae' et huiusmodi non sic debeatur Petro sicut Urbano et sicuti cuilibet alii summo pontifici, quos omnes saltem meritis Petro minores credimus et sentimus?

5   Nec vos moveat, humanissime princeps, quod tam mordaciter in illis litteris de hoc scripserimus dominatu et quod ob id in ecclesiam habere minus reverentiae videamur. Aliud est enim ecclesia, quam venerandam et colendam utpote sanctam—immo sacrosanctam—et credimus et fatemur; aliud est ista dominantium multitudo, quae sub ecclesiae titulo more furentis incendii per Italiam inundavit. Non enim plus habet ecclesiae venerabile nomen maiestatis et sanctimoniae quam illi crudelitatis atque saevitiae. Utinam licuisset, princeps optime, videre miserorum populorum oppressiones! Sed quid optamus rem infaustam et quae sacratissimos vestri culminis oculos polluisset? Longe quidem melius est celsitudinem vestram haec auditu quam visu oculis percepisse.

6   Vidisset enim vestra gloriosa maiestas et privatim et publice miserabiles populos spoliari, indici tributa extra ordinem et ordinaria severius exigi quam liceret hocque praetextu expelli patres familias domibus cum omni filiorum et coniugum comitatu et asperrimos exactores diripere substantias miserorum. Parva loquimur. Vidisset enim, ut breviloquio omnia concludamus, cunctis nihil esse de personis aut de rebus certum sed omnia indiscretis-

Besides, most glorious prince, why was it said that we show no 4
respect for the apostolic chair because we said his name, Urban,
without adding the formula "of good memory," when from ancient
times until today the usage is to employ one or the other equally?
The supreme pontiff himself customarily speaks in the same way
without circumlocution, using "of the Apostles Peter and Paul," as
though the expressions "of good memory," or "of happy memory"
and the like were as inappropriate to Peter as to Urban or to any
other supreme pontiff, all of whom we consider, at least as con-
cerns their merits, inferior to Peter.

And let it not influence you, most humane of princes, that we 5
have written about this matter in so biting a manner and that, on
this account, we might appear less than respectful toward the
Church. The Church is one thing, a thing that we believe and
confess should be revered and honored as holy, nay, sacrosanct;
but this crowd of men who are lording it over Italy, engulfing her
like a raging fire and claiming the title of the Church, is quite another. Just as majesty and holiness belong to the venerable name of
the Church, no less do cruelty and barbarism belong to them.
Would that you had been permitted, best of princes, to gaze upon
the sufferings of our unfortunate peoples! But why should we wish
for an accursed thing that would have polluted the most holy eyes
of Your Highness? It is far better that Your Highness has learned
of these things by hearing them rather than seeing them with your
own eyes.

Your Glorious Majesty must have known about the unfortunate 6
peoples pillaged both in public and in private; you know of the
special taxes imposed and ordinary taxes collected with undue severity; you know how fathers have been driven from their homes
on this pretext together with their wives and children; you have
seen these harshest of tax collectors seizing the goods of the
wretched. But there is worse. You must have seen, to put it in a
nutshell, how when everything is subject to the arbitrary and

simo et superbissimorum hominum arbitrio subiacere et denique
ipsos in cunctis civitatibus fovere et seminare discordias, hos inno-
centissimos per iniuriam poenis afficere, illos in magnis sceleribus
impunitate donare.

7   Quali autem caritate hi—quos Francis iniqua interpretatione in
vestrae gentis etiam dedecus admiscere conatur—populis praefue-
rint, hinc percipiat immensa vestra benignitas. Est enim insignis
quondam civitas in provincia Romandolae, nunc vero latronum
nidus et horrendum receptaculum barbarorum, nomine Faventia,
cuius incolae semper fidelissimi erga sanctam matrem ecclesiam
sunt reperti. Hanc nulla prorsus culpa vel culpae suspicione prae-
cedente sed inconcusse devotam et oboedientem rector provinciae
spoliandam—participaturus abominabili pactione rapinam—An-
glicis, quos ad sua stipendia tenet ecclesia, inaudita crudelitate
concessit.

8   Quid fuit videre, humanissime princeps, innocentissimum populum inermem obici gladiis armatorum, videre miseros in laribus
propriis obtruncari et suo sanguine nedum domesticos penates sed
vias et plateas tantae civitatis aspergere, videre super acervos mor-
tuorum flebiles mulieres totam urbem lacrimabili replere ploratu
et magnam hominum multitudinem saevissime trucidari. Sed felices illi qui in patria potuerunt occumbere! Mox enim quicquid
caedi superfuit et quicquid defessis occisoribus superavit, infinitum quidem vulgus etiam ultra numerum vigintimilium anima-
rum, ex urbe depellitur nudum, spoliatum et multis etiam vulneri-
bus miserandum.

9   Heu heu, quid fuit aspicere, in hoc semper deflendo recessu,
affectos plagis homines cum parvulis et coniugibus fugientes do-
mos et omnem substantiam suam latronibus in praedam dimittere,
videre miserum populum—praecedenti die in urbe florentissima
bonis omnibus abundantem—nudum et rebus omnibus spoliatum

ill-judged power of exceptionally arrogant men, all security of life and property is lost; you will know how they themselves sow and foster discord in every town, inflicting unjust sentences on the innocent while letting great criminals go unpunished.

The following episode may serve to illustrate to Your Immense 7 Benevolence the sort of charity displayed toward the people they would govern by these men, whom some try erroneously to identify as Franks to the dishonor of your people. The inhabitants of Faenza in the province of Romagna have always been perfectly true to Holy Mother Church, but this once-noble city has now become a den of thieves and a terrifying lair of barbarians.[25] The city had always behaved with unshakeable devotion and obedience, and had never given any sign or suspicion of guilt. Yet the governor of the province allowed this city to be sacked by English soldiers he had hired, an act of unheard-of cruelty, in order, by an unholy agreement, to share in the spoils himself.

Imagine, most humane of princes, an unarmed and innocent 8 people exposed to the swords of soldiers; imagine those wretches cut down in their own homes, their blood splattering the streets and piazzas of this large city, to say nothing of their household gods. Imagine wives weeping over the stacked bodies of the dead, filling the whole city with their wailing; imagine a multitude of men cut down with utter cruelty. But the fortunate ones were those who fell in their native land. For presently, those who had survived the slaughter, those who outlasted the weariness of the killers, a large crowd of more than 20,000 souls, were expelled from the city naked and destitute, many of whom were pitiably wounded.

How one laments to imagine this deplorable expulsion: men 9 being whipped along, fleeing their homes with their wives and little children, giving up all their property as plunder to thieves; to imagine a wretched people, who the day before had enjoyed abundance in a prosperous city, now naked and destitute, fleeing

fugere patriam et circumstantium urbes adire, videre finitimos tam
crudeli spectaculo lacrimantes occurrere, recipere in domibus miseros, esurientibus escam impendere et nudos donativis vestibus
coperire. Quid fuit videre matronas et puellas innuptas de parentum et virorum complexibus ad adulteria et stupra trahi religio-
nique astrictas mulieres a divino servitio removeri habitasque ludibrio infandis incestibus maculari.

10   Si haec igitur, clementissime princeps, et alia plura quae longior
inhibet series reprehendimus et mordemus, vestra sublimitas non
miretur. Caveant tamen illi qui volunt ex huiusmodi reprehensio-
nibus, quasi fuerint contra Francos adhibitae, serenitatem vestram
indignationem concipere, ne vestrae gentis nomini videantur non
mediocri diffamatione detrahere quam nos nostris litteris velint
interpretatione nimis extranea notavisse, et desinant quod de singulis dictum est et de illis solum qui in Italia crudeliter dominabantur, inter quos scimus nullum de gente fuisse Francorum, in
genus vel gentem aliquam maligne deflectere et praecipue in eos
quos nec nostra querimonia vel reprehensio potest attingere et
quos et aedificatione nostrae urbis et continuatione gratiarum et
etiam servitiorum usque ad caedes et effusionem sanguinis impen-
sorum multipliciter venerari debemus.

11   Si enim, prout alias scripsimus, scirent nos restitutionem civitatis Florentiae ab inclitae memoriae Carolo Magno — auctore sacra-
tissimae vestrae cognationis — agnoscere; si non lateret eos pro
libertate nostri populi multos de illustrissima vestra progenie
dimicasse ac, quod cum dolore recolimus, generosissimum
effundendo sanguinem occubuisse; si nos scirent continuata devotione fidelia semper servitia praestitisse; si nos sacri vestri vexilli

their homeland and going out to the nearby cities; to see their neighbors weeping to encounter so cruel a spectacle, receiving the wretched folk into their homes, feeding the hungry and clothing the naked. Imagine matrons and nubile maidens torn from the embraces of husbands and parents and forced into adultery and rape; imagine women under vows of religion taken from divine service, their habits stained in mockery from unspeakable acts of incest.

If therefore, most merciful of princes, we criticize and attack 10 these acts and much else which we omit for brevity's sake, Your Highness should not be surprised. The ones who should beware are the people who want to kindle Your Highness's ire on the basis of our criticisms, pretending they were directed against the Franks. They should beware lest they seem to be drawing no small dishonor on the reputation of your nation when they try to dishonor us by means of an extravagant interpretation of our letter. They should stop trying out of ill will to deflect on to another nation or people what we said about individuals and about persons governing Italy with cruelty — among whom, we know, were no members of the Frankish nation. Especially as our complaint and criticism could not possibly touch the French, to whom, moreover, we owe reverence on multiple grounds, as the builders of our city[26] and as a continuous source of favors and services to ourselves, even at the expense of life and limb.

If only, as we have written elsewhere, they knew that we ascribe 11 the restoration of our city of Florence to Charlemagne, of distinguished memory, the founder of your most holy line; if only it did not escape them that many of your illustrious house have fought for our people's freedom, some (as we recollect with pain) spilling their noble blood in death; if only they knew that we for our part have always with unbroken devotion lent you our faithful help; if only they recognized that in all our arduous public business,

cognoscerent praeferre in cunctis nostris arduis negotiis pacis et belli sanctissima signa, puderet illos de nobis haec inique confingere et quod aliquid in derogationem honoris Francorum scripserimus, depravando sententias aut corrumpendo litteras, obiectare.

12 Ceterum, iustissime princeps, ingenti iocunditate percepimus benignitatem vestram, non obstantibus processibus per apostolicam sedem facti contra nostrum commune, cunctis civibus et mercatoribus Florentinis securitatem plenissimam indulsisse. De quo non valemus quas celsitudo vestra meretur debita referre munera gratiarum. Sed Deus ille, totius orbis et tam ingentis opificii mirabilis fabricator, maiestati vestrae praemia digna rependat. Quod quidem certissime speramus et confidimus eum facturum.

13 Respexit enim throni vestri clementia causam filiorum qui, in excusatione nostra per sindicos nostri communis in praesentiam apostolicae sedis et sacri concilii cardinalium nuper facta, fuerunt etiam suis iustissimis defensionibus non auditi. Et cum obtulisset nostra devotio se contrarium omnium quae in nos impingebantur clarissime probaturam, nedum non fuit ad hoc faciendum terminus assignatus sed etiam omnis audientia denegata. Et ne rogati tabelliones de obiectis per sindicos nostros instrumenta conficerent, fuit terribilibus sententiis et comminationibus interdictum.

14 Quocirca serenitati vestrae humilitate debita supplicamus quatenus concessas gratias, ut speramus, dignemini conservare et communitatem nostram atque mercatores Florentinos, maiestatis vestrae devotos, sub alarum vestrarum umbra protectos favorabiliter suscipere commendatos.

Data Florentiae die xv mensis Maii xiiii Indictione mccclxxvi.

Ceterum super his et aliis gloriosissimae clementiae vestrae verbotenus explicandis sollemnes ambaxiatores nostros ad maiestatis vestrae praesentiam transmittemus, qui serenitatem vestram cum

whether in peace or war, we always carry the most sacred emblems of your holy banner — if they knew all this, they would be ashamed to invent these wicked lies about us and to claim, by twisting the sense and corrupting the text of our letters, that we had written something offensive to French honor.

However, justest of princes, we hear with great joy that Your 12 Benignity, despite the processes brought against our commune by the apostolic see, has granted to all Florentine citizens and merchants full and entire immunity. We cannot pay thanks enough to Your Highness for this. But that God who is the marvelous artificer of the whole world and of vast creation will repay Your Majesty with a fitting reward. We hope and trust with the greatest confidence that He will do so.

Indeed, the clemency of your throne has taken cognizance of 13 his children's case. We your children were not granted a hearing in the self-defense recently presented by the representatives of our commune in the presence of the apostolic see and the college of cardinals, even though our defense was completely just. Next, when we respectfully replied that we were ready to demonstrate the complete falsity of all the accusations laid against us, no deadline for action was set and the very possibility of a hearing was denied. On pain of terrible punishments and warnings the notaries were even forbidden to register our officials' objections.

Wherefore we humbly supplicate Your Serene Highness and we 14 hope that you may deign to confirm the favors already granted and may favorably receive and shelter under your wings our community and Florentine merchants who are devoted to you.

Florence, May 15, 1376, fourteenth indiction.

In order further to explain *viva voce* this and other matters to Your Most Glorious Clemency, we are sending our official ambassadors to Your Majesty's presence, who will speak about all these matters

reverentia de cunctis seriosius alloquentur, quam omnipotens Deus sua pietate conservare dignetur cum gloriosis felicium successuum incrementis.

: IV :

Papae Urbano VI

1 Sanctissime atque beatissime in Christo pater et domine, unice totius Christianitatis princeps vereque vicarie Iesu Christi. Redeuntes nuper oratores nostri communis a sublimitatis vestrae conspectu nobis inter innumera sanctitatis vestrae beneficia, quibus nos fuit vestra benignitas in ipsorum persona humanissime prosecuta, retulerunt maximos et excessivos honores quos eisdem tam privatim quam publice, semper cum nostrae humilitatis celebritate, quotidie magnis adiciendo maiora, quodam insatiabili benignitatis affectu, mirabiliter contulistis.

2 Pro quibus, quoniam superant undique modum et supra mortalium vires — veluti de quadam divinitatis altitudine prodeant — emerserunt, dignas rependere gratias non est nostri; retribuat autem ille qui solus cuncta potest quique infinitate bonitatis suae super merita nostra remunerans citra demerita semper punit. Ille retribuat igitur et fragilitatis nostrae defectum (imperfectum enim nostrum ipse novit) suae gratiae bonitate supplendo praemia digna ferat. Nos autem, quantum licet, agimus magnitudini vestrae gratias ex tota anima, ex tota mente et ex totis viribus nostris, ut — quamquam absit debitae retributionis effectus — non tamen cum omni gratitudine mentis, quantum nobis est possibile, desit affectus.

respectfully and in detail to Your Serenity, whom may almighty God in His mercy deign to preserve with glorious increase of your happy successes.

: IV :

To Pope Urban VI

Most holy and blessed father and lord in Christ, sole prince of all 1 Christendom and true vicar of Jesus Christ: On returning recently from the presence of Your Highness, the ambassadors of our commune brought with them — among Your Holiness's numberless favors which Your Benevolence with great generosity has bestowed upon us in their persons — extremely great and overwhelming honors which you conferred on them, both in private and in public, in a wondrous way, ever praising our humble condition, adding greater things to great on a daily basis with a kind of insatiable passion for kindness and goodwill.

In recompense for these benefits, since they exceed all bounds 2 and rise above mortal resources, proceeding as they do from a kind of divine highness, we cannot render due thanks. Rather may He requite you who alone can do all things and who from His infinite goodness always remunerates us above our merits and punishes us below what we deserve. May He then requite you and bestow upon you worthy rewards, supplying the defects of our weakness (for He knows our imperfection) with the goodness of His grace. We, for our part, as far as we may, thank Your Greatness with all our heart, all our soul and all our strength. We may lack the resources to requite you as you deserve, but all the gratitude and affection of which we are capable will never be lacking.

3   Nunc autem, beatissime pater, non potest nostra devotio cum
intrinseci doloris vehementia non moveri, videntes illum filium et
creaturam vestram, quem ad altitudinem regiam evexistis et in quo
tota sperabat Italia quemque videbamus fidei Christianae pugilem
et vestrae sanctitatis validissimum defensorem, tam crudeliter et
tam infeliciter periisse. Nam quamvis iuventutis lapsu malisque
deflexus consiliis, qui morbus cunctorum principum semper fuit,
visus forte fuerit de vestrae sanctitatis beneficentia demereri, videbamus tamen eundem taliter in gratiam reversurum, quod futurus
erat inter mortales unicum vestri status, ecclesiae Romanae et totius orthodoxae fidei firmamentum. Videbamus et ipsum—licet
turbatum, licet extra sanctitatis vestrae gratiam positum—fidelibus esse columen, adversariis frenum et status atque causae vestrae
solum et unicum fundamentum.

4   Sed heu, heu, 'nescia mens hominum!' Dum apud sanctitatem
vestram reconciliationis suae gratiam omni cum diligentia procu-
ramus, dum de corona regnorum Hungariae, sibi tanta cum
omnium populorum exsultatione collata, triumphalem laetitiam
apparatu mirifico celebramus, ille—feritate tamquam barbarica
circumventus—saevis percussoribus ac velut agnus immaculatus et
innocens victima iacuit. Nec sat fuit regiam aulam et reginarum
vultum cognato sanguine maculare, sed sceleratas manus in gene-
rosum illud corpusculum inferentes (heu pudor, heu dolor!) mori-
bundum regem in miseriam carceris intruserunt, ubi demum post
diem vigesimam sui martirii—non sine veneni suspicione, si quid
famae credi debeat—spiritum illum generosissimum exspiravit.

5   O dolor, o pietas! O Carole, sola cum filio miserando de Caroli
secundi fecunditate posteritas! O domus inclita tot regnis totque
regibus et principibus gloriosa, quis digne tuum flere possit

But now, most blessed father, our devotion cannot fail to be   3
shaken by a violent inward anguish when we see your son and
creature, whom you elevated to the royal rank[27] and in whom all
Italy placed its hopes, and whom we knew to be a fighter for the
Christian faith and a most valiant defender of Your Holiness, die
in such a cruel and unlucky fashion. For although through the
missteps of youth he was bent by bad advice — ever the disease of
all princes — and perhaps seemed little worthy of Your Holiness's
beneficence, we used to think nevertheless that he was going to
return to favor in such a way that he would have become the
unique foundation among mortals of your personal position, of
the Roman Church and of the whole orthodox faith. We also used
to believe that he — though turbulent, though out of favor with
Your Holiness — was still a column upholding the faithful, a brake
on your adversaries and the one and only basis of your position
and cause.

But alas, alas for "the ignorant human mind"![28] While we are   4
working with all diligence to reconcile him to Your Holiness, while
we are celebrating his coronation as king of Hungary with joyful
triumph and magnificent festivities, in the midst of rejoicing by all
peoples, he is surrounded by a kind of feral barbarity and is
knocked down like a stainless lamb and innocent victim by cruel
ruffians. Nor did it stop with staining the royal hall and the faces
of the princesses with their relation's blood, but criminal hands
were laid on that noble but frail body (and how shameful and
painful it was!) and they threw the dying man into a wretched
prison, where after twenty days of martyrdom (and not without
suspicion of poisoning, if the report should be believed) that noble
spirit breathed his last.[29]

O, the suffering and pity of it all! O Charles, you who were   5
the sole remaining issue, with your wretched son, of the line of
Charles II! O famous house, glorious for your many reigns, for the
number of your kings and princes: who could worthily bewail your

occasum? Sed haec omittamus. Certi quidem esse debemus, post-quam divinae dispositionis ordine cuncta reguntur, sic agi cum mortalibus ut oportet. Nam cum oculos nycticoracis etiam ad ea quae coram nobis sita sunt, sicut quotidie docemur per experien-tiam, habeamus, quid iudicare possumus de futuris? Supra conceptus existimationemque mortalium tanti principis caedem et tanti sceleris immanitatem, etiam postquam evenerint, quis non videt? Supra sensus etiam nostros est quantum et quale bonum sit eliciturus de tantis malis rerum omnium opifex atque rector. Maxima quidem bona de maximis malis eliciet Deus, si tamen, quantum in nobis est, quae restant prudenter — sicut rerum status exigit — disponantur. Videmus enim ex hoc, quantum sensus extenditur, infelicissimo casu multas mutationes multamque re-rum vertiginem secuturam, ut de stabilitione cunctorum oporteat magna cum circumspectione sanctitatem apostolicam cogitare.

6   Placet autem devotioni nostrae decretum vestrae sanctitatis quod iidem oratores nobis fideliter retulerunt. Et quantum licet humilibus filiis, deliberationem vestrae clementiae erga illustrissi-mum Calabriae ducem et unicum de felicis memoriae Carolo Primo superstitem masculum dominum Ladizlaum modis omni-bus collaudamus, sperantes indubie vestram benignitatem id to-tum, sicut deliberavit apostolica sublimitas, impleturam. Memine-rit autem circumspectio vestrae beatitudinis quantum periculum est in mora et quod iuxta poetae dictum 'semper nocuit differre paratis.'

7   Quod superest quodque devotioni Florentini populi debitum est, sanctitati vestrae totius nostrae humilitatis affectu reverendis-sime supplicamus quatenus ob honorem et gloriam regiae domus ac salutem animae dicti principis, nobis et toti mundo tanta cum martirii acerbitate praerepti dignemini sibi plenissime absolutionis beneficium impertiri, ut sublatis poenis si quas de iure forsitan incurrisset aut si quae per hominem latae sunt, restituatur nomen

fall? But let us leave this aside. We must be assured, since all things are ruled by divine order and control, that human affairs happen as they ought. For if we have eyes like the mole even for what is in front of us — as daily life teaches — how can we judge of the future? Who does not see as things beyond human imagining and reckoning, even after the event, the assassination of so high a prince and the bestiality of so great a crime? It is beyond the reach of our senses, too, to know how much and what kind of good the Creator and Lord of all things is going to elicit from such evils. God will surely elicit the greatest goods from the greatest evils, provided that, to the degree that we can, what is left to us is prudently arranged as the condition of affairs demands. For we see from this most unhappy mischance, as far as we can tell, that many changes and a great falling-off of affairs is going to follow, so that the Apostolic Holiness ought to ponder with great circumspection how it may stabilize the situation.[30]

We devoutly approve Your Holiness's decree that those same 6 orators of ours have faithfully reported to us. As humble children we praise highly Your Clemency's decision with regard to Ladislaus, the illustrious duke of Calabria and only surviving male child of Charles I of happy memory,[31] hoping that Your Benignity will doubtless carry it all out as the Sublime Apostolic Holiness has planned. But the circumspection of Your Beatitude will recall the dangers of delay and the saying of the poet, "to those who are ready it is always harmful to delay."[32]

What remains, and what is due the devoutness of the Floren- 7 tine People, is that we implore Your Holiness with the greatest reverence and in complete humility that you will deign to impart the blessing of a full absolution for the sake of the honor and glory of the royal house and the salvation of the soul of the said prince, snatched from us and the whole world in bitter martyrdom. Let all penalties be lifted, should he have incurred any under law or had them imposed by men. Let his name and reputation be restored,

eius et fama, consuetis honoribus ecclesiasticae sepulturae corpus et eius anima in sorte fidelium reponatur.

8   Nec de contritione sua dubitet apostolica sanctitudo, cum certi simus eundem post infelicia illa vulnera semper de sua morte sollicitum ad paenitentis cordis amaritudinem redivisse. Restituat eum supplicationibus nostris apostolica sanctitas, quae numquam clausit clementiae gremium supplicanti. Post huius equidem restitutionis munus, quod ardenti desiderio de vestrae benignitatis manibus exspectamus, nobis videbimur illum in pristinae sospitatis statu et vitae gloria recepisse. Sanctitatem vestram, cui nos devotissime commendamus, dignetur omnipotens Deus, qui suas vices vobis solis commisit in terris, ad unitatem ecclesiae suae feliciter conservare.

   Data Florentiae die v Aprilis VIIII *Indictione* MCCCLXXXVI.

: V :

Italicis

1 Tandem conceptum virus vipera complevit evomere; tandem, fratres et amici carissimi, serpens ille Ligusticus ex insidiis et latebris exiens suum non potuit propositum occultare. Nunc patet quid hactenus suis blanditiis instruebat; nunc manifeste conspicitur quid intendat. Apertum est illud ingens secretum quo comes ille Virtutum—si fallere, si violare promissa, si tyrannidem in cunctos appetere virtus est—apertum est, inquimus, illud ingens sub hypocrisi miranda secretum quo patruum et socerum quoque fratres et omnem suam necessitudinem decipiens cepit, ambiens deposuit et saeviens interemit.

and may his body be granted the usual honors of ecclesiastical burial and his soul placed among the portion of the faithful.

Nor need Your Apostolic Holiness doubt the prince's con- 8 trition; we are certain that, after being painfully wounded, the thought of his own demise pressed him to feel the bitterness of a penitent heart. May your Apostolic Holiness, who has never denied a suppliant the embrace of clemency, restore him to our entreaties. Once the gift of this restitution, which we await from the hands of your benignity with burning desire, has been effected, we may consider him restored to his prior state of salvation and received into glorious life. We recommend ourselves to Your Holiness with the greatest devotion; may God almighty, who charged you alone to act in His stead on earth, deign to preserve you in felicity, for the unity of His Church.

Florence, April 5, 1386, ninth indiction.

: V :

To the Italians

At last the viper[33] has shot the venom it was storing up; at last, 1 dear brothers and friends, that Ligurian snake, come out of its lairs and ambuscades, cannot hide its intentions. Now the plot it has been weaving hitherto with its flatteries stands revealed; now it makes plain what it aims at. Out is the huge secret of the Count of Virtue[34] — if it is a virtue to deceive, to break promises, to want to tyrannize over everyone — yes, out from under a cloak of astonishing hypocrisy is the huge secret, that by deceiving his closest relations he captured a man who was both his uncle and father-in-law, encircled him, deposed him, and put him to death in a fit of brutal rage.

2   Nam quamvis invasio domini Veronensis, quem pacificae inter-
positionis fabulationibus distraxit et hosti suo praebuit fatigan-
dum, eius animum potuit clarissime demonstrare, quia tamen
Veronensis civitas opportunitate quadam situs suis finibus immi-
nebat, potuit haec aggressio tolerari. Potuerit etiam impetitio domini Paduani—quem deceptum foederibus, occupata civitate Vin-
centiae, quae sibi de victoriae praemio debebatur, si in sua potentia
dimitteretur, habuisset verisimiliter formidare—potuerit (esto!)
corruptis tyrannorum moribus supportari.

3   Quid autem sibi nobiscum negotii est? Quid habet a nobis ex-
petere? Quid poterat aut debebat a communis nostri potentia formidare? Nos, popularis civitas soli dedita mercaturae, sed—quod
ipse tamquam rem inimicissimam detestatur—libera et non solum
domi libertatis cultrix, sed etiam extra nostros terminos conserva-
trix, ut nobis et necessarium et consuetum sit pacem quaerere, in
qua sola possimus libertatis dulcedinem conservare? Nos, sibi
nulla coniunctione finitima nec aliquarum offensionum iniuriis
inimici? Nos, capto per inauditam proditionem domino Ber-
nabove, secum ligam contraximus, quam qualiter observaverit nolumus replicare? Nos, in domini Veronensis oppressione, ne sibi
neve domino Paduano displiceremus, cum facile possemus occurrere, noluimus nostris viribus obviare? Nos, sibi, cum dominum
Paduanum offendi viderimus, quamvis amicus noster esset et nostri communis (tradito statu suis maioribus) creatura, tum sui tum
Venetorum intuitu nullo modo, de quo nunc poenas luimus, de-
creverimus contraire?

4   Cuncta permisimus quae concepit, nihil impedivimus quod tentavit. Et demum in ligam quam obtulit quamve videbamus per

Even though the attack on the lord of Verona revealed his true 2
intentions in the clearest possible light, since that lord was deceived by false promises of peaceful action only to find himself
turned over to his enemy to be worn down: still, since Verona
threatened him by the fact of being positioned on his borders, the
aggression might be tolerated. Similarly, the strike against the lord
of Padua could have been allowed (let us suppose) as within the
corrupt practices of tyrants. That lord had been deceived by treaties, and once Vicenza had been occupied, which was to have been
Padua's prize of victory, Visconti would likely have had something
to fear if it had passed into Padua's power.[35]

But what does this have to do with us? What does he want of 3
us? What could he or ought he have feared from the power of our
commune? From us, a city with a popular government and devoted to commerce? Granted we are something he detests and
cannot stand, that is, we are free and peaceful: we love liberty at
home and protect it beyond our borders, and we hold it needful
and normal to desire peace, for only with peace can we continue to
enjoy sweet liberty. Still, what does he want from us, who have no
shared border with him and are not his enemies for any offense
given? What does he want from us, who, after he had captured
lord Bernabò with an unheard-of act of treachery, still agreed to
form a league with him? — and how he chose to honor that we
prefer not to remember. From us, who during the attack on the
lord of Verona, so as not to displease either him or the lord of
Padua, chose not to oppose them with our forces? — though it
would have been easy to do so. From us, who when we realized
that he was attacking the lord of Padua, though the latter was our
friend and the creature of our commune (since his forefathers got
his state from us), decided not to hinder him out of respect for
him and the Venetians? — for which we now pay the penalty.

We allowed all his designs; we opposed none of his enterprises. 4
Finally, we consented with sincerity to the league he offered, even

malitiam peti, cum versutia tractari et tandem in duplicitate con-
cludi, sincera tamen mente consensimus et omnem removisse causam ac nubem discordiae gaudebamus. In cuius ligae tractatu quot
mutationes, quot decipulae quotque contra rectum et honestum in
nostram infamiam sunt non cogitata solummodo sed conficta!
Divulgavit ligam, cum vix erat in limine, convocavit colligandos, ut
nos posset facilius irretire.

5   Sed haec dimittamus; ligae quidem consensu purgata sint. Post
ligae vero contractum primum observationis et amicitiae signum
fuit Florentinorum expulsio, pro cuius rei iustificatione respondit—cum ad ipsum amicabiliter et quanta caritate dici potest
sinceritas nostra scripsisset—se compertum habere quod decreve-
ramus in nostris consiliis cum maximo pecuniarum profluvio ipsum aliquo secreto modo perimere et ob id nolebat cives Florentinos in suis finibus permanere. Prohibuit etiam Bononienses,
quamvis assereret ipsos tale facinus in suis consiliis nullatenus
agitasse. Cui calumniae, cum ad veneni flagitium tota suspicionis
conceptio flecteretur, postquam fuit per nos ample responsum hoc
nobis vel alicui Florentino non esse possibile, sed ipsum debere
tales insidias solum de suorum manibus formidare, se per alias
litteras convertit ad aliud, dicens nos de caede sua cum esset in
venatu vel aucupio cogitasse. Cui cum fuisset et abunde responsum, non difficultatem sed impossibilitatem evidentissime de-
monstrando, conticuit nec nobiscum post illa litteris disputavit.

6   Sed indulgeamus ista condicioni miserrimae tyrannorum: possint ipsi soli cum suspicione diligere, sit ipsorum magis amicos atque domesticos quam hostes et extraneos formidare; nec istud ad
argumentum inimicitiae, postquam sic est in ipsorum moribus,

though we saw that it was being sought in malice, negotiated with cunning and concluded in duplicity. We rejoiced that it had removed every cause and cloud of discord.[36] And as to the negotiation of the league itself, how many shifting accounts, how many traps and how many things contrary to justice and propriety, in defamation of us, have not only been thought of but simply made up! He made the league public when it had scarcely been set out, and he summoned a meeting of the signatories so that he might the more easily capture us in his nets.

But let all that go: all those machinations were excused in [our] 5 consent to the league. Yet once the league was agreed to, he immediately showed the stamp of his respect and friendship by expelling the Florentines. After we had written to him in a sincere and friendly way and with all possible charity, he responded, in justification of his act, that he had learned of a decision made in our assemblies to pay a large sum of money to have him assassinated, and on this account he was unwilling for Florentine citizens to remain any longer within his borders. He banished the Bolognese as well, though he admitted that they had debated no such crime at their meetings.[37] At that point all his suspicions were focused on poison, so we responded to this calumny in great detail, pointing out that neither we nor any Florentine was in a position to poison him, but that he ought to direct his fears toward plots among his own followers. He then wrote other letters advancing another theory, that we were planning to kill him when he was out hunting. When we responded to this charge as well, showing with the utmost clarity its difficulty or impossibility, he fell silent and thereafter stopped debating with us via letters.

But let us concede that all this befits the miserable condition of 6 tyrants: grant that their loves will always be mixed with suspicion; grant that they fear their own friends and household more than enemies and strangers. Since it is inevitable that they will act this

affirmamus, sed ipsam foederum observantiam prosequamur. Pro-
miserunt oratores sui, licet hoc non fuerit redactum in scriptis, de
quo Deum et ipsum mediatorem concordiae — magnificum fratrem nostrum dominum Petrum de Gambacurtis — imploramus in
testem, quod gentes omnes quas comes habebat in Tuscia, resoluta
societate domini Iohannis Haucud, sine dilationis intercapedine
revocaret. Numquam enim sine hac intentione certe nobis exhibita
secum nostra communitas, suspicione fervente de dimittenda nostra potentia, convenisset. Has non solum, illa societate dispersa,
non removit sed auxit, metuens scilicet — quod omnino futurum
esse cernebat — Senenses et Perusinos ad solitae fraternitatis affectum nobiscum et cum aliis reversuros.

7   Hinc filiis nostris Montepolicianensibus, quos ab omnibus sed
a Senensibus praecipue defendere tenebamur, et comiti Bertuldo
de Ursinis, filio et censuario nostro, quem nominatim in ligam
inclusimus, quam et ipse infra praefixum terminum approbavit,
rupta fide violataque liga bellum per ipsas gentes atque Senenses
illatum. Hinc alter censuarius noster dominus Cortonensis, a
Perusinis et gentibus eiusdem comitis inquietatus bellaciter et in-
vasus ⟨est⟩; et gentes quas solum ad defensionem amicorum suorum, si forsitan offenderentur, iuxta ligae foedera potuit desti-
nare — non in defensionem amicorum, contra quos nulla prorsus
erat offensio, sed in offensionem colligatorum, qui nostro nomine
ligam acceptaverant — et tenuit et transmisit. Nos autem sola defensione contenti, nostras gentes, ut ex liga licebat, ad offensos
misimus ut, quantum fas erat, suis machinationibus obviaremus.

8   Nec interim etiam nostri fines iniuriis et belli molestia ca-
ruerunt, sed quotidianis discursibus praedae abactae, capti agrico-
lae castraque nostra, adhibitis scalis, nocturni furti crebris insidiis
attentata. Quin et ipse fidelis promissorum observator comes per

way, we will not turn it into grounds for hostility. Let us rather focus on how he has kept the aforementioned pacts. His ambassadors promised that, after the company of Sir John Hawkwood had been dismissed, the count would remove all his troops from Tuscany without delay; this was never written down, but we call to witness the mediator, our magnificent brother Pietro Gambacorta.[38] In fact, our commune, given its anxiety about disbanding its military forces, would surely never have come to an agreement with him without getting an explicit undertaking. Yet, once Hawkwood's company was broken up, he increased rather than recalled those troops of his, fearing—and foreseeing with complete accuracy—that the Sienese and the Perugians were going to return to their customary fraternal devotion to us and to others.[39]

Thereupon he broke faith, violated the league, and made war   7 using his own troops and those of the Sienese. He attacked the people of Montepulciano, our children, whom we were obliged to defend against all but especially against the Sienese, and count Bertoldo Orsini, our son and subject, whom we expressly included in the league, which he approved within the time prescribed.[40] Next, another tributary of ours, the lord of Cortona, was threatened and invaded by the Perugians and by the count's troops. The terms of the treaty had obliged the count to use these troops only to defend allies under attack but in fact he kept his troops here and sent them out, not to defend his allies, who were not under attack, but to assault fellow members of the league, those who had accepted the league in our name. We, by contrast, observed the terms of the league and restricted ourselves to defense, sending our troops in aid of those who had been attacked, in order to oppose his designs as far as possible.

Nor, meanwhile, were our own territories spared the violence   8 and damages of war: plunder was carried off in daily raids, farmers were taken captive, our walled towns were ambushed and robbed by night using siege ladders. But the count himself—that faithful

manus infamis et insignissimi proditoris Iohannis de Ubaldinis occupationem arcis et castri nostri Sancti Miniatis cum quibus-dam proditoribus turpissime procuravit. Ipse comes oratores nos-tros quos mittebamus in Franciam ad illius serenissimi principis maiestatem capi fecit et, postquam duos ex ipsis cum litteris et scripturis insidias evasisse comperit, se huiusmodi capturae con-scium denegavit, rescribens etiam (quod erubescendum est!) do-mino Petro de Gambacurtis et aliis qualiter ipsos fecerat liberari; et forte pro liberatione scripsit, sed mox iubens oppositum ordina-vit sollemnius custodiri.

9   Causam autem praetendi fecit quod illi marchiones de Carretto, quod nullis umquam temporibus fuit auditum, a communi nostro recipere deberent nescimus quam pecuniae quantitatem, et quod debitum illud, sicut asserunt, sit antiquum viventium memoria. Cum tamen milies per illorum marchionum fines transitum ha-buerint Florentini cives, oratores publici mercatoresque privati, nulla prorsus alicui novitas fuit illata.

10   Quid plura? Die XXVII mensis Aprilis, omnibus coniunctis copiis, publice vexillis erectis, cum magna tam equitum quam pe-ditum multitudine noctu nostrum territorium attingentes contra castrum nostrum Sancti Iohannis in partibus vallis Arni, vana spe ducti de occupando castrum praefatum, hostiliter irruerunt. Ubi per Dei gratiam ipsis taliter fuit responsum taliterque nostrae gentes tamque celeriter affuerunt quod, nisi sequenti nocte fuga se turpiter commisissent, potentiam nostram cum ipsorum extermi-nio degustassent. Deinde vero die secunda Maii nobis fuerunt in-dicti belli litterae presentatae, quarum et responsionis, quam fieri fecimus, copiam praesentibus iussimus intercludi.

11   Habetis totius rei seriem. Videtis quali fide nobiscum incesserit comes iste Virtutum. Videtis quam possit contra nos iustitiam allegare. Videtis vos ipsi quid possitis de suae felicitatis successibus

keeper of his promises! — by the hands of that notorious traitor Giovanni Ubaldini, along with certain [other] traitors, brought about in the most disgraceful way the occupation of the city and citadel of San Miniato.[41] For his own part, the count caused to be taken captive the ambassadors we had sent to France to the Majesty of its Most Serene Prince, and when he found out that two of them were able to avoid the ambush along with their letters and documents, he claimed ignorance of the arrest, even going so far (what shame!) as to claim in a missive to Pietro Gambacorta and others that he had had them released. And perhaps he did indeed write in favor of their liberation, but soon he countermanded that order, and made sure that they were kept in strict confinement.

He advanced as a pretext the fact that the marquises Del Car- 9 retto were owed some sum of money by our commune and that the debt was an old one, though in living memory. This was something completely unheard-of. None of the Florentine citizens, ambassadors or merchants who had crossed into the marquises' lands thousands of times altogether had ever heard anything about it.

What more to say? On the twenty-seventh of April his com- 10 bined forces with unfurled banners crossed into our territory by night with a multitude of knights and infantry and attacked our fortified town of San Giovanni in the Arno valley, in the vain hope of taking it. By the grace of God our troops responded with such speed and effect that, had the attackers not fled shamefully the following night, they would have felt our great power and been wiped out. Then on May second we received a letter with the declaration of war; we took a copy of it and our reply and have bidden them accompany the present letter.

Now you have before you the succession of events. You see with 11 what faithfulness that Count of Virtue proceeded in dealing with us. You see what rights he could allege against us. You see yourselves what you may hope for if he proves fortunate and successful.

43

exspectare. Iustissima quidem sibi causa belli est posse vincere, posse fines suae tyrannidis ampliare. Nec exspectetis et vos fructus de suis manibus meliores. Scimus quod blanditur vobis, quod se coactum in bellum istud simulat incidisse, quod vobis perpetuam amicitiam et securitates, quascumque petiveritis, pollicetur. Fecit et similia nobis quando bellum intulit Paduano, sed mox, explicito bello, adeo vidimus hominem immutari quod ex tunc quae nunc aspicimus visione clarissima cerneremus.

12 Nec aliud, credite nobis, speretis ex ipso quam quod innocentiae et puritati nostrae videtis retribui reportare. Non incepit a vobis, quibus considerabat nos futuros esse subsidio; versus est in nos, quos sperat a vobis et ab aliis deseri, ut simul desertis possit et desertoribus dominari. Et credite nobis quod, qui solum ambitionis causa tam crudelis in suos exstitit tamque infidelis in omnes, vobis fidem, si potentiam nostram imminuet, non servabit. Concepit, ut vobis publicum esse debet, tyrannidem suam regii tituli splendoribus honestare; concepit et sine dubio totius Italiae principatum.

13 Quamobrem vos et totam Italiam ad opprimendum hoc monstrum, ad contundendam tantam superbiam et talem tantamque perfidiam puniendam altis et claris vocibus imploramus. Nam quamvis speremus Dei clementiam veritati et iustitiae nostrae, cum iniquitatibus semper obviet, astituram, nihilominus tamen gratissimum nobis erit hanc gloriam non solum communitati nostrae tribui, sed nos eam una vobiscum et cum aliis Italicis adipisci. In qua quidem re placeat sic oculos aperire quod infallibili periculo quod imminere vobis cernitis — cum potestis cumque caelum

For him the justest reason for war is the power to win it, the power to extend the borders of his tyranny. And do not expect that you will fare better at his hands than we have. We know that he is coaxing you with flattery, that he pretends to have been forced into the present war, that he promises you perpetual friendship and any kind of guarantee that you may ask. He did more or less the same with us when he made war on the lord of Padua, but presently, in the course of the conflict, we saw the man change so much that what he was before and what he is now came into the clearest focus.

Believe us, there is no hope of any greater profit from him than   12
we have received in reward for our innocence and sincerity. He did not start with you, whom he expected to receive help from us: rather, he attacked us violently in the hope that you and others would desert us, and that he could then lord it over both the deserted and the deserters. Believe us, too, that anyone who lets ambition make him behave so cruelly toward his own and so disloyally toward all others, if he manages to weaken us, will be no more loyal toward you. He is planning, as you must realize, to dignify his tyranny with the splendor of a royal title, and he doubtless aims to rule over all Italy.

Therefore we implore you and all Italy in a loud and clear voice   13
to suppress this monster, to blunt his huge arrogance, and punish his extraordinary perfidy. Although we hope that the divine clemency will stand up for the truth and our just cause, since it always opposes iniquity, it would nonetheless be most gratifying to us if the glory of resisting him should be credited not only to our community, but to us in concert with you and all Italians. Please, open your eyes! Stop the danger that you can see inexorably pressing in upon you. It is in your power to do it; heaven favors you; a

favet et praeparetur remedium—obvietis. Vobis etenim et toti
Italiae protestamur: hoc bellum nobis propter nos non inferri, sed
ut ⟨per⟩ superationem nostram possit vobis et aliis imperari.

Data Florentiae die xxv *Maii* xiii *Indictione* mccclxxxx.

: VI :

Regi Francorum Carolo VI

1 Non potuit contineri nostra devotio et illa sincerissima fides quam
cunctis retro temporibus erga sacratissimam Christianissimamque
domum Franciae semper habuit populus Florentinus, serenissime
atque gloriosissime principum et metuendisime domine; non
potuit contineri nostra devotio—cum videremus illa, quae tam
inhonesta totque permixta mendaciis contra culminis vestri celsitudinem scripsit fidelis ille maiestatis vestrae vassallus, immo regii
nominis detestabilis infamator Iohannes Galeaz, falsissimo nomine Virtutum comes—quin ea vestrae mansuetudini pandere-
mus, fidei et devotioni nostrae plus quam sacrilegum reputantes si,
cum tot et talia scribi de vestra magnitudine sentiremus, ea quocumque respectu duxerimus occulenda.

2 Et ut ad rem breviloquio veniamus, scripsit idem Iohannes suc-
cessori primi electi, qui summum pontificatum exercet in Urbe,
die XX mensis elapsi, quod cum vobis et eminentiae vestrae gu-
bernator Astensis infelicissimum casum vobisque non sine lacri-
marum effluvio recolendum caedis atque conflictus illustris quondam principis domini Iohannis Arminiaci et Convenarum comitis
celeriter quantum potuit intimasset, quod vestra maiestas infremuit et in semet spiritu, sicut scribit, excitato superbiae—

remedy is at hand. We solemnly declare to you and all Italy that he does not make war on us on account of anything we have done, but so that by our defeat he can bring you and others within his empire.

Florence, May 25, 1390, thirteenth indiction.

: VI :

To Charles VI, King of the Franks

The fervent and utterly sincere loyalty which the Florentine people   1
has in all times past had toward the most sacred and most Christian [royal] house of France has not been able to restrain itself, most serene and glorious of princes and most awesome lord. When we saw the dishonorable charges, mingled with numerous lies, that were written against Your Sublime Highness by your majesty's "faithful vassal"—or rather the hateful defamer of the royal name, Giangaleazzo, so wrongly known as the Count of Virtue—our sense of loyalty was not able to restrain us from reporting them to Your Benevolence. Once we had learned of these offenses against your great person, to have chosen to conceal them for any reason at all seemed worse than sacrilege in view of our own loyal devotion to you.

To come to the point: Giangaleazzo has written to the succes-   2
sor of the first elected, who acts as supreme pontiff in Rome,[42] the twentieth of last month, that when the governor of Asti notified Your Excellency with all possible celerity of the disastrous outcome of the battle and—something impossible for you to recall without overflowing tears—of the death of the prince Jean d'Armagnac, count of Comines, Your Majesty groaned and, inwardly provoked by the spirit of pride (so he writes), swearing we

praemisso nescimus quo iuramento—protulit amarum vehementissime vobis esse audivisse casum vestri dilecti comitis infelicem,
verum pro vestris viribus nullatenus remansurum quin propositum
vestrae sublimitatis per eundem inceptum circa statum ecclesiae
compleretis, et quod nuntio nova victoriae suae, sicut putat, felicia,
referenti vultum terribilem obiecistis prolatisque contumeliis (proh
nefas!) vos ipsum in maxilla, impresso pugillo, nobilissimis illis
vestris manibus percussistis.

3   In quibus quidem temperare non possumus quin contra tantam
audaciam exclamemus: O pudor, o dedecus, o nostri temporis ne-
fandissima turpitudo! Ergo reprehensibile vel superbum fuit excel-
lentissimo regi atque humanissimo infelici caede sui proceris sui-
que consanguinei vel infremere vel turbari? Christus, si nescis,
super Lazarum infremuit spiritu et turbavit semetipsum. Haec
autem pietas apud te non est, qui patruum eundemque socerum
tuum avumque serenissimae regiae conthoralis proditorie cepisti,
carcerasti crudeliter et supra omnis inhumanitatis facinus occi-
disti.

4   Noli de tua natura, tyranne saevissime, noli reges clemen-
tissimos extimare! Illis fides, illis pietas illisque supernaturalis
etiam mansuetudo, augentibus moribus quae innata sunt bonitate
naturae. Tibi autem infidelitas, tibi nulla religio tibique ferina crudelitas, corrumpentibus vitiis si quid boni plantat in homine geni-
tura. Et audes nec te pudet asserere quod rex inclitus et benignus
concussione vel contactu maxillae tui famuli suas manus serenissi-
mas macularit. Audes et ipsum dicere in superbiae spiritu concita-
tum, cum illa defleverit quae tu ipse, si quid in te virtutis esset et
si falsa ista felicitas te non extolleret et inflaret, debuisses—memor
humanorum casuum—abhorrere.

know not what, you burst out saying that it was a source of bitter pain to hear of the unhappy fate of your beloved count, but that you would use all available forces to complete your enterprise relative to the Papal State; and lastly, when the messenger brought good news (as he judged it) of his victory you turned to him with a grimace and a series of curses, punching him in the jaw (how wicked!) with your noble fist.[43]

In this matter we are unable to keep ourselves from exclaiming against this wicked act of audacity: O shame, O abomination, O greatest infamy of our time! Was it really something reprehensible, an act of pride, for an excellent and courteous king to groan and be troubled because of the death of a great dignitary, his own relative? Christ, you know, groaned in spirit and was inwardly troubled on Lazarus's account.[44] But a pious action means nothing to you [Giangaleazzo] — you who treacherously made prisoner, cruelly shut up in prison, and brutally killed a man who was at the same time your uncle, your in-law and the grandfather of the most serene consort of the [French] king.[45]

Your nature being what it is, fiercest of tyrants, you should not be passing judgments on most clement kings! To them belongs loyalty, to them piety, to them a kind of superhuman benevolence, thus augmenting with moral virtues the innate goodness of their nature. To you instead belong treachery, impiety and brutal cruelty, thus corrupting with vice the little of good that came to you from your birth. And you dare to assert, you have no shame in asserting, that that illustrious and benign king would have stained his most serene hands by contact with the jaw of your servant? And you dare to say that he was enraged by the spirit of pride when he wept for those calamities — calamities that should have horrified you as well, if you had but a touch of virtue, if false fortune did not buoy and puff you up, if you too were considerate of human misfortunes!

3

4

5   Sed haec satis. Nunc autem reliqua videamus. Subiunxit igitur
'non enim virus quod diu latuit potuit ulterius occultare; sed Deus
adiutor noster est,' et convertens verba ad illum cui scribit adiecit:
'qui sicut principes terrae cogitantes inania adversus sanctae memoriae dominum Urbanum Sextum abiecit velut pulverem quem
proiecit ventus a facie terrae, ita huius furorem propositi adversus
vestrae sanctitatis innocentiam suarum aquarum suffragio suffoca-
bit.' Haec sunt ad litteram verba sua, quae solum ex hoc volumus
in forma scribere, ne dicere posset nos aliquid de his quae scripserit depravare. Ergo benignissimus iste rex et—quod in te non
potes invenire—purissimus venenum occultat aut in sinu suo potest aliquid diu latere? Sunt hae tuae tyrannorumque aliorum, quorum tyrannicissimus es, artes atque latebrae; est et ista tua, quam
in illo praesumis defamare, duplicitas. Sibi vero, cum post Deum
nihil habeat formidare, cuncta sunt patula, cuncta sunt—sicut
decet magnanimitatem regiam—manifesta nec habet in cogitationibus suis—sicut tu, coluber tortuosissime fecundeque veneno—
Dei iudicium formidare.

6   Sed hos superbiae spiritus excitavit in ipso fortuita illa victoria
qua se reputat exsaltatum quaque, ni fallimur, si Deus omnis non
deleat domus Arminiacae memoriam potentiamque Gallorum,
praeceps dabitur in ruinam. Litterarum autem illarum exemplum,
quo possit vestra serenitas plenius informari, praesentibus iussimus intercludi. Super quibus, cetera ponderanda vestrae celsitudini relinquentes, verbum unicum attingemus. Et ut cum ipso loquamur, dic nobis, vipera virulenta, cur oportet nos subicere regis
imperio vel Gallorum? Nos devotione et fide nosque beneficiis sui

Enough: now let's look at the rest [of Giangaleazzo's letter]. He 5
then added, "In fact he could not hide the poison he had long
concealed, but God is on our side," and suiting his words to his
correspondent[46] he continued: "He who has driven, like the dust
that the wind drives from the face of the earth, the princes of the
earth who contemplated vain deeds against the Pope Urban VII of
holy memory, will choke, in the same way and with the help of his
waters, upon the violence of this enterprise against the innocence
of Your Holiness." I set down what he writes word for word in
order that we may not be accused of doctoring his missives in any
way. So: [you, Giangaleazzo, are claiming] that this most kind-
hearted and pure of kings—adjectives which certainly do not apply to you!—hid poison and was able to conceal things in his bo-
som over a long period? These are the sly arts and disguises of you
and other tyrants, of whom you are the most tyrannical; this duplicity, which you pretend to find in him, is your very own. For
him, since he has only God to fear, all lies open to view, all (as
befits the magnanimity of a king) is transparent, nor has he any
anxiety—unlike you, you sleek and venomous serpent!—regarding the judgment of God.

But this spirit of pride was aroused in [Giangaleazzo] by a 6
lucky victory, one by which he believes himself exalted but one by
which—if we are not mistaken, and if God does not wholly erase
the memory of the house of Armagnac and the power of the
French—will be the cause of his imminent ruin. We have bidden
a copy of the aforementioned letter to be enclosed with this missive in order that Your Serenity may be more fully informed. In
that regard we leave further reflections to Your Highness and only
mention it. And, to speak to the man himself: tell us, poisonous
viper, why ought we to submit to the command of the king or of
the French? Because we are his in devotion and loyalty; we are his

sumus. Nosti populum nostrum non magis Florentinum quam regium, quod exhorruisti, cunctis temporibus appellari. Nec mirum. Carolus quidem magnus, auctor regii sanguinis, hanc civitatem proditione regis Totilae crudelitateque deletam aedificavit, restituit et multis privilegiis exornavit. Carolus Primus, Ierusalem et Siciliae rex, nostros Guelfos extorres fidelissimos commilitones suos in hac civitate restituit, conservavit et auxit, Carolusque Valesiae et Alenconis comes, a quo vigentium regum gloriosa prosapia derivatur, Guelfos alborum degenerantium factione depulsos sua potentia in hac urbe reposuit et status, quem adhuc tenemus, iecit suis manibus fundamenta. Consueverunt regales Franciae hanc urbem non velle subditam sed devotam, non eius dominatum appetere sed suam contra cunctos defendere — etiam impensa proprii sanguinis, quod cum horrore meminimus — libertatem, velle (sicut habent) corda cunctorum, non imponere iugum, ut te pudere debeat talia scribere tamque manifestis falsitatibus materiam tuis mendaciis ampliare.

7   In his autem nihil petimus, gloriosissime princeps, nisi quod mentem huius tyranni — qui se, sicut clarissime testatus est, corona cupit et gloria regii nominis exornare — forte minus cognitam agnoscatis et dignemini nos atque Florentinos omnes, qui devotissimi vestri sunt, more maiorum vestrorum in peculiares agnoscere filios et favorabiliter suscipere commendantes.

Data Florentiae die xxviii Septembris Indictione xv mccclxxxxi.

thanks to the benefits he has done us. You know (however much it revolts you) that in all times our people has been called royalist as much as we have been called Florentine. And no wonder. Charlemagne, founder of the royal lineage, gave this city new life and endowed it with many privileges after the rapacious conquests and cruel destruction by Totila.[47] Charles I, king of Jerusalem and Sicily, restored the Guelf exiles who had been his faithful fellow soldiers, and preserved and increased their power; Charles, count of Valois and Alençon, head of the glorious line of the present kings, brought the Guelfs exiled by the degenerate White faction back to the city through his authority, and with his own hands laid the foundations of the political standing we enjoy today.[48] It is the custom of the French royal house to want this city, not to be subject to it, but loyal to it; not to desire to dominate its government but to defend its liberty against others (even, we shudder to recall, at the cost of its own blood); it wants to be loved by our citizens (as in fact it is), not to place them under a yoke. You should be ashamed to write such things and to enlarge the number of your lies with such manifest untruths.

O glorious prince, with this letter we seek nothing but to acquaint you, in case you are not fully aware of this, with the mind of this tyrant, a man who has made utterly clear that he seeks to dress himself in the crown and glory of the royal title. Just as your ancestors did, deign to recognize us and all Florentines, who are your most devoted followers, as your special children, receiving them benevolently as they recommend themselves to you. 7

Florence, September 28, 1391, fifteenth indiction.

: VII :

Papae Bonifacio IX

1 Sanctissime atque beatissime in Christo pater et domine vereque vicarie Iesu Christi. Sicut a maioribus nostris accepimus et experientia rerum, non opinione solum, certior sed omnium certissima rationum quotidianis docet exemplis, Deus et dominus noster, inferiora disponens, sic ecclesiae suae statum et nostrae libertatis ac populi Florentini felicitatem coniunxit, quod nec nos sine ecclesiae felicitate felices esse possimus nec nobis laborantibus prosperitas sanctae matris ecclesiae diu durarit; ut mirum non sit, postquam Deus taliter ista coniunxit, si semper veri vicarii Iesu Christi se nobis exhibuerunt favorabiles atque propitios et noster populus versa vice numquam spiritualiter a pontifice vero descivit et pro Romanae ecclesiae temporali statu veluti proprio dimicavit.

2 Quis enim populus opposuit se Manfredo? Populus Florentinus. Quis Fredericis summos pontifices impugnantibus restitit? Populus Florentinus. Quis summovit Henricum imperiales infulas non apostolica sed propria auctoritate quaerentem? Certe populus Florentinus. Quis scismaticum Ludovicum cum suo pseudopontifice, pseudocuria Romana, pseudoquecardinalibus persecutus est? Certe populus Florentinus. Quis in vestrae causae veritate numquam vel leviter titubavit? Populus Florentinus. Tacemus alia multa, tacemus infinita bella quae pro ecclesia gessimus, fidelia promptaque subsidia quae nos numquam denegasse recensere possemus. Sed surgente stirpe atque tyrannide viperarum quis ab

: VII :

To Pope Boniface IX

Most holy and most blessed father in Christ, father, lord and true   1
vicar of Jesus Christ: As we have learned from our forefathers and
from experience, not only from hearsay, we take it as certain — indeed the most certain of all things — as He teaches to us with daily
examples, that God our Lord, who disposes of all things in this
lower world, has bound so closely together the State of the Church
and the welfare of our liberty and of the Florentine people, that
neither can we be prosperous without the State of the Church's
prosperity, nor can the well-being of the Church last for long if we
are in difficulties. It is not to be marveled at, God having joined
together these two entities, that the true vicars of Christ have always shown themselves favorable and encouraging to us and, on
the other hand, our people has never separated from the spiritual
guidance of the true pontiff and has fought for the temporal state
of the Roman Church as if for its own.

And indeed, what people was it that opposed Manfred? The   2
Florentine people. Who resisted the several Fredericks when they
attacked the supreme pontiffs? The Florentine people. Who
turned back Henry, who sought to have the imperial crown of his
sole authority, not the pontiff's? The Florentine people, to be sure.
Who harried the schismatic Louis with his pseudopope, pseudocuria and pseudocardinals?[49] The Florentine people, of course.
Who has never had the slightest hesitation about the truth of
your cause? The Florentine people. We leave aside a multitude of
other things, we leave aside countless wars waged for the Church,
the reliable and prompt help that (as many could witness) we have
never denied. Who, since the race and tyranny of the vipers has

ecclesia Romana, dum hoc virulentum persequitur caput, numquam discessit semperque fuit secum in armis? Populus Florentinus. Nos archiepiscopum Mediolani, quondam cum Ludovico Bavariae publicum anticardinalem et occupatorem vestrae civitatis
Bononiae, armis fregimus. Nos tamdiu dominos Bernabovem et
Galeazium fuimus bellaciter persecuti quamdiu placuit ecclesiae
bellum illud deserere pacemque cum illis dominis renovare.

3   Sed quorsum haec, sanctissime pater? Ut certe sublimitas vestra
cognoscat populum Florentinum semper statum sanctae matris
ecclesiae promovisse quoniam et versa vice eadem benignissima
mater nostri populi libertatem semper dilexit, iuvit et fovit, non in
postremis reputans sibi populum Florentinum velut ecclesiae pugilem conservare. Nunc autem videt vestra sanctitas quam gravi
quamque laborioso bello vexemur et quam difficile nobis fuit singularissimum fratrem nostrum dominum Mantuanum eruere de
draconis ore cupientis ipsum et alios deglutire. Nec tamen finem
adhuc videmus malis nec pacem credimus faciliter secuturam. Licet enim illam modis omnibus exoptemus, tot tamen anguis illius,
cum quo bellum gerimus, sunt deflexus quod veram pacem, nisi
nocere non valeat, non speremus.

4   Quamobrem decrevimus nos, decreverunt et alii sanctitatis
vestrae filii, qui foedere iuncti sumus, bellum quantocius renovare
dareque gentibus nostris caput fidele sanctae matris ecclesiae,
Guelfum et libertatis atque status omnium zelatorem. Nec hoc
possumus nec volumus, etiam si possemus, sine sanctitatis vestrae
consensu, quam dispositi sumus veluti veri filii semper sequi.
Dignetur ergo vestra clementia nos et alios devotos filios vestros
in hoc quod quaerimus exaudire, videlicet quod magnificum
dominum Carolum de Malatestis ducem nostrorum exercituum

reared itself up, has never left the side of the Roman Church in its battle against this poisonous being, who has always fought alongside her?[50] The Florentine people. We have defeated in battle the archbishop of Milan, the former anticardinal in the service of Louis the Bavarian and invader of your city of Bologna.[51] We have constantly opposed in arms the lords Bernabò and Galeazzo down to the very moment when the Church elected to interrupt that war and make peace with them.

What is the point of this recital, most holy father? So that Your 3 Sublimity may know as a certainty that the Florentine people has always taken the side of the State of Holy Mother Church, just as the same very benevolent mother has always loved, helped and defended the liberty of our people, cognizant of how important it was for her to be able to count on the Florentine people as champion of the Church. Now, however, Your Holiness sees the serious and dangerous war that has struck us, and how difficult it has been for us to snatch the lord of Mantua, our well-loved brother, from the maws of the serpent that lusted to swallow him and others. We do not think the end of these misfortunes is in sight nor do we believe that peace will be easy to secure. However much we might long for it in every way, the serpent that we are warring against makes so many contortions that we can hope to reach a lasting peace only if he is made harmless.

Thus we, and other children of Your Holiness who have joined 4 us, have all resolved to go back to war as soon as possible, endowing our troops with a chief who is faithful to Holy Mother Church, a Guelf, and who is zealous for the liberty and well-being of all. But that we cannot do, and would not even want to do if we were able, without the consent of Your Holiness, whom we have ever intended to follow in the way of true sons. May it then please your clemency to fulfill this request of ours and of other true sons and name Carlo Malatesta as head of our armies.[52] Let him have

habeamus, idque non solum licentiam eidem indulgendo concedere, sed sibi, quod votis nostris assensum praebeat, imperare, firmissime tenentes quicquid felicitatis affulgeat nos umquam a vera tutaque pace, quam quaeritis et pro qua tam diu per vestros nuntios laboratis, nullatenus defuturos.

Data Florentiae die XIII *Septembris* V *Indictione* MCCCLXXXXVII.

: VIII :

Papae Bonifacio IX

1   Sanctissime in Christo pater et domine, vere et unice vicarie Iesu Christi. Temporum qualitas exigit ut pauca scribamus, quoniam res auxilio nimis indiget et, quod querelis abstineatur, vertigo rerum et subita novitas persuadet. Certi sumus quod sanctitas vestra persensit qualiter dux Mediolani vestram civitatem Bononiae potentissime diu vexavit et quod nostra communitas pro defensione civitatis illius et capitaneum nostrum et gentes in magna copia destinavit tandemque die lunae sexta et vigesima mensis huius, commisso proelio, cunctae gentes tam nostrae quam incliti domini Venetorum et magnifici domini Paduani victae superataeque sunt, captus capitaneus et omnium gentium duces et duo filii domini Paduani. Et sicut hodie relatum est, infelix Bononiensium civitas in manus hostium est deducta, quod quidem satis credimus, licet auctore certo nullatenus habeamus, et, si nondum est, propediem timemus infallibiliter id futurum et omnem belli vim in nos prospicimus recasuram.

2   Speramus tamen et unanimi voluntate decernimus nostram defendere libertatem, quam dispositi sumus etiam vitae praeponere

freedom of action and command him to assent to our wishes, with the certainty that whatever glorious success he may win, we for our part will always give our support to achieve that certain and lasting peace which you have so long striven to bring about through your emissaries.

Florence, September 13, 1397, fifth indiction.

: VIII :

To Pope Boniface IX

Most holy father and lord in Christ, true and sole vicar of Jesus 1 Christ: The temper of the times requires us to write briefly, as the state of affairs makes assistance exceedingly necessary and the shocking news and dizzying series of events urges us not to give way to complaints. We are certain that Your Holiness is well aware that the duke of Milan has for long been harassing your city of Bologna in a highly effective manner, and how our city, to defend Bologna, sent our captain and a large number of troops, and finally how the twenty-sixth last, Monday, all our troops together with those of the illustrious doge of Venice and the magnificent lord of Padua, were beaten and vanquished, and the captain and all other leaders of troops and the two sons of the lord of Padua taken prisoner. Today word has arrived that the unfortunate city of Bologna has fallen into enemy hands; the source is not official but we are inclined to believe it, and if it is not yet so, we fear it soon will infallibly be the case. We foresee that the full violence of the war will soon fall upon us.

Nevertheless we have hope and are unanimously resolved to 2 defend our liberty, which we hold dearer than our very lives, and

et eam, quam maiores nostri nobis relinquerunt, in posteros derivare. Et licet omnia quae videmus terribilia sint, non deficimus tamen animis, sed intentione defensionis nos ad omnia praeparamus, cogitantes quod tyrannicae felicitatis cursus hic consistet et quod nostra defensio cunctis statum suum diligentibus erit clipeus et iuvamen.

3   Nunc autem, sanctisime pater, dignetur vestra clementia nobis de gentibus vestris in quanto maiori poteritis numero, nostris etiam sumptibus, sine morae dispendio subvenire concedereque licentiam strenuo viro Paulo de Ursinis, quem in capitaneum habere proponimus, quod cum suis gentibus ad nostra possit servitia se conferre. Et si possibile foret, nostra devotio plurimum contentaretur et loco maximi subsidii foret quod mittendae gentes vexillum sanctae matris ecclesiae secum ferrent. In qua re, clementissime pater, dignetur vestra circumspectio versiculum Horatii reminisci: 'Nam tua res agitur paries cum proximus ardet,' et quod nihil resistere poterit, si vincamur, quin ista pestis et Romanam ecclesiam extrema calamitate pessumdet et totam Italiam redigat in deflendae miseriam servitutis.

Data Florentiae die xxx Iunii x Indictione MCCCCII.

: IX :

Francisco Novello domino Paduano

1   Magnifice domine, frater et amice carissime. Scimus vos optare debere, videmus et multis rerum experientiis vos optasse confusionem atque ruinam tyrannidis Mediolani vel, ut rectius loquamur, infaustae prosapiae Vicecomitum, qui tam diu civitatem illam magnamque partem Italiae crudeli turpique tyrannide pessumdarunt. Scitis vos, vidistis etiam totaque vidit et videt Italia

to pass that liberty on to future generations as our forefathers have left it for us. And however fearful the present prospects, we do not lack courage but are resolved to defend ourselves, standing ready for anything. We believe that the run of the tyrant's success will stop here, and that our resistance will be a help and a shield for all who love their own state.

Now, however, most holy father, may Your Clemency deign to 3 assist us without delay with as many troops as you can muster, even at our expense, whatever the cost, and give permission to the gallant Paolo Orsini, whom we desire as captain, to transfer his troops to our service. And if possible our devotion would take great comfort from it and would deem it the greatest help, if the troops sent were to bear the banner of Holy Mother Church. In this matter, most clement father, may Your Prudence deign to re-member the verse of Horace: "It is your concern if your neighbor's wall is on fire,"[53] and that, in the event of our own defeat, nothing at all can prevent this plague from ruining the Roman Church and bringing down all Italy into a pitiable condition of servitude.

Florence, June 30, 1402, tenth indiction.

: IX :

To Francesco Novello, Lord of Padua

Magnificent lord, brother and dearest friend: We know that you 1 must desire, and we see from many certain proofs that you have desired the downfall and ruin of the tyranny of Milan, or to be more precise, of the accursed spawn of the Visconti, who for so long have ruined that city and a great part of Italy with their cruel and shameful tyranny.[54] You know and you even see, and all Italy

solummodo populum Florentinum cursui suae felicitatis et intentionis annis iam ferme quindecim obstitisse. Certaque sit vestra fraternitas nos numquam quieturos donec eo redacta fuerit sua potentia quod eam non expediat formidare. Pro cuius rei effectu certa sit vestra dilectio nos nihil, nisi quod fuerit impossibile, dimissuros.

2   Quamobrem gaudemus statum eius, ut scribitis, vacillare laetique sumus ipsos propinquos esse ruinae laetioresque fiemus quando viderimus corruisse propeque speramus et cupimus esse diem. Cum autem mittamus istuc, iuxta requisita vestra, confestim oratores nostros, finem facimus; tractanda quidem per ipsos rebus omnibus formam dabunt.

Data Florentiae die XVII Decembris XII Indictione MCCCCIII.

has seen and sees, that the Florentine people alone, for almost fifteen years now, has been blocking the progress of his success and of his aims. Your brotherly person may rest assured that we will never rest until his power is reduced to the point where no longer needs to be feared. You can be certain, dear friend, that we will leave nothing but the impossible untried.

We rejoice that, as you write, his state shakes and we are happy   2 that it is close to ruin; we shall be happier still when we shall see it brought down and we hope and long for that day to be near. But since we are soon to send ambassadors to you, following your request, we add nothing more; the negotiations entrusted to them will clarify everything.

Florence, December 17, 1403, twelfth indiction.

DE TYRANNO

Praefatio

Coluccius Pieri cancellarius florentinus salutem dicit magistro Antonio de Aquila studenti in artibus Patavi.[1]

1   Quoniam rem arduam et scitu dignam quaeris, non possum, vir[2] (ut scripta tua testimonium afferunt) erudite,[3] negare responsum. Par equidem semper mihi visum est diligentem diligere[4] et rationabiliter interroganti debitae responsionis officium, si satisfacere valeas, non denegare.[5] Humanae siquidem societatis vinculum exigit—cum homo propter hominem, quem vidit, immo protulit Deus non esse bonum quod solus ut creatus erat foret, propagatus sit—ut nedum petentibus morem geras, sed etiam cures non petentes in his, quae possis, ut doceas, praevenire. Nec solum hoc debemus in his, quae respiciunt finem ultimum vel quae in finem illum dirigunt, agere, quod fidei communione tenemur, sed etiam in his quae praestare soleant civem bonum vel, quod patet latius, bonum virum. Uniunt equidem mortale genus fides, civitas et natura, quorum primum respicit salutem ultimam, secundum politicam societatem, tertium vero communionem humanam[6] et hominis perfectionem. Quo fit ut, cum id quod quaeris in haec singula per se vel per accidens dirigatur, responsum nec possim nec debeam non praestare.

2   Prius tamen litterarum tuarum initium, quo nimis mihi tribuis, ventilabo. Nam si petenti responsio neganda non est, idem debemus respondendi materiam exhibenti. Multa de me (blande vel stulte dixerim nescio) praedicas; multa fame multaque relatoribus

ON TYRANNY

Preface

Coluccio di Piero, chancellor of Florence, sends greetings to master Antonio of Aquila, student of the arts at Padua.[1]

Since you ask me something difficult to answer and yet worth knowing, my learned friend (for such your letter shows you to be), I cannot fail to reply. It has always seemed to me fair to repay esteem with esteem and, as far as one can, to make a proper reply to anyone with a reasonable inquiry. Indeed the very bond of human society—seeing that man is made for the sake of his fellow man, God having seen and indeed stated that it is not good that man should be alone as he was created[2]—requires not merely that you reply to those who ask, but also that, as far as possible, you foresee the needs of those who have not asked, in order that you might teach them. And this not only in things that relate to our final end or direct us toward that final end, given that we are all bound by the community of faith, but also in those which distinguish the good citizen or, more broadly, the good man. Faith, citizenship, and nature unite humanity; the first regards our final salvation; the second political society; the third the human community and the perfection of mankind.[3] Since, then, your inquiry touches in substance or accident upon each of these, I can not and must not fail to reply to it.

But first I must raise the subject at the beginning of your letter, in which you give me too much importance. For if we owe a reply to one who asks for it, we owe the same to one who furnishes us the material for a reply. You assume many fine things of me, out of

credens, quasi diligenter explorata, de me nimis affirmas. Nimis, immo plus quam nimis meis laudibus immoraris. Tu me cunctis in artibus homine libero[7] dignis, velut in singulis, principem non valere solummodo, sed abundare[8] confirmas. Tu me dicis unum, qui pro singulari ingenio, urbanitate et mansuetudine laudem ab omnibus adipiscar. Tu me, ut tuis utar verbis, praeter summam litterarum eruditionem, virum arbitratu omnium occupatum, parcere numquam laboribus dicis, neque—quod pro fundamento spei scriptionisque tuae sumis—etiam laborando quibus prodesse studeam considerare, quominus a me semper omnibus satisfiat. Tu me laborare, quo cunctis[9] prosim, affirmas, neque multum apud me referre, cum iuvare cupiam, cuius facultatis hominibus scribam. Tu meas epistolas quasdam[10] ad scolasticos multos scriptas memoras, quibus a me, quae per se vel per alios scire non poterant, didicerunt. Haec pro maiori securitate prae te fers, ut audeas a me aliquid postulare. In quibus quidem ne cuncta prosequar, multa quidem alia dicis, compatior errori tuo, qui de me sentiam te deceptum, qui, quod gallicae levitatis esse dici solet,[11] audita pro compertis habes, et illa mihi laudi ducis quae, licet in me fuerint, mea non sunt.

3   Quid enim habeo quod non acceperim, quodque gratis datum non fuerit, non ex meritis, sed ex gratia largitoris? Illum laudari velim, qui dator est et artifex, non me cui detur, quique sim opificis instrumentum. Quicquid sum, sive dixeris accidens[12] sive substantiam, eius est cuius opificium sumus, quod nostrum credere summa dementia nobisque ad laudem ascribere inexcusabilis superbia est. Quare facessas posthac ab istis, precor, nec aures meas decipi faciles hoc blandimento permulceas, ne forsitan obliviscar illa[13] quae laudaveris eius esse qui dederit et non mea. Qui se qui-

politeness or ignorance I hardly know whether to say. You speak too confidently of things that have come to you by common report,[4] as if you had carefully investigated them. You praise me too much, nay, more than too much. You say that in each and all the arts worthy of the liberally educated man I am not only the first, but exceedingly so. You declare that I have won the praise of all men by a singular talent, culture and courtesy. To use your own words, you say that besides my superior literary accomplishment, I am a man intent on the esteem of all men, never sparing any effort or labor, nor (and on this you hang the hope of a reply) even in working to be useful to some, do I ever fail to ponder if that pleases everyone. You say that I work for all, and that the abilities of the men to whom I write make little difference to me, provided only that I can be of service. You refer to certain letters of mine written to various scholars and containing things which they could not have learned from others or by themselves. You bring forward these things to give yourself greater confidence in making bold to ask me for something. I am truly sorry for your mistake in these matters and others which I pass over; for I do feel that you have deceived yourself, taking "with Gallic levity," as the saying is, things as proven which are only matters of hearsay, and praising me for talents that, even if I had them, are not really my own.

For what have I that has not been given to me, and *gratis* at 3 that, not for my own merit, but by the grace of the bountiful Giver?[5] I would rather have you give praise to Him who is the giver and the artificer, rather than to me the receiver and the mere tool of the craftsman's hand. Whatever I am, substance or accident,[6] is His, whose work I am; to say it is mine would be the height of folly; to take praise for it would be unpardonable conceit. Wherefore I beg you henceforth to have done with this sort of thing and not to flatter my all-too-ready ear with such blandishments, lest I forget that what you praise is not my own but His

dem didicisse quicquam dixerit studio suo et industria vel medita-
tione sua, primam se causam esse dicit, quo quantae sit dementiae
tu, qui studes in artibus, iudex esto. Tu me numquam in stultitiam
hanc induces. Instrumentum enim sum artificis, non efficiens[14]
causa vel operis vel actionis; licet, si velimus id quod per nos agitur
in quantum a voluntate nostra dependeat considerare, Deo veraciter cooperemur, ex quo nascitur operis meritum, quod retributionis non est causa sed mensura. Nam in eo quod ab actus integritate deficimus, ab aeternae legis regula deviamus, in eoque
deformitatem non agendo quod debemus inducimus, unde nos
aeternae legis suppliciis obligamus. Lauda nunc me, si potes, et
meum esse praetende quod a me[15] vides esse non posse. Si scio, vel
potius si me scire credideris, gratulare quod illud Dominus mihi[16]
dedit oraque quod permaneat gratia, ne—si subtracta fuerit—
ignorantia detegatur mea.[17]

4   Quod autem multos avaritiae clarissima ratione condemnas qui
docere nolint vel, si doceant, scribere saeculi felicibus soleant, cum
ceteros dedignentur, laudabiliter facis. Dignissimi quidem repre-
hensione sunt qui, cum sentire debeant Dei donum se gratis—si
non desipiant—accepisse, universalis causae munus in privatam
conantur redigere dicionem, et, quod detestabilius est, suis laboribus quaesisse gloriantur quod non possunt, nisi quantum Deo
placeat, conservare quodque vident aliis etiam magis laborantibus
non concedi. Sed illi maneant in errore suo; nos vero cum media-
tore Dei et hominum sentiamus: gratis accepistis; gratis date. Nec
postquam video rerum omnium principem hominibus, qui nihil
sunt, talia dona dare, quemquam velim in retributione talenti,
quod acceperim, posthabere. Nam si tanta maiestatis celstitudo
dignata fuit aliquid parvitati meae concedere, audebone sic ducere

who gave it. Whoever says he has learned anything by his own zeal or diligence or reflection declares himself to be the first cause, and what folly that is, you, a student in Arts, can judge for yourself. You shall never lead me into any such foolishness. I am the tool of the Master, not the efficient cause of the work or of the action.[7] And yet, if we think of the work in so far as it depends upon our own will, we truly cooperate with God, and from this comes all our merit in the work, not as a *reason* for recompense, but as a *measure* of it. For, in so far as we fail in the perfection of an action, we depart from the eternal law, and failing to do as we ought we cripple the work and thus incur the penalty of that law. Now then, praise me if you can, and pretend that is mine which you now see cannot come from me! If I have learning — or rather if you believe I have it — congratulate me that God has given it to me and pray that His grace may remain, lest if it were taken away my ignorance should be exposed.[8]

When you accuse many of selfishness, for the best of reasons,   4
because they are unwilling to give instruction or, if they do give it address themselves only to the fortunate of this world, neglecting the rest, you do well. They are indeed most worthy of reproof who, knowing, if they are not fools, that they have freely received the gift of God, try to bring under their own private control this favor of the universal cause, and what is worse, boast that they have gained by their own labor that which they could never keep except by God's favor and that which they see is denied even to others who work far harder than they do. But let them remain in their error, and let us follow the precept of the Mediator between God and man: "Freely ye have received; freely give!"[9] When I see the Lord of all things giving such gifts to men who are of themselves nothing, I could never wish to overlook any one of them in repayment for that talent which is mine. If majesty supreme has deigned to bestow some gift upon my insignificance, can I dare

meum sicque mihi putare concessum quod apud me remanere debeat, non per me potius publicari? Dedignaborne propter ignobili-
tatem tenuem sordidamque fortunam proximum, qui videam quod
me Deus tam infimum[18] et abiectum a sublimitate et excellentia
sua, licet maximus, non despexit? Non dedignabor te[19] nec alium,
licet ignotum qualis tu mihi es, qui quod scivero voluerit addiscere, nec cuiquam quod acceperim invidebo. Si veritatem eius
quod quaeris invenero, mecum poteris gratulari; sin autem non
satisfaciam ut exoptas, imputes ignorantiae meae, imputes et tibi,
qui plus de me[20] speraveris quam sperari potuisse rerum experientia te docebit. Haec hactenus.

5   Nunc autem ad id quod quaeris teque velle video venientes,
primo docebimus quid tyrannus,[21] tam de nominis proprietate
quam de rei essentia, ne forsitan in equivoco fluctuemus, adiciendo
quotuplex sit tyrannus;[22] secundo loco discutiemus an tyrannum
occidere liceat quacumque diffinire poterimus ratione; tertio de
principatu Caesaris disseremus et an Caesar inter tyrannos rationabiliter possit ac debeat numerari;[23] quarto numquid iure fuerit
an iniuria per suos invasores occisus; ultimo vero probabimus divi-
nissimum Dantem, civem et compatriotam meum, quod eos in
inferni profundum demerserit non errasse. Quibus explicitis,
cogito tibi similemque dubitationem moventibus satisfactum fore.
Quod autem ultimo loco quaeris, an scilicet Antenor et Aeneas
fuerint patriae proditores, quoniam non est controversia rationis,
satis erit quod ultimo loco faciam quid apud antiquos reppererim[24]
annotare. Quod quidem in postremis conabimur expedire.

think it was given me to keep to myself and not rather through me to be shared with others? Or shall I look down upon my neighbor on account of his humble station or his modest fortune, when I consider how God has not scorned me, low as I am and so far below His supreme excellence? I will not disdain you or anyone, even one unknown to me as you are, who may desire to learn what I know, nor will I begrudge to anyone what has been given to me. If I shall find out the truth of the matter about which you inquire, you may rejoice with me; but if I shall disappoint your expectations ascribe it in part to my ignorance, but partly also to yourself for having greater hopes of me than experience shall have shown to be warranted. Of this, enough.

Now, coming to your inquiry: I will first give a definition of a 5 tyrant, both as to the word and the thing itself, so that we may not be floating about in misunderstandings, and I will add also how many kinds there are. In the second place, we will discuss whether it is lawful to kill a tyrant for any definable reason. Third, we will discourse upon the rule of Caesar and whether he can and ought to be considered a tyrant. Fourth, whether he was rightly or wrongly slain by his assailants, and finally, we shall prove that Dante, my divinely gifted fellow citizen, was right in placing these assailants in lowest hell. When all this has been done I think you and all who raise similar questions will be satisfied. As to your final query, whether Antenor and Aeneas were traitors to their country, since this does not involve an argument, it will be enough if I make a note of what I could find about this in the ancient writers, and this I will try to do at the close of my treatise.

: I :

Quid sit tyrannus et unde dicatur

1 Haec dictio 'tyrannus' origine Graeca est, et tam apud ipsos quam etiam[25] apud nos idem significavit olim et hodie similiter idem signat. Nam cum 'tyros' idem sit quod 'fortis,' et ab initio quaelibet civitas atque gens rerum publicarum imperium, teste Trogo, penes reges habebat,[26] quos, ut Iustinus scribit, non ambitio popularis sed spectata inter bonos moderatio provehebat et ipsorum singulare munus esset defendere imperii fines, imperare quod iustum arbitrarentur et lites, si quas innocentia temporis fors[27] habebat, aequitate quae natura mentibus hominum inserta est[28] extinguere, quae quoniam tum corporis tum animi fortitudinem exigerent, apud Graecorum antiquissimos et priscos Italiae viros ab ista fortitudine reges tyranni dicti sunt. A regnando vero rex graece[29] 'vassileus'[30] appellatur; 'vassileuo'[31] quidem graece idem est[32] quod 'regno' latine.

2 Crescente vero malitia, cum superbe regnare reges incepissent, nomen tyranni restrictum est ad illos qui per insolentiam imperii viribus abutuntur. Cui rei testimonio sit optimus poetarum Maro: 'Gens,' inquit,

> bello praeclara iugis insedit Etruscis.
> Hanc multos florentem annos rex deinde superbo
> imperio et saevis tenuit Mezentius armis,

et subdit quod ad superbiam respicit:

> Quid memorem infandas caedes, quid facta tyranni?

: I :

What a tyrant is, and why he is so called

The word "tyrant" is of Greek origin and has the same meaning 1
among both the Greeks and ourselves, in ancient times and now.
For the word *tyros* is the same as "brave." Now, from the beginning,
as Trogus testifies, all city-states and peoples had the power of
their commonwealths under the control of kings, and these, as
Justin says, were raised to power, not through popular favor, but
by the well-considered judgment of good citizens.[10] Their special
function was to defend the frontiers of the realm, to rule justly and
to settle disputes, if the innocence of the time should produce
such, in accordance with that sense of equity which is implanted
by nature in the human mind; and since these duties required
bravery of mind and body, the most ancient Greeks and the earliest Italians called their kings "tyrants."[11] From his function as a
ruler the king is called in Greek *basileus*, for the verb *basileuo* in
Greek is the same as *regno* in Latin.

But then, as evil increased and kings began to rule oppressively, 2
the name "tyrant" was confined to those who abused their power
tyrannically.[12] On this point we have the witness of Vergil, greatest
of poets. He says:

A tribe, famed in war, making settlement upon an Etruscan
   hill,
flourished many years until King Mezentius held it down
with domineering rule and harsh force,[13]

and he adds, touching upon the idea of haughtiness:

Why record his unspeakable massacres or the tyrant's
   misdeeds?

Ecce quem 'superbum' primo regem dixerat, mox 'tyrannum' vocat qui prius de Aenea suo, quem pium et regem ubique vult, haec[33] dixerat:

Pars mihi pacis erit dextram tetigisse tyranni.

Et haec de ratione nominis dicta sint, ut quorumdam ignorantiam et somnia dimittamus.

3 Et ut ad diffinitionem eius quod per tyrannum intelligi debeat veniamus, ponam textum[34] divi Gregorii, qui librorum moralium[35] super Iob duodecimo, exponens illa verba[36] 'et numerus annorum incertus est tyrannidis eius,' quae leguntur Iob quinto decimo capitulo, tyrannum non diffinivit solum[37] sed plures eius species assignavit. Scribit enim divine prorsus, ut cetera: 'proprie enim tyrannus dicitur qui in communi re publica non iure principatur.'

4 Postque subiungit: 'Sed sciendum quia omnis superbus iuxta modum proprium tyrannidem exercet. Nam nonnumquam alius in re publica per acceptam potentiam dignitatis, alius in provincia, alius in civitate, alius in[38] domo propria, alius per latentem nequitiam hoc exercet apud se in cogitatione sua. Nec intuetur Deus quantum quisque mali valeat facere, sed quantum velit. Et cum deest potestas foris, apud se[39] tyrannus est, cui iniquitas dominatur intus,[40] quia etsi exterius non affligat proximos,[41] intrinsecus tamen habere potestatem[42] appetit ut affligat.'

5 Haec Gregorius. Et ut me prius de tyranni speciebus, quas ille ponit, expediam, principali sectione duplex videtur esse tyrannus: unus quidem habitu, sed alter est actu. Nam cui potestas deest, sed latente nequitia[43] tyrannidem exercet affectu, secum habet habitum sed non actum. Et hic est tyrannus, si recte respicias, solum secum; quae quidem deformitas apud Deum, 'qui scrutatur renes[44] et corda,' gravis est, quoniam non intuetur, immo non solum

You notice that the person whom he first called "a haughty king" is here called "tyrant," and previously he had said of his hero Aeneas, whom he everywhere describes as loyal and as a king:

For me a token of peace is to shake hands with the tyrant.[14]

Thus much I have said as to the meaning of the word in order to dispose of the ignorant fancies of certain persons.

Now, to come to the definition of a tyrant, I would cite a text 3 from St. Gregory, who, in the twelfth book of his commentary upon the [Book of] Job, expounding these words: "and the number of the years of his tyranny is uncertain" in chapter fifteen of Job, defines with divine accuracy not only the tyrant but also the various types of tyrant. He says: "Properly speaking a tyrant is one who rules a communal commonwealth without right."[15]

Then he adds "but everyone who rules pridefully practices tyr- 4 anny according to his own measure." "Sometimes a person may practice this in a commonwealth through an office which he has received, another in a province, another in a city, another in his own house, and another through concealed malignity, within his own heart. God does not ask how much evil a man does, but how much he would like to do. If outward power be lacking, he whose iniquity governs him inwardly is a tyrant at heart; for, although he cannot injure his neighbors outwardly, inwardly he desires to have power that he may injure them."[16]

Thus far Gregory. To dispose first of what he says as to the 5 kinds of tyrants, in his most important chapter the tyrant appears under two forms, one via an acquired capacity, the other via his activity.[17] If a man lacks power, and practices tyranny in his intentions by a hidden disposition to wickedness, he possesses the capacity but is not a tyrant in his activity. He is, properly speaking, a tyrant within himself, and this defect in the sight of God, "who trieth the hearts and reins,"[18] is a serious one, for

intuetur[45] Deus quantum quisque facere valeat[46] sed potius quantum velit. Et de hac in homine disproportione nihil ad praesens.

6   Actualiter autem et proprie tripliciter potest, sicut principatus dividitur, dispartiri. Est enim principatus regius, est politicus, est et despoticus. Nam aut quis dominatur iuxta prudentiae suae regulam et arbitrium voluntatis liberae[47] sine lege vel cuiusquam diffinitione legis aut hominis, pro subditorum utilitate, et hoc dominium est regale; aut auctoritate restricta legibus,[48] quam transgredi nefas sit, qui principatus politicus appellatur; aut illa ratione dominii, qua quis praesidet servis atque iumentis, in quo possesionis conservatio quaeritur et utilitas possidentis, quod regnandi genus proprie despoticum a Graecis appellatur, quod secundum finis rationem ad oeconomicam spectat.

7   In quibus quidem regnandi differentiis qui superbiam exercet convertitur in tyrannum, sicut volunt bene considerata verba Gregorii quae superius annotavi. Regium enim dominatum primo designat aliquem in re publica per acceptam potentiam dignitatis per superbiam commutare, politicum cum dicit in provincia vel civitate, despoticum autem cum subdit in domo propria. Non enim oeconomicus principatus contra regium, politicum vel despoticum distinguitur, sed illa tria potius amplexatur. Pater namque familias filio dominatur regie per dilectionem et amorem, uxori vero politice, secundum iuris determinationem, sed servis despotice, sicut in propriam possessionem. Tyrannus autem, licet omnibus opponatur, quia tamen eius proprium est pessundare leges,[49] superbe se

God considers not only what one is able to do, but still more what one desires to do. About this imbalance within man we say nothing for now.

Tyrannical activity properly so called, however, like regimes, can 6 be divided into three distinct types. For there is a monarchical, a constitutional, and a despotic regime.[19] For either one governs according to the standards of one's own prudence and the dictates of one's own will, freely and without laws or the limitations of any statutes or of any man, solely for the good of his subjects, and this rule is monarchical; or one governs with an authority limited by laws which it is a crime to break, which rule is called a constitutional government; or one rules by that system of government which is exercised over slaves and beasts, whose aim is the preservation of property and the welfare of its owner, which type of rule is specially called by the Greeks despotic rule,[20] because its ultimate purpose is similar to that of the head of the household.

Now in these several forms of government, he who rules pride- 7 fully becomes a tyrant, and that is the meaning of those words of Gregory above quoted, if we consider them carefully. For he indicates how it is that someone who takes on the power of an office in a commonwealth is altered through pride, first discussing monarchical power, next constitutional power in a province or city, adding lastly despotic power in one's own home. Now he does not set the government of a household against monarchical, constitutional or despotic rule, but the first rather embraces all three types.[21] The father of a family governs his son monarchically through his affection for him, his wife constitutionally according to the principles of right, but his slaves despotically as being his own property. The tyrant, however, although he is contrasted with all these, since it is his character to destroy laws, to behave

gerere suisque non subditorum utilitatibus providere, magis cum oeconomico convenit atque despotico, secundum finem, cuius est quae sibi conduxerint maxime sequi facultatesque proprias[50] ampliare; sed in eo quod ad voluntatis arbitrium spectat, cum regali congruit[51] principatu.

8   Proprium autem est tyranni non iure principari, quod quidem duplici ratione contingere potest: vel si non suum quis occupaverit principatum in communi re publica,[52] vel si regat iniuste, vel si, quod latius patet, leges et iura non observet. Audi tyrannum apud L. Annaeum Senecam de se loquentem:

> Ego rapta quamvis (inquit) sceptra victrici geram
> dextra geramque[53] cuncta sine legum metu

et cetera. 'Rapta sceptra' monstrant iniquitatem tituli; 'geramque cuncta sine legum metu'[54] respicit administrationis deformitatem, quae Gregorius formaliter dixit convenire tyranno, dicens 'qui non iure principatur.'

9   Concludamus igitur tyrannum esse qui invadit imperium et iustum non habet titulum dominandi et quod tyrannus est qui superbe dominatur aut iniustitiam facit vel iura legesque non observat; sicut e contra legitimus princeps est cui iure principatus delatus est, qui iustitiam ministrat et leges servat.[55]

haughtily toward his subjects and to consider his own welfare rather than theirs, comes nearest to the despotic government of a household as regards his main object, namely, to pursue what is specially profitable to himself and to increase his private wealth. As regards the action of his own will, on the other hand, he approaches more nearly a monarchical government.[22]

However, the particular quality of the tyrant is that he does not 8 rule according to law; and this may happen in either one of two ways: he may have taken possession of a communal commonwealth which he had no title to,[23] or else he may rule unjustly or generally speaking he may disregard laws and rights. Hear what a tyrant says of himself in the words of Seneca:

> Though I wield the scepter I have seized with a victor's hand,
> and though I administer all things without fear of the laws
>   [. . .]

and so on.[24] The words "scepter I have seized" show the unlawfulness of his title, and the words "administer all things without fear of the laws" show that corruption in administration which Gregory says is the mark of a tyrant: "one who governs outside of the law."

We conclude, therefore, that a tyrant is one who usurps power, 9 having no legal title to rule, and one whose governance is vitiated by pride or who rules unjustly or does not respect rights or laws; just as, on the other hand, he is a lawful prince upon whom governance is conferred by right, who administers justice and maintains the laws.[25]

: II :

An liceat tyrannum occidere

1   Et, ut ab invasoribus incohemus, quis neget et universum populum et seu maiorem civium partem aut etiam quamcumque municipum portionem quin immo singularem, vel, ut expressius loquar, singulum[56] et unum civem iure posse resistere libertatem populi vel principatum contra iustitiam invadenti? Nam si, ut optimi principum Diocletianus et Maximianus augusti scribentes Theodoro[57] statuerunt, ad defendendam possessionem, quam sine vitio quis teneat, licet recte possidenti propulsare vim illatam cum inculpatae tutelae moderatione, et, ut peritissimus iuris consultorum Ulpianus inquit, eum qui cum armis venisset armis repellere possumus (nam, ut scribit Cassius, licere vim vi repellere natura comparatum est), quis negare potest invadenti principatum[58] urbis, provinciae vel regni resisti per quemlibet iure posse?

2   Ergo licebit invasores unius hominis vel agri vi repellere et etiam perseverantem occidere, et illum — qui dominium civitatis aut monarchiam vel politicum principatum per vim occupare temptaverit — non poterimus armis et etiam cum caede vel sanguine[59] prohibere? Nimis iniquae leges essent, immo leges omnino non essent, si quod in periculis et iniuriis conceditur privatorum, conservationi libertatis et rei publicae negaretur. Quod si nocturnum furem, qui sic se telo defendat[60] quod occidens ei sine periculo suo — personae scilicet aut rerum — parcere non potuit, Ulpiano teste, licet impune perimere; si latrones publicos et militiae desertores Arcadius, Theodosius et Honorius permiserunt

: II :

Whether it is lawful to kill a tyrant[26]

Now, to begin with the question of usurpers: who will deny that   1
the people as a whole, or a majority of the citizens, or part of the
population of a town, or, to speak more exactly, even a single citizen may lawfully resist anyone who attacks the liberty of the people or usurps the government? For if, as those greatest of rulers,
the emperors Diocletian and Maximian, writing to Theodorus,
decreed, it is right for a lawful owner of property to which he is
entitled to repel force with force in just measure, in order to defend it by driving back opposition with the moderation of blame-
less guardianship;[27] and if, as Ulpian, the ablest of jurists, says,
one may forcibly resist an armed assailant; and if according to
Cassius it is a right of nature to oppose force with force,[28] who can
deny that any person may lawfully resist a person who usurps the
government of a city, a province, or a kingdom?

So shall it be permitted to repel by force someone who attacks   2
an individual or his land and, if he should persist, to kill him —
and yet we cannot prevent by use of arms or death itself a man
who tries to seize power in a state, whether it is monarchical or
constitutional? The laws would be very unfair, indeed they would
be no laws at all, if that which is permitted to private persons in
case of danger or abuse were forbidden for the preservation of
liberty or of the commonwealth. For if, according to Ulpian, it is
lawful to kill a thief in the night who defends himself with a
weapon in such a way that the slayer could not have spared
him without endangering his own person or property;[29] if Arcadius, Theodosius and Honorius permitted the killing of common

interfici, decernentes ius exercendae publicae ultionis pro quiete communi cunctis indultum, ut Hadriano praefecto praetorio[61] scripserunt;[62] si provincialibus[63] Valentinianus, Arcadius atque Theodosius liberam resistendi[64] tribuunt facultatem contra privatos et milites, ut qui agros nocturni populatores invaserint aut itinera frequentata insidiis aggressionis obsederint, permissa cuique licentia, digno supplicio subiungentur ac mortem, quam minabantur, excipiant permissa[65] sua cuilibet ultione, cum melius sit ante tempus occurrere quam post exitum vindicare, et quod serum esset punire iudicio praefatorum principum subiciatur edicto, quis esset legum tam iniquus interpres, quis iustitiae tam adversus, quis rei publicae communisque salutis tam obstinatis animis inimicus qui non censeat hoc idem contra tyrannidem inducere conantes esse permissum, et tanto magis quanto maior est salus publica quam privata?

3   Hoc vidit esse licitum inclitae famae Servilius Ahala, qui Spurium Melium, in affectati regni suspicionem adductum, quod in annonae penuria clientium hostiumque redemptis ministeriis ex Etruria frumentum advectum gratis, ut erat ditissimus temporum illorum, exemplo pessimo plebi romanae distribuit, cum—creato L. Quintio Cincinnato dictatore—vocatus ad iudicium[66] plebem in auxilium imploraret, nec lictori pareret, occidit non expectato iudicio, quod forte plebei[67] temeritas impedisset. Quod quidem Ahalae nedum fraudi non fuit, sed ad maximae gloriae laudem. Exstat[68] enim, renuntiata dictatori Melii caede, Cincinnati vox gloriosissima in Ahalae laudem. Inquit enim senex: 'Macte virtute,

thieves and deserters from the army on the ground that the right of public execution for the sake of the peace of the community is conceded by all—as they wrote to Hadrian, a praetorian prefect;[30] if Valentinian, Arcadius and Honorius granted the people of the provinces the right of resistance against citizens or soldiers, so that night raiders in the fields or highwaymen on the public roads might be put down by any person with suitable punishment (even the same kind of death that they had planned to inflict), on the clear principle that it were better to prevent an evil than to punish it after the fact, and that a crime which it would be too late to punish by the judgment of the praetors should be brought under a decree of the emperor[31]—if, I say, all these things are permitted, who could interpret the law so narrowly, who could counter justice, who could oppose the commonwealth and public security so implacably as to lay down that all these things are not lawful in regard to persons attempting to set up a tyranny—and all the more so because the security of the public is more important than that of individuals?[32]

A proof that this is true is found in the story of Servilius Ahala who murdered Spurius Melius, the richest man of his time, on suspicion of aiming at royal power. In a time of scarcity at Rome, Melius had brought in grain from Etruria through the hired services of clients and foreigners and had distributed it freely to the people, a most evil precedent. Afterward, when L. Quinctius Cincinnatus was made dictator, Melius was brought to justice and appealed to the people to rescue him from the lictor;[33] but Servilius Ahala, without waiting for a judgment, which might have been hindered by popular clamor, slew him on the spot. And this was not reckoned as a crime, but rather as a glorious deed. We have preserved the famous exclamation in praise of Ahala of Cincinnatus the dictator, when the murder of Melius was reported to

3

Servili, esto, liberata re publica tumultuante.' Moxque, advocata plebis et populi contione, pronuntiavit Melium iure caesum et eius bona auctoritate dictatoria publicavit. Quid memorem P. Scipionem Nasicam, qui Tiberium Gracchum, ex Cornelia superioris Africani nepotem, tumultu plebis concitato, tribunatum quem turbulente gesserat in sequentem annum prorogare in rei publicae perniciem satagentem, cum in illa turbatione caput suum tangeret, quasi regni coronam peteret, privata cura subegit? Consule quidem segnius resistente, praefatus Scipio sequi se cunctos, qui rem publicam salvam vellent, obvoluta sinistro brachio toga, comprimendi Gracchum nobilitatis optimatibus auctor fuit. In Capitolium enim fugiens Gracchus, fragminibus subselliorum percussus, occubuit ac inhumatus in Tiberim proiectus est.[69] Nec, quamvis Nasica iudicium et vindictam obtentu legationis effugeret, caedes ista dignissimo caruit laudatore; Africanus enim posterior Numantinum agens triumphum, a Gn. Carbone, Gracchanae seditionis et caedis vindice, interrogatus[70] quid sibi de affinis et consanguinei sui morte videretur, respondere non dubitavit sibi videri iure caesum. Adeo namque grave Romanis semper visum est rem publicam invadere, quod huius criminis suspicionem dignam ultimo supplicio iudicarint, ut civem omnino non putarent, sed publicum hostem, qui plus vellet posse legibus et senatu, vel regnum quaerere putaretur. Cuius rei coniectura M. Manlius, qui Capitolium contra Gallos summa virtute defenderat, cum privatis pecuniis aere alieno obstrictos liberaret et nexos exsolveret, affectati

him: The old man cried, "Well done, Servilius! Let it stand! The
state which was being thrown into confusion is now set free!"
Then calling an assembly of the people he proclaimed that Melius
had been lawfully put to death and, by his authority as dictator, he
declared his goods forfeit to the state.[34] And why need I mention
Publius Scipio Nasica, who by his own action put down Tiberius
Gracchus, grandson of the elder Africanus through his mother
Cornelia? Gracchus had stirred up the people and had plotted to
prolong his tribuneship, which he had used for purposes of agitation, into a second term, to the ruin of the commonwealth. In the
midst of the uproar he raised his hand to his head as if he were
seeking a kingly crown. The consul made only a languid protest,
but Scipio, calling upon all willing to save the commonwealth to
follow him, wrapped his toga about his left arm and, with the help
of the chiefs of the nobility, succeeded in crushing Gracchus, who
fleeing to the Capitol, was beaten to death with pieces of the
benches and thrown unburied into the Tiber.[35] Nor did this murder, though Nasica avoided a trial and punishment by claiming his
privilege as an ambassador, lack a most distinguished apologist.
The younger Africanus, in the course of his triumph after the
capture of Numantia, was asked by Gnaeus Carbo, a defender of
the uprising of Gracchus, what he thought of the killing of his
blood relation. He replied without hesitation that he thought he
had been justly put to death.[36] Thus it always seemed to the Romans such a serious matter to usurp the government of the commonwealth that the mere suspicion of this crime deserved the severest punishment. They did not regard as a citizen at all, but
rather as a public enemy, any man who would set himself above
the laws and above the Senate or who was believed to be aiming at
kingship. Upon this suspicion Marcus Manlius, who had once
defended the Capitol against the Gauls with consummate bravery,
charged with aspiring to a crown because he had used his private

regni reus, ex arcis Tarpeiae, qua Gallos armis summoverat, saxo proiectus est. Accessit et huic memorabilis decreti Manliae gentis nota: instituerunt equidem ne quis eius familiae post eum M. Manlius vocaretur.

4   Et ut ad Gracchum redeamus, notabile mihi dubium occurrit: quisnam Scipio Nasica Gracchanae caedis auctor fuerit.[71] Nam cum, teste Livio, Gn. Scipionis, qui cum fratre in Hispania caesus[72] occubuit, filius adolescens honestissimus, nomine P. Scipio Nasica, a senatu vir optimus iudicatus, matrem deorum accitam a Pessinunte quasi domestico susceperit[73] hospitio, quod fuit ante quam Africanus maior transmisit in Libyam tempore belli punici secundi, et inter bellum secundum et tertium, quod Romano cum Poeno fuit, intercesserint anni quinquaginta quadriennioque post Carthago deleta fuerit, tandemque bellum Numantinum, post cuius finem Tiberius Gracchus fuit occisus, annis quattuordecim gestum sit, facta diligenti temporum collatione ab anno, quo Nasica deae fuit hospes, ante finem secundi belli Punici, usque ad finem Numantini sexaginta et octo anni clarissime numerantur, quinquaginta scilicet, qui inter secundum et tertium Carthaginense bellum discurrerunt, quattuor, quibus tertium illud protractum est, et quattuordecim, quibus Numantina civitas Romano populo restitit; quibus si tempus adolescentiae Scipionis Nasicae cum annis quibus ante finitum secundum bellum deorum mater Romam advecta[74] est iunxeris, facile videbis tempore quo Tiberius oppressus est hunc Scipionem annum nonagesimum excessisse. Nunc autem quis affirmaverit hominem plus quam nonagenarium subito toga, sicut legitur, ad brachium obvoluta, iuventutis fuisse ducem et primarium in caede florentissimae aetatis viri, cum fuerat multitudo[75] simul fortissimorum civium superanda? Scio protervis hoc

property to release debtors and redeem those who were enslaved
for debt, was hurled from the very Tarpeian Rock from which he
had repelled the Gallic assault.[37] Moreover, the Manlian clan determined by a memorable decree that henceforth no member of
the family should bear the name of Marcus Manlius.[38]

But now to return to Gracchus: it seems to me to be decidedly   4
doubtful which Scipio Nasica was the leader in that murder. For
if, as Livy tells us, a son of that Gnaeus Scipio who was killed
with his brother in Spain, a most honorable youth named Publius
Scipio Nasica and declared by the Senate to be a nobleman, received the Mother of the Gods summoned from Pessinus into a
kind of adoption,[39] which event took place before the elder Africanus crossed over to Libya in the time of the Second Punic War;
and if we remember that fifty years intervened between the Second
and Third Punic Wars, and that Carthage was destroyed in the
fourth year after that interval, and finally that the Numantian
War, after the close of which Tiberius Gracchus was killed, lasted
fourteen years, an exact tally of these periods shows that from the
year in which Nasica played the host to the goddess before the end
of the Second Punic War to the close of the Numantian War was
a period of sixty-eight years: namely, fifty years between the two
Punic Wars, four for the duration of the second of these and fourteen during which the city of Numantia held out against the Roman people; and if we add to these the time of the adolescence of
Scipio Nasica and the years between the coming of the Mother of
the Gods and the end of the Second Punic War, you will easily see
that at the time when Tiberius Gracchus was put down this Scipio
must have been more than ninety years old. But now, who would
dare to say that a man of ninety would, as the account states,[40]
suddenly have thrown his toga about his arm and led young men
in the murder of a man in the prime of manhood and backed by
a crowd of the most powerful citizens? I am sure that the most

eripi non posse scioque pariter omnibus hoc tam mirum debere videri[76] quod inter non verisimilia facile debeat reputari. Et quoniam, si verum fuisset, inter senectutis laudes praecipuae celebritatis esset hoc facinus, non est credibile quod res exempli praeclarissimi, cui simile forte reperiri non posset, a cunctis esset obliterata silentio scriptoribus, praesertim colligendis[77] rebus singularibus occupatis. Verum invenio post virum optimum pontificem Nasicam alium P. Scipionem Nasicam, cui propter formae similitudinem, qua Serapioni victimario congruebat, Serapion cognomen datum fuit a Curiatio[78] tribuno plebis lusus gratia. Hunc satis credo prioris Nasicae filium fuisse. Forte fuerunt et alii, quos et historiarum amissio et similitudo nominum obscuravit. Nam unum omnino Nasicam fuisse si verum est et[79] Iugurthae Numidarum regi P. Scipionem Nasicam bellum indixisse, quod illatum constat anno ab Urbe condita sexcentesimo trigesimo quinto, cum secundum bellum Punicum finitum fuerit anno ab Urbe condita quingentesimo quadragesimo primo, sicut notat clarissimus historicorum[80] Livius, quo tempore extrema fuerat adolescentia Scipio Nasica vir optimus iudicatus, videretur hic Nasica non solum annis centum quindecim vixisse sed—quod trans omne miraculum esset—id aetatis consul rem publicam tenuisse. Quae cum verisimilia non sint, cunctis relinquo iudicii facultatem, et si placent eis quae diximus, boni consulant.

5   Si unum omnino velint cum Valerio P.[81] Scipionem Nasicam, dicant hunc 'togatae potentiae clarissimum lumen, qui consul Iugurthae bellum indixit, qui matrem idaeam e phrygiscis sedibus ad romanas aras focosque migrantem sanctissimis manibus excepit,' et reliqua quae capitulo de repulsis idem auctor in unius Nasicae laudem designationemque collegit, sive potius, sicut collecta per

violent critic could not force this conclusion, and I am equally sure
that everyone would agree that it is strange enough to be readily
classed as improbable. Furthermore, if it were true, it would have
been specially celebrated among the glories of old age, and it is
incredible that so marked an example as this, the like of which
could nowhere be found, should have been passed over in silence
by all writers, especially by those who were concerned with gather-
ing all remarkable events. I find, however, after the distinguished
pontifex Nasica, another Publius Scipio Nasica. It is he who so
closely resembled a certain Serapion, a dealer in cattle for sacrifice,
that the tribune Curiatius dubbed him "Serapion" by way of a
joke.[41] Now I am fairly convinced that this man was the son of the
elder Nasica. Perhaps there were others also whom the loss of records or similarity of names may have left in obscurity. For it is
incredible that there can have been but one Nasica, since in that
case—if it is true that Publius Scipio Nasica declared war on
Jugurtha,[42] king of the Numidians, which event certainly happened in the 635th year after Rome's foundation, while the Second
Punic War ended in 541 after Rome's foundation, as Livy, greatest
of the historians, states,[43] at which time Scipio Nasica, being then
at the close of his adolescence, was declared to be a nobleman—in
that case it would appear that this Nasica had lived one hundred
and fifteen years! And, what would be more than a miracle, he
would have been ruling the state as consul at that age! Since all
these things are not probable, I leave the decision open to all. If
they are pleased with what I have said let them be satisfied.

If they agree with Valerius [Maximus] that there was only one 5
Publius Scipio Nasica, let them call him "that most brilliant light
of the Roman power, who declared war against Jugurtha, who received with consecrated hands the Idean Mother when she came
over from her Phrygian home to the altars of Rome" and all the
other things which that author collected in his chapter "Of the
Excluded" to praise and characterize the one Nasica—or rather

alium repperit, dum omnia non explorat ad intimum annotavit. Dicant cum Valerio licebit seque tanto tueantur auctore.[82] Rationem tamen temporum, precor, reddant. Quam si nequeant[83] assignare, dicant potius sic scripsisse Valerium quam affirment, sicut ille scripsit, historiae consistere veritatem; et potius credant textum Valerii fuisse corruptum quam eum in tam supinum errorem, qui in tantae scientiae virum cadere non debuit, incidisse.

6   Dum enim ista rimarer, repperi clarum in capitulo de mutatione morum atque fortunae nominis eiusdem errorem. Scribitur enim communiter in omnibus Valerii codicibus quos aspexi Gn. Cornelium Scipionem Nasicam apud Liparas, cum consul classi Romanae praesideret, a Poenis captum fuisse, cum clarissime legatur apud Senecam (quem nescio qua re Florum dicunt), Eutropium et Orosium, non Scipionem Nasicam, sed Gn. Cornelium Asinam ab Hannibale maiore anno quinto primi belli Punici vocatum ad colloquium fraude Punica captum fuisse. Quod cum ita certissimum sit, puto quosdam cognomen illud Asina cum corrigere quaererent, in Scipionem Nasicam commutasse, quoniam tam deforme nomen eis in clara[84] familia forsan minus honorabile videretur. Qui si legissent apud Macrobium antiquitatis fidelissimum relatorem quod Cornelius, cum in foro emisset agrum[85] et sponsores pro pretio peterentur, e vestigio tantum aeris super asinam fecerit afferri quantum oportebat appendi et ex eo tempore Corneliae familiae—non in contumeliam sed ob facti magnificentiam—cognomen hoc Asina[86] datum esse non fuissent id cognominis admirati. Haec tamen tu et alii recipiant sicut libet. Nolo quidem aliquem mihi plus auctoritatis et fidei praebere[87] quam velit[88] sibique quod eligunt verum aut verosimile videatur. Ego

annotated after they had been collected by someone else, for he did not carefully investigate every point himself.[44] They may agree with Valerius and defend themselves with the authority of so great a writer; but I ask them to take into account the reckoning of time. If they cannot straighten this out, let them rather say: "Valerius wrote so and so" than say that what he wrote agrees with the truth of history. May they more readily believe that the text of Valerius is corrupt than that he could fall into such a thoughtless error, a thing which ought not befall a man of such great learning.

While looking into these matters I discovered a clear case of   6 error in regard to this same name in the chapter of Valerius "On the Change of Manners and Fortune."[45] In all the texts that I have examined Gnaeus Cornelius Scipio Nasica is said to have been captured by the Carthaginians at Lipara while commanding the Roman fleet as consul, whereas we read most plainly in Seneca — called, I know not why, Florus — in Eutropius and Orosius that not Scipio Nasica but Gnaeus Cornelius Asina was invited by Hannibal the Elder to a conference and then with Punic treachery was made prisoner in the fifth year of the First Punic War.[46] Now, since this is quite certain, I think someone must have changed the word "Asina" into "Nasica," thinking, perhaps, that such an ugly name would be a dishonor in so distinguished a family. If this person had only read in Macrobius,[47] a most faithful recorder of antiquity, how Cornelius, having bought a piece of land on the market and his bondsmen being called upon for the payment, ordered on the spot as much money to be brought on an ass's back as was necessary to pay the debt, and that from that time on the cognomen "Asina" was given to the Cornelian family, not in derision but in admiration for this noble action, he would not have wondered at the name. Still, you or anyone else may take this as you please. I am not asking anyone to put any more faith in me than he will. I want everyone to choose what seems true or probable to himself; for myself I am so sure of a corruption in the text

tamen corruptionis et mendi certus ex codice meo Valerii voces illas 'Scipione Nasica' sustuli et 'Asina,' sicut ab initio scriptum arbitror, annotavi. Nam etsi in capitulo de repulsis, ubi dicitur 'P. autem Scipio Nasica togatae potentiae clarissimum lumen, qui
consul Iugurthae bellum indixit,' addatur 'filius eius qui matrem
Idaeam' et cetera quae sequuntur, illa duo verba 'filius eius,' quae
potuit error scriptoris omittere, omnem auferunt dubitationem.

7   Sed ad propositum revertamur. Satis, ut arbitror, demon-
stratum est invadenti tyrannidem iure non a populi parte solum
sed a privato quolibet impune resisti posse,[89] tale monstrum armis
etiam cum caede et sanguine crudeliter opprimendo. Nec solum
cum invadit, sed etiam postquam invaserit, tametsi tempus inter-
cesserit, quo forte subsidia pro repellendo tyranno cum suis copiis
pararentur. Quod sapientissimus Ulpianus in privatorum causis
diffinivit; inquit enim: 'Sciamus non solum resistere permissum ne
deiciatur, sed et si deiectus quis fuerit, eumdem deicere non ex
intervallo sed ex continenti,' hoc est antequam ad extranea negotia
divertat. Sic enim Neratius actum continuum interpretatus est ut
aliquod momentum naturae[90] possit intervenire. Nam et, Ulpiano
auctore, cum patri liceat filiam in eius potestate constitutam in
domo, quam ipse vel gener habitat, in adulterio deprehensam in
continenti perimere, licet horis interpositis apprehensam, cum
persequeretur, occiderit, in continenti videbitur occidisse; licebit
ergo contra rem publicam invadentem insurgere, et non solum in-
vasionis tempore, sed in continenti connexisque negotiis, armis et
copiis obviare.

that I have stricken out of my copy of Valerius the words "Scipione Nasica" and emended the namer to "Asina" as I believe it was originally written. If in the chapter "Of the Excluded" where it reads: "Publius Scipio Nasica, that most brilliant light of the Roman power, who declared war against Jugurtha" we add: "son of him who received the Idean Mother etc.," those two words "son of," which a scribe may have omitted by error, entirely resolve our doubts.[48]

But let us return to our subject. It has thus, I think, been sufficiently demonstrated that anyone who sets up a tyranny may lawfully be resisted, not merely by a part of the people but an individual too,[49] and that such a monster may be put down with cruelty, even to the point of violence and murder. And this not only at the moment of tyrannical usurpation, but afterward,[50] even though an interval of time may have elapsed during which, say, the resources needed to repel the tyrant and his troops are being collected. This principle is most learnedly laid down by Ulpian in reference to private cases. He says: "It is lawful not only to resist in defense of one's property, but, even if one be ejected therefrom, to eject the intruder, not 'after a while' but 'without [unreasonable] delay,'" that is, before one is diverted to an unrelated item of business.[51] For Neratius interprets an "immediate action" as one in which some period of time may intervene.[52] We have it also on the authority of Ulpian that, since it is lawful for a father who detects a daughter under his authority in adultery in a house inhabited by him or by his son-in-law, to slay her without delay, he shall be viewed as having killed her without delay even if some hours shall have passed while she was being pursued and caught.[53] Therefore it must be lawful to rise up against a usurper of the commonwealth, and to resist him with negotiations, arms and troops not only at the moment of the usurpation but [afterward] "without delay."[54]

8   Quid autem dicendum est si dominationi tyrannicae incumbat[91] invasor et, populo per ignaviam patiente, non resistat aliquis invasori, sed aliquamdiu dominetur? Forte tacitus ille consensus et oboedientia, quoniam quae per vim vel metum extorta sunt — resistentia quiescente — non sint irrita, sicut leges statuerunt, ipso iure sequentique consensu tacito vel expresso purificentur et incipiant esse nec violenta nec meticulosa? Forte tacitus ille consensus, inquam, et oboedientia tanti fuerit quod, nisi prius superioris sententia contrarium declaretur, similitudinem iusti principis obtinebit?

9   Et quoniam dissentiente re publica plerumque contingit intestinum et civile certamen quotidianaque contentio, et tollendae discordiae gratia taedioque rerum praesentium[92] dominus eligitur, quandoque vero tumultuante populo sine consilio vel delectu quidam in principem sublimatur, quandoque praevalente factionis potentia, dum ad arma ventum est, uni summa rerum defertur et totius urbis regimen et gubernatio delegatur, dubitaret forte quispiam numquid taliter assumpti dici possint iustum titulum obtinere?

10   Super quo dicendum reor quod si sit princeps populus qui superiorem nec habeat nec agnoscat, quod maior pars populi fecerit ratum esse. Sin autem superioris in habente principem populo confirmatio subsequatur, legitimus erit procul dubio principatus. Eius vero deficiente consensu, sicut iure populus nihil agit, sic electus, si non expectata confirmatione se dominum gesserit, est tyrannus. Sin autem populus recognoscat principem[93] sed non habeat, cum non gubernet, sed maneat in remotis, forte iustus erit titulus, donec per principem contrarium declaretur.

But what shall we say if a usurper imposes a tyrannical govern- 8
ment, and yet no one resists him because the people are inured to
it owing to lack of spirit, and therefore his rule goes on for some
time? Perhaps this tacit consent and obedience — seeing that measures imposed by force or fear, once resistance has died down, are
not invalidated, as the laws require — following the same right,
may become purified by subsequent consent, express or implied,
and may begin to become less violent and fearful? Perhaps, I ask,
this tacit consent and obedience may be such in nature that, unless
a prior judgment of a superior authority declare the contrary, the
tyrant may come to have the semblance of a lawful ruler?[55]

When a state is torn by internal factions, civil strife with daily 9
conflicts generally takes place, and sometimes to quiet this discord
and out of weariness with the existing troubles a lord is chosen.
Sometimes through popular demonstration, without due deliberation or election a prince is set up. Sometimes one faction prevails
in armed conflict, and supreme power is conferred upon one person and the government of the whole city is entrusted to him. Is it
not, perhaps, to be doubted whether a person raised to power in
any of these ways can be said to hold a legitimate title?

On this point I think it should be said that if a people is sover- 10
eign and neither has nor recognizes any higher authority, the will
of the majority validates their action.[56] And if, in a people having
a superior authority the prince's confirmation ensues, then beyond
all doubt the rule in question will be a lawful one. If, however, this
consent is lacking, the people being without rightful authority of
its own, and if the person thus elected begins to govern without
waiting for confirmation from the higher authority, then he is a
tyrant.[57] On the other hand, if the people acknowledge a prince,
but are really without one because he does not rule but stays
abroad, then perhaps the title may be just until the contrary be
declared by the prince.[58]

11   An autem liceat contra dominum et superiorem insurgere, qui per superbiam abuti coeperit[94] principatu, licet titulum iustum[95] vel iustificatum habuerit, principalis nostra dubitatio est.[96] Et quod a superiore deponi valeat atque puniri, nullum crediderim denegare dummodo rite processum fuerit et legitime iudicatum. Quod si superior vel alius auctoritatem habens ipsum iudicaverit hostem, impune pelli poterit et occidi; per sententiam vero depositus absque superioris licentia nec exigi debet ne interfici nec offendi.

12   Civitas vero quae superiorem alium non agnoscit, abrogare sine dubitatione potest imperium praesidentis et ipsum expellere, iustaque subsistente causa fas erit occidere, sicut libet. Sic auctore Lucio Bruto Romanus populus ob Tarquinii Superbi filiorumque facinora regium depulit dominatum. Sic propter Virginiam—quae Claudii nequitia, sub calumniose servitutis obtentu, rapiebatur ad stuprum—ablata fuit auctoritas decemvirorum et ipsi legum latores modis variis profligati. Sic Nero, Caesarum ultimus, a senatu iudicatus hostis,[97] immissis percussoribus occidendus erat.

13   Et ne per exempla nimis expatier, quae collecta possunt tam ex sacris litteris quam gentilium et Christianorum historiis recenseri, quoniam licet infinitorum regum et principum caedes, qui iustissime praesidebant, possint facile numerari, non sunt attamen argumento quod reges aut tyranni sine scelere confici valeant, ad rationem potius veniamus. Scio quod

    ad generum Cereris sine caede et sanguine[98] pauci
    descendunt reges et sicca morte tyranni,

sicut inquit Aquinas. Sed caedium ista frequentia non concludit quod iustae[99] dici possint aut debeant reputari. Aliud enim est occisum aliquem esse, aliud iure caesum, ut mihi visus sit vir

But now, our chief problem is, whether it is lawful to rebel against a lord or higher authority who through arrogance begins to abuse his power, even though he has a lawful and approved title. That he ought to be deposed and punished by a higher authority I suppose no one could doubt — provided only that it be done by regular legal process.[59] For if the higher authority or any other having authority shall judge him to be an enemy of the state, he may with impunity be driven out or killed; at the same time a ruler deposed by a judicial sentence may not be banished or killed or injured without the approval of the higher authority. 11

A city-state which recognizes no higher authority may without doubt revoke the powers of its executive.[60] It may banish him or, for sufficient reason, may put him to death, as it sees fit. Thus the Roman people, on the motion of Lucius Junius Brutus, abolished royal power because of the crimes of Tarquinius Superbus and his sons.[61] So, on account of Virginia, who was dragged away by the wretch Claudius to be raped under the slanderous fiction of her slavery, the rule of the Decemvirs was done away, and the authors of the laws were themselves in various ways overthrown.[62] Thus Nero, the worst of the Caesars, declared a public enemy by the Senate, was marked for death by assassins who were set upon him. 12

I will not dwell too long upon illustrations which can be gathered from Holy Writ as well as from pagan and Christian histories because, though an infinite number of murders of lawful kings and princes may be cited, these are not arguments to prove that the murder of kings or tyrants is not a crime. Let us, therefore, go on to the question. It is true as Juvenal states: 13

Few kings descend to Ceres's son-in-law except by murder,
and few tyrants by a bloodless death.[63]

But the frequency of these murders does not imply that they are or ought to be considered lawful. It is one thing to kill a man and quite another thing to kill him lawfully. So that the learned

eruditissimus[100] Iohannes de Saberiis, qui libro — quem nescio quam ob rem dicimus *Policratum* — determinat tyrannum occidere iustum esse, dum hoc exemplorum multitudine probare nititur nihil agere. Non enim probant exempla tyrannos occidere iustum sed potius usitatum. Cum enim librorum illorum[101] tertio scripserit 'porro tyrannum occidere non modo licitum est sed aequum et iustum,' et[102] — quasi rationem reddat — subicit: 'Qui enim gladium accipit, gladio dignus est interire,' quam rationem vellem deduceret propositumque probaret. Mox autem declarans illud adiecit: 'sed accipere intelligitur qui cum propria auctoritate usurpat, non qui utendi eo accipit a Domino potestatem.' Hic indistincte videtur innuere quod tyrannos occidere sit concessum. In illius etenim tertii[103] libri calce, ne cuncta referam, sic scribit: 'Si enim crimen maiestatis omnes persecutores admittit, quanto magis illud quod leges premit, quae ipsis debent imperatoribus imperare? Certe hostem publicum nemo ulciscitur, et quisquis eum non persequitur, in se ipsum et in totum rei publicae mundanae corpus delinquit.' Haec ille; verum octavo, hoc est ultimo libro, materiam istam multorum capitulorum prolixitate tractavit. In quibus multus est et effusissimus in exemplis.

14   Alicubi tamen licentiam tyrannicae caedis certa ratione restringit. Capitulo quidem duodevigesimo, numeratis exemplis, ad fidem historiae se convertens subdit in haec verba: 'Quia semper tyranno licuit adulari, licuit eum decipere et honestum fuit occidere, si tamen aliter coerceri non poterat.' 'Non enim,' inquit, 'de privatis tyrannis agitur, sed de his qui rem publicam premunt. Nam privati legibus publicis, quae constringunt omnium[104] vitas, facile coercentur. In sacerdotem autem,[105] etsi tyrannum induat, propter reverentiam sacramenti[106] gladium materialem exercere non licet, nisi forte, cum exauctoratus fuerit, in ecclesiam Dei cruentam manum extendat.' Scribit et capitulo vigesimo primo:

John of Salisbury in his book called—I don't know why—*Policrat-icus*, in which he declares that it is right to kill a tyrant and tries to prove this by a multitude of examples, seems to me to reach no result.[64] His examples prove, not that the murder of tyrants is right, but that it is frequent. In his third book, having said that the murder of a tyrant is not only lawful but fair and just, he adds: "For he that taketh the sword shall perish by the sword." I wish he had carried out his reasoning and proved his point; but soon after in his exposition he adds: "but it is understood that he 'takes the sword' who usurps it of his own initiative, not he who receives the right to use it from a higher authority."[65] Here he seems vaguely to hint that it is lawful to slay a tyrant. At the close of this third book—not to quote the whole—he says: "If the charge of treason includes all oppressors, how much more the charge that a man suppresses the laws, which ought to govern even emperors? Certainly no one would avenge the murder of a public enemy, and anyone who should fail to punish him would fail in his duty to himself and to the whole body politic."[66] In the eighth and last book he treats the same subject in several chapters and in great detail, giving a multitude of examples.[67]

Occasionally, however, he sets certain limits to the right of ty- 14 rannicide. In the eighteenth chapter, after citing many cases from history, he notes "that it has always been proper to flatter a tyrant, to deceive him and honorable to slay him, if he could not otherwise be held in check. We are not," he adds, "speaking of tyrants in private life, but of such as oppress the state. For private persons can easily be controlled by the public laws, which govern the lives of all men. A priest, however, even though he plays the tyrant, may not be constrained by the temporal sword because of reverence for the sacrament of ordination, unless it so happens that after being deprived of his office he may have extended bloodstained hands against the Church of God."[68] But he also writes in the twenty-first chapter: "History teaches us, however, that we should

'Hoc tamen cavendum docent historiae, ne quis illius moliatur interitum cui fidei aut sacramenti religione tenetur astrictus.'

15   Videsne quantum idem hic auctor, quicquid habeat auctoritatis et fidei, ab illa tyrannorum perimendorum latitudine se restringit, ut indistincte non liceat in tyrannum manus inicere, nec an tyrannidem exerceat sit concessum cuilibet declarare? Ut si recte sentire volueris, praecedere debeat sententia[107] superioris, si potest adiri, vel decretum populi, si desit principantis auctoritas, expectari. Deprehensum autem cum coniuge vel filia in adulterium tyrannum non minus licebit occidere quam interficere liceat magistratum. Licet enim tyrannus maior pestis sit quam aliqua quae possit in populi vel rei publicae corpus insurgere, non debet tamen unus, non debent et plures, citra principis auctoritatem aut populi, statum — quem vel legitimum institutum vel populi placitum ordinavit vel oboedientia vel tacitus aut expressus consensus civitatis induxerit — auctoritate propria perturbare.

16   Praesumptuosum enim, immo superbum est, ceteris patientibus, contra dominantem insurgere, sit Nero licet, sit Encerinus, sit Phalarides vel Busiris. Et licet contingat eversionem tyrannicam a populo comprobari, licet summa felicitas liberatis[108] quaesita sit et liberatori vel liberatoribus summa laus praemiis etiam immortalibus cumulata, principium tamen, si iusta defuit ratio, fuit iniustum. Sed prosperum ac felix scelus virtus vocatur.

17   Me tamen iudice, sicut iuste tyrannum conficiens omni laude cumulandus et celebrandus[109] est, sic iniuste dominum, licet inique regentem, occidens omni supplicio omnique pena dignissimus dici debet. Nam, licet quilibet patriae[110] sit obnoxius, ut etiam vitam

beware of plotting the ruin of anyone to whom we are bound by an obligation of loyalty or by an oath."[69]

You see, then, do you not, how far this same writer, whatever the authority he possessed, would go in restricting the license of tyrannicide? He would not sanction laying violent hands upon a tyrant without due deliberation, nor would he think everyone authorized to decide whether a man be really a tyrant or not. So that, if you would proceed regularly, a sentence of the higher authority must first be obtained if possible, or if there be no princely rule, then a decree of the people must be waited for. A tyrant caught in adultery with a wife or a daughter may be slain just as lawfully as any regular magistrate would. For, though a tyrant is the worst plague that can infect the people or the commonwealth, nevertheless no single person nor even several together may, of their own initiative and without the authority of the people or the prince, disturb that civil order, whether this is established by a decree of the people or else by the obedience or consent (express or implied) of the community. 15

It would be a presumptuous, indeed, an arrogant act to rebel against a ruler while all the rest were willing to endure him, even if he were a Nero, an Ezzelino, a Phalaris or a Busiris.[70] And though it may happen that the overthrow of the tyrant is approved by the people, though the greatest happiness may be obtained by those who are set free, though the greatest praise may be heaped upon the liberator or liberators, with undying renown,[71] still, if a valid procedure be lacking, the undertaking was unjust. But a successful and fortunate crime passes for a virtuous deed. 16

Yet in my opinion, just as he who destroys a tyrant in a lawful way is to be loaded with honors, so he who unlawfully slays a lord, though the latter may be ruling unjustly, deserves the severest penalty. For, though every man is under such obligation to his country 17

debeat saluti rei publicae dedicare, nullum tamen vinculum nullaque obligatio cogit ut aliquid, licet utile rei publicae cognoscatur, debeat cum scelere procurari.

18   Tanta quidem honestatis vis est, legum et auctoritatis rei publicae[111] ut legamus, testimonio Ciceronis, dimittente Pompilio imperatore legionem, in qua Catonis filius militabat, cum ille pugnandi cupidine remansisset in exercitu,[112] patrem scripsisse Pompilio, si sibi placeret filium retinere, secundo deberet eum obligare militiae sacramento, quoniam functus esset primi debito iuramenti legione dimissa, et ob id iure cum hostibus pugnare[113] non posset.

19   Et quis erit qui sine licentia publica, sine imperatore vel duce se iuste putet, etiam ad liberandam patriam, arma movere? Non ponat igitur aliquis animam suam in manu sua, nec de voluntate sua faciat rationem et in dominum suum, licet etiam tyrannum se gerat, insurgat.[114] Auctoritate superioris aut populi[115] facienda sunt haec, non affectione propria praesumenda. Non potest enim morte dignus et publice criminosus iure a quolibet interfici, sed solum superioris edicto formaque quae fuerit publici legibus ordinata, quam qui dimiserit reus erit. Et haec de secundo nostrae promissionis articulo dicta suffecerint.

that he ought to devote even his life to the welfare of the common-wealth, nevertheless no bond or obligation demands that even a thing useful to the commonwealth has to be effected by commit-ting a crime.

So great indeed is the force of law, of honor and the authority 18 of the commonwealth that, as Cicero tells us, when Pompilius as general discharged the legion in which a son of Cato was serving, and the son in his zeal for the service remained in the army, his father wrote to Pompilius that if he wished to retain his son he ought to bind him by a second military oath, because with the discharge of the legion he had fulfilled the obligation of his former oath and no longer had the right to engage in combat with the enemy.[72]

And what person would suppose that without a public commis- 19 sion, without a general or a commander, he had the right to take up arms even to set his country free? Let no one, therefore, take his soul in his own hand or make a reason of his own will and so rise up against his lord, even though the lord be acting as a tyrant! This may be done only with the approval of a higher authority or of the people, not through the impulse of an individual.[73] Even a criminal publicly convicted as worthy of death may not be executed by anyone at all, but only by the edict of the higher au-thority and in the form prescribed by the laws of the state; who-ever ignores these is a criminal. Enough as to our second propo-sition.

: III :

*De principatu Caesaris et an ipse possit et debeat inter
tyrannos rationabiliter numerari*[116]

1 Iohannes de Saberiis, de quo proximo capitulo fecimus mentionem, cum decimonono capitulo libri octavi multa de Caesare
perstrinxisset, ferens super hoc expresse sententiam ait: 'Hic tamen,[117] quia rem publicam armis occupaverat, tyrannus reputatus
est, et magna parte senatus consentiente strictis pugionibus occisus in Capitolio.' Haec *Policratus.* Cicero vero noster, qui contra
Caesarem post eius mortem libentissime loquebatur, in officiorum
libris inquit: 'Quod enim est apud Ennium: 'Nulla sancta societas
nec fides regni est,' id latius patet. Nam quicquid eiusmodi est in
quo non possunt plures excellere, in eo fit plerumque tanta contentio ut difficillimum sit servare sanctam societatem.' Et subdit:
'Declaravit id modo temeritas C.[118] Caesaris, qui omnia iura divina et humana pervertit propter eum, quem sibi ipse opinionis
errore finxerat, principatum.'

2 Alibi tamen expresse dixit eum tyrannum, quod superius tacuit,
licet ipsum nullatenus nominarit. Secundo quidem librorum de
officiis scripsit: 'Multorum tamen odiis nullas opes posse subsistere,[119] si antea fuit ignotum, nuper est cognitum. Nec vero huius
tyranni solum, quem armis oppressa pertulit civitas apparet[120]
cuius maxime mortui, interitus declaravit quantum odium hominum valet ad pestem, sed reliquorum similes exitus tyrannorum.'
Possem et alia referre quibus idem Cicero, nimius defuncti Caesaris insectator, eum notat, persequitur atque mordet.

Concerning the principate of Caesar, and whether he may and must reasonably be accounted a tyrant

John of Salisbury, whom we mentioned in the previous chapter, 1 makes many references to Caesar in the nineteenth chapter of his eighth book[74] and expresses his opinions as follows: "Nevertheless, since he had seized upon the government by violence he was regarded as a tyrant and, with the approval of a majority of the Senate, was stabbed to death in the Capitol." Such is the view of *Policraticus*.[75] Our Cicero as well, who after Caesar's death gladly spoke out against him, says in his treatise *Of Duties:* "That saying of Ennius: 'In kingship no social bond, no loyalty, is respected,' is now clearer; for when things are in such a condition that but few persons can rise to eminence there is generally such great rivalry that the bonds of society are with difficulty preserved." And he adds: "This has recently been shown by the rashness of Caesar in violating all laws, human and divine, for the sake of a figment of his own mistaken judgment, that of supremacy."[76]

Elsewhere, however, Cicero expressly calls Caesar a tyrant, 2 which he does not do in the above passage, where he gives him no name at all. In the second book of his *On Duties* he says: "If until now we did not know that no power can stand against the hatred of the many, this has of late become clear. Nor does the downfall of this tyrant alone, whom the state, held down by force, endured and even now that he is dead obeys, but the fate of other tyrants also shows how powerful the hatred of men against this plague is."[77] I could cite further passages in which this same Cicero, pursuing too violently the memory of the dead Caesar, censures and condemns him.[78]

3   Verum, ut de *Policrato* sileam, Cicero noster ab academiae, quam colebat, institutione nimis assumpsit ex tempore loqui, nec solum nunc hoc nunc illud dicere, sed contraria mutatione temporum affirmare. Forte quidem qui diligenter ipsius scripta perspexerit, longe maiores Caesaris laudes inveniet quam detractiones; ferme quidem numquam eum vituperat quin et laudet vel extenuet aliqualiter acrimoniam invehendi.

4   Ante bella quidem[121] civilia se sibi semper gessit amicum; multa pro se, multa pro suis amicis ab ipso consecutus est. Accessit ad haec quod Q. Cicero, frater eius, sub eo militavit in Galliis et legationis est honoratus officio. Vide quid imperatori Lentulo scribat Cicero: 'Huc,' inquit, 'accessit commemoranda quaedam et divina Caesaris in me fratremque meum liberalitas, qui mihi, quascumque res gereret, tuendus esset; nunc in tanta felicitate tantisque victoriis, etiam si in nos non is esset, qui est, tamen ornandus videretur.' Haec de Caesare ante civile bellum Cicero. Et ad Quintum fratrem scribens ait: 'Scribis de Caesaris summo in nos amore; hunc tu fovebis et nos quibuscumque[122] poterimus rebus augebimus.'

5   Initio vero bellorum civilium, quoniam semper fuit auctor pacis, cui Caesar se facilem cunctis temporibus reddidit[123] et proclivem, credo quod, si suas illas orationes haberemus, inveniretur eius sine dubio collaudator. Bello vero civili, sicut idem Cicero testis est, officii gratia profectus est ad Pompeium. Vide quid super hoc scribit M. Caelio; nam, cum iste suspicari videretur Ciceronem iturum ad Caesarem idque Ciceroni, quantum ex suis litteris conicere licet, scripsisset, respondit: 'Sed tamen qua re acciderit ut ex meis superioribus litteris id suspicareris quod scribis nescio. Quid enim in illis fuit praeter querelam temporum,[124] quae non meum animum magis sollicitum haberet[125] quam tuum?' Et post pauca:[126] 'Illud miror adduci potuisse te, qui me penitus nosse

Truly, to leave aside the *Policraticus*, this Cicero of ours, accord- 3
ing to the teaching of the Academy which he followed, took upon
himself to speak too much offhand, saying now this and now that
and contradicting himself as circumstances changed. It may well
be that a careful examination of his writings would show far
greater praise of Caesar than blame. Certainly Cicero never attacks
Caesar without at the same time praising him or somewhat modi-
fying the violence of his invective.

Before the civil wars he always affirmed his friendship for him 4
and received from him many favors for himself and his friends.
Further, his brother Quintus Cicero served under Caesar in Gaul
and was honored with the post of legate. Cicero himself wrote to
the general Lentulus: "I must mention the divine generosity of
Caesar toward me and my brother. Whatever he may do I ought
to support him, and now that he is in such great good fortune and
has won such victories, even had he not done for us what he has,
I think honor should be shown to him."[79] That is the way Cicero
spoke of Caesar before the civil wars. Writing to his brother Quintus he says: "You speak of Caesar's great affection for us; you cher-
ish it, while I will try to increase it in every way that I can."[80]

At the outset of the civil wars Cicero was always an advocate of 5
peace,[81] to which Caesar showed himself readily inclined, and I
believe that if we had his speeches on the subject we should find
him taking Caesar's part. But, in the course of the civil wars, as
Cicero himself testifies, his sense of duty carried him over to the
party of Pompey. Notice what he writes on this point to Marcus
Caelius, who seems to have suspected that Cicero would go over
to Caesar and to have written him to this effect, as we may judge
from Cicero's reply: "Why you should suspect this from my former letters, as you say you do, I have no idea; for what was there
in them but complaints against the times, which I am sure cause
you as much anxiety as they do me?"[82] A little farther on he says:
"I wonder that you should have brought up this matter, you who

deberes, ut existimares aut me tam improvidum qui ab excitata fortuna ad inclinatam et prope iacentem descisceram aut tam inconstantem ut collectam gratiam florentissimi hominis effunderem a meque ipse deficerem[127] et, quod initio semper fugi, civili bello interessem.' Et post plura: 'Quod cum ita esset, nil tamen umquam[128] de profectione—nisi vobis approbantibus—cogitavi.'

6   Nec multis locis tacuit amicitiam quam cum Caesare habuisset. Exstant inter eos mutuae familiares et amicabiles epistulae. Multis in locis de Caesaris beneficentia et virtutibus loquitur, et se causam eius in senatu fovisse testatur. Nec invenies apud Ciceronem,[129] praeter principatum et bella civilia, quicquam Caesaris illaudatum. Quid autem de Pompei sentiret exercitu, quid de Pompeiana victoria vincentiumque minis quantumque de ipsorum insolentia crudelitateque suspicionis et formidinis concepisset multis in locis aperit et testatur. Nam quod supra rettulimus ex verbis Arpinatis nostri de Caesaris principatu, nonne cum inquit eum id sibi opinionis errore finxisse maxima culpa liberat Caesarem, cum ei non dolum sed opinionis errorem imponit? Sine comparatione quidem graviora sunt quae culpa contrahit quam quod per errorem susceptum est. Et eo loco quo sibi tyrannum imposuit, nonne nomen Caesaris tacuit, quasi vereretur expresse dicere quod tamen volebat omnibus persuadere?

7   Mihi vero cuncta cogitanti videtur Cicero Caesarem semper, dum viveret, multis laudibus affecisse, non solum ante bella civilia sed postquam illis quinque triumphis finis armis impositus est. Lege, si placet, orationes eius[130] pro M. Marcello vel Q. Ligario. Lege, precor, et eius epistulam ad Servium Sulpicium; cum enim

ought to know me too well to suppose that I should be so impru-
dent as to turn from a well-established cause to one that is failing
and almost ruined, or so fickle as to throw away the favor of a
most successful man after I had once gained it, to be untrue to
myself and to throw myself into civil strife, from which I have always stood apart."[83] And again: "Even if things stood in this way, I
should never have thought of a defection from Pompey without
your approval."[84]

Nor does he hide in many passages the friendship he had with   6
Caesar.[85] Many intimate and cordial letters between them are still
extant.[86] Cicero often refers to Caesar's generosity and good qualities and says that he supported his cause in the Senate.[87] Nowhere
in his writings can you find any unfavorable criticism of Caesar
except in regard to political leadership and the civil wars. On the
other hand, his views about Pompey's army and the menace of a
victory on his part and how greatly he suspected and dreaded the
violence and cruelty of his troops are revealed and affirmed in
many passages. Indeed, from his words quoted above in regard to
Caesar's supremacy, where he says that Caesar conceived this design through a "mistaken judgment," does he not thus free him
from the greatest reproach by ascribing to him a blunder rather
than a crime? What is done through wrongdoing is beyond comparison more serious than what happens through a mistake. And,
in that passage where he calls him a tyrant, does he not suppress
the name of Caesar as if he feared to assert openly what he nevertheless was trying to make everyone believe?

In my opinion, as I think the whole matter over, as long as   7
Caesar lived, Cicero was always heaping praises upon him, not
only before the civil wars but after an end had been put to that
struggle in five great triumphs.[88] Read, if you please, his speeches
on behalf of Marcus Marcellus and Quintus Ligarius.[89] Read
also, I beg you, his letter to Servius Sulpicius. Speaking of the

de restitutione Marcelli mentionem fecisset inquit: 'Ita mihi pulcher hic dies visus est ut speciem aliquam viderer videre quasi reviviscentis[131] rei publicae.' Nec hoc tacuit oratione qua gratias egit[132] Caesari[133] pro restitutione Marcelli; nam cum Caesar iactare diceretur satis se diu vel naturae vixisse vel gloriae, 'Satis,' inquit Cicero, 'si ita vis fortasse naturae; addo etiam, si placet, et gloriae. At, quod maximum est, patriae certe parum,' ut statum illum rei publicae qui resedit in Caesare non ad tyrannidem sed ad rem publicam pertinere vir libertatis avidissimus iudicarit.

8   Nec dissimilem condicionem rerum[134] futurarum[135] sensit, si triumphasset Pompeius. Vide quid super hoc M. Marcello scribat.[136] Ait enim: 'Primum tempori caedere, id est necessitati parere, semper sapientis est habitum; deinde non habet, ut nunc quidem est, id vitii res. Dicere fortasse quae sentias non licet, tacere plane licet. Omnia enim delata ad unum sunt. Is utitur consilio ne suorum quidem sed suo. Quod non multo secus fieret si is rem publicam teneret quem secuti sumus. An qui in bello, cum omnium nostrum coniunctum esset periculum, suo et certorum hominum minime prudentium consilio uteretur, eum magis communem censemus in victoria futurum fuisse quam incertis in rebus fuisset?' Et post aliqua in eamdem sententiam subdit: 'Omnia sunt misera in bellis civilibus, sed miserius nihil quam ipsa victoria quae, etiam si ad meliores[137] venit, tamen eos ipsos ferociores impotentioresque reddit, ut etiam si natura tales non sint, necessitate esse cogantur. Multa enim victori eorum arbitrio, per quos vicit, etiam invito facienda sunt. An tu non videbas mecum simul quam illa crudelis esset futura victoria?'

restitution of Marcellus he says: "So glorious did that day appear to me that I seemed to see, as it were, the vision of a restored commonwealth."[90] In the speech in which he thanks Caesar for the restitution of Marcellus he says the same thing; Caesar supposedly boasted that he had lived long enough to pay the debt of nature and of glory, and Cicero replied: "The debt of nature perhaps enough, and I will add, if you insist, the debt of glory, but, what is of the highest importance, your debt to the fatherland, little"[91] as if this most ardent champion of liberty believed that the form of state which Caesar represented belonged not to a tyranny but to a commonwealth.

Nor did he think that any different state of affairs would have 8
been produced by a victory of Pompey. Observe what he writes on this point to Marcus Marcellus: "First, to suit oneself to the times, that is, to obey necessity, is ever the task of a wise man. Second, this evil is irrelevant as things now stand. One cannot, perhaps, speak out what one feels, but one is at perfect liberty to keep silence. Everything is referred to a single man. He follows his own opinion, not taking counsel even with his own followers. And there would be no great difference if he whom we have followed [i.e., Pompey] were master of the commonwealth. Now can we suppose that the man who, in the thick of war, when we were all exposed to the same dangers, acted upon his own opinion and that of certain most unwise counselors, would be more tractable in victory than when his fortunes were in doubt?"[92] After some further remarks to the same effect Cicero adds: "Civil war is deplorable in every way, but the most deplorable part of all is the victory, which, even if it falls to the better party, renders them more cruel and headstrong, so that even if they are not so by nature, they are forced to become so. The victor is obliged, even against his will, to do many things at the will of those who made possible his victory. Did you not see at the same time that I did, what a cruel victory that [of Pompey] would have proved to be?"[93]

9   Respice, frater optime, quid Cicero de victoria Pompeiana sentiret! Quae cum ita fuerint, videtur mihi laudatissimis illis Romae principibus necessarium fuisse non pugnare pro partibus sed consiliis, opibus conatibusque cunctis[138] ne pugnaretur obsistere vel civile certamen armis iustis et pro sanguine prohibere, quando quidem non omnino ne quisquam, sed uter regeret et rerum summam et moderamen assumeret, certabatur. Non solum enim

signa, pares aquilae et pila minantia pilis,

sed utrimque par impietas, par furor et aequalis ambitio, par votum opprimendi concives, tollendi leges et illud aequum ducere quod placeret prodessetque victoribus. Non tuendae rei publicae sed opprimendae certamen illud fuit.'

Quis iustius induit arma
scire nefas,

ut ille ait. Nunc quoniam cives, in duas secti factiones, quinam imperaret[139] decertare voluerunt, Dei dispositione factum est ut victor Caesar fuerit.

10   Qui quidem, quod nemo negaverit, mira clementia teterrimum bellum ac arma civilia, quibus nihil potest esse crudelius,[140] compensavit. 'Vicit enim is,' ut inquit Cicero, 'qui non fortuna inflammaret odium[141] sed bonitate leniret.' De cuius felicitate benignaque natura non dubitavit Arpinas dicere: 'Vidimus tuam victoriam proeliorum exitu terminatam; gladium vagina vacuum in Urbe non vidimus. Quos amisimus cives, eos Martis vis[142] perculit, non ira victoriae, ut dubitare debeat nemo[143] quin multos, si fieri posset, C. Caesar ab inferis excitaret, quoniam ex eadem acie conservat

Do you see then, my worthy brother, what Cicero thought 9
about the possible success of Pompey? In view of this it seems to
me that it was necessary for those two most praiseworthy leaders
of Rome not to engage in partisan warfare but to strive with all
their counsels, efforts and resources to prevent such a conflict and
to avert civil war and bloodshed by lawful arms. The fact is, their
struggle was not about whether some one man should rule and
have supreme control of the state, but which of the two it should
be. For not only were the same

> ensigns, eagle standards and pikes ranged against each other,[94]

but on both sides were found also equal disloyalty, equal fury and
self-seeking, an equal desire to oppress the citizens, to set aside
the laws and to think anything right which was pleasing and of
benefit to the victors. It was a contest, not to preserve the commonwealth, but to destroy it.

> Which takes up arms in the better cause,
> it is forbidden us to know,

says the poet.[95] Now, when the citizens, divided into hostile
camps, determined to settle by force which should rule, it came to
pass by the will of God that Caesar conquered.

No one will deny that he compensated for the horrors of civil 10
strife, than which nothing can be more cruel, by his wonderful
magnanimity. For, as Cicero says: "He conquered, yet did not ex-
cite hatred in his good fortune, but rather allayed it by his leniency."[96] Speaking of his geniality and his gentleness of nature
Cicero did not hesitate to say: "We saw your victory decided by
the fortune of war; your sword we have never seen unsheathed
inside Rome. The citizens whom we have lost perished in the heat
of battle, not in the fury of victory; so that no one can doubt that,
could he, Caesar would call many of them back to life from the
realm below. In fact he is protecting as many of the hostile camp

quos potest.' Et quis iudicat hos mores, hos affectus, haec gesta tyrannidem appellari?

11   Sed quaeris titulum. Audi Senecam, quem quidam Florum vocant. Ipse quidem historiae Romanae compendio post bella Caesaris sic concludit: 'Hic aliquando finis armis fuit; reliqua pax incruenta pensatumque clementia bellum. Nemo caesus imperio praeter Afranium (satis ignoverat semel) et Faustum[144] Sullam[145] (docuerat generos timere Pompeius)[146] filiamque Pompeii cum patruelibus[147] ex Sulla (hic posteris cavebatur). Itaque non ingratis civibus omnes unum in principem[148] congesti honores, circa templa imagines, in theatro distincta radiis corona, suggestus in curia, fastigium in domo, mensis in caelo. Ad hoc[149] pater ipse patriae perpetuusque dictator. Novissime—dubium an ipso volente—oblata pro rostris ab Antonio consule regni insignia.'

12   Hicne titulus Caesaris violentus atque tyrannicus, quem grata civitas tradidit? Qui cum iure pro meritisque fuerit evectus tantaque humanitate non in suos solum sed in hostes, quia cives erant, usus[150] sit, dicine potest appellarique tyrannus? Non video qua ratione possit hoc, nisi iudicare voluerimus ad libidinem, affirmari. Quare concludamus hoc articulo Caesarem non fuisse tyrannum, quoniam iure—non iniuria—in communi re publica tenuit principatum.

as he can."[97] Who then can reckon that such behavior, such affection, such deeds are to be called tyranny?

But you ask me to give it a name. Hear what Seneca—whom 11
some call Florus—says. In his compendium of Roman history,
after describing Caesar's wars, he concludes as follows: "Here at
last was an end of fighting, a bloodless peace, a war counterbalanced by clemency. No one was put to death by order of the commander except Afranius (he had forgiven him once already), Faustus Sulla (Pompey had taught him to be afraid of sons-in-law),
and the daughter of Pompey together with her uncles on Sulla's
side (here, he was taking precautions against offspring). Thus,
with the approval of the citizens, all kinds of honors were heaped
upon this one man: statues around the temples, a crown with radial spikes in the theater, a raised seat in the Senate, a decorated
gable for his house, his name given to a month of the year; besides
these the titles of 'father of his country' and 'perpetual dictator';
finally—whether by his own consent or not is uncertain—the insignia of royalty that were offered him by the consul Antony before the rostra."[98]

Was this title [of king] tyrannical or acquired by violence when 12
it was offered him by a grateful state? Can a man raised to power
through his own merits, a man who showed such a humane spirit,
not to his partisans alone but also to his opponents because they
were his fellow citizens—can he rightly be called a tyrant? I do
not see how this can be maintained, unless indeed we are to pass
judgment arbitrarily. We may, therefore, conclude with this proposition: that Caesar was not a tyrant, seeing that he held his supremacy in a communal commonwealth lawfully and not by abuse
of law.

: IV :

An Iulius Caesar iure fuerit occisus

1 Quoniam ergo Caesar non potest inter tyrannos legitime reputari, qui gratitudine civium eo devectus est unde continuatis honoribus ceteri principes, quos nemo tyrannos iudicat, in successionem imperii ducti sunt, quis affirmare possit quod iure fuerit occisus? Qui non dicat eius percussores non iure sed iniuria sceleratissimas manus in patriae patrem et in orbis iustissimum principem iniecisse? Quod scelus, teste Cicerone, longe maius est quam patrem proprium trucidare. Vide quae superius de tyrannicido dicta sunt et facile concludes non licuisse coniuratis illis senatoribus perpetuum occidere dictatorem.

2 In quibus quidem rebus peculiariter censeo ponderandum quod praecipui Caesaris occisores Brutus et Cassius ceterique Romanorum praeturas, pontificatus, quaesturas et alia publice gubernationis officia, quae Caesar decreverat, tenuerunt actaque dictatoris omnia senatus consulto confirmata sunt et cuncta quae fecerat aut etiam facere destinaverat, quae redegisset in actis,[151] rata mansuerunt. Et quis ferat Ciceronem et alios contra Caesarem obloquentes cum ipsos et alios videamus, quos ius victoriae privaverat tam dignitatibus quam civitate, restitutionem et honores — vel a Caesare noviter delatos vel confirmatos ab eo[152] — tamquam concessos[153] legitime tenuisse? Ubi, precor, illa legum observantia, libertatis amor odiumque tyranni postquam ea quae victis et civibus confirmata vel delata sunt ab illo reputari legitima voluerunt?

: IV :

Whether Julius Caesar was killed lawfully

Since, therefore, Caesar cannot legitimately be accounted a tyrant, 1
seeing that he was raised by the gratitude of his fellow citizens to
that level from which other princes, whom no one considers as
tyrants, were carried on, by continuity of office, to the imperial
succession, who can maintain that his murder was justified? Who
will not say that his assailants, not lawfully but unlawfully, laid
their wicked hands upon the father of the country, the most righteous ruler on earth? That is a crime, as Cicero declares,[99] far
more atrocious than the murder of one's own father! Think over
what has been said above about tyrannicide and you will readily
conclude that those senatorial conspirators had no justification for
the murder of the perpetual dictator.

I think we should consider particularly that the leading as- 2
sassins of Caesar — Brutus, Cassius and other Romans — kept
the praetorships, priestly offices, quaestorships and other government offices which had been established by decrees of Caesar; further, that all the acts of the dictator were confirmed by
decrees of the Senate, and that everything he had done or even
planned to do and for which he had drawn up written documents, remained in force. Who, then, can bear with patience
to hear Cicero and others speaking against Caesar, when the
very same ones, and others whom the law of conquest had deprived of their honors as well as of their citizenship, received
from Caesar restitution or new positions or confirmation of former ones as legitimately acquired? What, I ask you, became of
that devotion to the laws, that love of country, that hatred of
the tyrant, when they were ready to accept as lawful grants or
confirmations made by him to citizens whom he had overcome?

Discurre per omnes historias; dic, si potes, aliquem beneficia Caesaris, quoniam regnaret iniuste tyrannusque fuerit, recusasse.

3   Scipio Nasica et C.[154] Figulus—hic ex Gallia, ille revocatus a
Corsica[155]—consulatum resignaverunt quoniam monente Tiberio[156] Gracco deprehensum est comitiis consularibus vitiose taber-
naculum captum esse. Camillus autem non prius etiam ab exilio
venit Veios quam omnia rite facta circa dictaturam eius comperis-
set. Et L.[157] Quintius Cincinnatus senatum contra leges in sequentem annum continuare volentem consulatum, quem egerat,
repressit et honore quem leges prohibebant abstinuit. Et quis tunc
repertus est qui causaretur dictatorem vitio factum reluctantibus-
que legibus rite nihil facere potuisse ob eamque causam delatos[158]
honores etiam post illius caedem recusasset?[159]

4   Quae cum ita fuerint, miror Ciceronem meum in tantam rabiem contra memoriam dictatoris accensum quod ipsum non[160]
solum dixerit iure caesum sed etiam omnes bonos mortem eius[161]
vel procurasse consiliis vel optasse votis[162] vel sententiis appro-
basse; sic enim, disceptans cum Antonio,[163] secunda Philippica-
rum affirmat. An mors dictatoris placuit bonis omnibus, cum Romana plebs a funere ad domum Bruti et Cassii cum facibus[164]
impetum faciens aegre repulsa fuerit? An in tota plebe nullus bonus, o Cicero? An in omnium bonorum favore atque consensu
Capitolium, securitatis causa, percussores[165] cum coniuratis in
Caesarem, postquam illum occiderant, occuparunt? An cum prae-
ferentium in funus munera suffecturus multitudini dies non esset
signum est caedem eius omnibus placuisse? An senatus consul-
tum, quo simul omni sibi divina et humana delata sunt, signum

Search through all the histories and tell me, if you can, of a single person who refused a favor from Caesar because he ruled unjustly or as a tyrant!

Scipio Nasica and Gaius Figulus, were called back—the one 3 from Gaul the other from Corsica—and resigned their consulates because, on the motion of Tiberius Gracchus, it was discovered that in the elective assemblies the auspices had not been regularly selected.[100] Camillus would not even return from his exile at Veii until he learned that all measures relating to his dictatorship had been legally carried out.[101] Cincinnatus checked the Senate's desire to renew for a second term the consulate which he had completed, thus denying himself an honor forbidden by the law.[102] And was there anyone at the time who took the fact of being a dictator, even one created in an irregular manner and opposed to the laws, as a pretext for his not taking any valid action or as a reason to refuse after his death honors conferred by him?

This being so I marvel that my Cicero should have been so 4 stirred to fury against the memory of the dictator as to say, not only that he was lawfully slain, but that all good men either counseled his death or desired it in their hearts or approved it by their declarations. This statement he makes in his discussion with Antony in his second Philippic.[103] Was the death of the dictator pleasing to "all good men," when the Roman plebs, returning from his funeral, attacked the houses of Brutus and Cassius with torches and were with difficulty held in check?[104] Was there not in the whole plebs a single "good man," O Cicero? Was it with the favoring consent of all good men that the assailants of Caesar and their accomplices, after they had murdered him, took over the Capitol to protect themselves?[105] When the day was not long enough for the vast number of those who brought gifts to the funeral, was that a sign that his murder was pleasing to everyone?[106] Was the decree of the Senate conferring upon him all honors human and

non est publicae dilectionis? Nonne quod matronae ornamenta quae gerebant liberorumque suorum praetextas et bullas, et legionarii milites ac veterani arma, quibus ornati funus celebrabant, rogalibus[166] flammis ingesserint amoris, non odii, signa sunt? Nonne luctu publico gentium exterarum continuis noctibus bustum illud frequentatum est? Et quis dixerit imperii Romani subditos funeri tyranni bonis omnibus odiosi, qui suis in his rebus utilitatibus semper student, in bonorum omnium displicentiam tantum officii praebuisse?

5   Quid mihi, Cicero, verba iactas? Quid de secreto mentium coniectaris cum rebus atque factis contrarium videamus? Te vincas oportet in dicendo, Cicero, si volueris eloquentia consequi quod coniecturae et verba factorum evidentia non vincantur. Coniuratorum enim metus et occupandi Capitolii cautio signa non sunt illam caedem bonis omnibus placuisse. Et quis credat omnes bonos, qui liberalitate Caesaris affecti sunt et tum vitae beneficium tum dignitatis ornamenta receperant, sic ad unum ingratos fuisse quod omnes eum mortuum optaverint et probarint?[167] Constanter affirmem, si forsitan id fuerit, dignissimos fuisse, qui liberalitate benignitateque principis orbati in servitutem foedissimam truderentur.

6   Mihi vero, quicquid sequentis civicae dissensionis rabies per Ciceronem aut alios delatrarit, rerum progressum et exitum conferenti indubitanter occurrit, sic sibi Caesarem beneficiis suos, hostes clementia cunctosque prudentia et animi magnitudine devinxisse, quod paucissimis grata fuerit eius caedes. Placuit omnibus contrariae factionis, arbitror, non odio Caesaris[168] sed spe potius

divine not a sign of the public devotion?[107] And was it not a proof of affection rather than of hatred that matrons threw upon the funeral pile the ornaments they were wearing, together with the robes and amulets of their children, and legionaries and veterans the arms they had carried at the funeral service?[108] Was not his tomb visited night after night by people of foreign nations as a token of the public grief?[109] Who could say that subjects of the Roman Empire, always on the lookout for their own advantage, would have shown such interest in the funeral of a tyrant hateful to all good men and thus have given offense to all these good people?

But what words do you fling at me, Cicero? Why do you specu- 5
late upon the secrets of men's minds when we see the opposite from the facts and deeds? You will have to be a greater master of oratory than you are, Cicero, if you expect to make guesswork and mere words overcome the evidence of facts. The terror of the conspirators and their precautions in occupying the Capitol are not indications that the murder pleased "all good men." Who can believe that all those good men who had experienced Caesar's generosity and had received from him the gift of their lives and honorable distinctions would all, to a man, have been so ungrateful as to have desired and approved his death? I would resolutely affirm, in that had been the case, that they deserved to be deprived of the generosity and kindness of their principal citizen and thrown into the most abject servitude.

For myself, in spite of the snarlings of Cicero and the others 6
expressing the anger of the civic strife that followed, the more I study the development of events and their outcome, the more fully I am convinced that Caesar so won over his followers by kindness, his enemies by leniency and all by his wisdom and magnanimity, that his murder would have been welcome to only a very few. It pleased all of the opposing faction not, in my judgment, because of their hatred of Caesar, but because they hoped to recover their

recuperandi status et dignitatis, quam se videbant illo principe parem victoribus habituros omnino non fore. Assumptam credo licentiam contra Caesarem[169] obloquendi[170] non hominis odio sed studio libertatis et ut omnes ab appetitu principatus exemplo Caesaris terrerentur.

7 Sed quis est opus verbis? Nonne in Caesaris ultionem homines, caelum, superi[171] et inferi consensisse videntur? Omnes enim eius percussores et qui coniuraverunt in eum[172] infra triennium ad unum, modis variis, non sine caede et sanguine perierunt. Maximaeque laudi datum est Octavio quod, ceteris parcens civibus, reos paternae caedis contentus fuerit punivisse.

8 'Sed,' inquies, 'nonne percussores illi libertatem publicam intenderunt? Et quid? Nonne debemus patriae quicquid possumus, quicquid sumus? Et quid maius quidque divinius exhiberi patriae potest quam quod[173] ipsam eximamus miseriae servitutis? Tantum est hoc bonum, tam excellens et universale, quod ei nihil possit aut deceat comparari. Fecerunt ergo Cassius atque Brutus,[174] Trebonius et alii coniurati quod magnanimitatem eorum[175] decebat quoque maius praestare rei publicae non valebant.'

9 Cui quidem obiectioni respondeat optimus principum divus Augustus. Fertur enim cum in domum M. Catonis ob tanti civis memoriam intravisset et assentatorum qui tunc aderant multitudo Catonem uno ore reprehenderet, quod nimis obstinatis animis Pompeianae factionis vindex et assertor fuerit, in excusationem eius[176] astantibus protulisse: 'Qui praesentem statum civitatis mutari non optat et civis et vir bonus est.'

10 Tot quidem calamitates sequi solent totque scandala concitari cum status rei publicae commutatur, quod omnia satius tolerare

positions and their honors, which they saw would never be equal to those of the victorious party while he ruled. I believe that the freedom that was taken in speaking out against Caesar sprang not from hatred for the man but from zeal for liberty, in order that the example of Caesar might frighten everyone from the desire for supremacy.

But why so many words? Does it not seem as if men and gods, the powers above and below, conspired to avenge the death of Caesar? In the space of three years all of his assailants and the conspirators against him, to a man, met their deaths in various ways, but in every case by bloodshed or murder.[110] Octavius was specially praised for contenting himself with punishing those directly guilty of parricide and sparing the rest.

"But," you might say, "were not his assailants aiming to secure the freedom of the commonwealth? Do we not owe to our country all that we are and all that we can do? And what greater, what more divine service can we render to our country than to deliver it from the misery of servitude? So great, so excellent, so all-embracing a good is this that nothing else can or ought to be compared with it. Therefore Cassius and Brutus and Trebonius and the rest of the conspirators did what was appropriate for men of great spirit and performed the greatest possible service to the commonwealth."

To this objection let the greatest of emperors, the godlike Augustus, answer. It is reported that when he visited one day the house of Cato in respect for the memory of that great citizen, surrounded by the throng of flatterers all criticizing Cato as too insistent an advocate and sustainer of Pompey's faction, Augustus said in his defense: "He who does not choose to change the existing order of the state is a good citizen and a good man."[111]

Truly, when the regime of a commonwealth is changed, usually so many misfortunes follow and so many scandals are stirred up

sit quam in mutationis periculum devenire. Numquam enim quisquam tantae potentiae fuit vel prudentia tam divina cui mutatio
civitatis ad intentionis propositum responderet. In magna quidem
civitate varia sunt ingenia, dissonae mentes[177] et multiplices voluntates, et in iaciendo rei publicae fundamenta quilibet dignitati
commodisque suis studet. Nec est aliquis qui decens non putet
sibi contingere quicquid optat. Quo fit un antequam in unam con-
sonantiam veniatur et omnium quietetur ambitio multi sint motus, infinitae discordiae et innumerabiles, non sine periculorum
apparitione, conatus, etiam si cessent arma, nec etiam pleniter ad
sanguinem veniatur, ad quem cum perventum fuerit nihil crudelius atque calamitosius potest accidere.[178] Quarum rerum metu,
tolleranda potius hominis vita fuit, non Caesaris solum, qui tanta
clementia — sicut legitur — utebatur, sed etiam Sullae vel Marii,
qui non poterant civili sanguine satiari.[179]

II   Volo tecum parumper, mi Cicero, super hoc — si placet — rationis examine disputare. Vidisti totum Romanae rei publicae corpus
in duas discissum partes, armis non civilibus solum sed consangui-
neis et cognatis vel, ut usitatiore loquar vocabulo,[180] plusquam civilibus decertare. Vidisti victum confectumque Pompeium, vidisti
Catonem et alios — partis victae reliquias et fragmenta bellum in
Africa pertinaciter renovantes — simili clade prostratos. Vidisti
Pompeianum nomen et factionem in Hispania renovatum altius
quam per victarum partium residua sperari poterat aspirare et,
cum fortuna videretur miram rerum vertiginem polliceri, non
eventu dissimili quam conatus reliquos[181] profligatum. Vidisti,
positis armis, bellorum civilium finem et rem publicam debilita-
tam in unius principis potestatem, utpote de letalis belli morbo
resurgentem, velut in quietem certam et necessariam reclinasse.

that it is better to bear all ills rather than risk the dangers that come with change. There never was anyone possessed of power so great or prescience so divine that a political revolution unfolded according to his intention. In a large city-state there are varied talents, differences of judgment, a multitude of wills, and in laying the foundations of a commonwealth every man aims at his own honor and his own advantage. Nor is there any man who does not think it suitable to appropriate everything that he desires. For this reason, before an agreement can be reached and the ambitions of all can be met, there will be many tumults, endless contentions and countless plots, leading to peril—even if fighting may have ceased and no acts of bloodshed have been attempted—for this state of things is itself the most cruel and ruinous that can occur. To avoid these evils, it is preferable to spare the life of a man—not just the life of a Caesar, whom as we read showed such leniency, but the life of a Sulla or of a Marius, who could not have enough of their fellow citizens' blood.

Allow me, then, my Cicero, to examine this argument with you 11 for a moment. You saw the whole Roman body politic split into two parties and engaged in a conflict, not merely between fellow citizens, but between blood relations, or, to use a more common expression, in a worse than civil war.[112] You saw Pompey defeated and overthrown; you saw Cato and others, the broken remnants of the defeated party, obstinately renewing the fight in Africa, beaten with equal slaughter. You saw the name and faction of Pompey in Spain renewed and reaching greater success than could have been hoped for by the remnants of a conquered party; and then, just as fortune seemed to promise them the very height of prosperity, they were thrown down by a disaster not unlike those which befell the other attempts. You saw, after the laying down of arms and the end of civil war, the exhausted commonwealth rising as if from the disease of mortal conflict to rest peaceful and secure in the power of one principal citizen.

12   Responde — precor — Cicero, quem portum tam diu tempestati-
bus iactatae naviculae videbas offerri nisi quod ad unius victoris
arbitrium, pro victoriae freno victaeque partis securitate, res publica redigeretur? Dic mihi, nonne quinquennalem Sullae memi-
neras dictaturam? Quae licet fuerit cruenta[182] victosque omnes
paene confecisset, fuit tamen alicui[183] rei publicae firmamento.
Quid autem in perpetua dictatura Caesaris desiderasti quod optari
posset a victis? Nonne fuit prostratis illa praesidio, victoribus
freno? Nullos dictatura perdidit, quae multos in vita et dignitate
servavit. Fuit illa timentibus praesidium, grassantibus frenum,
cunctis salus et principi laus. Quotidie bonum crescebat publicum
iamque dignitatibus et honore victi victoribus aequabantur.

13   An recordaris, Cicero, quod et tu ipse dixisti? 'Omnia sunt exci-
tanda tibi, C.[184] Caesar, uni, quae iacere sentis, belli ipsius impetu,
quod necesse fuit, perculsa atque prostrata: constituenda iudicia,
revocanda fides, comprimendae libidines, propaganda soboles; omnia quae dilapsa iam defluxerunt severis legibus vincienda sunt.
Non fuit recusandum in tanto bello civili tantoque animorum ar-
dore et armorum, quin quassata res publica — quicumque belli
eventus fuisset — multa perderet ornamenta dignitatis et praesidia
stabilitatis suae multaque uterque dux faceret armatus, quae idem
togatus fieri prohibuisset. Quae quidem nunc tibi omnia belli vulnera curanda[185] sunt, quibus praeter te mederi nemo potest.'

14   Haec omnia verba tua[186] sunt, longe magis vere dicta quam
blande. Quis enim his mederi poterat nisi Caesar? Senatus enim
in partes sectus, aut equestris ordo, vel populus aut plebes[187] eadem factionum contrarietate laborantes, inter victos atque victores

Now answer me, Cicero, I ask you: What other harbor did you   12
see for the ship of state so long tossed by storms except bringing
the commonwealth under the control of one victor, as both a
check to the victorious party and a protection of the defeated
party? Tell me, had you forgotten the five years of Sulla's dictatorship? Which, however bloody and fatal to most of the vanquished,
nevertheless sustained the commonwealth? What indeed did you
find lacking in the perpetual dictatorship of Caesar which the defeated could have asked for? Was it not a protection to the conquered and a bridle upon the victors? His dictatorship ruined no
one, but rather preserved the lives and the fortunes of many. It was
a protection to the timid, a restraint upon the cruel, safety for all
and a glory to the principal citizen. The public welfare increased
daily, and already the conquerors and the conquered were being set
upon an equal level of offices and honors.

Do you remember, Cicero, what you yourself said: "By you   13
alone, O Caesar, can all those interests be revived which you see
overthrown by the fury of that inevitable war and now lying pros-
trate. The courts are to be reopened, credit restored, license re-
pressed, a new generation brought into being. Whatever has gone
to ruin is to be reestablished by stringent legislation. It was inevitable in the thick of so great a civil war, in such heat of opinion
and of arms that the battered commonwealth, whatever the outcome of the conflict, should lose many marks of its dignity and
many guarantees of its stability, and that both leaders should do
many things while under arms which in serving civic office they
would have prohibited. All these wounds of war are now to be
healed by you, and there is none except you who can heal them."[113]

These are your own words, and they were far more than mere   14
flattery. For who but Caesar could have cured those evils? The
Senate, divided as it was into factions? The knightly order? Or the
middle and lower classes, struggling in the same factional conflict,
fighting between victors and vanquished, with interests not merely

non diversis sed adversis pugnantes studiis, quomodo poterant ista perficere? Vanam, crede mihi, nullumque felicem exitum habituram spem rei publicae concipiebas aliam quam victoris clementiam et aequitatem. Poterat fortasse locus esse concordiae si non hominum vi et iniuria Caesar occubuisset. Quam occasionem istorum tuorum, quos in infinitum laudas, liberatorum Urbis et orbis rabies — dum illum auferunt, qui te teste solus adhibere poterat[188] medicinam — non solum impediverunt sed ingratitudine, proditione et scelere penitus abstulerunt.

15   Tu quidem ipse, Cicero, pro Plancio tuo causam agens, cunctis — ut abritror — probantibus divine prorsus sanctissimeque dixisti: 'An cum videam navem secundis ventis cursum tenentem suum,[189] si non ea eum petat portum quem ego aliquando probavi sed alium non minus tutum atque tranquillum, cum tempestate pugnem periculose potius quam illi, salute praesertim proposita, obtemperem et pareaem?'[190] Haec est tua[191] sententia. Nunc autem, cum res publica tamquam navis non secundis ventis sed belli civilis fluctibus agitata non quem volebas sed aequalem forteque meliorem portum intrasset, fuitne iterum in mare turbidum et civicam tempestatem e portu trudenda?[192] Magna belua imperium est et quae non facile possit ad arbitrium flecti vel regi.

16   Sed per immortalis Dei maiestatem, nullusne est rei publicae status in monarchia? Nullamne Roma rem publicam habuit donec sub regibus fuit? Nullamne post Caesarem habitura fuit sub alicuius quemvis sanctissimi principis dominatu? Nonne politicum est et omnium sapientum sententiis diffinitum monarchiam omnibus rerum publicarum condicionibus praeferendam, si tamen contingat virum bonum et studiosum sapientiae praesidere? Nulla libertas maior quam optimo principi, cum iusta praecipiat, oboedire.

diverse but in direct opposition—how could they have accomplished the result? Believe me, you could have imagined no hope
for the commonwealth that would have had a favorable outcome,
except in the clemency and justice of the conqueror. There might,
perhaps, have been a chance for concord if Caesar had not fallen a
victim to the violence and vengeance of men. But the opportunity
for this was not only hindered by the fury of those liberators of
yours of the city [of Rome] and the world, whom you praise to the
sky, once they took hold of the only one you yourself admit was
capable of providing a remedy, but was lost through ingratitude,
treason and crime.

Why, you yourself, Cicero, in defending the cause of your   15
friend Plancius, with the approval, I believe, of all, put it in divinely fitting language: "If I see a ship holding her course with favoring winds, not toward the harbor which I had formerly chosen,
but toward another equally safe and tranquil, should I risk a fight
against the storm rather than give way to it and seek safety first?"[114]
Such is indeed your judgment. But now, just when the ship of
state, not under favorable winds, but buffeted by the waves of civil
war, was nearing a harbor, not that of your choice but one equally
good if not better, would you have had it pushed out again into
the troubled sea of civil commotion?[115] A mighty beast is imperial
rule, not easily guided or controlled at will.[116]

But, by the majesty of the everlasting God! Is it not the case   16
that one constitutional form of a commonwealth is to be found in
monarchy? Was there no commonwealth at Rome while it was
under kings?[117] Was there to be none after Caesar under the rule
of a single one of the holiest emperors?[118] Is it not sound politics, approved by the judgment of all wise men, that monarchy is
to be preferred to all other forms of government, provided only
that it be in the hands of a wise and good man?[119] There is no
greater liberty than obedience to the just commands of a virtuous
prince.[120]

17   Quod si nihil divinius et melius quam mundus regitur uno solo
praesidente Deo, tanto melius est humanum regimen quanto pro-
pinquius ad illud accedit. Illi vero similius esse non potest quam[193]
unico principante. Nam et multorum regimen nihil est nisi in
unam sententiam conveniat multitudo;[194] si quidem nisi praecipiat
unus et ceteri pareant, non unum erit sed plura regimina. Quid[195]
abhorres hoc,[196] Cicero, quod apud Aristotelem didicisti? Scis inter species principandi tam natura quam ordine, subditorum utilitate necessitateque rerum omnibus antecedere monarchiam? Natura quidem exigit ut, cum aliqui nati sint servire et aliqui
principari, quoad[197] debitae proportionis aequalitas inter omnes
observetur, ad meliorem perveniat principatus.[198]

18   Si fuisset enim vobis, o Cicero, princeps unus, numquam inter
vos civile bellum tantaque discordia succrevisset. Potuit, immo
debuit, vos docere Sullanorum temporum vastitas proximaque dissensio ad illa tollenda necessarium fuisse monarcham, in quem
ordine debito totum corpus rei publicae dirigeretur. Nam in illa,
quam diligebas, politia vel aristocratia malorum remedium vel esse
non poterat, dissidentibus animis, vel tam difficulter[199] et periculose quod nihil minus tempori conveniret. Sicut, occiso Caesare
ruptaque monarchici[200] principatus harmonia, rerum experientia
clarum fecit; mox enim ad bella civilia fuit reventum, ut nedum
utile sed necessarium fuerit ad unum devenire[201] principem,[202] in
cuius manibus tot rerum motus et animorum contrarietates, iustitia et aequitate regnantis, simul discerent convenire atque coales-
cere.

As there is no better or more divine rule than that of the universe under one God, so human sovereignty is the higher the more nearly it approaches that ideal. But nothing can be more like this than the rule of one man. For a popular regime is nothing unless the multitude are united in one common view, and unless one commands and the rest obey, there will not be one regime but several. Why, Cicero, should you condemn what you have learned from Aristotle? You know that among the kinds of government, various both in their nature and in the order of time, considering the welfare of the subjects and the very nature of things, the monarchy has precedence over all the rest. It is a law of nature that since some are born to serve and others to rule, in order that equality may be preserved among all in due proportion, government should be in the hands of the better man.[121]

If in your time, O Cicero, there had been a single leading citizen, you would never have had a civil war and such great disorder. You might, in fact you ought, to have learned from the devastations of the Sullan period and the party conflict which followed, that in order to remove these evils a monarch was needed, through whom the whole body of the commonwealth should be guided in due order. In that polity or aristocracy[122] of which you were so fond there could have been no remedy at all for the ills of the state on account of the conflict of opinions, or it would have been accompanied by such difficulties and dangers as to be wholly unsuited to the times. This was clearly shown by experience after Caesar had been slain and the harmony of a single rule had been destroyed. At once civil strife broke out again, so that it was not merely useful but necessary to resort to a principal citizen in whose hands so many disturbances and such diversities of interest might be reconciled and harmonized through his justice and equity.

19   Quod si factum in Octavio non fuisset, numquam Romana
rabies quievisset, numquam fuisset²⁰³ finis malis²⁰⁴ coeptumque
civile certamen ad confectionem ultimam Romani nominis proces-
sisset. Cumque legamus Octavium de restituenda re publica multotiens cogitasse, nihil crediderim eum ab illius intentionis propo-
sitio demovisse nisi quod videbat in contentionem omnia reditura.
Non erat enim expiatum fermentum illud nec animi civium a
commotione tanti fremitus requierant. Quod advertens Maro divi-
nissime, sicut reliqua, dixit:

Pauca tamen suberunt priscae vestigia fraudis
quae temptare Thetim ratibus, quae cingere muris
oppida, quae iubeant telluri infindere sulcos

et cetera. Quod autem 'fraudis' dixit, non 'deceptionis' intelligi debet sed 'fraudis,' id est 'culpae,' in quo sensu penes Livium saepe
reperitur vocabulum istud 'fraus.'²⁰⁵

20   Quare concludamus illos Caesaris occisores non tyrannum occidisse sed patrem patriae²⁰⁶ et clementissimum ac legitimum principem orbis terrae, et tam graviter contra rem publicam errasse
quam grave et detestabile potest esse²⁰⁷ in quiescente re publica
civilis belli furorem et rabiem excitare. Nec illis imponere volo superbiam spiritus, qua nedum meliorem supra se perpeti non poterant sed secum etiam nec parem. Non imponam et ambitionem,
qui non solum honores ac magistratus sperabant sed inter summos
Romae senatus populique Romani principes numerari; hanc optabant, hanc intendebant²⁰⁸ gloriam.²⁰⁹ Sed ea non parricidio, non
scelere, non superbia, non ambitione paranda fuit; veram gloriam
vera virtus gignit, nec alibi quam in verae virtutis laudibus reperitur. Et haec de quarto quem promisimus articulo dicta sufficiant.

If this had not been done by Octavius, never would the Roman   19
fury have quieted down; never would there have been an end of
evil days, and civil strife once begun again would have gone on to
the final ruin of the very name of Rome. We read that Octavius
many times considered the plan of restoring the commonwealth,
and I am persuaded that nothing could have turned him from that
purpose except the conviction that everything would then have
fallen into confusion.[123] The earlier agitation had not subsided,
and the minds of citizens had not recovered from that terrible
shock. Referring to this, Vergil, speaking as always with divine
genius, says:

> Some traces will remain of that ancient deceit,
> urging men to challenge Thetys with boats, encircle towns
> with walls, draw plows across the earth.[124]

We must note that he says "deceit" and not "error," and deceit implies wrongdoing, in which sense it is often found in Livy.

Wherefore we may conclude that the murderers of Caesar slew,   20
not a tyrant but the father of his country, the lawful and most
benevolent ruler of the world, and that they sinned against the
commonwealth in the most serious and damnable way possible by
kindling the rage and fury of civil war in a peaceful community.[125]
I am not blaming them for their proud spirit in refusing to tolerate
one who was their better — or even an equal. I will not blame
them for their ambition in hoping for honors and offices and de-
siring to be counted among the leaders of the Roman Senate and
people. That was the glory they desired and worked for; but these
are not things to be gained by parricide, by criminal practices, by
pride and ambition. True glory is the offspring of true virtue and
is found in the reputation for true virtue. So much for the fourth
article we proposed to discuss.

: V :

Quod Dantes iuste posuerit Brutum et Cassium in inferno
inferiori tamquam singularissimos proditores.

1 Quoniam ergo Caesar,[210] ut luculentissime probatum est, tyrannus
non fuit titulo, quem grata non coacta patria sibi delegit in principem, non fuit et superbia, qui clementer et cum humanitate rege-
bat, clarum est quod sceleratissime fuit occisus. Unde Dantes
noster spiritualem designans vitam, attento quod proditio, quae
numquam obrepit sine fidei violatione, omnium peccatorum gra-
vissimum est, congelatos glacie proditores infimo statuit in inferno,
ubi Luciferum tricipitem totius mundi locavit in centro, formans
tria illa capita:[211] medium coloris rubei,[212] sinistrum vero nigerri-
mum, dexterum autem inter album et croceum, quae coloris qualitas pallor est. Iudam autem, qui Christum prodidit, figuravit Dantes mediis daemoniis immersum faucibus, capite per Luciferum
mordicus arreptum, miserabiliter affici; Brutum sinistri, Cassium
dexteri rictu capitis apprehensos pedibus aeterne commestionis
supplicio lacerari.

2 Quae quidem omnia per poetam singularissimum divinae rationis examine ficta sunt. Hos enim proditores—quorum unus ae-
terni Dei filium, patrem et creatorem omnium,[213] praetio prodidit,
alii patrem patriae,[214] Brutus autem etiam patrem proprium scelere
proditionis occiderunt—loco personaque Luciferi punientis ae-
quavit. Modo vero capitibusque[215] quibus torquentur sic eos secre-
vit quod gravitas peccati per singulos discernatur. Et colores quidem trium capitum referri possunt ad tres effectus qui gignuntur
in mentibus peccatorum: primus est rubor ex morsu conscientiae,

: V :

That Dante correctly placed Brutus and Cassius in lower Hell as extraordinary traitors

Since, then, Caesar, as has been most abundantly proved, was not   1
a tyrant by defect of title, seeing that a grateful country chose him
for its principal citizen, nor by reason of arrogant pride, because
he ruled with clemency and humanity, it is clear that his murder
was an utterly wicked act. Hence our own Dante in his description of the spiritual life, remembering that treason, which always
slithers in through a breach of faith, is the gravest of all sins,
placed traitors in his lowest Hell, where also in the center of the
universe he put three-headed Lucifer, distinguishing the three
heads thus: The middle one he made red, that on the left the
deepest black, the right-hand one a color between white and yel-
low, known as "pallor." Then Dante represented Judas, the betrayer
of Christ, as plunged by the head in the central jaws of the demon
and wretchedly stuck there; Brutus in the maw of the left head
and Cassius of the right, are caught by the legs and torn by the
torture of this perpetual feast.[126]

All this is conceived by the supreme poet by a weighing of   2
the divine account. For he made those traitors equal in place
and in person with the Lucifer who is punishing them. One of
them had for a price betrayed the son of the eternal God, father
and creator of all things; the others had murdered the father of
their country, and Brutus even his own father, with the added
crime of treason. Further, the poet so distinguished them by
the heads in which they were tormented that the enormity of
their offenses was made clear individually. The colors of the three
heads may be related to the effects produced in the minds of the
criminals. The first is redness from the gnawings of conscience;

secundus est pallor ex metu poenae, tertius est nigredo,[216] qui color est nota ex macula culpae. Quae licet omnibus peccatoribus communia sint, inter hos tres tamen specialiter dividuntur. Iudas enim in rubeo capite, quod primum est, immersus caput Luciferi faucibus poenas luit. 'Iuda' quidem, ut ex libro Philonis probat Hieronymus, hebraice scriptum 'laudatio' sive 'confessio' latine dicitur et interpretatur, 'Iudas' autem 'confitens' sive 'glorificans.' Hic enim, poenitentia ductus, referens triginta argenteos inquit: 'Peccavi tradens sanguinem iustum.' Vox quidem confitentis est[217] 'peccavi tradens,' glorificantis autem sive laudantis vox fuit 'sanguinem iustum.' Is ergo qui poenitens laqueo se suspendit, primo rubeoque capite[218] punitur immersus.

3   Cassius, de quo legitur quod cogitans Brutum esse devictum et ob id metuens in manus hostium devenire, uni de proximis caput praebuit abscidendum. Historia quidem habet quod illa pugna Brutus exercitui occurrit Octavii, quem repulsum atque confectum castris exuit; vidente tamen C. Cassio[219] equites ad capienda castra cum impetu recurrentes, cum fugisse crederet, actum de Bruto ratus, in tumultum se redegit et, exploratore tardius redeunte, metu se contulit ad mortem voluntariam subeundam. Qua consideratione fuit a Dante capiti pallido deputatus. Brutus vero, licet Octavii victor, cum superatum videret Cassium[220] et licet sero sciret eadem die maritimo bello se fuisse victores, omnia tamen languescere cernens et Cassium mortuum, scelere et impietate causae victus, hauriendum latus uni sociorum exhibuit. Et quoniam nota criminis maior[221] eidem inusta fuit, eo quod Caesaris filius[222] putaretur, ipsum nigro capiti[223] Dantes, ut cernitur, assignavit. Et quod filius eius fuerit, qui sciunt Caesari cum matre Bruti lasciviae fuisse

the second pallor from fear of punishment; the third blackness from the stain of the offense itself. These effects, though common to all sinners, are apportioned among these three in a peculiar sense. For Judas, plunged in the red head, which is the first, pays the penalty with his head in the jaws of Lucifer. In fact the word *juda*, as Jerome proves from the book of Philo, taken in the Hebrew sense means in Latin *laudatio* or *confessio*, and therefore Judas means "confessor" or "glorifier."[127] Now, when he was overcome by remorse and returned the thirty pieces of silver, he said: "I have sinned and have betrayed innocent blood," the word of confession being "I have sinned and have betrayed" and the word of praise or glorification being "innocent blood."[128] And so he, being penitent, and having hanged himself with a cord, is punished by being plunged into the first head, the red one.

As to Cassius, it is said that, believing Brutus to be beaten and fearing to fall into the enemy's hands, he begged one of the bystanders to cut off his head. But history tells us that in the fight Brutus met the army of Octavius and drove it out of its camp beaten and destroyed; yet Cassius, seeing horsemen hurrying back to occupy the camp, supposed they had taken flight and thinking it was all up with Brutus, betook himself to a little hill, and there, his scout being too late in returning, took his own life.[129] Therefore he is assigned by Dante to the pallid head. Brutus, although victorious over Octavius, and though he learned at a late hour that his party had won a naval victory on the same day, when he saw that Cassius was beaten and learned of his death, perceiving that his own fortunes were declining and overcome by the baseness and treachery of his cause, begged one of his companions to pierce him in the side.[130] Since, therefore, he was branded with the mark of an especially heinous crime, being reputed to be the son of Caesar, Dante assigned him to the black head.[131] That he was Caesar's son those may readily convince themselves who know that Caesar used to sleep with the mother of Brutus[132] and who read that at the

consuetudinem et qui legunt caesariana caede dictatorem, cum
ipsum stricto in se videret gladio irruentem, dixisse graece, ut
Graecam vocem Latinis exprimam litteris: 'Kai su, teknon?', hoc
est 'Et tu, fili?', quod graece sic scribitur: 'Καὶ σύ, τέκνον;' satis
habere debent verisimiliter persuasum. Accedit ad[224] deformitatis
rationem singulare quiddam in Bruto; historice quidem legitur
quod, illato lumine, cum aliquid de nocte secum ageret, meditanti
quamdam imaginem atri coloris apparuisse, quam, cum quaenam
esset interrogasset, respondisse ferunt: 'Malus genius tuus.' Iure
Dantes igitur sibi nigram faciem deputavit.

4   Quis reprehendat igitur Dantem si perditissimos homines —
qui morali ratione tam graviter peccaverunt occidendo proditorie
Caesarem,[225] patrem patriae, gerentem tanta cum clementia principatum, quem ei, maxima necessitate ponendi finem malis[226] ex-
tinguendique bella civilia,[227] senatus Romanusque populus detu-
lerunt — in inferni profundum submerserit maximoque supplicio
condemnarit? Ceterum illic, ubi princeps diabolicae creaturae, qui
per superbiam in Deum et proprium opificem insurrexit, ab eodem sui poematis ordine relegatus est, rationabiliter demersi sunt
Iudas, qui Deum hominem prodidit, et Cassius atque Brutus,[228]
qui proditorie Caesarem, quoddam quasi divinitatis vestigium iure
principatus et accumulatione beneficiorum, quae largissime con-
gessit in eos, destruentes rem publicam ac orbantes patriam,[229]
occiderunt. Denique satis abunde sufficeret Danti nostro Maronis
auctoritas, quem sibi ducem proposuit et magistrum; inter ultimos
enim quos in infimo ponit inferno vult esse 'quique arma secuti / impia nec veriti dominorum fallere dextras.'

5   Postremo qui poetico artificio res pertractant[230] solent a negotiorum eventibus, sive veri sive ficti sint, celebrare viros[231] et gesta
virorum obscurareque. Sic Homerus Achillem Hectori praetulit,

moment of his death the dictator, seeing Brutus rushing at him with drawn sword, cried out in Greek—if I may express the Greek words in Latin letters—*kai su, teknon?* that is, "You too, my son?" which is written in Greek thus: Καὶ σύ, τέκνον?[133] In the case of Brutus, beside the reason of his shameful conduct there is added a certain strange incident: it is recorded in history, that, as he was brooding at night, after a light had been brought, a dark figure appeared to him, and when asked what it was, answered: "I am your evil spirit!"[134] Dante, therefore, was right in assigning the black face to him.

And who can criticize Dante for thrusting into the depths of 4 hell and condemning to extreme punishment those abandoned men who sinned so grievously in treacherously murdering Caesar, the father of his country, while he was administering with such clemency the government which the Senate and people of Rome had conferred upon him in a desperate crisis to put an end to the evils of civil war? It was a reasonable idea to plunge Judas, Cassius and Brutus into the same place to which the prince of the world of demons, who through pride had rebelled against God his maker, was relegated in the plan of the poem. For Judas betrayed God made man, and Cassius and Brutus treacherously slew Caesar, the image, as it were, of divinity in the rightfulness of his rule and in the multitude of favors which he had abundantly heaped upon them, thus destroying the commonwealth and bereaving the fatherland. Finally, we may find sufficient authority for Dante in the words of Vergil, whom he chose for his guide and master. For among the very last of those whom Vergil places in the lowest hell he puts those "who took up arms disloyally and did not hesitate to deceive the hand of their masters."[135]

Those who treat events with the art of the poet are wont to 5 praise or blame men and their deeds according to the success of their undertakings. Thus Homer sets Achilles above Hector;

sic Aeneam Mezentio Vergilius Turnique laudibus anteponit. Sic et ipse idem Antonium postponit Octavio, Pallantem Turno, sic et omnes alii victores victis laudibus praestantiores conantur ostendere. Nunc autem quis vult Dantem nostrum eos, quos victoria stravit et praevalentium sequax obscuravit felicitas, celebrare? Ut quos hominum potentia perculit, Dei dispositio non infelices solum sed impios et sceleratos ostendit, Marte iudice testimonioque fortunae, poemate suo Dantes erigat vel laude dignos esse contendat?

6 Verum cum auctor iste doctissimus Christianus videret ex rerum effectibus, qui divinae voluntatis verissimi testes sunt, Deum decrevisse res hominum sub una Romanorum redigere monarchia, nonne debuit eos, qui conati sunt huic ordinationi—qua ratione potuerunt—obsistere, veluti dispositioni Dei contrarios, inter damnatos er reprobos deputare? Quare concludamus in hoc, sicut et in aliis, Dantem nostrum nec theologice nec moraliter longeque minus poetice damnando, sicut fecit, Brutum et Cassium erravisse; immo non solum non errasse sed iuste sine dubio iudicasse.

7 Postremo nunc restat quod de Antenore dubitas et Aenea paucis, sicut promisimus, expedire. Principio quidem historicorum antiquissimi Dares Phrygius et Gnosius Dictys, qui Troianam scripserunt historiam, non ambigue sed plane clarissimeque testantur ipsos de prodenda patria cum Graecorum principibus pepigisse. Quo minus indignor Guidoni de Columna Messana, quod secutus hos auctores ambobus illis principibus notam proditionis inusserit, credoque quod, florentibus tandem[232] Romanis Juliaque familia in humanarum rerum cacumen evecta, quoniam Aeneam inter auctores suos praecipue fuisse iactabant, scriptores quosdam Aeneae nomini pepercisse. Inter quos singularis est Sisenna, qui refertur solum Antenorem Troiae proditorem, non alium, voluisse.

Vergil prefers Aeneas to Mezentius and Turnus, and places Antony below Octavius and Pallas below Turnus. So all the rest try to show that the victors were better men than the vanquished. Why, then, should we expect our Dante to praise persons laid low by defeat and relegated to obscurity by the fortune that ensued to the victors? Or why should we suppose that in his poem he would restore and render praiseworthy persons brought down by the strength of man and persons whom the will of God, through the arbitration of war and the evidence of fortune, shows to be not only unfortunate but impious and criminal?

Further, since that most learned and Christian poet saw from 6 natural effects — the most certain witness of divine will — that God had decreed that all the affairs of men should be brought under the one single government of the Romans, was he not bound to place among the damned, as men working against the divine plan, those who tried in every possible way to oppose this order? For which reason we may conclude that our Dante, in this matter as in others, made no mistake either theologically or morally — still less poetically — in condemning Brutus and Cassius as he did. Indeed, not only did he make no mistake, but beyond question he rendered a just judgment.

It remains, finally, to dispose in a few words of the question 7 you raise about Antenor and Aeneas. In the first place, those most ancient historians Dares Phrygius and Gnosius Dictys state in no doubtful terms but plainly and clearly that those men negotiated with the Greeks to betray their country. For this reason I cannot blame Guido delle Colonne of Messina, who follows these authors, for branding both with the marks of treason.[136] It is my belief that later, when the Romans had prospered and the Julian family had reached the summit of human glory, since they boasted Aeneas as their ancestor, certain writers spared the memory of his name. Among these is Sisenna, who is said to have represented Antenor and no one else as the betrayer of Troy.[137]

Livius autem, nobilissimus auctor, utrosque duces illos excusat, dicens conservatos a Graecis[233] hospitii iure, quod apud antiquos sanctissimum fuit, et quoniam paci restitutionique rerum ablatarum et Helenae se semper favorabiles praebuissent. Honesta quidem excusatio, quae quoniam Capys, Helenus et alii plures, qui numquam sunt inter proditores reputati ab[234] Troia, patientibus victoribus Graecis, incolumes evasere, necessaria non fuit Antenori vel Aeneae, nisi quod alio vitio laborabant. Inter haec tu et quilibet iudex esto. Potes ipsos cum Dicte Dareteque[235] proditionis reos habere, si libet; potes,[236] auctore Sisenna, liberare, si placet, Aeneam, vel ambos excusare cum Livio et Dictem Cretensem atque Daretem[237] Phrygium inter apocryphos reputare. Veritatem enim ad solidum non credo posse per ea quae legerim reperiri, stante praesertim vigintiquinque saeculorum fama, quae non solet, si falsum effuderit, permanere.

8   Habes, Antoni carissime, meum super utraque dubitatione iudicium, in quo, si tardior fui, meis occupationibus, quas tu ipse commemoras, imputato. Sin[238] autem non satisfecerim, ut arbitror, ignorantiam accusa meam;[239] sum enim paratior addiscere quam docere.[240] Vale felix et conare, precor, in virum summum evadere, quo sis tuis decus et omnibus carus.[241]

Then Livy, a most famous author, exonerates them, saying that they were protected by the Greeks in accordance with the law of hospitality, which the ancients held especially sacred, and because they had always favored peace and the restoration of booty and of Helen.[138] An honorable excuse indeed, but not needed by either Antenor or Aeneas, seeing that Capys, Helenus and many others who have never been considered traitors passed safely out of Troy, being allowed to do so by the victorious Greeks[139] — unless, indeed, they were guilty upon some other charge. Between these various opinions you or anyone else may judge. You may, if you please, with Dictys and Dares, regard these men as traitors. You may, if you prefer, on the authority of Sisenna, acquit Aeneas, or with Livy acquit them both and treat Dictys the Cretan and Dares the Phyrgian as apocryphal writers. I do not believe that the precise truth can be ascertained from the books that I have read, especially since the tradition has lasted twenty-five centuries, and tradition does not ordinarily persist if its report is false.

Such, my dear Antonio, is my judgment upon these two problems. If I have been rather late in giving it, lay this down to those occupations of mine which you refer to. If I have not given you satisfaction, ascribe this to my ignorance; for I am always more ready to learn than to teach. Farewell! Live happily and strive, I beg you, to show yourself the best of men, a credit to your family and beloved by all.

ANTONII LUSCI

INVECTIVA IN
FLORENTINOS

1   Illucebitne umquam dies, perditissimi cives, vastatores patriae et
quietis Italiae turbatores, quo dignam vestris sceleribus poenam
meritumque supplicium consequamini? Dabiturne aliquando, vestrae cuiuspiam calamitatis insignis exemplo, sic vestri similes deterreri et sic in aerumnis vestris suum formidare discrimen, ut calamitas vestra videatur non solum iusta in ultione, sed etiam utilis
in exemplo? Eruntne ullo tempore sic vestra detecta atque delusa
praestigia, in quibus omne vestrum praesidium collocatum est, ut
oculatae ceterae gentes appareant, vos, ut estis, vanissimi et caecutientissimi videamini?

2   Sic erit profecto, non fallor: advenant tempora, fata sunt prope,
pleno cursu appropinquat diu exoptata mortalibus ruina vestrae
superbiae. Videbimus, ecce videbimus illam vestram in defendenda
quadam foedissima libertate vel potius crudelissima tyrannide constantiam fortitudinemque Romanam; hoc enim nomine superbire
soletis et vos genus praedicare Romanum, quod quam impudenter
faciatis alio dicendum erit loco. Nunc prosequor; videbimus, inquam, illam inanem atque ventosam iactantiam et insolentiam
Florentinam et quam virtuti vere respondeat a vobis, praeter ceteros mortales, propriarum rerum semper usurpata laudatio cognoscemus.

3   Non possunt amplius homines sine stomacho vestrum nomen
audire; non potest pati Italia eos incolumes videre qui, cum eam
cladibus multis afflixerint, ad extremum suffocare turpissima

144

ANTONIO LOSCHI

INVECTIVE AGAINST THE
FLORENTINES

Will that day ever dawn, O most evil citizens, enemies of your 1
country and disturbers of the peace in Italy,[1] when you will pay
the penalty your crimes deserve, when you will have to undergo
the punishment you merit? Will it ever come about that the example of your special undoing will frighten those like you and
make them comprehend, in light of your disasters, the risks they
run, such that your ruin will be not only a fitting vindication but
also a useful example? And will your deceptions be revealed and
thus foiled, deceptions that you rely upon wholly, so that other
nations may be found to be clear-sighted and so that you may appear to be what you are: utterly empty and utterly blind?[2]

So shall it surely be, I am certain; the times have arrived, 2
destiny is about to be fulfilled, and with great strides there approaches the collapse of your pridefulness, long wished-for by the
human race.[3] We shall see—and how we shall see!—your celebrated constancy and "Roman" tenacity in defending that repulsive
liberty, or rather cruel tyranny. You are accustomed to boast of the
name of Rome and declare to all that you descend from the Romans. This impudent lie I will refute another time. Now I continue: we shall see, I say, that Florentine presumption and insolence is empty as the wind, and we shall learn how much the
praise that more than any other nation you claim for yourselves,
truly corresponds to virtue.

People can no longer hear your name without vexation; Italy 3
can no longer bear that those who have afflicted her with many
disasters, and in the end even sought to strangle her with wretched

145

servitute conati sunt; non potest denique vos ferre diutius divina
iustitia. Quomodo igitur stare possint non video, contra quos omnium fere hominum vota ac studia accensa sunt; quos vexata per
vos et ad servitutem vocata Italia detestatur; in quos denique tantis
flagitiis irritata ira caelestis armatur. Haec, mihi credite scelerati,
contra vos militat; haec nocentissimum sanguinem vestrum sitit;
haec extremam ruinam insidiosissimae et flagitiosissimae gentis
exposcit, atque ideo tantam hanc furiam mentibus vestris iniecit,
ut de excidio sacrosanctae matris ecclesiae, de mutatione Romani
imperii, de ruina gloriosissimi ducis, perniciosa consilia tractaretis.
Quid enim aliud cogitandum est, nisi divinum numen, iam iam
sceleribus vestris infensum, vos occaecatos in tantam insaniam
impulisse, ut odia et arma illa contra vos excitaret, quorum viribus
non solum non possetis resistere, sed nec etiam ferre fulgorem?

4   Atque, ut omittam ceteros vestros inimicos, quibus nihil videtur
antiquius quam ut aliquando de cruento illo superbiae scopulo
corruatis, ecce contra perfidiam vestram venit his armis et copiis
hisque armorum ducibus instructus exercitus, ut maiori multo potentiae quam vestra sit (ea qua tamen adeo superbitis ut arrogantia
vestra tolerari vix possit) extimescendus esse videatur. Venitque
non tam avide eo missus quam desideratus atque exspectatus a
vestris; vestris, inquam, si ita sunt appellandi quorum cum in fortunas et corpora crudele et avarum habeatis imperium, nihil minus quam animos possidetis. Sperant equidem hoc uno assertore
suae libertatis exercitu, vobis prolapsis in servitutem, dignitatem
pristinam, quam sibi per vos ereptam lugent, tandem esse recuperaturos. Itaque arma haec omnes hi populi, quos sub acerbissima
tyrannide suffocatis, exspectant, ut cum tempus occasionemque
prospexerint, excutiant iugum illud servitutis, quo manente nihil
ipsis potest esse iocundum. Etenim quid delectabile videri potest miserrimae servituti,[1] cui speciose amplaeque fortunae, quae

slavery, remain unpunished; divine justice herself can no longer tolerate you. I can hardly see how you can hold out when the yearnings and hopes of nearly all humanity are aroused against you; if Italy—which you harassed and summoned to servitude— hates you, and if heaven's wrath itself, vexed by so many misdeeds, is in arms against you. Yes, heavenly wrath too makes war upon you, believe me, wicked ones; it too thirsts for your guilty blood; it too requires the total ruin of the most scheming and criminal of nations. That is why it has injected this madness into your minds, so that you hatch pernicious plots to destroy Holy Mother Church, to undermine the Roman Empire and ruin the most glorious of dukes. What else can one imagine but that God Himself, outraged by your wickedness, has blinded you, driving you to the height of madness, so that he might arouse hatred and arms against you? You cannot bear even the gleam of your enemies' arms, to say nothing of their power.

And leaving aside other enemies, for whom nothing seems 4 more desirable than for you to topple from that bloody eminence of arrogance, behold an army is advancing against you, strong enough in arms, soldiers and commanders as to strike you down in fear of a power much greater than your own, despite your intolerable arrogance. It is advancing, driven not just by its own eagerness, but because it is desired and awaited by your allies—if you can call "allies" those whose souls you by no means possess, though you exercise a cruel and greedy empire over their bodies and fortunes. Indeed, they hope that, thanks to this army of liberation, you will finally be enslaved and they may recover that ancient dignity which, as they lament, they saw you tear from them. All the peoples whom you are choking with your unbearable tyranny await these forces, and as soon as the moment and opportunity arise, they will throw off the yoke of your tyranny, under which they can have no joy. Besides, what enjoyment could exist under the most wretched slavery, with the pain of seeing riches

magnam afferre solent voluptatem, aut summo dolori ablatae aut, ne eripiantur, aeterno metui sint oportet? Quid uxore, quid liberis dulcius? Quam tamen ex his sentire dulcedinem potest is qui se videt nuptias ad alterius petulantiam comparasse, liberos ad alienam libidinem procreasse? Patria vero, quae unicuique debet esse iocunda, infinitam affert tristitiam atque maerorem in servitute conspecta, ubi non solum non auditur ulla vox libera, sed nec etiam ulli sunt liberi cogitatus. Haec quidem cum ab uno pati sit miserum, miserius est a multis, miserrimum vero ab his quorum avaritia, libido, crudelitas, post hominum memoriam, tyrannorum omnium malitiam excessere. Ergo hi, quos hac tam infausta vitae condicione sub iugo intolerabilis servitutis opprimitis, omnes in speculis sunt, observant praestolanturque opportunitatem qua sese in libertatem asserere possint, quibus quantam spem praestiterit huius adventus exercitus difficile dictu est. Affecti enim sunt inextimabili atque incredibili alacritate seseque iam pedes posuisse in possessionem desperatae quondam libertatis existimant.

5   Neque vos tantum Sancti Miniatis oppidi extollat illa quidem oppidanis infelix — vobis, ut videtur, fortunata — receptio quantum terrificet tam cito properata rebellio, ex qua quid animi sit reliquis municipiis atque urbibus pari servientibus calamitate licet intelligatis. Quibus, mihi credite, illius magnanimi quidem sed vel precipitis nimium vel proditi atque deserti liberatoris patriae exsilium nequaquam prae metu voluntates exstinguet, sed admonebit ut diligentius cogitent suis rebus esse consulendum.

6   Age, postquam ad hunc locum pedetemptim fluxit oratio, ut in quem formidabilem casum prolapsi sitis et in quam praecipitem foveam incideritis, si adeo estis dementes ac caeci ut non videatis, ostendat. Respondere vos cupio quibus e locis quibusve de horreis

and properties gathered with such care — ordinarily a great source of happiness — taken away, or else with the constant fear of having them snatched away? What is sweeter than a bride and children? But how can they make for happiness when someone sees that he has prepared his nuptials to minister to another man's wantonness, and given birth to children to satisfy a stranger's lust? Our own country, which should be a source of joy to everyone, instead causes us sadness and grief when we see it enslaved, without free speech or even a single free thought. It is sad if a single person should inflict all this, sadder still if many do so, but the saddest thing of all is when it is done by a people whose avarice, lust, and cruelty defeats the malice of every tyrant in human memory. This, then, is why all those whom you are oppressing in this accursed condition of life, under the yoke of intolerable bondage, are now upon the watchtowers, anxiously awaiting the chance to reclaim their liberty, and it is hard to say how great is the hope the arrival of our army is offering them. They are moved by a boundless enthusiasm, and they reckon they have already taken steps to repossess the liberty they thought forever lost.

And boast not of the surrender to you of the town of San 5 Miniato — a happy circumstance for you, but sad for the inhabitants.[4] Rather, may the sudden revolt that followed afterward fill you with terror, so that you may come to understand the kind of spirit that animates other towns and cities subjected to a like calamity for those enslaved. Believe me: the exile of that magnanimous liberator of his country — even though he was too hasty (or perhaps was just betrayed and abandoned) — far from blunting their wills with fear, will just teach them that they need to be more careful when taking counsel about their own affairs.[5]

Come then! My discourse has arrived step by step to the point 6 where it should show you — if you are not so insane and blind that you don't see it yourselves — the fearful collapse that is upon you, the steep pit into which you have fallen. I would like you to tell me

inediae vestrae subveniendum iri existimatis, cum ager hic omnis
quem aratis suapte natura sit Cereri adversus, ut pace integra atque secura ad victum urbis ipse non suppetat; hostilibus flammis
ardebit et undique belli clade vastabitur, nisi forte Siciliam, horreum populi Romani vestrumque frumentarium, hac aetate praesidium subventuram esse putetis. Sed videte eo vos portu esse
privatos quo vitam et spiritum ducere solebatis et per Alpium iuga,
ex agro Flaminio, quomodo satisfieri possit tantae multitudini iudicate, cum sit transitus ipse difficilis etiam omni carens molestia
belli. At si ad difficultatem viarum accesserit itinerum infesta turbatio, quae cessare in bello longe lateque diffuso non potest, cogitare non possum, nisi Iupiter ipse vobis de caelo pluat fruges, vos
vel fame sola non esse perituros.

7   An fortasse fines vestros tueri posse confiditis? Ego sane non
video tantum virium vobis esse ut quattuor equitum legionibus,
tot enim contra vos armantur, possitis obstare. 'At socii ferent
opem rebus afflictis.' Digna quidem res in summo periculo auxilia
implorare sociorum. Sed quis umquam vobis socius fuit cui vestra
superbia non invisa sit? Quem non tergiversationum vestrarum
fastidia satiarint? Qui non vos oderit? Qui non vestra calamitate
laetetur, ut si sine suo periculo fieri possit, vos deleri funditus atque ex orbe terrarum exturbari non optet? An inania fortassis et
falsa fingo? Bononienses velim hac in parte respondeant, qui iam
annos novem vobiscum societate et foedere sunt coniuncti, qui
primo, cum inter eos ducemque Liguriae dissensio nulla esset,
vestram societatem amicitiamque secuti, priori sese bello non necessario implicuerunt, et cum pace in summa possent spectatores
esse alienae fortunae, suam pro salute vestra in discrimen adducere

where and what supplies of grain you will draw upon in order to feed the population, since your territory is by nature infertile, too poor to meet the needs of the city even in times of peace.[6] Your enemies will set fires and make raids everywhere, unless you think Sicily, granary of the Roman people and your main source of cereals,[7] will help you this time. But you need to recall that you may no longer count on the port from which you used to draw life and breath,[8] and consider how difficult it would be to transport grain for so great a multitude from Emilia Romagna across the Apennines, a difficult track even without the obstacles caused by a war. But if to the difficulty of transport you add the hostile disturbance of travel typical of a war waged over a wide territory, I really don't know how you can help dying just from famine, unless Jupiter in person delivers grain from the skies.

Are you perhaps confident you can protect your borders? I 7 don't think you quite have sufficient forces to be able to resist four legions of horse, for those are the forces being armed against you. "But the allies will rush to help us in our afflictions." Nothing forbids invoking the help of allies when the situation is desperate. But have you ever had an ally that did not begrudge you your pride? Is there perhaps a single one that is not disgusted by your continual hesitations? That does not hate you? That does not rejoice at your misadventures, that would not want to see you defeated once for all and chased off the face of the earth, if it could happen without danger to themselves? Are they falsehoods and pure inventions, these words of mine? I would like to hear the reply of the Bolognese, who for these nine years now have been tied to you in a pact of alliance.[9] By the mere fact of having united themselves with you and become your friends, they found themselves involved in that first conflict, against their will and without there having been any reason for discord with the Duke of Liguria; indeed they could well have stood aside as peaceful spectators but chose instead to risk their security for the sake of yours,[10] and

maluerunt et eo in bello cuius molem paene totam suis humeris substinendam esse viderent. Quam enim aliam offensionem dux iste Ligusticus, cum bellum indiceret, illis obiecit nisi quod aequo nimis vestram amicitiam foventes sese vestros omnino sequaces effecissent? Qua re dubitandum est nemini, si sese a vestris foederibus abscidissent, illius belli onus sibi nequaquam fuisse subeundum. Sed valuit sociorum integritas, valuit amor, valuit opinio. Itaque in rebus duris atque asperis vos, contra quod dignum erat, praepotenti et vicino domino, magno cum suo periculo, praetulerunt.

8   Vos vero contra hos amicos et socios tam propitios, tam constantes, tam veteres, tam probatos, quales deinde in media pace fueritis ipsi norunt et omnis, non sine stupore quodam, vidit Italia. Hoc mihi, quamquam sitis impudentissimi, non negaturos esse confido: vos cum his tam fidelibus sociis non mediocrem controversiam habuisse vestra culpa susceptam, parumque abfuisse quin bello atque armis totam eam causam decerneretis, neque ullum amicitiae vetus officium, non communium fortunarum laborumque memoriam—quae una in coniungendis animis hominum valeat plurimum—non concordiae curam, non ullius gratiam societatis, non denique religionem foederum tenuisse, sed metum. Hic unus vobis contra socios, contra fidem, contra divina et humana iura furentibus extorsit arma de manibus.

9   Hi ergo nunc socii humeros suos ruinae vestrae subiciant? Non sunt adeo, ut opinor, insani ut pro his, quos non sine ratione deletos atque deperditos velint, arma suscipiant. 'Sed accurrent,' dicet aliquis, 'ad commune periculum repellendum, ad commune incendium restinguendum.' Primum quidem intellegunt neque periculum neque hoc bellum esse commune quod vos propriis furoribus

that in a war where the greater burden was clearly to be their own. In fact what accusation did the said Duke of Liguria make against them, in declaring war, but that of having shown excessive friendship for you, more than was fair, and so becoming your followers entirely? Truly no one doubts that if they had dissolved the alliance made with you they would never have been forced to uphold that burdensome war. But their integrity as an ally prevailed, their affection prevailed, their concern for reputation prevailed. And so, in dire and stressful circumstances, they preferred you to a most powerful lord and near neighbor, contrary to what was the appropriate course and exposing themselves to a grave threat.

On the other hand, how you have behaved in times of peace 8 toward these friends and allies — so benevolent, so faithful, of such long standing and trustworthiness! — they well know and all Italy, not without astonishment, has seen. I trust that, despite your incredible effrontery, you will not deny what I am about to say: with these faithful allies you engaged in a controversy of no little moment through your own fault, and you were nearly at the point of resolving the question by armed warfare. But you were held back, not by any sense of duty toward old friendship, not by the memory of shared successes and labors — that which does the most to unite the hearts of men — not by the desire for harmony, not by any special favor owed to the alliance, still less by the sacred bond of treaties, but simply by fear. It was this alone that tore the arms from your furious hands, keeping you from war against your allies, against your oath, and against all law, human and divine.[11]

And these allies are now to lift you on their shoulders and save 9 you from ruin? I do not consider them so foolish as to take up arms to help the very ones they should want to see, not without reason, defeated and destroyed. "But they will come running," someone will say, "to repel a common danger and extinguish a fire that threatens them as well." In the first place they understand that neither the danger nor this war is a matter of common concern: it

accendistis, atque ideo vobis solis substinendum non iniuria existimabunt. Deinde, si qua suspicio occupabit animos et fueritis in ea fingenda fortunati quod sine ulla intermissione temptatis efficere, profecto magis erit eis curae pro suis defendendis finibus, quam pro vestris liberandis praesidia comparare.

10 A tribus vero tyrannis quid auxilii sit sperandum, non satis intelligo; alterius enim tenues atque afflictae sunt, alterius nondum reintegratae fortunae, ut hi ope aliena magis indigeant. A tertio vero tantum abest ut quicquam exspectetis auxilii, ut cum ipse circumsaeptus undique in medio belli flagrabit incendio, Florentinam opem ac fidem frustra imploraturus esse videatur. Qua re desinite vobis spes vanas et inutiles conflare de sociis, sed cogitate potius qua ratione, qua spe, quo denique fato atque fortuna vos soli tantam belli magnitudinem subeatis.

11 Nisi forte vobis ferociores animos facit Gallicanum foedus. Miror in hominibus, qui se haberi volunt et prudentes et callidos, tantam insedisse dementiam ut spes omnes suas in gente levissima collocarint. Mirarer in Italis tantam perversitatem exstitisse naturae ut de Gallis bene sperare possent, nisi vos venenum ac faecem Italorum, iam diu inimicos salutis Italiae, cognovissem. Sed per Deum immortalem, cum pollens et fortis exercitus agrum vestrum populetur, cum castra hostium in vestris finibus habeatis, cum iam denique pro tectis ac moenibus patriae dimicaturi paene de muris armorum strepitum sentiatis, quid auditis e Gallia illa Transalpina? Afferuntur, credo, quotidie rumores ac litterae; cuius, quaeso, sententiae? Legati regiam regemque sollicitant, opem ex foedere debitam, cadentibus paene rebus, implorant, ne a summo

was something your own furies ignited, and they will reckon, not without justice, that you alone should wage it. Then, if they start to harbor doubts and you turn out to be lucky in the plots you are continually trying to bring off, they will surely be much more concerned to guard their own borders than to liberate yours.

In addition, I fail to understand what help you expect to get 10 from three tyrants, one of whom is weak and ruined in his fortunes, while another has yet to recover from his misfortunes, so that both stand themselves in need of help. From the third there is so little hope of assistance that it will likely be he, trapped on all sides amid the fires of war, who will beg for Florentine aid and loyalty — and in vain.[12] So leave off concocting these great and useless hopes about your allies and think rather in what way, with what likelihood of success, and with what fate and fortune you may endure a war on so large a scale.

Unless, perhaps, it is a treaty with the French[13] that is making 11 your hearts more fierce. I'm surprised that such insanity should take hold of men who wish to be thought prudent and astute, so that they place their hopes in a people so fickle.[14] I would be surprised to find Italians so enormously wrongheaded as to trust the French if I hadn't long since recognized that you are the poison, the dregs of the Italians, the enemies of the security of Italy.[15] But — by the immortal God! — when a strong and powerful army devastates your territory, when enemies are encamped inside your borders, when you are close to the point of having to defend your very homes, hearing from the walls the clangor of arms,[16] what news arrives from the much-sung Transalpine Gaul? Words and letters arrive every day, I imagine, but of what tenor? The ambassadors supplicate the court and the king, beg for the help owed them by treaty, and, when the situation deteriorates, demand that the high king not desert them in their clear and present danger —

rege—quem sibi unum defensorem et dominum, spreto Caesare, neglecta Romana ecclesia, concupiverunt—in tanto et tam propinquo periculo deserantur expostulant. In armis hostem esse popularique iam fines eius; nisi succurratur, omnia brevi esse ruitura significant; esse eum regem in terris, qui saluti suae consulere possit, praeter eum neminem. Obsecrant obtestanturque per sacratissimi diadematis maiestatem ne desertos ac destitutos ludibrio dedat inimici; eius, addunt, inimici qui eis ob hoc maxime infensus sit, quod se et fortunas suas maiestati regiae, summa cum devotione, commiserint.

12   Miris deinde modis animos Gallorum, suapte natura leves ac tumidos, inflare student, miris suasionibus adhortari, si anniti parum velint, venisse tempus et apertam esse occasionem non solum Italiae capiendae sed ad manum suam imperii transferendi et ad nutum ecclesiae redigende; sese cum Ianua, cum magna Italiae parte esse iam suos; nihil reliquum, oppresso duce Liguriae, quod terra marique suae magnitudini possit obstare; ducem autem ipsum, quamquam magnum aliquid videatur, primo belli impetu esse casurum. Itaque quibus parum est spei parumve consilii ad solum patriae defendendum, liberam possessionem Italiae atque orbis terrae imperium pollicentur.

13   Non sum dubius ad haec omnia benigna et grata responsa suscipiunt: regi salutem amicorum esse cordi et foedera nuper icta memoriae; bono se illos animo esse iubere, nequaquam eorum necessitati maiestatem regiam defuturam. Et fortasse, cum armatis legionibus egeatis, Galli legationibus prius pro vestra salute intercedendum putant, quod etiam si impetratis est maximum. Interim stabunt illi suis occupati deliciis, fruentur opima in pace opibus suis, dum vos miseri in tanto bellorum incendio conflagratis. Sed age: tueri velint non solum nuda auctoritate sed armis! Ut

the king whom they longed to have as their sole defender and lord, disdaining his imperial majesty and ignoring the Roman Church. The enemy — they cry — has taken to arms and lays waste to his[17] lands; if help is not given soon, all will be lost. He is the only king in the world who can save them, there is no other. They pray and implore the king, in the name of his most holy crown, not to leave them alone and defenseless at the mercy of the enemy, that enemy who (they add) is particularly hostile to them because they have entrusted themselves and their fates to his royal majesty, with the greatest devotion.

Next they seek in wondrous ways to stir up the hearts of the   12 French, a people by nature frivolous and conceited, to exhort them with wondrous rhetoric. If they but exert themselves a little, the time is ripe and the moment propitious not only to take Italy captive but also to transfer the Empire into their own hands and to remake the Church at their command; Genoa and a great part of Italy is already theirs; with the Duke of Liguria defeated, no force by land or by sea could oppose his power; that duke, strong as he may seem, will fall at the first attack. Thus, to precisely those who have little hope and few means of defending the soil of their own country,[18] the Florentines promise complete control of Italy and world dominion.

I do not doubt that all this may provoke friendly and pleased   13 replies, such as: the king has at heart the security of his friends and does not forget pacts recently signed; he urges them not to lose heart, for His Majesty the king will never fail to come in their aid. It may even be the case, although you need armored legions, that the French decide to intervene for your security by first sending legations, which is the most you will get for your entreaties. In the meantime they will stand around, taken up with their pleasures, enjoying their wealth in plentiful peace,[19] whilst you wretches burn in the conflagrations of war. But come: they may [after all] want to protect you with their arms as well as their mere

omittam qualis animus Caesaris totiusque Germaniae futurus sit, si quis Gallorum motus ad Italiam fiat, cum sibi pro dignitate imperii — cuius in Italia caput est — viderit subeundum esse certamen; ut, inquam, omittam hoc, quod vero propius est omnem Gallorum impetum non solum posse tardare sed tollere atque cohibere. Veniant certe Galli et affletur vobis ab Occidente aura illa salutaris, per quam in summa malorum anxietate respirare possitis; venient tamen eo tempore ut non ad defendendam vestram salutem sed ad deplorandum casum et exsequias celebrandas venisse videantur.

14   Quae tamen est ista dementia tanta, tam abhorrens ab omni sensu rationeque perversitas, ut cogitare possitis amplissimum regem — officiorum plurimorum, sanctissimae societatis atque affinitatis immemorem — ita Florentinas opes tuendas ampliandasque suo periculo suscepisse ut, ceterarum rerum omnium negligens, vestrae tantum salutis et gloriae studiosissimus videatur? Quod si tantam levitatem in eo rege putatis exsistere, ut pro hoste eum ducat, quem avus quondam suus dignitate decoravit et regia sibi affinitate coniunxit, quem ipse paulo ante socium atque amicum habuit, cui denique illustre singularis benivolentiae monimentum regalia dedit insignia ad generis et sanguinis Vicecomitum laudem sempiternam, si regem hunc, inquam, tam leviter, tam repente mutatum esse putatis, ut hunc, sibi sanguine et recenti admodum societate coniunctum — nulla prorsus ad id impellente causa nisi ut avertat a capitibus vestris impendens malum — bello temptet invadere, videte ne nimis magno errore ducamini.

15   Potuit fortasse vestra calliditas et illa immoderata fingendi mentiendique licentia, qua in rebus omnibus privatis ac publicis praeter ceteras gentes utimini, in mente regia aliquid suspicionis affigere, quo ipsum abalienatum aliquantulum a duce Ligustico

authority! I won't say how the emperor and all Germany would take it if the French were to make any move against Italy; they would have to contest any invasion to defend the prestige of the empire, whose capital is in Italy. I don't say it, but this fact alone could go far, not only to delay any French invasion, but to eliminate and suppress it. Let's allow that the French come; let's allow that salutary Western wind to blow toward you. It might let you breathe amid your great anxieties; yet they will likely come at a time when they will not be safeguarding you but weeping for your downfall and celebrating your funeral.

What sort of madness is this, an obstinacy devoid of any sense 14 or reason, that should lead you to think that so important a king—a man forgetful of so many of his duties, of the bonds of holy religion and the ties of blood—should undertake at his own peril to protect and enlarge the resources of the Florentines, to the point where he becomes utterly committed to your security and glory alone, neglecting all his other affairs? And if you think this king can be so fickle that he deems as his enemy a man upon whom his grandfather once conferred a title of nobility and with whom he made a marriage alliance,[20] one whom he himself not long ago held to be his ally and friend, to whom he gave royal insignia [for his coat of arms] as a noble pledge of special affection to the eternal honor of the Visconti line[21]—if indeed you think this king so fickle, so suddenly changeable, as to try to make war upon one to whom he is tied by marriage and a recent pact—and for no other reason than to keep an impending doom from falling on your heads—then watch out that you don't commit an irretrievable error.

It may be that your craftiness and ungovernable license[22] to 15 lie and engage in conspiracies—of which you make use in all matters public and private, more than any other people—have succeeded in fixing a shade of doubt in that sovereign's mind and alienating him in some small measure from the Duke of Liguria.

redderetis. Sed absit ut tantum vestrae temeritati atque impudentiae datum sit ut ad libidinem mentis vestrae arma rex moveat
bellumque suscipiat. Erit sibi ante oculos recens foedus quod pro
utriusque principis dignitate, ad nullius iniuriam atque perniciem,
ictum fuit. Obversabitur avi imago, gravissimi illius quondam et
sapientissimi regis, cui olim, in rebus difficillimis adversisque temporibus, pater huius, Galeaz ille magnanimus, liberrima voluntate
se obtulit et qua potuit ope non defuit. Redibit in mentem cum
regio sanguine bina coniunctio. Subibit animum, quem putatis
vestris mendaciis obsedisse, veteris amicitiae recordatio aliquandoque etiam recognoscet vestras insidias et intelliget vos pro vestra
libidine tam multa de duce optimo et principe clarissimo fuisse
mentitos.

16   Qua re non modo suis copiis vos non defendendos esse (non!)
existimabit, sed omni dignos supplicio iudicabit tantumque aberit ut vobis corruentibus manum det ut etiam optet assurgentes
opprimere. Quod si in regia illa Transalpina vestra fraus plus
quam amplissimi ducis integritas fidesque valuerit poteruntque
vestra praestigia omnium officiorum et necessitudinum memoriam obscurare, mihi credite, nobis est animus sic Gallis obsistere,
ut intelligant quod maiores sui saepissime experti sunt: perfacile
Gallis Italiam petere, victores redire difficile. Unde proverbium
illud a nostris hominibus usurpatum scimus: Italiam sepulcrum
esse Gallorum. Non exigit locus hic ut ad priscas historias et
Romanae virtutis exempla vos revocem; quae ipsi nudius tertius
vidimus, proferamus in medium. Venit in Italiam dux Andegavensis ille, quem non solum patris regis nomen ornabat, sed qui multos per annos regia fretus potestate tantis thesauris atque opibus

But may God avert it that your temerity and impudence should succeed in the king's taking arms and starting a war at your pleasure! He will be well aware of the pact only recently agreed to in defense of the dignities of both princes, without seeking to offend or harm the interests of anyone. There will arise before his mind's eye his forebear, that king in his time most noble and wise, whom the present duke, the magnanimous Giangaleazzo, volunteered to help in very difficult and uncertain circumstances, and whom he aided in every way possible.[23] He will think of the double marriage alliance that ties that man to his royal line.[24] The memory of this ancient friendship will come over his mind, which you think to have besieged with your lies, and eventually he will realize what you are plotting and he will recognize for what they are all the lies you have told, for your own depraved purposes, about that excellent duke and most illustrious prince.

On this account he will not only not reckon that you must be defended by his troops,[25] (no!), but he will judge you worthy of every punishment, and so far from helping you prevent your ruin, he will rather choose to suppress any who might rise up to do so. And if the fraud you are perpetrating in that transalpine royal palace should prevail over the upright and loyal behavior of the most noble duke, and if your deceptions should succeed in darkening the memory of all the obligations and affections that tie one to the other, believe me, we are resolved to oppose the French, so that they may understand what their ancestors have experienced many times, that it is very easy for the French to enter Italy, but difficult to return thence victorious. Whence our popular proverb: Italy is the tomb of the French.[26] No need to recall to you the ancient stories and exemplars of Roman prowess; I limit myself to note those which we have ourselves witnessed recently. There came to Italy the famous Duke of Anjou, remarkable for his father's royal title but also because, after many years of support from the royal power, he boasted of such riches and treasure that

16

abundabat, ut a ceteris Galliarum principibus formidabilis videretur; et venit tanto cum equitatu Gallico, tam valido et florenti exercitu, ut non modo de regno ad quod properabat spem haberet, sed de universae Italiae dominatu. Neque enim facile intelligebant homines quisnam tot armatis legionibus, tanto splendori nominis, tantis opibus auderet obstare. Contra erat qui animo et virtute sua maius praesidium non habebat: Karolus ille rex optimus, regum decus eximium, quo nihil umquam sol in terris vidit illustrius. Et erat novus in regno, nec eo quidem integro, sed intestinis factionibus procerumque discordiis iam diviso; auri praeterea inops, sed ingentis animi virtute ditissimus. Hic paucis admodum Italorum copiis fretus, ita saepe Gallos afflixit, ita ad extremum contudit ac dissipavit, ut ex tanta multitudine pauci in patriam redire potuerint, plerique ferro caesi, multi laboribus inediaque consumpti. In quibus ipse dux periit, hoc uno felix, ne tantae vivus ignominiae dedecorique restaret.

17   Vos etiam priore bello quod cum duce gessistis egregiam Gallorum in Italiam manum nobilissimumque et fortissimum Arminiacensem equitatum, pretio et pollicitationibus, conduxistis, eoque freti praesidio spes animo vanas insulsasque capiebatis. Sed cum iam superbiam vestram Italia tota non caperet, sparsit in auras Deus cogitationes inanes atque impias. Vidistis ut repente vir belli atque pacis artibus illustris, Iacobus de Verme, quem honoris causa nomino — et quo, pace ceterorum dicam, clarius militiae iubar non habet Italia — et hostium ducem cepit et, luce altera, reliquum fugientem subsecutus exercitum, ubi primum attigit, dissipavit ac vicit. Illa, illa fuit insignis salutarisque victoria per quam non solum Cisalpina haec Gallia, sed omnis Italia ab ignominia

the other French princes regarded him as formidable; and he came with so large a troop of French knights and such a famous and strong army that he hoped to establish lordship, not only over the lands of the Kingdom he was marching upon, but all Italy.[27] In fact men could not think of anyone who would dare resist so many armed legions, such an illustrious name, and so many resources. On the other side was a man who had no greater protection than his own courage and strength: Charles, best of kings, the glory of royalty, than whom the sun has seen none on earth more illustrious. At the time he had but recently come into his kingdom and lacked full control of it, as it was torn by internal conflict and disagreement between dignitaries; poor in gold but rich indeed in virtue and greatness of spirit. Although supported by very few Italian troops, he so often harassed the French, he so blunted and scattered their forces, that in the end only a few of that great multitude were able to return home; most were cut down by the sword, worn down by fatigue and hunger. Among the dead was the duke himself, fortunate only in this: that he did not survive to witness his own shame and ignominy.

Already in the last war you Florentines fought against the duke, you hired, using both pay and promises of pay, a noteworthy force of the French and the famous and powerful cavalry of Armagnac to come to Italy, and supported by their protection, you acquired empty and foolish hopes.[28] But now, since all of Italy has not been won over by your arrogance, God has thrown to the winds your vain and impious plans. You have seen how suddenly that man celebrated for the arts of peace and war, Jacopo dal Verme, whom I mention here for honor's sake — than whom, with all due respect to the rest, Italy has no more brilliant military light[29] — captured the enemy commander; the day after he pursued the remainder of the fleeing army and no sooner did he catch up with it than he scattered and defeated it. This, this was the victory, famous and blessed, that saved our Cisalpine Gaul and all Italy from shame

17

et vastitate liberata est, quae principis huius Ausonii in omnibus terris ac nationibus clarum, vobis etiam formidabile, nomen fecit, in qua denique, si quid haberetis sanitatis, nisi vos caecos et miseros in praecipitium ageret infinita temeritas, praesentissimo potuissetis exemplo cognoscere quam vanum quamque ridiculum sit Gallicanis auxiliis contra Italos sperare victoriam.

18   At vos furor et rabies et impatientia quaedam pacis oblivisci faciunt omnium salutarium exemplorum; non tenetis ista memoriae nihilque nisi impium, crudele, nefarium[2] mente cogitationibusque versatis. Potuistis quidem soli, et in vestris manibus situm erat, Italiae pacem dare, sedare tumultus, auferre discordias, res denique Italas tanta tranquillitate componere quanta non fuerant patrum avorumque memoria. Nam cum in Italia vos post Liguriae principem scire multa, posse omnia videremini essetque ille etiam quam dignitati et splendori sui nominis conveniret pacis avidior—propter quam non sine amicorum suorum stomacho ita se haberet humiliter, ita et quaedam indigna quotidie patientissime toleraret, ut et vobis cervices erigeret, qui paci eratis adversi—et eorum, qui melius sentiebant, corda posset inflectere, nil prohibebat, si vobis pacis studium placuisset, pacem perpetuam esse futuram. Sed abhorrebant curiae vestrae a consilio quietis, et animos vestros urgebant conceptorum scelerum stimuli et aures vestras sanioribus monitis obstruebant atque oculos occaecabant Furiae illae pestiferae quas peccata vestra de sedibus Tartareis excitarant.

and devastation, which made celebrated (though for you terrifying) the name of this Ausonian leader[30] in every nation and place of the globe! This victory could have furnished the clearest possible example—if you had any sense, if your limitless rashness did not drive you, blind and wretched, to the precipice—of how ridiculous and vain it is to hope to defeat Italians by reliance on French aid.[31]

But the fury, rage[32] and intolerance of peace that afflict you make you forget all salutary examples. The latter you forget, while you turn over in your mind and thoughts nothing that is not indecent, cruel and wicked.[33] You alone—and the choice lay in your hands—could have brought peace to Italy, quelled uprisings, erased conflicts, and in short, brought back the kind of tranquility to Italian affairs of state such as only our fathers and grandfathers remember.[34] Since, next to the prince of Liguria, you seemed the most well informed and the most effective power in Italy, and since he was more eager for peace than befitted his title and his resounding fame—so much so that his conciliatory attitude irritated his allies, and he would bear each day with the greatest patience charges he did not deserve, for example, that he had stiffened your stubborn hostility to peace—and since he was able to influence the hearts of right-thinking people, nothing stood in the way of a durable peace, had your desire for peace been genuine. But your Signoria shrank from counsels of quiet, and the thought of the crimes you had planned goaded you on, deafening you to wiser advice, and your eyes were blinded by the plague-ridden Furies whom your sins had aroused from their Tartarean homes.[35]

18

19   Itaque semper contra salutem Italiae, contra pacem, contra bonorum consilia, contra patriae vestrae statum ac requiem sic fuistis
accensi ut sine dubitatione videremini non pro cura et conservatione vestrae rei publicae vigilare, quod unum volebatis intelligi,
sed ad civitatis et libertatis voluntarium interitum festinare. Qui
quidem ita iam proximus est ut et vos iam iam impendentis ruinae
terrore concutiat et universam Italiam ad spectaculum vestrae calamitatis attollat.

In brief, you have always been so hostile to the welfare of Italy, 19
so opposed to peace, so deaf to the counsels of good men, so indifferent to the prestige and tranquility of your fatherland, that you
are not standing guard out of concern for the preservation of your
commonwealth, as you wish to have believed, but you are hastening toward the voluntary destruction of your city and your liberty.
This fate is now nigh, so much so that you are already stricken
with terror at your impending collapse, and you are raising up all
of Italy to watch the spectacle of your undoing.

COLUCII PIERI SALUTATI

EPISTULA AD PETRUM TURCUM

1   Iussisti, vir insignis filique carissime, quod obiurgatori illi petulan-
tissimo, qui Florentinorum nomen et gloriosissimam hanc patriam
tam insolenti maliloquio pupugit gloriamque, sicut arbitror, iniuria nostra quaesivit, iuxta suae insaniae merita responderem. Quod
quidem cum viderem rebus magnum, oratione longum obiurgan-
dique necessitate fecundum, licet patriae moveret iniuria debi-
tumque quo tenemur huic mysticae genitrici—cui, quicquid im-
penderimus, non possumus non obligati magis atque perpetuo
remanere—cogeret et urgeret, steti diu[1] dubius quidnam facturus
essem. Dicebam enim: 'Quid, Line Coluci, facies? An septuagena-
rius (Februarius enim mensis septuagesimum et tertium adducet
annum), qui neminem hucusque tuo nomine nisi iocose laeseris,
incipies, discedens ab habitu tam longae consuetudinis, insanire?
Tune privatum stilum tuum, qui neminem hactenus offendit, ad
mordacitatem invectionis translaturus es?'

2   Quae mecum agitans non poteram tuis hortatibus obsequi du-
rumque nimis videbatur invehendi procacitatem profiteri; sed urgebant litterae caritatis tuae dilectioque patriae requirebat quod
illam offensam iniuriis, oneratam maliloquiis totque mendaciis ac-
cusatam sine defensione saltem derelinquere non deberem. Horre-
bam tamen Antonii Lusci nomen, quem scribebas in patriam illo
scripto tam mordaciter invexisse, quoniam ipsum ut filium diligo
cupioque non iniuria patriae (id etenim nemini possem optare)
sed bonis artibus et alia ratione quod in clarissimum evadat virum.

168

LETTER TO PIETRO TURCHI[1]

You have enjoined me, distinguished man and dearest son, to reply   1
as he deserves to that mad and impudent critic who has insolently
attacked the good name of the Florentines and of this most glorious country with the hope, I imagine, of winning glory by injuring
us. As this seemed to me, on the one hand, an act of defamation
large in its implications, requiring a long treatment and richly in
need of rebuke, while on the other, I was compelled to act by the
offense given to my country and by my sense of duty toward this
our mystic mother — to whom we must feel ourselves eternally in
debt, whatever the sacrifice[2] — I was long uncertain about what to
do. In fact I asked myself: "What will you do, Lino di Coluccio?
You have never attacked anyone under your own name except as a
joke, and now that you are over seventy (seventy-three next February) are you to lose your wits, changing a lifetime's habits? Are you
to turn your private pen to composing a biting invective, you who
have never yet offended anyone?"[3]

Prey to such thoughts, I could not comply with your exhorta-   2
tions; it seemed too hard to take on the role of polemicist. But I
was spurred on by the affectionate words of your letter, and my
love of country would not allow me to leave her injured, loaded
down with so many insults, lies and accusations without someone
at least to defend her.[4] Yet I felt horror at the thought that (as you
write) it was Antonio Loschi who had attacked my country with
such violence in this piece of writing, since I love him as a son and
hope that he will reach high fame, not through insults against my
country (I could wish that for no one) but through literary skill
and by another path. But if the style suggests that we might be

Et cum stilus satis arguat quod Luscus sit, tot tamen mendacia quibus insultat, tot vitia—quae suam non decent eruditionem—quibus invectio sua scatet, tot maledicta quot excandescit, sed imperitia potius dissuaserunt, immo persuaserunt cum ipso mihi non esse sermonem.

3   Equidem, si habuissem eum refellere, dixissem invehens: 'Unde tibi, Lusce, tanta procacitas? Tune luscus Florentinos caecos vocas? Tune tot mendaciis potuisti innocentem hanc patriam insectari? Nonne sciebas ex hoc tibi mecum certamen fore? Putabasne pro filio, pro amico dilectissimoque, quisquis fuerit, viro me patriam relicturum, cuius caritas non solum omnes necessitudines amplexa est, sed praeterit et excedit? Errabas, carissime Lusce, et quem publicae causae nostrae defensionis gratia videbas domino tuo publicis scriptionibus non pepercisse, sperare potuisti privatim provocatum causae meae cunctorumque civium defuturum? Moneo hortorque caritatem tuam quod quieto tranquilloque scribendi genere, non contentioso, boniloquioque, non maliloquio, cum refellendi confutandique locos et facultatem videas sciasque non responsorem unum, sed plurimos esse posse, gloriam quaeras, non unde scire possis et debeas, laudis incertus et dubius, certissima tibi iurgia indubitabilesque contumelias proventuras. Scio tamen quantum assumpserim oneris, qui me dictaque mea simili carpenda ratione qua tua pexerim tibi necnon et tuis exposui.'

4   Sed in hoc volo potius quidcumque futurum sit discriminis incurrisse, quo corrigar atque discam, quam deserere patriam, quam illum (sive Luscum, ut dicitur, sive quemvis alium) dimittere, quod gloriabundus, quasi victor, maliloquiis fruatur suis; voloque, si

dealing with a Loschi, so many are the mendacious insults, so many are the grammatical faults, unworthy of a man of his erudition, that riddle the invective, so many are the enraged but ignorant taunts that disfigure it, that I was dissuaded from believing, or rather I was persuaded not to believe, that he could be the author.

Indeed, if I had had to refute him, I would have taken the of- 3 fensive and said: "Why such insolence, Loschi? Do you, blind fellow, call the Florentines blind?[5] Could you have dared attack this innocent country with all those false accusations? Didn't you know that by so doing you were going to get into a contest with me? Did you believe that from regard for a son, a friend, a loved one — for anyone' sake — I was going to abandon my country, love of which not only embraces other relationships but rises above and transcends them all?[6] You were mistaken, my dear Loschi. And how could you have hoped that man who had not spared your lord in his public writings for the sake of defending our public cause was not going to react to a private provocation with a defense of his own cause and that of his fellow citizens? I advise and exhort you, my friend, to chase after glory by writing in a calm and peaceful, not a polemical way, affable and not adversarial; you should see to it that there be occasion and ability to reply and rebut, and you should know too that the respondents may be not one but many. Do not write on subjects from which, as you probably know and should know, the praise you earn will be uncertain and doubtful, but the obloquy most sure and the insults inevitable. I know, too, what a burden I have taken on, leaving my person and my claims open to be criticized by you and your fellows in the same way I have treated you."

But in this matter I prefer to incur risk, whatever may come of 4 it, so that I may be corrected and learn, rather than to desert my country and let that fellow (whether Loschi, as they say, or someone else) go, so that he may strut about boasting as though he

nostra fors viderit et victoriam speret, congrediatur audacter: non enim labor erit, quotiens provocaverit, respondere.

5   Nunc autem ad te veniam, qui iuvenis demandasti seni quod tu ipse facere debuisti. Gaudeo tamen hoc mihi fuisse reservatum; forte quidem alius non ita libere et rerum gestarum nescius non potuisset ad quaedam apposite respondisse. Mitto igitur, immo remitto tibi, sicut postulas, invectivam in nos factam mittoque responsum, quod velim prius relegas quam de prolixitate condemnes. Credo quidem te facile iudicaturum, quo tot rebus idoneae satisfacerem, tum ad intelligentiam tum ad persuasionem brevius fieri non potuisse. Vellem autem apud te privatim esse, nisi maledici illius invectio prodisset in publicum. Tu tamen rei consule et rescribe.

Vale, Florentie, III idus Septembris.

were the victor, profiting from his malicious tongue; and I wish, if my luck will see to it and will have hope of victory, that he may join battle boldly; for it will be no effort for me to respond, however many times he shall summon me to the fight.

Now I come to you [Pietro], a youth who has asked an old man to do what you yourself ought to have done. Yet I am happy that the task has fallen to me. Maybe another could not have responded so freely or, ignorant of the facts, could not have responded precisely to certain charges. I send you, then, or better I send back to you, the invective written against us and I send you the reply. I would like you to read and reread it before you make the judgment that it is too long. I believe indeed that you will readily agree that to reply fully to each point, explain matters and to be convincing, it could not have been briefer. I would like you to keep it to yourself, unless the invective of that detractor should begin to circulate publicly. At all events, consider the matter and write back to me.

Stay well. Florence, September 11 [1403].

CONTRA MALEDICUM ET OBIURGATOREM QUI MULTA PUNGENTER ADVERSUS INCLITAM CIVITATEM FLORENTIAE SCRIPSIT

1 Fuit nuper per quosdam insignes et venerabiles viros mihi trans-
missum invectivae cuiusdam exemplum quod sumptum ab exem-
plari verissimo carissimi fratris mei Antonii Lusci Vicentini certissime dicebatur, quam aiebant, ut res ipsa docet, eum contra nomen
et gloriam Florentinorum, immo certissimum asserebant impetu
quodam mentis et voluntatis mordaciter dictavisse, rogantes obnixius ut ob patriae decus ad singula responderem. Ad cuius quidem rei annuntium et hortatum fateor me fuisse permotum ut
scriberem, indignatione magis an dolore nescio; me quidem
utrumque simul invasit. Dolebam enim quod in meam patriam
praesumeret aliquis maledicere indignabarque Antonium meum
gratis talem provinciam accepisse.

2   Sed postquam scriptum illud legendo percurri, videns in maledictis illis nullum ordinem, nullum finem, nihil ibi probatum nihilque penitus persuasum, et exordium, ut omittam vulgare atque
commune, clara ratione commutabile, quod scilicet inversis solum
nominibus magis appositum sit adversario quam scribenti, risi
mecum dixique: 'Iuvenis est iste dictator vel doctrina vel tempore,
qui nullo dictionis vel rationis nervo, sed solo voluntatis impetu
moveatur; qui sic adversarium maledictis oneret quod, si narrata
negentur, inveniatur protinus nil egisse, sed oporteat eum alium

COLUCCIO SALUTATI

REPLY TO A SLANDEROUS DETRACTOR WHO HAS WRITTEN MANY WOUNDING THINGS AGAINST THE RENOWNED CITY OF FLORENCE

Certain distinguished and venerable men have placed in my hands   1
a copy of an invective, transcribed from an authoritative copy, said
to be the work of my dear brother Antonio Loschi of Vicenza; an
invective, they said, written against the good name and the honor
of the Florentines, as the text itself makes clear. The author, they
added, had most certainly written with the desire and intent to
defame, and they besought me to write a reply to every accusation
in defense of my country. Informed of the matter and exhorted to
act, I confess that I felt at once the impulse to write, whether
driven more by indignation or by pain I know not: both attacked
me at the same time. I was pained that someone dared to defame
my country, and I was indignant that my Antonio had elected to
take on such a task without pay.[1]

   But once I had scanned the text and found that there was   2
no foundation to the accusations, no order or purpose, nothing
proven or convincing, and that the beginning, to leave aside its
commonplace clichés, could easily be turned upon the accuser just
by reversing the names,[2] I had to laugh to myself and think: "The
fellow who dictated this is immature either in age or in learning,
motivated entirely by impulse and lacking any power of speech or
reason; the accusations cast in the face of his enemy are so weak
that simple denial would be enough to disprove them all, and he

orationis filum texere, et ab initio, quasi nil prorsus dixerit, omnia retractare.'

3   Puerile quidem est sic multa dicere quod, unico negationis verbo, causa de manibus auferatur. Non stat dicendi virtus in eo quod solum dicitur vel ipsius dictionis ornatu, sed si probes, si persuadeas sique fidem facias et irrefragabiliter dicas. Quid enim est sceleris aut vitii quod non possit de quocumque, licet omni vitio crimineque careat, enarrari? Nec sufficit ad fidem ornatus, qui quidem falsis et veris possit aequaliter adhiberi. Quibus firmissime teneo, sicut verosimili ratione coniecto, numquam Luscum meum, qui non natura solum sed eruditione doctrinaque valeat, in tam futilis orationis nugas vel tam mordacis obiurgationis petulantiam incurrisse, quamvis verba sic redoleant iuxta corticem — non medullitus — Ciceronem, quod difficile sit alium ab Antonio meo, qui talia referre sciverit, assignare. Cum enim sententiarum soliditas et argumentationum vis desit, credere non possum hoc ab Antonio scriptum esse. Nam, ut alia omittam, quis credat gente Luscum caecutientes dicere Florentinos?

4   Dimittamus, ergo, Luscum nostrum, et cum illo, quisquis fuerit qui Spartam hanc — ut Graecum proverbium habet — susceperit, contendamus. Perdo tamen occasionem pulcherrimam et oratoribus exoptatam cum adversarii persona, contra quam multa saepe dicere licet, auferatur. Utar tamen in eum, quisquis ille sit, utarque liberius quia nescio plane qui sit, dignis pro meritorum suorum fraude nominibus, ut cum se viderit per universum huius responsionis nostrae corpus veris rationibus laceratum, paeniteat eum aliquando temeritatis et audaciae suae discatque parcius maledicere, cum contra se cognoverit semel ultionis debitae laqueum

would have to retract them and start all over again from the beginning, as though he had said nothing at all."

Indeed it is schoolboy error to speak at such length without 3 realizing that, by simply denying what is said, the entire case falls to pieces.[3] The force of an argument lies not only in what is said and how prettily, but in whether you prove it, whether you persuade, whether you give incontrovertible evidence of what you say. Is there a sin or a vice that cannot be attributed to anyone, however immune from vice or crime?[4] Moreover, neither is elegance of style enough to produce belief, since it can be applied equally to true things and to false. All this leads me to affirm without the least doubt that my Loschi — who is an able man not only because of his natural gifts but thanks to culture and education — could never have gone in for such trifling and petty speech or such impudently caustic reproaches.[5] To be sure, the words *do* bear a superficial resemblance to Cicero's, such that it would be hard to attribute them to anyone besides Antonio, who knows how to write in that manner. But, again, the lack of both coherence in the discourse and force in the arguments makes it hard for me to believe that Antonio could have composed it. For example (to mention nothing else), who would have thought that a man whose family name was Loschi would call the Florentines "blind"?[6]

So let us leave aside our Loschi and address ourselves to who- 4 ever has seen fit, as the Greek proverb says, "to take on Sparta."[7] But not knowing the name of my adversary takes from me a splendid opportunity, dear to all orators, who may often attack their opponents at great length.[8] Nevertheless, I will not hesitate to upbraid him (even more freely since he is nameless), adopting the epithets that he has earned by fraudulent action, in order that, finding himself torn to shreds by the incontrovertible proofs in my reply, he may eventually repent of his rash boldness and learn to be more cautious in making accusations, since he will feel the consequences: the noose of a just revenge and infamy, instead of the

intendisse ac unde stulte quaesiverit, ut arbitror, gloriam, infamiae turpis notam in se perceperit esse conflatam. Compatior tamen stultitiae suae, qui se maliloquio suo prodiderit cunctisque sua legentibus se cupiverit esse ludibrio, inscitiae quidem singularis documentum et malae mentis perspicuum argumentum. Quis enim non ut inscium et malignum irrideat homunculum quemdam os in caelum apponere et unum populum — singulare decus Italiae, quem metuant hostes, socii velut numen aliquod in terris degens colant, orbis universi principes multi faciant, legationibus visitent cunctisque prosequantur honoribus — tam stulte, tam procaciter violare?

5   Nescio videre tuae praesumptionis aut ambitus rationem. Hominis est, enim, ut cuncti volunt tam theologi quam philosophiae studiosi, quicquid egerit agere propter finem vel propter aliquid quod tandem in verum finem hominis reducatur. Nunc autem dic, obsecro, quem finem his obiurgationibus intendisti? Numquid in verum illum et ultimum finem omnium — qui beatitudo perpes et eterna est, perpes dono, quod in tempore traditur, sed eterna partecipatione, quoniam sine principio fuerit id quod datur — illa te dirigunt vel perducunt? Contra caritatem quidem proximi, ni fallor, est eum non diligere; quanto magis illi maledicere vel famam eius etiam leviter maculare? Tu vero non unum quempiam sed innumerabilem populum gentemque non suis contentam moenibus sed quae totum sparsa per orbem est, veluti gloriosum aliquid, non levi dicto sed gravibus contumeliis insectaris. Quod equidem non credam ad ultimum illum finem pertinere te, licet desipias, reputare. Cumque qui dixerit fratri suo 'racham,' veritate teste, 'reus sit iudicio,' quid te movet qui tanto populo maledicas?

glory that I suppose he foolishly hoped to acquire. I feel compassion for him in his foolishness, for he has betrayed himself by his own malicious tongue and made himself a laughingstock to anyone who reads his work, evidence indeed of his unique ignorance and a clear proof of his evil intentions. How not to despise as inexperienced and ill-willed any little man who dares to set his mouth against heaven[9] and throw words that are so absurd and offensive against an entire people, and one that is the pride of all Italy, feared by its enemies, venerated as a divinity by its allies, and respected by rulers of all the world, who send it embassies and accord it every honor?[10]

I am unable to understand the reasoning behind your presumptuous parade of words. It is a characteristic of man, after all, according to theologians and philosophers, to act for some goal or in view of something that may eventually be related to the true ends of mankind.[11] But tell me, I ask: what goal did your insults serve? Can they perhaps help you to reach the true and ultimate end of all mankind, which is lasting, eternal beatitude—lasting with respect to the gift, since it happens in time, but eternal by participation, since that which is given had no beginning?[12] It is against charity for one's neighbor, if I'm not mistaken, not to love him. Why is it not much more against charity, then, to speak ill of him and to stain, even slightly, his good name? But then, as though it were some glorious deed, you attack, not with a jest but with grave insults, not a single person but a numberless people, a clan that is not content to stay at home but is scattered through the whole world. I don't think that even you, however foolish, can view such actions as directed to that final goal that has been mentioned. And if "he who insults his brother," as the Bible states, "shall be held in judgment,"[13] what can have moved you to insult so noble a people?

6   Nec video — cum pro domino tuo et, fas sit vera dicere, pro tyranno contra civitatem liberam et libertatis vindicem obloquaris —
quem finem beatitudinis politicae maledictis intendas tuis. Nec
cum, ut scripta testantur tua, non mediocriter eruditus esse vi-
deare — sine ratione tamen dicendi quam te, certum est, vel parte
minima non tenere puto — cogites quod haec via sint vel instrumentum ad speculationis apicem vel virtutem? Ut cum nullus tibi
finium qui laudantur praepositus esse possit, restet ut in hoc tamquam homo nullatenus sis locutus, sed ut animal, quod ratione
penitus non utatur. Curasti forsan domino tuo placere, cui non
crediderim fuisse gratum audire maliloquia vel contextum tot et
talium falsitatum. Tanta quidem in illo circumspectio fuit talisque
prudentia quod quae veritati nixa non esse cognosceret, sine dubitatione videret non solum cum infamia peritura fore sed etiam in
assentationem eius, qua nihil suspectius sapientibus dominis esse
debet, vel malitiose vel pueriliter ordinata.

7   Nullus, ergo, tibi finis nisi malitia frui tua, nisi latratu rabido —
cum vitiosissimus esse debeas; talis est enim habitus mentis intus
quales sermones produnt foris — latratuque foedissimo persequi
virtuosos, ut rabidam bestiam te possim, si recte loqui voluero,
vocitare. Licet enim bestia sis, non tamen es cicurris, id est humana, sed rana: non simplex bestia, sed omnino bestia bestialis.
Accedit huic inhumanitati tuae — vel, ut rectius loquar, procacitati — summa quaedam dementia. Nam cum stultum sit maledicere mortuis propter posteros, stultius est offendere vivos, licet
aliquando morituri sint, propter utrosque, praesentes scilicet et
futuros. Stultissimum vero vivis maledicere, qui numquam sint
successione continua morituri. Talis est, ni fallor, populus Florentinus, quem difficile sit ad unum penitus interire. Capta quidem,

Since you are attacking a free city and a champion of liberty on   6
behalf of your lord and (it would be God's truth to say) on behalf
of a tyrant, I don't see what end of political happiness you are aiming at with your insults. And since you are a man of considerable
education, as your writings attest—though they lack logic, something I am sure you have no understanding of at all—are you
thinking that these insults of yours are a path or a vehicle to the
apex of contemplation or to virtue?[14] Not having set yourself any
praiseworthy end, we are forced to deduce that you speak as an
animal, not as a man, that is, without making any use of reason.
You may have hoped to please your lord, but I doubt that it
pleased him to hear insults and a tissue of gross falsehoods. He
was indeed so circumspect and prudent that he doubtless saw that
the things which he knew were not supported by the truth were
not only going to perish, to his discredit, but also that they had
been designed, whether maliciously or ingenuously, to flatter him,
flattery being among the greatest dangers for wise rulers.

In short, you have attained no end except satisfying your mali-   7
cious instinct, except a rabid howl—and a vicious creature you
must be, as the quality of one's language reveals one's real character[15]—a dirty howl with which you vent yourself on upright people, deserving the label of "raging animal," if we wish to state how
things really are. You are indeed an animal, but not even a swine
domesticated for human use, but a toad: not an ordinary animal
but a wholly brutish beast. This subhuman, or more properly, this
shameless attitude of yours is accompanied by total madness. If it
is like a fool to slander the dead because of their descendants, it is
even more like a fool to attack the living, although they shall die
some day, because of both present and future generations. The
most foolish thing of all is to slander the living whose number will
never decrease, since their issue cannot end. The latter is the case,
if I mistake not, of the Florentine people, whom it would be hard
to kill off entirely, all at once. Even if Florence should ever be

quod Deus avertat, dirutaque Florentia, tot sunt extra Florentiam
Florentini quod viris et opibus novam possent alteris vel refectis
moenibus Florentiam excitare quique si, veluti loquacitate tua
mereris, bellum indixerint, stultitiae tuae locum non relinquent
tibi tutum sed etiam in domini tui curia te conficere poterunt et
punire. Tutus enim vix in castris suis fuit contra Romanum unicum rex Porsenna, nec in tabernaculo suo feminae manus evasit,
maximo comitatus exercitu, dux ille formidabilis Holophernes.

8   Sed haec relinquamus. Securus enim es, quoniam Luscus is, de
quo dicitur, fuisse non crederis, et si forte prodibis in medium
detegasque quis sis, vilitas et stultitia tua te reddet omnibus inof-
fensum. Sed his omissis, stilus ad id quod intendimus deflectatur.
In cuius quidem rei principio, quoniam de te perpauca dixi, de me
non est consilium subticere; docendus enim es — et quicumque
nostra haec scribenda perlegerit — cur ergo me defensioni tuisque
refellendis nugis, cum me non provoces, offeram, ne te videar eadem qua tu Florentinos libidine persequeris impetisse. Scripsi
praesentis orationis fronte me rogatum obnixius quod in patriae
decus deberem ad singula respondere, ut tam iusta rogantibus
honestum non fuerit morem non gerere. Sed vehementius tamen
urget — tacens licet — patria, cui non praestare nullo modo possumus quod debemus, ut armis meis ipsam protegam nec in tam
acerbae sugillationis iniuria derelinquam ipsam, tot diffamatam
mendaciis, indefensam; ut sicut hactenus commissa sequens dominorum meorum, publicae scriptionis officio causas incidentes,
etiam cum hostium diffamationibus, ut iubebar, defendere sum

conquered and destroyed (God forbid), the Florentines outside of Florence are so strong in men and resources that they could rebuild its walls and summon forth a new Florence. And if they were to make war, which would be the response your raving deserves, they would leave no place safe for you and your foolishness; they could hunt you down and punish you, even at the court of your lord. Even surrounded by his camp and facing a single Roman, King Porsenna was not safe, nor, tented amid his mighty host, did the powerful general Holofernes escape a woman's attack.[16]

But leave that aside. You *are* safe, since you won't be believed to   8
have been the aforementioned Loschi, and if perhaps you shall show your face in public and reveal your identity, your vileness and stupidity will render you harmless to everyone. But, putting these matters aside, let us turn our pen to the subject intended. In the first instance, it were well that I speak a little of myself, having said a few things about you. You, and all who shall read me, ought to know the reasons why I decided to take on the burden of responding to your impertinences — even if I was not challenged directly — so that I do not seem to be attacking you with the same unbounded license you have shown in attacking the Florentines. I said at the start that my obligation to respond to every charge against my country's honor had been pressed upon me, and it would have been disgraceful not to comply with so just a request. But my country herself also strenuously urges me on, silent though she is; we absolutely cannot refuse what we are obliged to give to our country, which asks me to protect her with my weapons and not to abandon her, defenseless, when she is receiving so nasty a beating and has been defamed by so many calumnies. Therefore, just as hitherto I have tried to defend her, carrying out the charges given me by my lord priors, and undertaking cases as I was bidden in my office of chancellor, including cases of defamation by

conatus, ita nunc, cum privata laceratur lingua, privatim tuear et defendam.

9   Quis enim patienter ferat, cum eius intersit, patriam, cui cuncta debemus, contra veritatem ab eo cuius non intersit tam turpiter diffamari? Vellem autem hanc causam coram aliquo principum inscribere et ipsorum hostium oculis ventilare; vellem ipsos audire qualeque principium mendaciis illis facerent intelligere, quas probationes et argumenta sumerent; ornarem eos, ni fallor, meritis suis, efficeremque quod patriam verbis non laederent, quam adhuc non potuerunt, nec per Dei gratiam poterunt, etiam ea quam tu iactas potentia, superare. Cumque civis quilibet sit civitatis et populi sui portio, non extraneus, causam patriae, quam quilibet defendere tenetur, assumo, rogans quibus vacabit haec legere quod me benigne ferant pro veritate, pro iustitia, pro patria disputantem. Et sicut moleste vel, quod non arbitror, patienter impietatem adversarii tulerint, sic pietatem meam aequis animis et patientissime dignentur ferre; quoque dicendorum ordinatio pateat, ponam prius adversarii verba, sicut scripsit, ad litteram, de membro in membrum, et articulatim ad ea que dixerit respondebo, ut cum unum elisero, mox alium cum sua confutatione subnectam.

10   Incipis, ergo, venenum quod conceperas evomens in haec verba, videlicet:[1] *Illucebitne umquam dies, perditissimi cives, vastatores patriae et quietis Italiae turbatores, quo dignam vestris sceleribus poenam meritumque supplicium consequamini? Dabiturne aliquando, vestrae cuiuspiam calamitatis insignis exemplo, sic vestri similes deterreri et sic in aerumnis vestris suum formidare discrimen, ut calamitas vestra videatur non solum iusta in ultione, sed etiam utilis in exemplo? Eruntne ullo tempore sic vestra detecta atque delusa praestigia, in quibus omne vestrum praesidium collocatum est,*

enemies, so now, since she has been abused by the tongue of a private citizen, I shall protect and defend her as a private citizen.[17]

Indeed, what responsible person could bear it patiently when 9 his country, to which we owe everything, is irresponsibly made subject to shame and defamation? I would like this case to be brought before a prince and tried under the eyes of our very adversaries; I would like to hear them out and to understand the starting point of those lies and the proofs and arguments they are assuming; and unless I'm mistaken I could set them off in proportion to their merits and cause them not to defame our country — a country they have hitherto been unable to defeat and, please God, never shall, even with that military power of which you boast. And as every citizen, so far from being extraneous to his state and his people, is a constituent element of them,[18] I take on the defense of my country, as each is called upon to do, and I pray all who may read these lines to be well-disposed toward me as I speak for truth, justice, and country. And just as they have borne with patience or (as I suspect) with annoyance the wicked assertions of my adversary, let them likewise bear with equanimity and utter patience my holy ones. So that my discourse may be easier to follow, I will first cite my opponent's affirmations word for word and line by line, then respond point by point to his accusations, passing from disproof of one assertion to exposition of his next, followed by its rebuttal.

You begin spewing the poison you've stored up with these 10 words: *Will that day ever dawn, O wicked citizens, enemies of your country and disturbers of the peace in Italy, when you will pay the penalty your crimes deserve, when you will have to undergo the punishment you merit? Will it ever come about that the example of your special undoing will frighten those like you and make them comprehend, in light of your disasters, the risks they run, such that your ruin will be not only a fitting vindication but also a useful example? And will your deceptions be revealed and thus foiled, deceptions that you rely upon wholly, so that other nations may*

ut oculatae ceterae gentes appareant, vos, ut estis, vanissimi et caecutientis-
simi videamini?

11   Principio quidem, sicut dictis verbis exprimitur, in huius orationis auspicio tribus votis, velut accensus in iram, mirabiliter
excandescens — non aliter quam si Diras, quod extremae despera-
tionis est, exoptes et clames — Florentinis indignas poenas immeri-
taque supplicia verbis acerrimis imprecaris. Cupis sic ipsos alicuius
calamitatis exitio sui similibus exemplo fore, quod videntes metuant et iusta sit pro factis ultio, nec non utilis in exemplo. Cupis
sic nostra denudari praestigia, quod oculatae ceterae gentes appareant et Florentini vanissimi, sicut sunt, atque caecutientissimi videantur. Qui quidem tuae narrationis introitus quam ineptus sit
quidque legentibus afferat paucissimis edocebo. Quis dominus
quisque princeps quaeve communitas est in quam non possit hoc
idem, si quis debacchari voluerit, iaculari? Si tuum in dominum
haec eadem verba scribantur, quis inconvenienter posita causaretur? Quid erit necessarium immutare, nisi pro 'civibus' 'tyrannum'
et pro plurali ponere numerum singularem?

12   Sed illum et mortuos dimittamus, cum quibus decet mitius
agere quam si vivant. Dic, obsecro, nonne te Florentinis verbis tuis
prodis et detegis inimicum, et capitalem ac teterrimum inimicum?
Nunc autem fare, precor, quam personam induis: accusatoris an
testis? Et testis, cum te offeras planeque te geras et declares his
tuis optatibus illorum quos insequeris inimicum, quem locum
relinquis ut tibi vel levissima fides detur? Accusator autem quis
tantae gravitatis umquam fuit, qui vel criminationis vel invectionis solo contextu potuerit culpabilem reddere quem accusat? Sit
Cicero, sit Demosthenes, sit summae vir integritatis Cato, sit

be found to be clear-sighted and so that you may appear to be what you are: utterly empty and utterly blind?

At the start of your oration, then (as expressed in the forego- 11 ing), exactly as though you were invoking the Furies — a sign of utter desperation — and like one in the grip of awesome rage, you curse the Florentines in the bitterest terms, with triple vows, calling down upon them unjust punishments and unmerited torments. You desire that their ruin might be an example to others like them, a frightening sight and a worthy as well as a useful vindication of wrongs done. You hope that our deceptions may come to light, that other peoples show themselves clear-sighted, that the Florentines show themselves as they really are, thoroughly untrustworthy and blind. It won't require much for me to show that this is an inept beginning and what effect it has on readers. Is there any lord, any prince or any community at all against which the same accusations could not be hurled, if one wants to give way to uncontrollable rage? If the selfsame words were directed against your lord, who would make the case that they are wide of the mark? What else has to be changed but the word "tyrant" in place of "citizens" and the singular for the plural?

But let us leave in peace him and all the dead, with whom it is 12 fitting to be gentler than with the living.[19] Tell me, pray, doesn't your mode of address give you away and reveal you to be an enemy of the Florentines, indeed a deadly and loathsome enemy? And declare now, please, which role you are assuming: that of prosecutor or witness?[20] If you play the witness, how can one have any trust in you at all, since you show yourself, prove yourself and even declare yourself, with these desires of yours, the enemy of those against whom you bear witness? On the other hand, since when has a prosecutor possessed authority of such a kind as to render the defendant guilty by the mere fact of accusing and attacking him? Even were he Cicero or Demosthenes, or that Cato of

Antonius aut Crassus, sit Demosthenis insectator Aeschines vel quicumque togatus aut palliatus plus umquam in curia pro rostris vel subselliis valuit; sint, si placet, et omnes simul, numquam, nisi probaverint, reum damnabunt. Quamobrem vide recognosceque tuam inscitiam, tuum errorem, disceque, rabida stultissimaque bestia, quod etiam in iudiciis senatu vel populo nulla fides accusatori vel testibus qui se gesserint inimicos soleat vel debeat adhiberi, quamvis etiam saepe sint iudices, sit senatus aut populus illi quem quis accusaverit subiratus. Ut quotiens accusator vel vocati testes hoc inimicitiae virus, quod tu tam manifeste prodis, prae se tulerint, vel se stulti non sentiant insanire vel auditores ut insanos reputent et in suam inclinare stultitiam et in insipientiae supinae notam aut iniquitatis infamiam trudere meditentur.

13 Quis enim adeo demens vel rerum humanarum ignarus qui credat accusatori vel testi qui profiteatur aut eius, quem insequitur, se detegat inimicum? Tu vero, cum non unum aliquem dominum vel iudicem, non unum vel aliquos populos sed universum genus hominum, quos haec tua legere contigerit, alloquaris, nonne (si putas te sapere, sicut credo; talia quippe non scriberes nisi tibimet de scientia atque prudentia blandireris) stultissimus es si speras haec illis te persuasum iri? Nonne tibi similes arbitraris vel, quod malignius est, iniquos ducis? Cavebimus omnes, igitur, teque cum tua stultitia relinquemus; nec usquam fidem merebere, nisi forsitan apud stultos. Quae cum ita sint (negari quidem non possunt, orator egregie), nonne primo tam elegantis orationis ingressu te rabidam bestiam probas, ut superius diffinivi? Sed haec omittamus

supreme integrity, Antony or Crassus, Aeschines against Demosthenes, or any other Roman or Greek orator who proved himself in the curia, senate, or tribunal: were he able to unite all their strengths, he still could not get an accused person condemned without any proof. So recognize and accept your own ignorance and error, and learn, raging and stupid animal, that when there is a trial, neither the senate nor the people consider reliable a prosecutor or witnesses who conduct themselves as enemies of the accused, even though there is often prejudice against the accused on the part of judges, senate or people.[21] And any time the prosecutor or the witnesses called show the venom of hostility [toward the accused], as you clearly do, [one of the following holds good]: either, stupid as they are, they remain unconscious of their own madness; or else they reckon their audience is mad and study how to push them into their own brand of stupidity, so that they acquire the stigma of passive foolishness or the infamy of active injustice.

Whoever could be so mad or naive as to believe a prosecutor or 13 a witness who shows himself or confesses himself to be enemy of the person he speaks against? Now, since you are addressing yourself, not merely to one lord or one judge, not to one or several peoples, but to every human being who may happen to read your text, and assuming you believe yourself wise, as I believe (for surely you wouldn't write stuff like this if you didn't flatter your own learning and wisdom), aren't you actually rather a dunce to believe you can convince them with these arguments? Isn't it the case that you either think them like you or — even more maliciously — unjust? Then let's all be careful and leave you to your stupidity; nor will you ever deserve trust, unless perhaps among those who are equally stupid. Since that is undeniably how things stand, my fine orator, haven't you proven yourself to be a rabid beast, as above defined, from the outset of your elegant oration? But enough of this. Granted you are completely untrustworthy, let

et quamvis omni fide careas, videamus an vocabula quae Florentinis imponis vere vel idonee[2] sint his, quos insequeris, attributa.

14 'Perditissimos cives, vastatores patriae turbatoresque pacis Italiae' Florentinos vocas. 'Perditissimos,' inquis, 'cives.' Si cunctos Florentinos increpas, falsissimum est quod dicis; licet enim aliquibus hoc nomen forte convenire possit, qui sua prodigant, male vivant et pravitate morum ac sceleribus delectentur, sine comparatione tamen longe plures sunt quos perditos, si vera loqui velis, nequeas appellare multosque tutemet fatebere qui possint, immo debeant, non perditi sed boni cives omnium iudicio vocitari. Sed hosti nostro non congruit hoc querelae genus; nostrum est ista conqueri vel dolere, quorum interest cives non perditos habere sed utiles, sed bonos, sed tales quibus possit res publica se iuvare. Relinquas igitur hoc nobis, relinquas et id quod sequitur, 'patriae vastatores.' Quid enim aliud est vastare patriam quam patriam exhaurire? Ut, si de patria nostra sentias, optandum hoc esse tibi debeat, non dolendum! Si vero de Liguria, Flaminia Venetiaque, domini tui pressis iugo, forsan intelligis, doleas, obsecro, non reprehendas, optesque tibi tuisque partibus tales hostium patriae vastatores, nec reliquam ex hoc deplores Italiam. Habent tot Ausoniae gentes quae tuo non subiacent domino, fines suos habent et ora habent et qui dicere noverint atque possint; et quis umquam illarum partium dominus aut populus hoc quod nobis imputas fuit conquestus? Quis personam eorum tibi commisit et vices?

15 Ut in hoc non sis, etiam si verum dixeris, audiendus: si pacem turbaremus Italiae, sicut scribis, totam haberemus Italiam inimicam; quod cum non sit, sed ubique qua iurivorae serpentis iugum

us now see if the words with which you have been attacking Florentines are truthfully and fitly applied to them.

You call the Florentines *wicked citizens, enemies of their country and*   14
disturbers of the peace in Italy. "Wicked citizens," you say. If you are
upbraiding all Florentines, this is absolutely untrue. The word
might apply to some of them if they wasted their patrimony,
conducted themselves deplorably, took delight in perversion and
crime. Still, if you wanted to tell the truth, those who in no way
merit such an accusation are incomparably more numerous, and
indeed you really ought to admit that there are many who can be,
and indeed should be called, by anyone's judgment, not "wicked"
but "upright citizens."[22] In addition it is hardly the business of our
enemies to make such a complaint: we should be the ones to be-
moan or regret any such state of affairs, since it behooves us in the
first place to have not wicked but good and upright citizens, such
as can serve the state. Leave this to us, and also the next part
about "enemies of their country." What can "enemies of their country" signify except those who bring it to ruin? If you mean our
country's ruin, that ought to be something desirable for you, not a
source of pain. But if perhaps you mean Liguria, Emilia Romagna
and the Veneto, regions oppressed by your lord, you should feel
sorry for them, not attack them; and you should be wishing for
such enemies of your enemies' country for your own sake and that
of your region, not lamenting the behavior of the rest of Italy on
that account. Many are the Italic nations which are not under your
lord's rule, who are masters of their shores and borders and who
know how to speak and can speak: when has any lord or people of
those regions brought out the imputations that you do? Has any
one of them entrusted their persons or their fortunes to you?

Even if you were speaking the truth, your claim on this head   15
could not be accepted: if we were the "disturbers of peace in Italy,"
all Italy would be against us. But as that is not the case—on
the contrary, wherever the yoke and the venom of the legality-

venenumque non attigerit maneant habeanturque carissimi suis
commerciis Florentini, nonne patet haec, quae iactas, te contra
manentem rerum evidentiam comminisci, ut te deceat vocabulum
illud 'praestigia' quod attribuis Florentinis, quod quidem 'occultam
fraudem,' ut arbitror, esse vis? Non enim detegenda tuis optares
votis, nisi praestigiorum ludificationes sentires occultas. Sed quis
te docuit hostibus haec obicere? Dolus an virtus, quis in hoste re-
quirat? Dic tamen ubinam vel tuum dominum vel aliquem alium
res publica Florentina decepit? Quas umquam aliis, praeterquam
hostibus, struxit insidias? Nil te prohibet haec omnia de quibuscumque tibi placuerit delatrare. Non dicas, sed probes oportet
ista quae scribis, ut verum dixisse videaris, non maledixisse. Sed
quis te praestigiosior, qui cum Florentinos tibi sic proposueris
diffamandos, quod credi non velis omninoque credendus non sis,
omnes qui faciant quae reprehendis infamia, quam Florentinis
imponas, notandos sine dubio derelinquas? Quid enim aliud in-
tendit qui mordet aliquem de vitio—cui nec re nec audientium
opinione talis, in quem invexerit, sit affinis—nisi reprehendere vitium et omnes qui damnato illo vitio sint infecti? Ut si turbare
pacem Italiae, destruere subditos et vastare vicinos dominum tan-
gat tuum, in ipsum illa votorum tuorum acrimonia, non in illos
qui tali culpa careant, inveharis, praesertim cum sic Florentinos
arguas quod nil probes. Qui damnat quidem vitia, damnat procul
dubio vitiosos, si qui sint vel evidentia rerum vel opinione publica
tali vitio criminosi. Bene ergo tibi iam est de totius tam elaboratae
dictionis introitu, cum illa sumpseris in unum quae cunctis convenire possint quaeque communia sint tam accusatori quam etiam
accusato, saltem verbis paucissimis immutatis; cum te faciens ac-
cusatis inimicum fidem perdas, et illos, quos alloqueris, aut insanos

devouring serpent has not yet reached, the Florentines remain loved and respected for their commerce[23] — isn't it obvious that you are mixing together your boasts with countervailing evidence, so that this word "tricks" you use to characterize Florentine acts really suits you. "Tricks" is a word you would like to have mean, I think, "hidden acts of fraud." Indeed, you could hardly want them exposed unless you knew that there were hidden swindles in the first place. But who instructed you to make these accusations against an enemy? Whose business is it if an enemy be virtuous or evil? Tell me, when, pray, has the Florentine republic ever deceived your lord or anyone else? Whom, except enemies, has it ever plotted against? Nothing forbids you from barking accusations like this against anyone you like. But you have to prove them, not just make them, if you want to show you are telling the truth and not simply throwing out calumnies.[24] But really, who is trickier than you are? When you would expose the Florentines to defamation in such a way that your charge is entirely lacking in credibility, surely you are letting everyone else who acts in the way you condemn escape the infamy you are putting on the Florentines? After all, what aim can one have in accusing a certain party of a vice to which it has no inclination in fact or in public opinion, except to condemn the vice itself and all those who are infected by it? So if to upset the peace in Italy, ruin one's subjects and plunder one's neighbors apply to your lord, you must direct your acrimony against him, not against those guiltless of these things, all the more so as not one of your accusations against the Florentines stands proved. He who condemns the vice condemns also those who practice it, if they are incriminated of such a vice by clear evidence or public opinion.[25] Quite a start for your elegant oration: you attribute to a sole party things that may be said of many, such that by changing a word here and there they apply to the accuser; next you show how you are not to be trusted by revealing your opposition to the accused; and last you let it be known that

reputes aut facere coneris iniquos. Quae quantum oratoriae facultatis sint, tibi, si forsan haec nostra videris, relinquo cunctisque qui nostra haec legerint tribuo iudicandum.

16   Sed iam ulterius procedamus videamusque quid post haec vota tua, sive maledicta, subnectas: *Sic erit profecto, non fallor: adventant tempora, fata sunt prope, pleno cursu appropinquat diu exoptata mortalibus ruina vestrae superbiae. Videbimus, ecce videbimus illam vestram in defendenda quadam foedissima libertate vel potius crudelissima tyrannide constantiam fortitudinemque Romanam; hoc enim nomine superbire soletis et vos genus praedicare Romanum, quod quam impudenter faciatis alio dicendum erit loco. Nunc prosequor; videbimus, inquam, illam inanem atque ventosam iactantiam et insolentiam Florentinam et quam virtuti vere respondeat a vobis, praeter ceteros mortales, propriarum rerum semper usurpata laudatio cognoscemus.*

17   Quibus quid responderim nisi quod cum oratoris officium deseras — diffidentia scilicet, ut arbitror, probationum — eadem stultitia, qua dicere cepisti, nunc incipias divinare? O singularis orator, qui primis orationis tuae verbis, cum nihil probaturus omnino sis, probare quidem non potes, tibi fidem abstuleris et, etiam si quid posses orationis dulcedine vel artificio consequi, stultitia tua perdas! Quis te docuit oratorem exuere teque transferre, quod est perridiculum, in prophetam? 'Sic erit,' inquis, 'profecto.' Quis hoc tibi stulte promisit? 'Non fallor,' adiicis, quasi quae turbatus optas sic tibi comperta sint quod in illo malivolentiae tumultu nec falli valeas nec errare. Fabellam ursi, cum nugas tuas relego, reminiscor: cum enim pyrorum anni futuri secum copia laetaretur, interrogatus unde presciret respondisse

you believe your audience is either mindless or malleable enough to act unjustly. How far all these exordia belong to the art of public speaking I leave it up to you to judge, should you ever read this text, and to any other readers I may have.

But let us proceed to see what you add to these wishes of yours, 16 or rather curses: *So shall it surely be, I am certain; the times have arrived, destiny is about to be fulfilled, and with great strides there approaches the collapse of your arrogance, long wished-for by the human race. We shall see — and how we shall see! — your celebrated constancy and "Roman" tenacity in defending that repulsive liberty, or rather cruel tyranny. You are accustomed to boast of the name of Rome and declare to all that you descend from the Romans. This impudent lie I will refute another time. Now I continue: we shall see, I say, that Florentine boastfulness and insolence is empty as the wind, and we shall learn how much the praise that more than any other nation you claim for yourselves, truly corresponds to virtue.*

How else can I respond to accusations like these except to point 17 out that, having once decided to abandon the obligations of an orator (presumably for want of evidence), you now put on the airs of a prophet, still brandishing words in the same foolish fashion as before?[26] What an extraordinary orator you are! From your very first lines, you can prove absolutely nothing at all, since it is impossible; you do your utmost not to be credible, and even when you might achieve something through sweetness and verbal artifice, you lose it all with your stupidity! Who counseled you to drop the cloak of orator and put on the (perfectly laughable) mantle of prophet? *So shall it surely be*, you say. And who was fool enough to promise it to you? *I am certain*, you add, as if the things you were wishing for in your confusion were made known to you in such a way that you were able neither to err nor be deceived in the tumult of your malevolence. These inanities remind me of the little story about the bear bursting with happiness that next year would bring a bumper crop of pears; when asked why it was so

fingitur: 'Quoniam opto.' Tu, non aliter quam ursus ille, quae concupiscis affirmas, ut non minus bestialiter sentias quam loquaris.

18   Sed subdis: 'Adventant tempora, fata sunt prope, pleno cursu appropinquat exoptata mortalibus ruina vestrae superbiae.' Adventant tempora, immo labuntur, immo currunt. Inquit enim Naso:

> Tempora labuntur tacitisque senescimus annis
>   Et currit freno non remorante dies.

Adventant, fateor; immo tempora, quae tunc adventare nuntiasti, tuis (per Dei gratiam) inania votis et optatibus advenerunt. Vide tecumque considera quid loquaris mementoque quod non sit tuum scire tempora vel momenta, quae Pater noster, qui in caelis est, in sua potestate recondit. 'Fata sunt prope'; stultissime Lombardorum, quid nomine fatorum intendis? An ea Pater omnipotens Phoebo, tibi Phoebus Apollo praedixit, ut nobis haec tu, Furiarum maxima, pandas? Sed audiamus ulterius vecordem vementemque novum hunc vatem.

19   'Videbimus, ecce videbimus illam vestram in defendenda quadam foedissima libertate vel potius crudelissima tyrannide constantiam fortitudinemque Romanam; hoc enim nomine superbire soletis et vos genus praedicare Romanum. Quod quam impudenter faciatis alio dicendum erit loco.' 'Videbimus,' inquis; immo videras, vides atque videbis plus quam Romanam fortitudinem atque constantiam populi Florentini in defendenda dulcissima libertate, 'quod caeleste bonum,' ut ille dixit, 'praeterit orbis opes,' quam mens est omnibus Florentinis ut vitam, immo supra vitam, opibus ferroque defendere nostrisque posteris hanc hereditatem optimam, quam a maioribus nostris accepimus, relinquere — Deo favente — solidam et immaculatam. Adeo placet nobis haec quam

sure of this, it replied "because I wish it." Just like that bear, you assert as true the things you hope for, and your ideas are no less bestial than your language.

Next you add *the times have arrived, destiny is about to be fulfilled,* 18 *and with great strides there approaches the collapse of your arrogance, long wished-for by the human race.* Oh yes, the times have arrived, they are slipping by, they run. As Ovid writes:

The times slips by, we grow old amid the silent years,
   And the day runs on, held back by no rein.[27]

The times have arrived, true; indeed, the times you have announced are now here and, lo!—thanks be to God—they are empty of all your hopes and wishes. Think well and reflect on what you say; recall that it is not for you to know the times or the seasons, which our Father, who art in heaven, hides within his power.[28] *Destiny is about to be fulfilled,* but what, foolish Lombard, do you mean by the word "destiny"? Did the omnipotent Father vouchsafe this prophecy to Phoebus Apollo, and Apollo to you, in order that you, as chief of the Furies, might divulge it to us? Well, let us listen further to this mad new seer as he raves.

We shall see—and how we shall see!—your celebrated constancy and 19 *"Roman" tenacity in defending that repulsive liberty, or rather cruel tyranny. You are accustomed to boast of the name of Rome and declare to all that you descend from the Romans. This impudent lie I will refute another time.* "We shall see," you write, and indeed you have seen, you do see and you shall see the more than Roman constancy and tenacity of the Florentines in defending sweet liberty, "the celestial good exceeding all the wealth in the world," as [Aesop] says.[29] It is the resolve of all Florentines to defend liberty with their sword and substance as they defend their own lives, indeed beyond their own lives, and to leave this finest inheritance to their posterity, an inheritance we have received from our ancestors—through God's favor—undiminished and unstained.[30] So much do we treasure

foedissimam vocas, omnium hominum stultissime, libertatem, quam inexperti solum, qualis es, nec alicuius momenti faciunt nec cognoscunt, quam solum Lombardorum genus, sive natura, sive consuetudine, sive forsan utraque fiat, nec videntur diligere nec optare. Tu vero solus hoc summum divinitatis munus foedissimum reputas et abhorres, cuius sententiae non arbitror te socium invenire, etiam sub tui principis dominatu, adeo naturale est diligere libertatem. Quo mihi videtur, non humilitate sed vitio, te posse 'servorum servum,' immo debere rationabiliter appellari.

20   Sed cur 'servum' te voco, qui tam valde servitute delectaris tua, quod non pudeat vocare 'foedissimam' libertatem? Immo, quod stultius est, non es veritus eam 'tyrannidem crudelissimam' appellare. Quod verbum, cum omnes risum isse vel ire certus sim, ferre non potui. Numquid aliquam nosti vel in Italia vel alibi libertatem quae sit Florentinorum libertate liberior aut integrior, vel quam nostrae libertati possis, ne comparare dixerim, anteferre? Talisne est tyrannis illa domini cui servis, quod tyrannidem audeas Florentinorum dicere libertatem? Scio quod gravis et instar servitutis est custos legum libertas—gravis et instar servitutis est effrenae iuventuti, quae cupit suam libidinem evagari, quae passionibus ducitur atque vivit, ut te facile putem et tui similes non solum non intelligere libertatem quid sit, sed rem et nomen, veluti tetrum aliquid, abhorrere.

21   Cui rei testis est Livius, cum proditionem de reducendis regibus solido illo stilo suo referret: 'Erant,' inquit, 'in Romana iuventute adolescentes aliquot, nec hi tenui loco orti, quorum in regno libido solutior fuerat, aequales sodalesque adolescentium Tarquiniorum, assueti more regio vivere. Eam tum aequato iure omnium licentiam querentes, libertatem aliorum in suam vertisse servitutem

this liberty which you, most foolish of men, call repulsive. Only those who have never experienced it, people like you, can fail to appreciate it or know its worth, and it is precisely the Lombards who seem the only people (whether from nature, custom, or both) not to love it or long for it.[31] But it is you alone who regard as repulsive and shrink from this highest gift of divinity; and I don't think you will find any who share your sentiment, even within the domain of your lord, so natural is love of liberty. That is why it seems to me that you could be styled — indeed you ought with good reason to be styled — the "servant of servants," but as a mark of moral weakness rather than humility.

But why do I call you "servant" when you are so pleased with   20
servitude that you unashamedly define liberty "most hateful"? Still worse, you call it "cruel tyranny." This is really unbearable and I am sure everyone has laughed and will laugh at it. In all Italy and elsewhere is there a freer and more intact liberty than the liberty enjoyed by the Florentines, a higher liberty or even an equal one? Or is the tyranny of the lord you serve such that you dare call the liberty of the Florentines a tyranny? I know a liberty that stands guard over law may appear burdensome and like slavery — burdensome and like slavery for dissolute youth who want only to follow their lusts and live dragged about by their passions. So I can easily understand how you and your kind not only do not understand the essence of liberty, but shrink from its reality and reputation as though it were something repulsive.

To all this Livy bears witness when he describes, in that lapi-   21
dary style of his, the plot to bring back the monarchy: "There were among the young men of Rome a number of youths, the sons of families not unimportant, whose pleasures had been less confined under the monarchy, who, being of the same age as the young Tarquinii and their cronies, had grown used to the untrammeled life of princes. This license they missed, now that all enjoyed equal rights, and they had got into the way of complaining to each other

conquerebantur.' Haec et alia, quae tantus auctor scripsit, puto te, sicut sunt ingenia mortalium ad ea quae desiderant curiosa suntque proclivia, tecum iugiter meditari, cogitantemque talia te rerum dulcissimam libertatem crudelissimam tyrannidem ducere taleque tantumque bonum, quo nihil pulchrius esse potest, rem foedissimam appellare; quae quam inepte quamque contra veritatem dicta sint tibimet relinquerem, si te tantum hominem gereres, iudicandum. Cunctis tamen ista legentibus exhibeo dirimenda.

22   Verum cum negare videaris Florentinos genus esse Romanum, dic, precor, ubinam contrarium repperisti? Cur nobis invides quod, praeter te solum, tota consentit Italia, quod nullus umquam, nisi tu, teterrima belua, contradixit, quod urbs Roma Romanique principes nullis umquam temporibus negaverunt, sed nos filios, carnem ex carne sua et ossa ex ossibus suis etiam in singularem sui nominis honorem et gloriam reputant atque vocant? Quoque te pudeat hoc in dubitationem stultissime revocasse, volo referre quid sentiam de tantae civitatis origine et his auctoribus, quos adducere potero, confirmare ut, postquam alio tibi dicendum loco reservasti quam impudenter praedicemus nos genus esse Romanum, et auferam tibi delirandi materiam et occasionem exhibeam rectius sentiendi.

23   Nunc autem relaturus originem civitatis Florentiae, rem quidem obscuram multaque temporum antiquitate sepultam, sine dubitatione crediderim de parvo principio, sicut contingit in reliquis, gloriosissimum hunc populum urbemque celeberrimam quam habemus, non tamen ignobili, processisse. Verum cum antiquissima civitas Faesulana in urbis huius corpus, sive bello, ut fama est, sive pace, captis montanis civibus amoenitate loci,

that the liberty of the rest had resulted in their own enslavement."[32] I'm sure that this and other passages of this great author
led you to long introspection—the thoughts of mankind being
inquisitive and inclined to the things they desire—and brooding
upon the matter you came to view as a most cruel tyranny that
liberty which instead is the sweetest of all things, and to define as
hateful so great a good, indeed the most precious of all. The ab-
surdity and falseness of these views I would leave to you to adjudi-
cate, were you capable of acting like a human being. Still, I offer
them for dissection to everyone who reads these pages.

But since you seem to deny the Roman origins of the Floren-   22
tine people, tell me, please, wherever did you find the contrary
view? Why do you envy what all Italy (save you) grants us, what
no one except you, filthy beast that you are, has ever doubted?
Why be jealous of what the city of Rome and the Roman emperors have at no time denied, so that still today they call us and regard us as their children, flesh of their flesh and bones of their
bones,[33] a source of pride and honor to their name? And in order
to make you ashamed of the doubts you have foolishly raised, I
want to tell you my views about the origin of this noble city and
confirm them by means of authorities I shall be able to cite, so
that I may remove from you, who have "kept for another time"
your demonstration that we wrongly take pride in descent from
the Romans, any grounds for your ravings and give you the opportunity to adopt more correct views.

In undertaking to set out the origins of Florence, an obscure   23
question that is buried in the depths of antiquity, I am prepared
to believe that this people rich in glory and their celebrated city
will have come from small beginnings (as is often the case), but
not ignoble ones. Yet if the most ancient city-state of Fiesole
left its dwellings and came flooding down into the site of our

confluxerit sedesque suas reliquerit, nemini dubium esse potest urbem hanc augustius quam putetur initium habuisse. Quod si nos lateat, non est mirum. Nam, ut externa pertranseam, urbis Romanae primum principium, dic mihi, quis novit? Legimus Evandrum et Archadas — cum fatis, ut aiunt, auctore Carmente, per Tyberim intrantes Italiam appulissent — ubi postea condita Roma fuit oppidum invenisse quod Latino nomine 'Valentia' dicebatur, vocabulum cuius Archades vertentes in Graecum, iuxta verbi significationem, 'Rhomen' pro 'Valentia' vocaverunt, unde creditum a nonnullis est inclitum Romae nomen, non a Romo, sicut communiter traditur, descendisse. Auctori quidem urbis verum nomen non Romulus sed Romus fuit, unde 'Roma,' non 'Romula' dicta est; et Varro plane 'Romum' vocat et 'Romulum.' Quis autem legit quemnam auctorem habuerit antiquissimum illud oppidum quod Valentia dictum fuit? Quis verum eius oppidi principium valeat assignare? Ut hereditarium nobis sit ignotam habere nostrae conditionis originem, sicut Roma, quod quidem antiquitatis est validissimum argumentum.

24   Quod autem haec urbs Romanos habuerit auctores, urgentissimis colligitur coniecturis, stante siquidem fama, quae fit obscurior annis, urbem Florentinam opus fuisse Romanum: sunt in hac civitate Capitolium, et iuxta Capitolium Forum; est Parlasium sive Circus, est et locus qui 'Thermae' dicitur, est et regio Parionis, est et locus quem 'Capaciam' vocant, est et templum olim Martis insigne, quem gentilitas Romani generis volebat auctorem (et templum non Graeco, non Tusco more factum, sed plane Romano). Unum adiungam, licet nunc non extet, aliud originis nostrae signum, quod usque ad tertiam partem quartidecimi saeculi post incarnationem mediatoris Dei et hominum Ihesu Christi apud pontem qui 'Vetus' dicitur erat: aequestris statua Martis, quam in

city — whether driven by war, as report says, or peacefully, because those citizens of the mountain became enamored of its pleasant situation — no one can doubt that this city had a more august beginning than is thought. It's not surprising that this has been overlooked. To take an outside example, tell me, who knows what the first beginnings were of the city of Rome?[34] We read that Evander and the Arcadians, driven via the Tiber into Italy by the Fate, under the guidance of Carmenta, discovered a village in the place where Rome was afterward founded, called in Latin "Valentia." The Arcadians translated this into Greek, keeping the etymology, and renamed the village "Rome" instead of "Valentia," this being according to some the derivation of the noble name of Rome — not from "Romus," as is commonly thought. The true name of Rome's founder was "Romus" not "Romulus," which yielded "Roma" not "Romula"; and Varro, clearly, also calls Romus "Romulus."[35] But who, pray, has read that the ancient town called Valentia had a founder? Who is able to fix the real beginnings of this town? It belongs to our birthright not to know the origins of our city, just as for Rome, and this in itself is strong proof of its antiquity.

That this city was founded by the Romans may be gathered   24
from weighty arguments, so long as the tradition lasts (which grows darker with each year) that the city of Florence was the work of the Romans. There exists in this city a capitol, and next to it a forum;[36] there is an amphitheater or circus[37]; there is a place called the Baths;[38] there is the area called Parione, a place called Capacia, and an important temple, in ancient times dedicated to Mars, according to the pagans the father of the Roman people, a temple not in Greek or Etruscan style but wholly Roman.[39] I may add yet another indication of our origin, no longer extant but which stood, until the third part of the fourteenth century after the Incarnation of Jesus Christ, mediator between God and man, visible near the Ponte Vecchio: an equestrian statue of Mars, torn

memoriam Romani generis iste populus reservabat, quam una cum pontibus tribus rapuit vis aquarum, annis iam complendis pridie nonas Novembrias septuaginta. Quam quidem vivunt adhuc plurimi qui viderunt.

25 Exstant adhuc arcus aquaeductusque vestigia, more parentum nostrorum, qui talis fabricae machinamentis dulces aquas ad usum omnium deducebant. Quae cum omnia Romanae sint res, Romana nomina Romanique moris imitatio, quis audeat dicere, tam celebris famae stante praesidio, rerum talium auctores alios fuisse quam Romanos? Exstant adhuc rotundae turres et portarum monimenta, quae nunc episcopatui connexa sunt, quae qui Romam viderit non videbit solum, sed iurabit esse Romana, non solum qualia sunt Romae moenia, latericia coctilique materia, sed et forma. Non mirum ergo si, tot astipulantibus rebus, constans et inextinguibilis fama est urbem nostram opificium esse Romanum oppositum Faesulanis, quos Romanis fuisse contrarios et adversos clarissimum facit, quod sociali bello legamus Faesulas et alia quaedam oppida fuisse deleta; ut Romanum opus esse Florentiam plane sit stultissimum dubitare.

26 Legitur enim apud Sallustium, certissimae veritatis historicum, L. Catilinam quemdam C. Manlium praemisisse Faesulas ad exercitum comparandum, qui 'sollicitans in Etruria plebem, egestate simul et dolore iniuriae novarum rerum cupidam, quod Sullae dominatione agros bonaque omnia amiserant;[3] praeterea latrones cuiusque generis, quorum in ea regione magna copia erat, nonnullos etiam ex Sullanis coloniis, quibus libido atque luxuria ex magnis rapinis nihil reliqui fecerant,' magnum paravit exercitum. Quibus Sallustii verbis, Ciceronis nostri ditissimum eiusdem rei testimonium, si placet, adiciam ut, his collatis, clarius efficiam quod intendo. Scribit ergo Tullius oratione secunda, quam ad populum Romanum habuit contra Catilinam, dum qualitatem exercitus, quem habuit hostis ille perditissimus patriae, per membra

away along with three bridges by violent floods exactly seventy years ago this November fourth, a statue that our people had preserved in memory of the Romans; many who are still alive today have seen it.[40]

In addition there are the arches and remains of the aqueducts 25 built in the accustomed fashion of our ancestors, who by means of these structures made drinkable water available to all. Given all these Roman remains, these Roman names, and the imitation of Roman customs, and with the protection of a famous tradition still standing, who would dare say that the founders of all this were any people other than the Romans? There are still extant the round towers and remnants of the gate, today attached to the bishop's palace, which anyone who has seen Rome will swear to as Roman, not just because they show the identical materials as Roman walls (brick and terracotta) but also style. It is no surprise to me, with so much supporting evidence for it, that there is a unbroken and unbreakable tradition that Florence was built by the Romans in opposition to the Fiesolans, who were famously hostile to the Romans. We read that in the Social War Fiesole and certain other towns were destroyed. In short, it is absurd to doubt that Florence was built by the Romans.[41]

In fact we read in the entirely trustworthy historian Sallust that 26 Lucius Catiline sent one Gaius Manlius to Fiesole to recruit an army, which he did "by stirring up the common people, desirous of revolt because of their poverty and the many offenses they had suffered, having lost their lands and possessions under Sulla; also robbers, a great many of whom infested the area, as well as members of Sulla's colonies, who in feeding their vices and appetites had dissipated all their ample gains from thefts," and so assembled a large army.[42] Allow me to add to Sallust's words the very rich testimony of our Cicero on the same topic, as comparison of the two will better clarify what I mean to show. For in his second oration to the Roman people against Catiline, Cicero writes,

designat, in haec verba, videlicet: 'Tertium genus est aetate iam
affectum, sed tamen exercitatione robustum, quo ex genere ipse
Manlius, cui nunc Catilina succedit. Hi sunt homines ex his coloniis quas Faesulis Sulla constituit, quas ego universas civium esse
optimorum et fortissimorum sentio.'⁴

27   Respondeat velim nunc vel dementissimus ille, qui negat Florentinos esse Romanos, vel quivis alius cui placuerit ista conten-
dere, negetque, si potest, Faesulanis in finibus Romanas colonias
esse deductas, et ubi velint assignent eas—praeter Florentiam—
Romanis congruentes nominibus, aedificiis atque notis, et Marte
praeside, quem iste populus in illo gentilitatis errore religiose colebat. Quod cum facere nullo modo valeant, famam sequantur tot
vigentem saeculis, et rem notissimam, tot fultam adminiculis, oro
non negent, nec contra Ciceronis sententiam arbitrentur et dicant
viles illos milites agricolasque fuisse, sed cum tantus auctor 'cives
illos optimos et fortissimos' esse dicat, cum ipso sentiant id, quod
decet, et audiant quid sequatur.

28   Subdit enim immediate post illa quae proxime rettuli: 'Sed tamen hi sunt coloni qui se insperatis ac repentinis pecuniis sump-
tuosius insolentiusque iactarunt; hi dum aedificant tamquam
beati, dum praediis, lecticis, familiis magnis, conviviis apparatis
delectantur, in tantum aes alienum inciderunt, ut si salvi esse velint Sulla sit his ab inferis excitandus; qui etiam nonnullos agrestes,
homines tenues atque egentes, in eandem illam spem veterum ra-
pinarum impulerunt.' Haec Cicero, quibus facile capi potest quale
genus illud optimorum fortissimorumque civium Romanorum
fuerit quibus illae coloniae fuerint tunc temporis assignatae.

describing the sort of army that perfidious enemy of his country possessed: "The third category consists of men advanced in age but vigorous in their activity, among them this same Manlius, whom Catiline is replacing. They are men from the colonies which Sulla founded in Fiesole, all of them, I think, consisting of the finest and bravest citizens."[43]

Now I would like to hear that raging madman respond who 27 dares deny that the Florentines are Romans, or anyone else who would like to defend that view: let him deny if he can that the Romans founded colonies within the territory of Fiesole; let him say where else besides Florence they would have put those colonies, so close to the Romans in names, building types, and features, and under the aegis of Mars whom this people, led astray by pagan error, venerated most highly. But since they will find this impossible, let them follow a tradition kept alive for many centuries, and may they kindly refrain from denying something which is widely known and amply borne out by much evidence, and not dare to contradict the opinion of Cicero by speaking ill of the soldiers and country folk whom this great author calls "good and earnest citizens." Let them accept his opinion as is proper and listen to what follows.

Directly after this passage, Cicero adds: "But these I speak of 28 are the colonists who, finding themselves suddenly rich, well beyond all expectation, took to fast and pretentious living; by dint of immoderate construction, and squandering on properties, litters, slaves, and sumptuous banquets, they piled up debts so massive that they would have to call Sulla up from Hades to save their skins. What's more, they also compelled many simple country people, humble and needy, to hope for quick gains, as with the robberies of olden times."[44] Thus Cicero, and from his words can be understood the excellent and honest mettle of these Roman citizens to whom these colonies had at that time been assigned.

Cumque nulla prorsus colonia supersit cuius vestigia sint praeter Florentiam, credant Sullanos illos milites, quo possent resistere Faesulanis, in huius unius aedificationem consensisse. Nec quem ad male sentiendum de maioribus nostris moveat quod nonnulli, sicut vult Sallustius, vel qui male rem gesserant, ut tradit Cicero, contra patriam adhaeserint Catilinae; neuter, enim, ipsorum 'omnes' dixit, sed 'aliquos,' quos, scilicet, ad illud nefas rei familiaris angustiae perpulerunt, quos credibile sit illa pugna taeterrima, quam in agro Pistoriensi commissam legimus, periisse.

29   Verum nomen forte quaeris; fateor id in historiis quas habemus me nullis temporibus invenisse. Puto tamen, quoniam Florentinus ager suapte natura feracissimus liliorum sit, flores occasionem nominis praebuisse. Huius nominis autem auctor optimus, Ptolemaeus Philadelphius, qui claruit temporibus Antonini Pii, claram facit libro tertio *Geographiae* suae (qua priorum omnium scripta diligentia et veritate superavit) — huius, inquam, nominis facit et civitatis Florentiae mentionem. Inquit, enim, ubi Tuscorum mediterranea enumerat breviloque,[5] sicut et in ceteris, ut quaedam omittam, 'Luca, Lucus Feronis, Pistoria, Florentia, Pisae, Volaterrae, Faesulae, Perusia, Arretium, Cortona.' Ut cum multas urbes alias oppidaque maxima tacuerit, forte quia tunc non forent aut memoratu digna non essent, Florentiam, quia iam ad dignitatem memoriae subcrevisset, notabiliter nominavit. Forte etiam cum astrorum peritia, cuius studiosissimus fuit, videret urbem hanc ad tam notabilem[6] magnitudinem perventuram, noluit, futuri praescius, rem adeo mirabilem subticere.

30   Quod autem apud Plinium legitur, cum oras Tusciae diligentissime scribit, in haec verba videlicet: 'Fluentini profluenti Arno appositi,' forte corruptum est et scribi debuit 'Florentini,' quodque sequitur, 'profluenti Arno appositi,' non minus librariis dare potuit corrumpendi materiam quam auctori 'profluentis' vocabulo ei, quod 'Fluentini' dixerat, alludendi. Nam cum inter

And since the remains of no colony except Florence survive in the area, they should trust that the soldiers of Sulla shared in its construction as part of the resistance to the Fiesolans. Nor should one be moved to think ill of our forefathers because a few of them (according to Sallust) or those who had conducted themselves badly (as Cicero reports), had joined Catiline against their country: neither writer says "all" but "some," that is to say, those brought to this crime by economic difficulties, only to die (we suppose) in the great battle fought in the countryside near Pistoia.[45]

You may perhaps ask about the name, and I admit to not find-   29
ing it in the historical sources we know of. Very likely, as the fields around Florence are naturally fertile with lilies, its flowers gave rise to the city's name. At all events the city is mentioned under this name "Florentia" precisely by Ptolemy, the fine author of the period of Antoninus Pius, in the third book of his *Geography*, a work surpassing all earlier ones in clarity and precision. He says, with some omissions, when describing Mediterranean Tuscany in brief form (as elsewhere) the following: "Lucca, Lucus Feronis, Pistoia, Florence, Pisa, Volterra, Fiesole, Perugia, Arezzo, Cortona."[46] Note that besides leaving out many other important cities and large towns, perhaps because they did not exist or were not worthy of attention at the time, he clearly mentions Florence, proof that it was worthy of note. Perhaps too, when thanks to his knowledge of celestial bodies, a subject to which he had devoted great study, he saw that this city would achieve conspicuous greatness, he preferred not to remain silent about so marvelous a circumstance, knowing the future as he did.

When in his careful description of Tuscany Pliny writes "the   30
Fluentini situated on the Arno River flowing by,"[47] there may be a corruption and it should have been written *Florentini*, because the phrase that follows, "situated on the river Arno flowing by," could easily have led copyists into error because of the resemblance between *profluenti* and *Fluentini*. Now given that the city had been

Africum, Munionem et Arnum aliquosque torrentes,[7] qui iam extincti sunt, haec civitas sita fuerit, cui mirum si 'Fluentia' forsan ab initio dicta fuit et quod a florum copia maluerint eam posteri 'Florentiam' appellare? Nec putet aliquis Plinium de Florentia non sensisse. Cum enim dixisset 'Clusini veteres, Clusini novi,' mox adiecit 'Fluentini profluenti Arno appositi, Faesulae' et cetera quae subnectit. Quod adeo verum est quod etiam auderem dicere, nisi rationi[8] temporum Ptolemaei repugnaret auctoritas, priscum nomen illud in 'Florentiam' commutatum quando, mense Ianuario, singulari Dei miraculo certum est ulmum efrondem ad feretri vel sandapilae contactum, quae corpus sanctissimi patris nostri Zenobii continebat, traditur floruisse; ut ex tunc pro 'Fluentia' 'Florentia' coeperit vocitari.

31   Nec hoc a Romani nominis sono vel institutis abhorret. Habent enim et ipsi non ignobilem Urbis partem quae vulgo dicitur 'Campus Flore' vel, ut hodie dicitur, 'Campus Floris,' ut consonum satis sit Romanis rationem illius nominis placuisse. Potuerunt et esse quamplures ex regione Campi Flore qui, tali nomine delectati, causa nominis exstitere. Licet etiam cogitare Deum, qui cunctarum rerum efficiens causa est, talis nominis sonum[9] et faciem inspirasse, sciens quo potentiae, pulchritudinis et honoris erat suam Florentiam perducturus. Et cum 'Nazareth,' Hieronymo teste libro quem transtulit atque composuit cui titulus est *De Hebraicis nominibus et ipsorum etymologia*, interpretetur 'flos' sive 'virgultum,' et ipsa sit, eodem auctore teste, 'viculus in Galilea unde Salvator noster 'Nazarenus' vocatus est,' ut in locorum libello scripsit, quis dubitet, attenta fide qua semper floruit super alias Italiae civitates urbs nostra Florentia, illum rerum omnium opificem Deum nomen hoc futurae cultrici Christi Florentiae tribuisse, quod Latine significaret idem quod Hebraice 'Nazareth' dicitur importare?

founded in a position between the Affrico, the Mugnone, the Arno and other streams now extinct, would it be strange if the city had first been known as *Fluentia* and later, because of the abundance of flowers, its later inhabitants preferred to call it *Florentia*? Nor should it be supposed that Pliny had in mind a place other than Florence, for after stating "the inhabitants of old Chiusi and those of the new Chiusi" he at once adds "the *Fluentini* situated on the river Arno flowing by, Fiesole" and so on.[48] This is so true that I would even dare say, if Ptolemy's authority did not conflict with the chronology,[49] that the old name was changed to *Florentia* in that month of January when, as tradition attests, a bare elm tree burst into flower by a special divine miracle, as the pall or bier holding the body of our most holy bishop Zenobius brushed it,[50] and from then on one began to say *Florentia* instead of *Fluentia*.

The sound of the name does not distance it from Roman 31 names or practices. Rome itself has, for example, an area of some importance in the city called "Campofiore" or as one says today "Campo dei fiori," so that such a name [as *Florentia*] could well have seemed suitable to the Romans. It is not to be excluded that some denizens of Campofiore came here to settle, attracted by the name. One may also suggest that God, efficient cause of all things, inspired the sound and look of the name, knowing the height of power, beauty and fame that would be attained by his Florence. Now since, as Jerome relates in the book he composed and translated, *Of Hebrew Names and their Meanings*, the word "Nazareth" means "flower" or "bud"[51] and this is (following the same author's brief text on places) "the village in Galilee from which Our Savior took his name 'Nazarene;'"[52] then given the faith thanks to which our city of Florence has always flourished more than any other in Italy, who could ever doubt that the Artificer of all things assigned to this future devotee of Christ that name, "Florentia," which is the Latin equivalent of the Hebrew "Nazareth"?

32   Videtis, ut cunctis loquar, immo digito tangitis nostrae civitatis exortum Romano genere, civibus optimis atque fortissimis ex coloniis Faesulanis! Videtis quot originis Romanae vestigia clament et consentiant illud idem; videtis insignem tam gloriosi nominis rationem, habetis famam constantissimam atque latam, cuius initii memoria non existit! Quis ergo poterit, inter tot veritatum suffragia, super hoc amodo, si nostra haec legerit, rationabiliter dubitare? Cum enim omnia consonent veritati nihilque prorsus sit quod in huius originis contrarium possit adduci, quis intellectus potest, nisi desipiat, dissentire? Verum, dicet aliquis, nonne legitur apud Senecam — quem quidam Florum vocant — ubi civile bellum, quod inter Sullam ac Marium gestum est, non minus conqueritur quam describat: 'Municipia Italiae splendidissima venierunt: Spoletium, Interamnium, Praeneste, Florentia. Nam Sulmonae vetus oppidum, socium atque amicum, o facinus indignum, nondum expugnatum, ut obsides iure belli et modo morte damnati duci iubentur. Sic damnatam civitatem iussit Sulla deleri'? Scio quod sic aliquibus in codicibus scriptum est; alibi vero, quod emendatius arbitror, non 'Florentia' legitur sed 'Florentina,' cuius quidem nominis adhuc est in Campaniae finibus oppidum, quod dicitur 'Florentinum,' ut tam similitudine nominis, quam locorum aliorum vicinitate, quae pestis illa confecit, doceamur potuisse talem errorem faciliter irrepsisse, praesertim cum antiquissimo codice legerim 'Florentina.' Accedit ad haec quod urbs nostra summo magistratu, sicut olim Roma per consules, regebatur usque ad exactos annos incarnationis divinae sapientiae mille ducentos octoginta duos, ut hoc etiam arguat originem a Romanis.

You can see (and I am addressing everyone), indeed you can   32
touch with your finger[53] the Roman origins of our city, founded by
the finest and bravest citizens from the Fiesolan colonies! You can
see how many Roman remains cry out and harmonize with the
very same conclusion; you can see the noble explanation of a name
so glorious and you can grasp its unbroken and widespread tradition whose beginning is lost in the night of time. Who, in the face
of so many certain proofs and after reading these pages of mine,
could henceforth harbor any doubts on the matter? If, as we have
seen, all points to this one truth about the origin of Florence and
no counterargument may be sustained, what person of understanding, who but a fool could ever disagree? And yet, someone
will object, is not the following passage to be read in Seneca
(whom some call Florus)? In this passage, during the war between
Marius and Sulla, he writes (or better, laments) that "the finest
cities in Italy came up [for auction]: Spoleto, Terni, Praeneste,
Florence. As for Sulmo, an allied and friendly city of long standing, Sulla, instead of storming or besieging it according to the
rules of warfare, committed an act of base injustice in condemning
the city and ordering its destruction, even as those condemned to
death were ordered to be led to execution."[54] This, I know, is the
reading found in many manuscripts; however, in others one reads
Florentina in place of Florentia, and I think this is a better reading; still today there is a village in Campania known as Florentinum.[55] Hence, because of the similarity of these names and of the
proximity of the other places struck by that disaster, an error of
this kind may easily have come about, especially if we keep in
mind that I have read in a very old codex the form "Florentina."[56]
Finally, we may add that our city was governed by a chief magis-
tracy, just as Rome was one time under the consuls, until the year
1282 after the Incarnation of divine wisdom,[57] and this is further
proof of our Roman origin.

33   Nunc ad tua reditum faciens, adicis: 'Videbimus, inquam, illam inanem atque ventosam iactantiam et insolentiam Florentinam, et quam virtuti vere respondeat a vobis praeter ceteros mortales usurpata laudatio cognoscemus.' Inanem dicis et ventosam iactantiam Florentinam. Et quis umquam Florentinum regimen aliquid dicere potest, tot quas per orbem sparsit litteris, iactavisse? Iactare futurum respicit, quod tibi relinquimus tibique similibus faciendum. Gravitatis enim Florentinae non est inania divinando iactare, sicut tu facis, quod quidem in tempus aliud differamus. Quod si iactantiam et insolentiam gloriationem intelligis, sicut credo, quis in Italia dominus aut in orbe populus est qui possit rebus pace belloque gestis verius et honestius gloriari quique se minus umquam curaverit exaltare? Quae vero laus inanis et ventosa minus est quam quae procedit ex meritis? Quam ea quam nemo possit increpare mendacem? Quae princeps iste populus pro libertate gessit sua, vel in defensione etiam sociorum, tam sponte sua, sicut multotiens, quam ex foedere, sicut semper (numquam enim in hac parte defecit), nonne licitum moribus est, improperatione sequestra, in aliorum exhortationem et exemplum et in consecutionem vicissitudinis recensere? An inane vel ventosum est id quod nititur veritate? Si vellem domini tui (tua nequeo, cum ignorem) si vellem, inquam, domini tui facta dictaque, quibus iactantiam et insolentiam prae se tulit, hac in parte colligere, crede mihi, nihil simile posses Florentinis vel privatim vel publice, nisi more tuo ad fingenda confugeres, imputare. His ergo dimissis, quam vera post haec prosequaris videamus.

34   Subdis ergo: *Non possunt amplius homines sine stomacho vestrum nomen audire; non potest pati Italia eos incolumes videre qui, cum eam cladibus multis afflixerint, ad extremum suffocare turpissima servitute conati sunt; non potest denique vos ferre diutius divina iustitia. Quomodo igitur stare possint non video, contra quos omnium fere hominum vota ac*

To return to your text, you proceed: *Now I continue: we shall see,* 33
I say, that Florentine boastfulness and insolence is empty as the wind, and
we shall learn how much the praise that more than any other nation you
claim for yourselves, truly corresponds to virtue. You call the boastfulness of the Florentines "empty as the wind." But who could say
that the Florentine government has ever been boastful in the numerous letters it sends around the world? Boasting always looks to
the future, an attitude that we leave to you and your like. Indeed it
is no part of Florentine seriousness to throw out empty and boastful predictions, as you do; it is something we put off to another
moment. And if, as I suppose, by "boastfulness" and "insolence"
you mean to show pride in one's own merits, what lord in Italy or
what people in the whole world can more justifiably and more
honorably pride itself on its own accomplishments in peace and in
war, and what community has ever shown less interest in self-
promotion? Besides, what praise is less empty and windy than
that based on merit — praise that no one can call dishonest? All
that this sovereign people has done to defend its own liberty and
to protect its own allies — either spontaneously (as so often) or in
fulfillment of agreements (always honored) — isn't it right for the
sake of good morals to rehearse these actions to show the outcome
of events and also as an example and encouragement to others? If
I wished to speak of your lord — *you* I don't know and can't speak
of — if I wished to bring up here all the deeds and words of your
lord which put his boastfulness and insolence on display, believe
me, you could impute nothing like that to the Florentines, either
in public or in private, unless you took refuge in fictions, as is your
wont. Now let us see if there is any truth in your next lines.

You go on: *People can no longer hear your name without vexation;* 34
Italy can no longer bear that those who have afflicted her with many disas-
ters, and in the end even sought to strangle her with wretched slavery,
should remain unpunished; divine justice herself can no longer tolerate you.
I can hardly see how you can hold out when the yearnings and hopes of

studia accensa sunt; quos vexata per vos et ad servitutem vocata Italia de-
testatur; in quos denique tantis flagitiis irritata ira caelestis armatur. Haec,
mihi credite scelerati, contra vos militat; haec nocentissimum sanguinem
vestrum sitit; haec extremam ruinam insidiosissimae et flagitiosissimae
gentis exposcit, atque ideo tantam hanc furiam mentibus vestris iniecit, ut
de excidio sacrosanctae matris ecclesiae, de mutatione Romani imperii, de
ruina gloriosissimi ducis, perniciosa consilia tractaretis. Quid enim aliud
cogitandum est, nisi divinum numen, iam iam sceleribus vestris infensum,
vos occaecatos in tantam insaniam impulisse, ut odia et arma illa contra
vos excitaret, quorum viribus non solum non possetis resistere, sed nec
etiam ferre fulgorem?

35   'Non possunt,' inquis, 'amplius homines sine stomacho vestrum
nomen audire.' O vir mirabilis, primis orationis tuae partibus optas; secundis, veluti prophetans, futura praedicis; nunc te subli-
mius elevans, quod solius Dei est, scrutaris renes et corda. Nec
solum hominum affectus refers, sed etiam, quasi divinae mentis
arcanum agnoscas, ais:[10] 'Non potest, denique, vos ferre diutius
divina iustitia.' 'Non possunt,' ut dicis, 'amplius homines sine stomacho nomen audire' nostrum. Sed possunt viri, possunt, crede
mihi, nostrum audire nomen homines virtuosi; nec possunt solum,
sed volunt, sed cupiunt, sed delectantur. Scio quod Guelforum,
quos habet Italia, multitudo populum Florentinum, huius sanctissimae conglutinationis caput, columen atque principem, et hi vehementius quos Gebellinae factionis crudelitas premit, quales infiniti sunt, qui tuo domino subiacent, non solum gratulanter
Florentinum nomen audiunt, sed adorant, sed victoriam et felicitatem eius cupiunt; nec solum cupiunt, sed expectant. Gebellini
vero, nisi desipiant, qui tyrannico iugo subiacent, Gebellino quidem favore mallent, sed si non detur, etiam Guelforum manibus
eligerent liberari.

nearly all humanity are aroused against you; if Italy—which you harassed
and summoned to servitude—hates you, and if heaven's wrath itself, vexed
at so many misdeeds, is in arms against you. Yes, heavenly wrath too
makes war upon you, believe me, wicked ones; it too thirsts for your guilty
blood; it too requires the total ruin of the most scheming and criminal of
nations. That is why it has injected this madness into your minds, so that
you hatch pernicious plots to destroy Holy Mother Church, to undermine
the Roman Empire and ruin the most glorious of dukes. What else can one
imagine but that God Himself, outraged by your wickedness, has blinded
you, driving you to the height of madness, so that he might arouse hatred
and arms against you? You cannot bear even the gleam of your enemies'
arms, to say nothing of their power.

People can no longer hear your name, you say, *without vexation.* You   35
are quite remarkable! In the first part of your speech you advance
wishes; in the second part prophecies; now in the third part you
are rising higher to scrutinize minds and hearts, a role that belongs to God alone.[58] Not only do you relate the sentiments of
mankind, but, as if you knew the hidden mind of God Himself,
you add: *divine justice herself can no longer tolerate you.* According to
you, people cannot hear our name without vexation. But men can,
believe me, they certainly can heed our name if they are men of
virtue: not only can they, but they want to, desire to, hope to, and
are delighted to! It is certain that the numerous Guelfs of Italy,
especially those oppressed by the cruelty of the Ghibelline party
(too numerous to count) and those subject to your lord, are happy
to heed the name of the Florentine people as to the brains, support, and leader of that most holy alliance. Not only do they heed
it, they adore it; they desire its victory and felicity; and not only
do they desire it, they look longingly for its coming. As for Ghibellines under a tyrant's yoke, only the fools among them would
not prefer a Ghibelline tyrant or, failing that, to be freed even by
Guelf hands.

217

36   Sed addis: 'Non potest pati Italia eos incolumes videre, qui cum eam cladibus multis afflixerint, ad extremum suffocare turpissima servitute conati sunt.' Verissimum est hoc, inquam; non enim quae vera dixeris denegabo. Restat tibi quod probes, vel ratione liquidissima declaretur, quinam sint qui Latium cladibus afflixerint, et ipsum conati fuerint subicere servituti. Quod postquam ostenderis, si conviceris hos esse Florentinos, tunc in ipsos dicito quicquid libet. Et quoniam hoc alibi commodius disserendum est, donec illuc pervenero sum contentus quilibet Italus secum examinet qua vexatione Florentia, sicut ais, afflixit Italiam, quis ipsam cogitaverit occupare vel sibi subicere servitute.

37   Sed coniecteris et asseras de rebus hominum quicquid libet; quis tibi secretum divinae iustitiae revelavit? Sed quis praeter te, foedissima belua, diceret quod non possit diutius nos divina iustitia sustinere? Non potest divina iustitia, quae sine misericordia divina non esset, quaeve sustinet diabolum, idolatras, inimicos sui nominis et alios peccatores, nos diutius sustinere? Vel quoniam velle et posse in Deo realiter unum sunt, non potest quia non vult, vel non vult quia non potest? Stulte nimis et impertinenter de Deo loqueris. Stultissime nobis iram Dei, quae donec venerit semper occulta fuit, veluti rem certissimam minitaris. Quod si, ut inquit Cicero, 'nihil est principi illi Deo, qui mundum regit, quod quidem fiat in terris acceptius quam concilia coetusque hominum iure sociati, quae civitates appellantur,' sique, ut testatur tragicus, 'victima haud ulla amplior potest magisque opima mactari Iovi quam rex iniquus,' quid domino tuo quidque nobis potest metui vel sperari, non tibi, qui non capis, sed omnibus recte sentientibus exhibeo iudicandum.

But you add, *Italy can no longer bear that those who have afflicted her*   36
with many disasters, and in the end even sought to strangle her with
wretched slavery, should remain unpunished. This is perfectly true, I
admit, for I shall not deny what you are saying is true. There only
remains for you to prove or make clear with lucid arguments just
who are they who have brought so many ills to the peninsula and
tried to enslave it. After you give your demonstration, if you have
proven convincingly that these men are Florentines, then say whatever you will against them. And since there will be another better
occasion on which to discuss it, until then I am happy for any
Italian to ponder both the evils that, according to you, Florence
supposedly has inflicted on Italy, as well as the question of who, in
fact, has been planning to take control of and enslave it.

Speculate and hold forth as you like about human affairs, but   37
who was it who revealed to you the secrets of divine justice? Who
besides yourself, filthy beast, would dare say that divine justice can
no longer tolerate us? Divine justice, which without mercy would
not be divine, and which tolerates the devil, idolaters, enemies of
its own name and other sinners, can no longer tolerate us? Since
to will and to be able are one and the same thing in God, is it that
He can't because He doesn't want to, or is it that He doesn't want
to because He can't? Your talk of God is silly and impertinent. It
is utter foolishness to threaten us by bringing in divine ire as
though it were an accomplished fact, when in fact it is always hidden until it appears. And if, as Cicero says, "nothing that happens
on earth is more pleasing to that supreme God who governs all
than communities and associations of human beings assembled
according to law that are called states,"[59] and if, as a tragic poet
claims, "no victim is finer and more pleasing to Jupiter than an evil
king who is to be immolated,"[60] then I leave it to all those of correct understanding, not to a witless fellow like you, to decide what
is to be wished or feared by us or by your lord.

38   Sed, ut ad reliqua veniamus, adicis: 'In quos denique tantis
flagitiis irritata ira caelestis armatur.' Ab ira divina descendis ad
caelestem, sed quid est armari caelestem iram in nos? Irasciturne
caelum, aut quasi metuat, cum offendere decrevit, armatur? Scio
quod nihil divina maiestate dignum, quoniam inenarrabilis est,
proferre possumus, sed de illo, velut homine quopiam, quicquid
loquimur enarramus. Cavendum est tamen, quod si quid de ipso
dixerimus, tam sobrie talique moderatione relatum sit, quod nec
includat impossibile nec ineptum. Quid autem est dicere: 'Haec,
mihi credite, scelerati, contra vos militat; haec nocentissimum sanguinem vestrum sitit; haec extremam ruinam insidiosissimae et
flagitiosissimae gentis exposcit'? Si Deus iratus contra nos militat,
ut affirmas, quomodo potuimus aut possumus una hora consistere? Si sitit nostrum sanguinem, cur non bibit, cur non eruit? Si
ruinam nostram exposcit, quis obstare potest divinae manui, cum
scriptum sit: 'Voluntati eius quis resistet'? Mox autem velut ab effectu probare niteris quae dixisti. Scribis enim: 'Atque ideo tantam
furiam mentibus vestris iniecit, ut de excidio sanctae matris ecclesiae, de mutatione Romani imperii, de ruina gloriosissimi ducis,
perniciosa consilia tractaretis.' Unde tibi — quo de duce tuo, cuius
utinam ordinare potuissemus excidium, dimittamus — unde tibi
tot, inquam, comperta sunt et tanta mendacia? Nosne de excidio
sanctae matris ecclesiae cogitamus, qui semper opibus[11] et subsi-
diis nostris illam fovimus, iuvimus, auximus? Florentinine possunt
aut cogitant de mutatione Romani imperii providere? Quis nobis
hanc auctoritatem dedit potentiamque concessit? An forte tanta
dementia nos invasit quod sumptibus et expensis nostris prae-
sumamus quod ad nos non attinet quodque nec de iure nec de
facto possumus sed totum ex aliena pendeat potestate? Dic, obsecro, vel in medium proferas, quosnam principes ob hoc adivi-
mus, vel ubi super hoc colloquium commune nostrum tenuit aut

But to continue, you next add: *heaven's wrath itself, upset by so* 38
many misdeeds, fights you. You move from divine to heavenly wrath,
but what exactly does it mean for heavenly wrath to take up arms
against us? Heaven is enraged with us or, as though it is fearful, it
takes up arms and has decided to attack? I well know that we
do not have words suitable to divine greatness, it being indescribable, and so when we speak of it we fall to speaking as if of a person. But we must still be careful to speak with the greatest care
and circumspection to avoid impossible or unsuitable statements.
What sense have phrases like: *Heavenly wrath too makes war upon*
you, believe me, wicked ones; it too thirsts for your guilty blood; it too re-
quires the total ruin of the most scheming and criminal of nations. If God
is enraged with us and—as you state—wars upon us, how could
we have held out for even an hour? If He desires our blood, why
doesn't He take it, and spill it? If He wants our undoing, what
ever can hold back the hand of God, if it is written "Who can oppose His will?"[61] Next you try to demonstrate *a posteriori* what you
have just stated, and you write: *That is why it has injected this mad-*
ness into your minds, so that you hatch pernicious plots to destroy Holy
Mother Church, to undermine the Roman Empire and ruin the most glori-
ous of dukes. Where have you found—let's leave aside your duke,
and would that we *could* have brought about his ruin!—where, I
say, have you found so many enormous lies? *We* plotted to destroy
Holy Mother Church? *We*, who have always fostered it, helped it,
strengthened it with every means at our disposal?[62] Do the Florentines have the intention or capacity to plan for the overthrow of
the Roman Empire? Who gave us this authority or allowed us so
much power? Have we been gripped, perhaps, by such a fit of
madness that we are presuming, at huge cost to ourselves, to do
what is none of our business and what is in law and in practice
impossible, something that rather depends wholly upon others?[63]
Tell me, please, or make known publicly, what rulers we have ap-
proached to this end? Just when has our commune debated or

tractatum? Non possunt haec, cum a potestate nostra non pendeant, a nobis incipi. Ridiculum, immo stultum et inane nimis, immo prorsus et impossibile[12] foret a nobis, quae facere non possumus, inchoari.

39   Quae cum ita sint, quid immoror diutius super hoc, quod prorsus nec persuaderi potest, cum non sit verisimile, nec probari,[13] cum omni careat veritate? Nec nobis obicias bellum quod contra quosdam officiales sanctae matris ecclesiae—qui sic terras eis in Italia commissas pessumdabant, quod subditos miserabili servitute prementes et nostram et aliorum cogitarent extinguere libertatem—Florentinum populum suscipere fuit necesse! Satis enim illa causa per Italiam et omnia Christianitatis regna ventilata fuit et, ut per effectum patuit, universus orbis commendavit et vidit populi nostri iustitiam, et illud non in exitium sanctae matris ecclesiae, sed in nostrae libertatis defensionem iudicavit, non in aliud ordinatum. In quam quidem obiectionem si forte pergas, referam socios, referam alia multa bella, quae tam intentione quam causa turpissimam his, quibus nolles, notam inurent multaque scelera renovabunt, quae quidem pudore, non metu, urbanitate, non formidine, subticentur. Scimus quibus fautoribus damnatae memoriae Ludovicus,[14] quem 'Bavarum' vulgus dixit, contra ius et voluntatem ecclesiae conatus sit Romanum imperium occupare. Scimus quem antipapam sibi constituit quosque scelus et monstrum illud anticardinales habuit et praelatos. Scimus aeternam illam Gebellinae factionis infamiam, quam renovabimus et in notitiae lumen, sepultam licet tenebris obscuratamque lapsu temporum, detegemus. Et cum voluerimus malefactis veritate nixi—non mendaciis, ut tu—maledicere, aliter nos videbis quam te tuis nugis et fictis adinventionibus resonare.

negotiated on this subject? We certainly cannot embark upon any such thing, since it does not depend on our own authority. It would be ridiculous, indeed foolish and worse than useless — indeed quite impossible — for us to commence something we cannot do.

This being so, why dwell further over something which, being 39 improbable, can convince no one, and being quite devoid of truth, cannot be demonstrated? And kindly don't advance as an objection the war which the Florentine people were compelled to fight against some officials of Holy Mother Church, who had so cruelly brought low the lands entrusted to them that they were forcing their subjects into despicable slavery, with the aim of destroying our own and others' liberty![64] Much about this has been said in Italy and in all the states of Christendom and, in light of the outcome, everyone recognized and praised the justice of our people and believed that the war had been undertaken, not to destroy Holy Mother Church, but only to defend our liberty, nothing else. And if you wish to press this accusation, I shall bring forward many allies, many other wars that in terms of aims and causes shall throw the greatest discredit upon those you would least like to, calling back to mind many crimes that we pass over in silence out of a sense of decency, not fear; out of courtesy not cowardice. We know with whose help that Louis of accursed memory, commonly called "the Bavarian," attempted to possess the imperial crown against all right and the express will of the Church.[65] We know what antipope he set up for himself, and what anticardinals and prelates that criminal and monstrous creature had about him. We know the eternal shame of the Ghibelline Party and we shall bring it back to life and drag it into the light of notoriety, buried though it is in the shadows and obscured by the passage of time. And as it is our aim to condemn crimes like these on a foundation of truth, not of lies as is your way, you will see our account reechoing widely in a way quite different from the response to your trifling fictions.

40   Sed haec satis; si sapienter enim te gesseris, satis erunt. Nolo
tamen — cum sciam (latere quidem me non potest) nos esse prorsus ab offensionibus tam ecclesiae quam imperii, quicquid oggan-
nias, alienos — nos terreas et ob hoc scribas: 'Quid enim aliud
cogitandum est, nisi divinum numen, iam iam sceleribus vestris
infensum, vos occaecatos in tantam insaniam impulisse, ut odia et
arma illa contra vos excitaret, quorum viribus non solum non possetis resistere, sed nec etiam ferre fulgorem?' Indigebat, ergo, Deus
caecitate et insania nostra, quo contra nos arma, quae minaris,
excitaret? Impellitne Deus in scelera nos, vel alios mortales, ut
puniat, an potius mentem inspirat, quo cavere possimus, declinare
malum et facere bonitatem? Non sapit oratio tua stultitiam solum,
sed blasphemiam, sed haeresim, cuius apud Gebellinos facilis est
iactura, sed summum supinumque mendacium. Nec Martium
hunc populum, qui tot bella sustinuit totque gessit, non posse resistere vel armorum splendorem ferre dicas; restitit, enim, et resis-
tit, et adeo splendorem armorum non exhorret quod armis arma,
sicut solet, obicientem tua iam sensit et per Dei gratiam sentiet
Lombardia.

41   Sed iam ad reliqua procedamus: *Atque, ut omittam ceteros vestros
inimicos, quibus nihil videtur antiquius quam ut aliquando de cruento illo
superbiae scopulo corruatis, ecce contra perfidiam vestram venit his armis et
copiis hisque armorum ducibus instructus exercitus, ut maiori multo potentiae quam vestra sit (ea qua tamen adeo superbitis ut arrogantia vestra
tolerari vix possit) extimescendus esse videatur. Venitque non tam avide eo
missus quam desideratus atque expectatus a vestris; vestris, inquam, si ita
sunt appellandi quorum cum in fortunas et corpora crudele et avarum habeatis imperium, nihil minus quam animos possidetis. Sperant equidem hoc
uno assertore suae libertatis exercitu, vobis prolapsis in servitutem, dignitatem pristinam, quam sibi per vos ereptam lugent, tandem esse recuperaturos. Itaque arma haec omnes hi populi, quos sub acerbissima tyrannide*

But enough of this, and if you conduct yourself wisely, it will be   40
enough. Yet I won't have you frightening us — since I know (what
can hardly have escaped me) that we are completely innocent of
any plots against Church or Empire, for all your chatter — and to
that end writing: *What else can one imagine but that God Himself,
outraged by your wickedness, has blinded you, driving you to the height of
madness, so that he might arouse hatred and arms against you? You cannot
bear even the gleam of your enemies' arms, to say nothing of their power.*
So God will stand in need of our blindness and insanity to set
against us the armed force you speak of in your threats? God
drives us and other mortals to commit crimes in order that he may
punish us; or rather he inspires in us an intention so that we
might learn caution, turn aside from evil and do good? Your
speech seems to smack not only of stupidity, but blasphemy and
heresy — a charge easy to suppose in the case of Ghibellines — and
utter, helpless mendacity. And do not say that this martial people,
which has endured and conducted so many wars, cannot fight
back or bear to see even the gleam of your arms. It has resisted
and does resist, and so far is it from cringing at the gleam of your
arms that Lombardy has already felt her armed resistance to your
arms, as usual, and will continue to feel it, by God's grace.

But now let us pass on to the rest: *And leaving aside other enemies,*   41
for whom nothing seems more desirable than for you to topple from that
bloody eminence of pride, behold an army is advancing against you, strong
enough in arms, soldiers and commanders as to strike you down in fear of
a power much greater than your own, despite your intolerable arrogance. It
is advancing, driven not just by its own eagerness, but because it is desired
and awaited by your allies — if you can call "allies" those whose souls you by
no means possess, though you exercise a cruel and greedy empire over their
bodies and fortunes. Indeed, they hope that, thanks to this army of libera-
tion, you will finally be enslaved and they may recover that ancient dignity
which, as they lament, they saw you tear from them. All the peoples whom
you are choking with your unbearable tyranny await these forces, and as

225

suffocatis, exspectant, ut cum tempus occasionemque prospexerint, excutiant iugum illud servitutis, quo manente nihil ipsis potest esse iocundum. Etenim quid delectabile videri potest miserrime servienti,[15] *cui speciosae amplaeque fortunae, quae magnam afferre solent voluptatem, aut summo dolori ablatae aut, ne eripiantur, aeterno metui sint oportet? Quid uxore, quid liberis dulcius? Quam tamen ex his sentire dulcedinem potest is qui se videt nuptias ad alterius petulantiam comparasse, liberos ad alienam libidinem procreasse? Patria vero, quae unicuique debet esse iocunda, infinitam affert tristitiam atque maerorem in servitute conspecta, ubi non solum non auditur ulla vox libera, sed nec etiam ulli sunt liberi cogitatus. Haec quidem cum ab uno pati sit miserum, miserius est a multis, miserrimum vero ab his quorum avaritia, libido, crudelitas, post hominum memoriam, tyrannorum omnium malitiam excessere. Ergo hi, quos hac tam infausta vitae condicione sub iugo intolerabilis servitutis opprimitis, omnes in speculis sunt, observant praestolanturque opportunitatem qua sese in libertatem asserere possint, quibus quantam spem praestiterit huius adventus exercitus difficile dictu est. Affecti enim sunt inextimabili atque incredibili alacritate seseque iam pedem*[16] *posuisse in possessionem desperatae quondam libertatis existimant.*

42   Nunc autem ad ineptias rediens tuas, adhuc minis omnia terrens, de secreto mentium subditorum nostrorum male sentis, peius auguras et pessimum minitaris. Inquis enim: 'Atque, ut omittam ceteros vestros inimicos, quibus nihil videtur antiquius quam ut aliquando de cruento illo superbiae scopulo corruatis, ecce contra perfidiam vestram venit his armis et copiis hisque armorum ducibus instructus exercitus, ut maiori quidem potentiae quam vestra sit (ea qua tamen adeo superbitis ut arrogantia vestra tolerari vix possit) extimescendus esse videatur. Venitque non tam avide eo missus quam desideratus atque exspectatus a vestris.'

soon as the moment and opportunity arise, they will throw off the yoke of your slavery, under which they can have no joy. Besides, what enjoyment could exist under the most wretched slavery, with the pain of seeing riches and properties gathered with such care — ordinarily a great source of happiness — taken away, or else with the constant fear of having them snatched away? What is sweeter than a bride and children? But how can they make for happiness when someone sees that he has prepared his nuptials to minister to another man's wantonness, and given birth to children to satisfy a stranger's lust? Our own country, which should be a source of joy to everyone, instead causes us sadness and grief when we see it enslaved, without free speech or even a single free thought. It is sad if a single person should inflict all this, sadder still if many do so, but the saddest thing of all is when it is done by a people whose avarice, lust, and cruelty defeat the malice of every tyrant in human memory. This, then, is why all those whom you are oppressing in this accursed condition of life, under the yoke of intolerable bondage, are now upon the watchtowers, anxiously awaiting the chance to reclaim their liberty, and it is hard to say how great is the hope the arrival of our army is offering them. They are moved by a boundless enthusiasm, and they reckon they have already taken steps to repossess the liberty they thought forever lost.

Coming back now to your nonsense: still spreading terror everywhere with your threats, you discern evil in our subject populations'[66] secret thoughts, predict worse, and threaten the worst. In fact you state: *And leaving aside other enemies, for whom nothing seems more desirable than for you to topple from that bloody eminence of pride, behold an army is advancing against you, strong enough in arms, soldiers and commanders as to strike you down in fear of a power much greater than your own, despite your intolerable arrogance. It is advancing, driven not just by its own eagerness, but because it is desired and awaited by your allies.* 42

43   Et unde, precor, ista coniectas? Iam bis bellum cum domino tuo gessit, immo sustinuit, populus Florentinus, et nunc tertium pendet. An primo forte bello tales nostros vidisti subditos ut ex ratione praeteriti possis illa, quae scribis, inferre? Sed verba, quae praemittis, ante omnia ventilemus: 'Ut omittam,' dicis, 'ceteros vestros inimicos.' Ubi sunt, obsecro, nostri nominis inimici, si dominum tuum tollas, sique, sicut decet, auferas quos invidia nostrae felicitatis excoquit et pellacitas tui ducis ascivit? Exosos invidia facit, offensio vero generat inimicos; ut cum nullos enumerare possis, quibus dederimus ex iniuria causam quod inimici sint, non potueris omittere quod non est, nec debueris Florentinorum nomen talibus mendaciis onerare, licet ipsos gratis (cur enim? assignare non potes!) elegeris inimicos. Quod autem addis — 'quibus nihil videtur antiquius' — dicas mihi velim, oratorum optime, quid ibi significet hoc nomen 'antiquius'; et cum per ipsum significare velis, ut arbitror, non praerogativam temporis sed affectus, si nihil eis videtur optabilius quam ut aliquando de cruento illo scopulo corruamus, non succedat magis eis in ipsorum[17] optatibus aliis quam in isto, immo tanto minus quanto magis hoc duxerint exoptandum. Credo te forte tamen illud optare, sed meliora vota divinaque misericordia praevalebunt et nos a servitutis laqueo, quem nobis parari denuntias, praeservabit.

44   Et ut ad exercitum, quem minaris, redeam, 'Venit,' inquis, 'non tam avide eo missus quam desideratus atque exspectatus a vestris; vestris, inquam, si ita sunt appellandi quorum cum in fortunas et corpora crudele et avarum habeatis imperium, nihil minus quam animos possidetis. Sperant equidem hoc uno assertore suae libertatis exercitu, vobis prolapsis in servitutem, dignitatem pristinam, quam sibi per vos ereptam lugent, tandem esse recuperaturos.

And from where, pray, do you get this inference? The Floren-   43
tine people have fought two wars with your lord—or rather, they
have had two wars forced on them—and now a third is imminent.[67] In the first war, did you perchance see our subject population acting in a way that you could infer what you wrote from
what happened? But let's first give an airing to the opening words
of your discourse, *And leaving aside other enemies*. Who, if you
please, are these enemies, if we leave aside your lord and, as is fitting, those who are boiling with envy at our successes or have been
seduced by your duke? Envy makes people hate you, but it's an
offense that creates enemies; and as you are unable to name anyone who is our enemy due to injuries received from us, you cannot
help talking of things that are nonexistent; nor should you have
heaped such lies upon the good name of the Florentines, although
you have selected enemies for us free of charge—but only because
you could not send anyone the bill! And in that phrase *for whom
nothing seems more desirable*, I would like you to say, greatest of the
orators, just what the word *more desirable* means in this context;
and since you mean to signify by it, I think, a preference of sentiment, not of time,[68] if nothing is more desirable for them than for
us to fall from our bloodstained precipice, may this wish not be
realized in this any more than in the other cases; or rather, may it
be realized the less, the more they believe it to be desirable. I believe perhaps it is you who wish this, but better prayers and divine
mercy shall prevail and shall preserve us from the noose of servitude that you announce is being prepared for us.

To return to the army that you threaten us with: *It is advancing,*   44
driven not just by its own eagerness, but because it is desired and awaited
by your allies—if you can call "allies" those whose souls you by no means
possess, though you exercise a cruel and greedy empire over their bodies and
fortunes. Indeed, they hope that, thanks to this army of liberation, you will
finally be enslaved and they may recover that ancient dignity which, as
they lament, they saw you tear from them. All the peoples whom you are

229

Itaque arma haec omnes hi populi, quos sub acerbissima tyrannide suffocatis, exspectant, ut cum tempus occasionemque prospexerint, excutiant iugum illud servitutis, quo manente nihil ipsis potest esse iocundum.' Ergo, domini tui tyrannique crudelis exercitum desideratum et exspectatum a nostris putas? Vidisti priore bello per effectum quantum secundo posses deberesque sperare de nostrorum mentibus subditorum. Vidisti quidem, et nisi fores insensata belua potuisti plus quam satis addiscere quid sperandum de mentibus subditorum nostrorum, ut — cum quo possis exemplo quae somnias sperare vel dicere omnino non habeas, sed ex praeteritis oppositum monearis — certum sit te captum ambitu splendoreque verborum tam stulte quam reprehensibiliter delirare.

45   Nam quod nostros subditos, dignitate pristina spoliatos, dicis acerbissima tyrannide suffocari, tale quidem est quod te tam falsa dicere si quis arguerit, non habeas quid excuses. Tyrannidene suffocantur aut dignitate pristina spoliati sunt Florentinorum subditi quos vel urbs nostra constituit atque fecit vel de tyrannorum manibus eruit aut recepit? Qui sunt vel nobiscum in libertate nati vel de miserrimae servitutis angustiis in dulcedinem libertatis asciti? Num iugum excutere cupiunt, quod non habent, vel dulce libertatis frenum — quod est iure vivere legibusque, quibus omnes subiacent, oboedire — desiderant in tyrannicum domini tui iugum, ut arbitrari te simulas, commutare? Desino nunc mirari quod multotiens summo cum stupore mecum conquestus sum. Conquerebar enim tot gentes, tot urbes, tot oppida quot domini tui iugum premit saevae nimis tyrannidi subiacere, mirabarque quod infinita Dei benignitas hoc tam longo tempore toleraret. Sed ex te video mihique firmiter persuasi vos adeo servitute delectari, quod

choking with your unbearable tyranny await these forces, and as soon as the
moment and opportunity arise, they will throw off the yoke of your slavery,
under which they can have no joy. Do you therefore believe that our
people desire and await the army of your cruel lord and tyrant?
You saw from the first conflict what you could and ought to expect
from the state of mind of our subjects. You have seen it and, if you
were not a blind beast, you could have learned well enough how
much hope to place in our subjects' state of mind; and as there are
no grounds at all for entertaining such hopes and dreams, and as
experience teaches you the exact opposite, there is little doubt
that, enamored of your own lofty words, you are raving on in a
way that is as mad as it is despicable.

To assert as you do that our subjects have lost their ancient 45
dignity and are suffocating under an insufferable tyranny is so
manifestly false that you would be unable to reply to anyone who
contests your affirmation. The subject peoples of the Florentines
—the very ones who founded and built our city or who accepted
or wrested it from the hands of tyrants—*they* are supposed to be
smothered under a tyranny and deprived of their original liberty?
They, who were either born free along with us or were adopted
into sweet liberty out of the poverty of a wretched servitude? We
are to suppose that they would shake off a yoke they do not have
and would long to exchange the sweet restraint of liberty—which
is to live in accordance with [natural] right and to obey laws to
which all are subject—for the tyrannical yoke of your lord?[69] Here
I cease to wonder at something that I have so many times de-
plored numbly to myself. It used to embitter me, in fact, that so
many peoples, cities, and villages oppressed by the yoke of your
lord, were subject to tyranny beyond measure, and I would ask
how infinite divine goodness could allow this for so long a time.
But thanks to you I see and am firmly persuaded that you delight
so much in servitude that you can only live in submission to an
overlord, and you don't understand how to abide within the sweet

non possetis sine domino vivere nec sciretis in libertatis licentiosa dulcedine permanere. Legibus obsequi, quae cunctos aequalitatis iustissima ratione respiciunt, grave vobis iugum et horrenda servitus est; oboedire vero tyranno, qui cuncta pro suae voluntatis moderatur arbitrio, summa vobis est libertas et inextimabilis dignitas. Et ob id putas illam populi Florentini partem quae degit extra nostrae civitatis moenia vel in municipiis vel in agris, quos nescis quanta libertate fruantur, appetere, quia subditi sunt urbi nostrae, sub vestro dominio servitutem.

46   Abest, et absit oro, tantus furor tantaque dementia ab eis quorum singularis gloria sit, vel nativitate vel lege vel incremento donoque fortunae, quod, quoniam nostri sint, se possint dicere Florentinos. Quid enim est Florentinum esse nisi tam natura quam lege civem esse Romanum et per consequens liberum et non servum? Proprium enim est Romanae nationis et sanguinis divinitatis munus quod libertas dicitur et adeo proprium quod qui desierit esse liber nec Romanus civis nec etiam Florentinus rationabiliter dici possit; quod donum quaeve gloriosa nomina quis velit amittere, nisi qui nihil curat de libero servus esse? Desinas, igitur, divinare tam stulta quae nec potes de praeteriti ratione percipere nec vides iuxta blanditias tuas, licet tempus illud iam longe transierit, evenisse.

47   Nec scio quam probabiliter dixeris tyranni crudelis exercitum libertatis assertorem et quod subditi debeant nostri, nobis prolapsis in servitutem, dignitatem pristinam, quam sibi per nos ereptam lugeant, recuperare. O verbum oratorium, tyranni crudelis exercitum libertatis assertorem, quod sit plus quam ridiculum, appellare! Quos credis legentibus stultitias tuas, cum ad id verbum venerint, te moturum esse cachinnos? Miror quod aliquando tua haec relegens te numquam intellexeris erravisse. Quis enim non

license of liberty. To obey the laws, which treat everyone in accordance with the most rightful principle of equality, for you is a heavy yoke and revolting servitude; but to obey a tyrant, who controls everything arbitrarily by his will, is for you the highest liberty and honor beyond price. This is why you believe that the part of the Florentine people living outside our city walls, in the villages or farms, with how much liberty you have no idea, simply because they are subject to our city, yearn for enslavement under your lord.

Never has it come to pass, and I pray it never may, that such 46 folly and madness take hold of those whose singular glory it is, because they are our subjects, to be able to call themselves Florentines, whether by birth or by legal right or by an increase or gift of fortune. What does it mean to be Florentine except, by nature and by law, to be a Roman citizen and hence free and not a slave?[70] It belongs to the people and bloodline of Rome to have that divine gift called liberty, and so much does it belong to them that whoever ceases to be free can no longer rationally be described as a Roman or Florentine citizen. And who would ever wish to lose this gift and these glorious titles but someone to whom it makes no difference to pass from the condition of a free man to that of a slave? So leave off these absurd predictions which have no basis in past events and which you will not see coming to fruition in accordance with your flattering blandishments, although the time for that is already long past.

I have strong doubts that the army of that cruel tyrant is a de- 47 fender of liberty, as you say, and also that our subjects, who lament that we took away their ancient dignity, after we ourselves had fallen into slavery, would be able to regain it. What an absurd piece of rhetorical trickery, to call a cruel tyrant's army a defender of liberty! Did you think you were going to arouse guffaws when readers of your nonsense reached this passage? I wonder that you never understand the mistake you had made when rereading what you'd written. Who was not going to see how inappropriate it was

videt quam inepte coniungatur exercitui tyrannico assertio libertatis? Quis non dicat te tibi contrarium esse cum exercitu, quem
assertorem libertatis dicis, nos in servitudinem prolapsuros esse
confirmes? Assertorne libertatis in servitutem trudit? Aut tam
stulti subditi nostri sunt quod servitute nostra sperent maiorem
habere quam obtineant libertatem?

48   Sed ulterius accedentes videamus quomodo probes quod, manente subiectione subditorum nostrorum, nihil ipsis possit esse
iocundum. Subdis namque: 'Etenim, quid delectabile videri potest
miserrime servienti, cui speciosae magnaeque fortunae, quae magnam afferre solent voluptatem, aut summo dolori ablatae aut, ne
eripiantur, aeterno metui sint oportet? Quid uxore, quid liberis
dulcius? Quam tamen ex his sentire dulcedinem potest is qui se
videt nuptias ad alterius petulantiam comparasse, liberos ad alienam libidinem procreasse? Patria vero, quae unicuique debet esse
iocunda, infinitam affert tristitiam atque maerorem in servitute
conspecta, ubi non solum non auditur ulla vox libera, sed nec
etiam ulli liberi cogitatus. Haec quidem cum ab uno pati sit miserum, miserius est a multis, miserrimum vero ab his quorum
avaritia, libido, crudelitas, post hominum memoriam, tyrannorum
omnium malitiam excessere.'

49   Haec omnia tua sunt, quae quidem si negaverim esse vera me-
metipsum te stultiorem vanissimumque fatebor. Verissima namque
sunt, quibus adicias velim quod nihil miserius esse potest quam de
vita neceque, de statu vel splendore dignitatis, arbitrio,[18] crudelitate vel etiam bonitate cuiuspiam qui tyrannus sit die noctuque
pendere. Quis enim securus comedit, securus vigilat vel securus
dormit, qui capiti suo continuo videt imminere securim, qui videt
quod ad domini sui voluntatem illa sit in iugulum descensura, qui
minimo dominicae suspicionis motu de vita periclitetur, qui se

to link a tyrant's army with the defense of liberty? Who could fail to call out how you'd contradicted yourself when you asserted that we would be enslaved by the army you were calling a defender of liberty?[71] What, does a defender of liberty enslave people? Or is our subject population so foolish that it hopes through our enslavement to have greater liberty than it has [already] obtained [from us]?

But let us move forward and examine how you prove that, so 48 long as our subjects remain in subjection, they can enjoy no happiness.[72] You add, *Besides, what enjoyment could exist under the most wretched slavery, with the pain of seeing riches and properties gathered with such care—ordinarily a great source of happiness—taken away, or else with the constant fear of having them snatched away? What is sweeter than a bride and children? But how can they make for happiness when someone sees that he has prepared his nuptials to minister to another man's wantonness, and given birth to children to satisfy a stranger's lust? Our own country, which should be a source of joy to everyone, instead causes us sadness and grief when we see it enslaved, without free speech or even a single free thought. It is sad if a single person should inflict all this, sadder still if many do so, but the saddest thing of all is when it is done by a people whose avarice, lust, and cruelty defeats the malice of every tyrant in human memory.*

These are all your words, and if I denied their truth I would 49 show myself to be still more foolish and untrustworthy than you are. For these words are most true indeed,[73] and I would only like to hear you add that nothing is more wretched than to be dependent, night and day, for death and life, for one's position and success, on the arbitrary choices, the cruelty and even the goodness of a tyrant. For who indeed could eat in security, stay awake or sleep in security, knowing that a blade always hangs over his head, knowing that it may fall upon his throat at the whim of his overlord, who is in danger for his life at his lord's least suspicion, who sees that he has to fear the tale-bearing of all those who have his

videt cunctorum, qui dominantis aures possint imbuere, formidare relatus, quibus letale sit domino suo vel leviter displicere? Haec et alia quae recenses sine scrupulo te tuosque conservos respiciunt et dominum notant tuum, sub cuius imperio sunt omnia quae verissime deplorasti quaeve de tyrannorum subditis annotavi.

50   Quae quidem verba, quoniam contra propositum tuum sunt, credo Deum, qui plenitudo veritatum est, tibi taliter inspirasse quod tacere non potuisti, quin scriberes; fors etiam ex proposito factum est, ut praestigiosissimus es, quod in tuorum admonitionem ista proferres. Utcumque tamen fuerit, certum est te verbis illis elisisse domini tui causam, deterruisse nos et nostros ut mortem prius quam ea, quae desideranda praedicas, eligamus simulque conservos tuos quid optare quidque moliri debeant monuisti. Habeo tibi gratias easque non magnas solummodo sed ingentes, qui talia scribere—licet minus oratorie, licet contra causam quam tueris, in hoc te gesseris—non es veritus, sed libere, sicut veridicum decuit, ausus es. Nihil enim maius pro nobis quisquam posset vel efficacius affirmasse.

51   Sed instabis: 'Nonne cum miserum dixerim esse haec ab uno pati miserius a multis addidi miserrimumque ab his, qui tyrannorum malitiam excessere?' Dixisti, fateor; sed cum de nobis nullam facias mentionem et notum sit omnibus, nisi forsitan omni sensu caruerint, eorum aliquid quae dixisti quaeque ego ipse subieci statum nullo modo respicere popularem, publicumque sit et notorium nullum orbis populum magis impatientem esse talium rerum quam genus et populum Florentinum, nolo quod nos non tangit quodque nobis non imponis nec possis imponere (nam esset omnino supervacuum) excusare, relinquoque tuis dominis et ipsorum dominio talem notam—sive fuerit unus, cui talia licuerint, sive

lord's ear, for whom it would be fatal to displease their lord in the slightest way? These and the rest of the horrors you describe without scruple really regard *you* and your fellow slaves and brand with infamy *your* lord, under whose rule occur all the things you, with complete truth, deplore, and all the things I have condemned regarding the subjects of tyrants.

As these assertions fly in the face of your purpose, I well believe   50
that God, in whom is the fullness of truth,[74] inspired you in such
a way that you could not be silent and couldn't help writing them
down. Perhaps you even did this on purpose, tricky fellow that
you are, to warn your fellow slaves. In any event, writing thus you
clearly spoke against the interests of your lord and convinced us
and ours to prefer death to embracing the course of action you
declare to be desirable; and at the same time you warned your fellow slaves what to wish for and what to undertake. I give you, not
just great, but enormous thanks for daring to write such things,
fearlessly, freely, as befits the truth — although you've conducted
yourself in the matter without oratorical skill and without aiding
the cause you were defending. No one could have spoken more
convincingly and more forcibly on our behalf.[75]

But you will object: "Did I not say, *it is sad if a single person should*   51
inflict all this, sadder still if many do so, and I added, *the saddest thing of*
all is when it is done by those who exceed the malice of tyrants?" So you
said, I admit, but since you made no mention of us, and everyone
who has any sense in their head knows that what you said and
what I added have no relevance whatever to a popular state, and
since is it public knowledge that there is no people on earth who
tolerate less the state of affairs we described than the Florentine
nation[76] and people, I don't want to defend against this state of
affairs that doesn't apply to us and that you can't impute to us
(that would be useless). I leave to your lords and their domain the
task of defending against these charges — whether it be one person
to whom they may apply or many, or whether there exist those

237

sint multi, sive fuerint etiam qui tyrannorum omnium malignita-
tem excesserint—excusandam, tibique concedo, requirens obnixius
quod nos doceas apud quem rhetorem legeris vel apud quem inve-
neris oratorem, cum officium in aliquem invehendi susceperis, illi
maledicere pro quo loquaris, vel singulariter adversariis imponere
quod ipsi possint, evidentia rerum omniumque consensu, in illos
reflectere quos tueris, ut ridendum sit quod, veluti concludens, in
huius loci materia subiecisti.

52   Scribis etenim: 'Ergo hi, quos hac tam infausta vitae condicione
sub iugo intolerabilis servitutis opprimitis, omnes in speculis sunt,
observant praestolanturque opportunitatem qua sese in libertatem
possint asserere, quibus quantam spem praestiterit huius adventus
exercitus difficile dictu est. Affecti enim sunt inextimabili atque
incredibili alacritate seseque iam pedem posuisse in possessionem
desperatae quondam libertatis existimant.' Non potest ex stulte
praemissis sequi nisi stulta conclusio. Stulte dixisti, nec solum
stulte sed false, nostros subditos esse servos; stultius resumis quod,
infausta vitae condicione, iugo servitutis intolerabilis opprimantur,
nec stultius solum sed mendacius; stultissime vero subinfers quod
omnes in speculis sint, observent et praestolentur nescio quam
opportunitatem ut se possint in libertatem asserere. Quae vel ubi
sunt hae speculae? Quanam ex orbis parte nobis eas, si quaerere
voluerimus, assignabis? In quam maiorem libertatem subditi nostri se possunt asserere?

53   Difficile dictu dicis quantam spem eis praestiterit adventus
huius exercitus. Non difficile solum fateor sed impossibile; quod
enim non est, quomodo veraciter dici potest? Difficile quidem dicere quot sint in mari pisces; quot autem ibi stellae vel sidera sint,
cum nulla prorsus sint, non est aliquo modo possibile. Solus enim
Deus novit quot astra maris ambitu non continentur. Ipse quidem,

who exceed even the malice of tyrants. I concede all that to you, asking only, with firmness, that you instruct us in what rhetor you read or in what orator you found, when you took up the role of attacker, the device of calumniating the very person you are defending, or of imputing to your adversaries the very charges which, in view of the evidence and by universal consent, you yourself could turn on the very persons you are defending.[77] Thus you've made ridiculous the theme that you put at end of the passage above.

For you write, *This, then, is why all those whom you are oppressing* 52 *in this accursed condition of life, under the yoke of intolerable bondage, are now upon the watchtowers, anxiously awaiting the chance to reclaim their liberty, and it is hard to say how great is the hope the arrival of our army is offering them. They are moved by a boundless enthusiasm, and they reckon they have already taken steps to repossess the liberty they thought forever lost.* From a silly premise only a silly conclusion can follow. Senselessly (senselessly and falsely) you say that our subjects are slaves; even more senselessly (more senselessly and even more falsely) you add that these unfortunates are under the yoke of an intolerable slavery; most senselessly of all you claim that they are on the watchtowers, trembling in expectation of some sort of chance to regain liberty. And just where are these watchtowers? Can you say in what part of the world you will be allotting them to us if we wish to seek them out? And where is this greater liberty to be found that our subjects can reclaim?

According to you it is difficult to say how many hopes they 53 harbor for the arrival of this army. I say it is not only difficult but impossible. For who can speak truthfully of something that doesn't exist? It is hard to say how many fish there are in the sea, but to say how many planets or stars are in the sea is utterly impossible, since there aren't any at all; God only knows how many stars *are not* contained by the broad ocean. Indeed even He, who has the

qui summa et perfectissima notitia rerum et veritas est, sicut scire non potest quod aliqua sidera sint ibi, cum nulla sint, sic scire non potest quot sint. Et nedum extimari non potest alacritas quae nulla sit, sed nec etiam assignari nec sperare possunt nostri subditi maiorem quam habeant libertatem nec umquam potuerunt quam habeant desperare; spes enim et desperatio sicut quod non habemus respiciunt, sic eorum, quae fuerint in manibus nostris, omnino non sunt. Alias autem spes esset in patria quae solum habetur in via.

54   Sed iam ab his, quae nobis ex tuis praescripsimus, facessendum est et ad alia, quae sequuntur, per ordinem quem promisimus veniamus. Subdis ergo: *Neque vos tantum Sancti Miniatis oppidi extollat illa quidem oppidanis infelix — vobis, ut videtur, fortunata — receptio quantum terrificet tam cito properata rebellio, ex qua quid animi sit reliquis municipiis atque urbibus pari servientibus calamitate licet intelligatis. Quibus, mihi credite, illius magnanimi quidem sed vel praecipitis nimium vel proditi atque deserti liberatoris patriae exsilium nequaquam prae metu voluntates exstinguet, sed admonebit ut diligentius cogitent suis rebus esse consulendum.*

55   'Neque vos,' inquis, 'tantum oppidi Sancti Miniatis extollat illa quidem oppidanis infelix — vobis, ut videtur, fortunata — receptio quantum terrificet tam cito properata rebellio.' Infelixne terrigenis illius oppidi fuit mutatio[19] de servitute in libertatem, de rabie civilis belli deque obsidionis urgentissimae periculis in dulcedinem securitatis et pacis? Fuit, fuit illa, si nescis, exclusio qua viperam saevientem tyrannidemque Ligusticam ex illo potentissimo castro praecipitem dedimus, gloriosissima nobis, optatissima faustaque

highest and most perfect knowledge of all things, and is very Truth, cannot know that there are some stars where none at all exist, and likewise cannot know their number. And eagerness cannot be measured where it does not exist, and our subjects cannot hope for or be allotted a greater liberty than they [already] possess, nor will they ever be able to lose hope in the liberty they possess; for hope and despair are not emotions that refer to what we already possess; thus hope and despair are both emotions that look to things we do not have, and so are entirely unrelated to things which we already possess. The hope to be in one's home country one can only have when away.[78]

But it is time to set aside what we have learned from your own 54 words and proceed as promised to your next words: *And boast not of the surrender to you of the town of San Miniato — a happy circumstance for you, but sad for the inhabitants. Rather, may the sudden revolt that followed afterward fill you with terror, so that you may come to understand the kind of spirit that animates other towns and cities subjected to a like calamity for those enslaved. Believe me: the exile of that magnanimous liberator of his country — even though he was too hasty (or perhaps was just betrayed and abandoned) — far from blunting their wills with fear, will just teach them that they need to be more careful when taking counsel about their own affairs.*

And boast not of the surrender to you of the town of San Miniato — a 55 *happy circumstance for you, but sad for the inhabitants. Rather, may the sudden revolt that followed afterward fill you with terror.* So, then, it would have been an unhappy change for the natives of that town, to pass from slavery to liberty, from the fury of civil war and the dangers of an oppressive siege to the sweetness of safety and peace? It was precisely that expulsion — in case you didn't know it — that allowed us to throw the cruel viper and Ligurian tyrant[79] headlong out of that most powerful fastness; it was a moment of high glory for us, highly desired and auspicious for the those townsmen, who were dying of biting hunger and being oppressed

municipibus illis, qui saeva fame peribant iugoque crudelissimae
tyrannidis premebantur. Fuit toti patriae salutaris vobisque, si rectum aliquid saperetis, exemplo, ne spem tentandi vel acquirendi
sumeretis in posterum illa quae non potuit vestra potentia, recenti
victoria tumens moenibusque nostris imminens et infesta, tueri.

56   Et ut rem totam certa ratione cognoscas—forte quidem nondum editus eras in lucem—paucis accipe summam rerum. Cum
populus Sancti Miniatis contrariis factionibus dissideret, tandem
inter principes factionis quae potentior erat, quam Ciaccionum
dicebant, orta contentio sceleratissima movit arma, cuius rei causa
populus ille coepit novae sectionis studiis dissidere; cumque caedes horrenda commissa fuisset, occisores cum paucis exclusi sunt
tantaque fuit paucorum rabies quod numquam concordiae modus
repertus est, his conquerentibus inexcusabiles, ut eis videbatur,
caedes, aliis ponderantibus tantae rei causas, quas dignas non
ducebant ut ab altis deberent animis tolerari. Cumque malum hoc
intestinum in dies cresceret, pullulantibus quotidie magis indignationibus quas augebant iniuriae, succendebat invidia spesque variae
nutriebant, eo deventum est ut unius sectionis arbitrio, ceteris patria pulsis aut in patria ipsa prostratis, illa res publica regeretur.
Nec contenti sunt intra se furere, sed venenum suum contra nos
evomentes, quasdam imperatoris Caroli Tertii copias, quas prae-
missas in Etruriam rabies illa susceperat, spe praedae nostros in
fines hostiliter impulerunt.

57   Post imperatoris vero discessum, cum maneret alta Florentini
populi mente repostum vulnus illud iniuriae, commune nostrum—ascitis, quos intrinsecorum expulerat superbia, captis montibus circa castrum illud—multa castellorum opera, cunctos aditus

by the yoke of the cruelest of tyrants. It was salutary for the whole country and a good example for you too, if you could understand anything aright, that you should not in future take it upon yourselves to try and acquire things that your power cannot protect, puffed up though it was with its recent victories and placed though it was in a position to threaten our walls.

And in order that you may have a true account of events, since 56 perhaps they predate your birth, I will relate briefly what happened.[80] When the people of San Miniato were already split by the contending factions it came to pass one day that a conflict arose among the leaders of the more powerful faction, called the Ciccioni faction, and they came to wicked arms against each other, with the effect that the people began to be divided by partisanship for the new sect. After a series of terrible murders the assassins and a few others were exiled, but a small group of citizens was seized by a hate so violent as to make peace impossible. Some complained bitterly, saying that the murders seemed to them inexcusable, while others, pondering the causes of these terrible deeds, felt that high-minded people ought not to tolerate such unworthy behavior. As the conflict between citizens daily sharpened and acts of injustice increased, angry outbursts on a daily basis, rancor and all kinds of expectations were fostered. It came to the point that one faction took public affairs into its own hands, having exiled the other or suppressed them within the city. And not content with pillaging each other, they spat out their poison against us, and drove within our borders in hope of plunder some troops of Emperor Charles III which that outburst of madness earlier had brought into Tuscany.

After the emperor's departure, at a moment when the Floren- 57 tine people remained deeply wounded by this unjust act, the foreigners, whom the pride of the natives had expelled, captured the mountains around that fortress, and our commune shut down all the approaches to the town by siege works, forming a system of

obsidionis indagine clausit. Tunc autem domini tui socer et pa-
truus Bernabos, aeterna nepotis et generi sui nota, castrum illud
de manibus imperialis vicarii suscipiens, sic obsessum magna gentium suarum potentia munit. Florentini versa vice obsidionem ur-
gent, castella multiplicant, munitiones extendunt fameque cogunt
populum et inclusa tyranni subsidia laborare. Compulsus igitur
Bernabos obsessis opem ferre, Iohannem Haukud — Anglicorum,
qui latrociniis vexabant Italiam, ducem — stipendio magno con-
duxit; cumque Pisarum in finibus haberent castra, Florentini sperantes victoriam ad expugnandum eos omnes suas equestres copias
et capitaneum transmiserunt.

58   Sed nullis in rebus mortalium votis ordinationibusque re-
spondet minus spes et audacia quam in bellis. Aquarum enim
copia caenosum solum et itineris defatigatio et sui fiducia, cum
infestis signis nostrae gentes nimis audacter in hostes ruunt, ex-
spectantibus victoriam dedit captoque capitaneo cunctisque nostris copiis profligatis, post biduum excurrunt hostes obsidionem
solvere liberareque conclusos. Florentini vero, quo Romanum genus scias, maiorum nostrorum more rebus adversis animosiores,
novis praesidiis cuncta firmaverant moxque, conspectis hostibus,
non sicut mos est victis sed animo quo victores, non stant, quod
satis erat, pro vallo solum sed extra munitiones occurrentes hostibus manus conferunt, vim repellunt, et mirantes resistentiam hostes retrocedere pedemque sistere coegerunt.

59   Interea venit dux hostium, rei bellicae peritissimus, considerat
castri situm, munitionum opportunitatem, audaciam obsidentium
nihilque minus ratus quam cum illis temptare fortunam, via, quae
dabatur, aliquos in oppidum mittit, qui vix obtento transitu

castles.[81] At that time your lord's uncle and father-in-law, Bernabò, source of eternal infamy to his nephew and son-in-law,[82] had received the fortress from the hands of the imperial vicar and had garrisoned the besieged place with a large force of his men-at-arms. The Florentines in response stepped up the siege and multiplied their castles, adding more outposts and forcing the inhabitants, and the tyrant's troops with them inside, to suffer hunger. Thus compelled to aid to the besieged, Bernabò decided to hire, at great cost, John Hawkwood, leader of the English [mercenaries] then harrying all Italy with their depredations; since they had their camps in the territory of Pisa, the Florentines in hope of victory sent their entire cavalry and their commander to capture them.

But in no affairs do hope and audacity correspond less to the 58 wishes and plans of mortals than in warfare.[83] The ground, muddy with heavy rainfall, the fatigue of travel, and excessive confidence all gave victory to the besieged and not to our soldiers, who had met the enemy attack with too much boldness; two days later, with our captain a prisoner and the army put to rout, the enemy advanced with the aim of lifting the siege and liberating the captive population. But the Florentines, to show you what Roman ancestry means, were in the Roman way made even bolder by adversity. They strengthened their fortifications with new emplacements; and then, as the enemies advanced, with the spirit of victors and not of the vanquished, they were not satisfied with standing in front of the ramparts, but went out beyond the defenses to meet the enemy and engage him in hand-to-hand combat, repelling his attack. The enemy, amazed at this resistance, were compelled to fall back and stop their attack.

Meanwhile there arrived the enemy commander, who was 59 highly experienced in warfare, and after pondering the location of the town, the chances offered by the siege works, and not least the boldness of the besiegers, he decided, rather than tempting fate with them, he would instead send a few men into the town by a

tandem intra suorum moenia recepti sunt. Ex consilio quidem, cum intrantes oneri futuros obsessis scirent, plena resistentia facta non est; satis enim fuit ostendere quod poterant facile prohiberi. Processit ergo dux illarum gentium et castra movens infestis signis urbem nostram petit et, cum nullus esset resistendi modus, portis imminet et agros undique populatur. Interea nostri—fide et industria simplicis cuiusdam hominis, cui Luparello nomen erat, oppidi muro fracto—nocturnum occupant aditum; fit ingens intra municipium clamor, caeduntur vigiles, magna pars exercitus nostri irrupit intus subitoque totum obtinet oppidum et quicquid ibi[20] tyranni copiarum fuit nostris praeda fuere, nisi qui potuerunt ad arcis praesidium penetrare.

60   Nuntius huius insperatae victoriae post ortum solis venit in urbem moxque tanta fuit in civitate laetitia, tantus plausus[21] quantum calamus non posset exprimere. Simul et hostes, exercitus scilicet Anglicorum, occupationis accepta notitia, tanta rerum novitate perculsus abiit et versus amissum oppidum, si quid forte recuperari posset, properanter pergunt. Nostri vero cum oppidanis arcem et quod ibi praesidium erat magis undique clamoribus aggrediuntur et expugnare parant. Illi suis viribus locoque—licet munitissimo et inexpugnabili—diffidentes, deditionem faciunt et recedunt illaesi; nostri, potiti loco, viperam vestram, quae flabellante vexillo turri summae celsitudinis insidebat, in praeceps deturbant, tanta letitia tantoque oppidanorum favore et alacritate quantam vix fecisse Graecia legitur cum T. Quintius Flamininus edicto consulari cunctas Graeciae civitates quae Philippi iugum tulerant liberas et immunes esse pronuntiavit.

way that had opened up; these men, having with difficulty gotten through, were at length received within the walls of their allies. Our side, realizing that inside the walls these soldiers would be more a burden than a help to the besieged, intentionally avoided strong opposition, content to show them that if they had wanted, they could have stopped them easily. Thus the commander of the enemy forces set out, and breaking camp, he headed for Florence under hostile standards. Since there was no way for her to resist, he threatened her gates and devastated the countryside on all sides. In the meantime, our forces entered the town by night through a breach, thanks to the loyalty and efforts of a humble man called Luperello. A great commotion broke out inside the town, the sentinels were slaughtered, and a great part of our army entered and quickly took hold of the town. They took as plunder whatever belonged to the troops of the tyrant, except for those who were able to penetrate to the citadel of the city.[84]

Word of this unexpected victory reached the city after dawn, 60 and the joy and the jubilation in the streets were indescribable. In the meantime the enemy—the English army—having learned the news of the occupation of San Miniato, were thoroughly shaken by the novelty of the situation and went away and hastened in the direction of the town they had lost to see if there was anything they could recover. But our troops, with the townsmen, marched out with great clamor on all sides and made ready to capture the citadel with its garrison. The enemy did not trust their own strength or their situation, well-defended and impregnable though it was, so surrendered and marched away unharmed. Our forces took control, throwing down the standard displaying your viper that had been flapping from the top of the tower, to the joy and approval of the whole populace, and an eagerness even greater than in Greece when (we read) Titus Quintius Flamininus announced that the cities once under Philip were, in fulfillment of a consular edict, made free and exempt from tribute.[85]

61   Haec fuit nostra Sancti Miniatis receptio; quod quidem divina
manu datum recepimus, nec rebellionem devotissimus ille populus
ullis umquam temporibus attentavit, sed novitati — quam impro-
bus ille proditor, quem liberatorem patriae vocas, anno nonage-
simo sexto praeteriti saeculi turpiter temerereque tentavit — solus
populus Sancti Miniatis, sine nostris aliis gentibus, mira concordia
restitit, et eum igni ferroque circumsaeptum viriliter expulit et nisi
socios deseruisset, beneficio noctis aufugiens, ipsum virum (ut
opinaris) magnanimum, confecissent.[22] Ut mirandum sit qua ratione post illa verba quae rettuli, 'tam cito properata rebellio,' subie-
ceris: 'Ex qua quid animi sit ceteris municipiis atque urbibus pari
servientibus calamitate licet intelligatis. Quibus, mihi credite, illius
magnanimi quidem sed vel praecipitis nimium vel proditi atque
deserti liberatoris patriae exsilium nequaquam prae metu voluntates exstinguet, sed admonebit ut diligentius cogitent suis rebus
esse consulendum.'

62   Ex tam cito properata rebellione deducis nobis licitum intelligere 'quid animi sit reliquis municipiis atque urbibus pari calamitate servientibus.' Si verum est exemplum, tenendum est nobis
omnibus subditis nostris animum esse firmissimum ut nihil mutari cupiant et quod futuri sint cunctis res novas tentantibus inimici. Fuit ille vir magnanimus, de quo sentis, in palatio vicarii.
Mactavit optimum virum — cuius nomen, cum pro patria oppetie-
rit, nulla umquam delebit oblivio — proditor infandus iste, quem
laudas; mactavit, inquam, senem iuvenis amicabiliter receptus, armatus inermem, confidentem perfidus, bellicosus imbellem, multis
stipatus sociis paene solum, provisus incautum, ut nihil indignabi-
lius, ut nihil effeminatius et inhonestius, ut nihil pusillanimius, ut

Such was our recapture of San Miniato: we took that which   61
was given us by the divine hand, nor did that devoted populace
ever try to rebel; on the contrary, by itself and without asking help
of our other subjects and with remarkable concord among the inhabitants, the people of San Miniato opposed the coup attempt of
that low and mad traitor—whom you call liberator of his country—in '96 of the last century. It surrounded him brandishing
torches and arms and drove him out, and if that magnanimous
man (as you think him) hadn't fled under cover of darkness, abandoning his followers, it would have killed him.[86] I am surprised to
read that after the phrase just cited, *the sudden revolt that followed
afterward,* you add, *so that you may come to understand the kind of spirit
that animates other towns and cities subjected to a like calamity for those
enslaved. Believe me: the exile of that magnanimous liberator of his country—even though he was too hasty (or perhaps was just betrayed and
abandoned)—far from blunting their wills with fear, will just teach them
that they need to be more careful when taking counsel about their own affairs.*

According to you from *the sudden revolt that followed afterward* we   62
ought to understand *the kind of spirit that animates other towns and
cities subjected to a like calamity for those enslaved.* But if we may rely
upon this example, we ought to deduce that all our subjects are
firmly resolved not to change government and will be hostile to
anyone with subversive aims. That man you call magnanimous was
at the time in the vicar's palace. This miserable traitor, whom you
exalt, killed a most excellent citizen, whose sacrifice for his country will make his name remembered forever.[87] More precisely, after
having been received kindly, a young man killed an old man, an
armed man a defenseless man, an evil man a good man, a violent
man a peaceful man, a man supported by henchmen a man practically alone, a schemer a trusting man. The traitor could have committed no act more low, womanish and dishonorable; no act more

nihil illaudabilius, ut nihil ignavius, ut nihil ingloriosius, ut nihil timidius et tandem nihil undique sceleratius potuerit perpetrari.

63   Magnanimum licet hunc voces qui scelestas manus contra patriam movit pro tyranno Florentinis pro naturalique Florentini nominis inimico, non ut dominaretur, quod saltem alti spiritus est, sed ut, quo nihil miserius cogitari potest, in servitutem submersa patria tanti mali causa sceleratiore quam alii servitute serviret. Sperabat, tamen, ingentes forte divitias, magna stipendia, maximam domini confidentiam et altissimum sibi statum et alia multa, quae scelerata facinora cogitantes sibi proponunt quibusque quandoque promissis potitum iri sine dubitatione confidunt, quae tamen licet plerumque magna ex parte succedant, semper in uno deficiunt. Numquam enim proditores confidentiam assequi potuerunt; semper namque formidolosi sunt ne redeuntes ad ingenium fidem rumpant.

64   Et, ut hanc particulam concludamus, semel Dei digito castrum illud in fidem protectionemque recepimus, occupantem ipsum vestram viperam excludentes, nulla per Dei gratiam umquam oppidanorum rebellio fuit secuta, sed semper in fide manserunt. Aliquotiens per improbos quosdam, culpa et scelere domini tui, cum in pace secum essemus, fraudulens temptata proditio; et illa 'tam cito properata rebellio,' de qua tangis, rebellio quidem properata non fuit: viginti septem, enim, annis iam exactis, postquam castrum illud additum nobis est, rebellionem attentavit proditor ille patriae quem magnanimum vocas. Melius tamen praecipitem dicis; non desertum, ut ais, sed plane desertorem honoris, famae, patriae sociorumque quos fugiens prodidit atque deseruit. Attentavit enim rebellionem, non perfecit; erat in palatio, quod praesidium quoddam est, et non mediocre praesidium, magnanimus ille tuus proditor et, sicut erat unius factionis princeps, clamat et invocat ille suos; hortatur omnes ad libertatem ad finemque

cowardly, blameworthy, and base; no act more shameful, no act more weak and, to sum it all up, no act more utterly evil.

Call magnanimous, if you like, a person who conspired wick- 63 edly against his own country in order to assist the natural enemy of Florence who was seeking to become tyrant of Florence — call magnanimous a man who so acted, not in order to become a lord (which at least would have been a sign of a noble spirit) but — pathetic beyond imagination — to be a slave to another man, and the very man responsible for the enslavement of his own country to boot. That "magnanimous" man hoped as well, perhaps, to gain great sums of money, rich rewards, the complete trust of his lord, high place and so forth, all such things as are sought by men who plot crimes like this and who feel sure of success when promised such rewards. Often they do succeed, but one thing always evades their grasp: traitors have never inspired trust and there are always those who fear they will return to their old ways and break faith.[88]

And, to finish off this section, once we had taken that town 64 under our protection and safekeeping by the finger of God, turning the viper out of its new lair, no episodes of revolt by the citizens ever took place afterward, thank God, and they stayed completely faithful to Florence. It is true that some rascals have tried now and then to mount acts of delusive treachery, spurred by your lord in time of peace, but that *sudden revolt that followed afterward* which you write of hardly followed immediately: it was twenty-seven years after our conquest of the town that the traitor of his country you call magnanimous tried to spark a revolt.[89] You do better to call him "hasty"; he wasn't "abandoned," however; if anything he is the one who abandoned honor, fame, his country, and his companions, whom he betrayed and abandoned in his flight. He tried to foment a revolt, in fact, but he failed; he found himself in the palace of your magnanimous traitor, that is in a garrison and not a mean one, and as head of a faction he collected and appealed to his men, exhorting them to retake their liberty, spurring

tributorum et onerum, quae gravissima quidem sunt malitia temporum, omnes oppidanos invitat, quibus cogitabat ut facile poterat
animos audientium[23] permovere. Clamat, inquam, ille; silet populus et utraque factio, depositis contrariis dissensionum studiis, in
unum coeunt, arma sumunt, palatium circumdant et illum — suorum requirentem fidem, promittentem omnibus omnia — cuncti
clamoribus, igni ferroque petunt, palatii pontem et portam incen-
dunt. Ille dimissa sociorum parte per posticum fugit.

65   Eiecta peste sublatoque periculo, cuncti laetitia simul exsul-
tantes superis gratias agunt; dominis suis, a quibus petebant auxilia, rem significant. Et quis in illa rerum novitate de tanto populo
repertus est, qui non summis studiis exitium eius intenderet, ser-
varet fidem dominis et exclusionem proditoris non laetaretur, fu-
gam salutemque doleret? Quae cum ita sint (clarissima quidem
sunt), quam 'Sancti Miniatis fortunatam receptionem' vocas, immo
vocare potes, nisi primam illam, quam seriose descripsi? Quam
'properatam rebellionem' appellas, quae cum secuta non sit, rebellio dici nequit? Nam si defensionem illam contra maledicti proditoris illius conatus factam Sancti Miniatis receptionem intelligis, si
conatus illos acceleratam forte nimis rebellionem dicis, cur ad
verba confugis quae non possint significare quod intendis quaeque
non possint rebus gestis, ut ipsas exprimant, convenire? Nihil minus oratorium est quam dubiis et aliud quam intendas significanti-
bus verbis uti. Sibyllarum et oraculorum est hoc, non oratorum,
quibus vel maximum vitium est, ut inquit eloquentiae summae
Cicero, 'a vulgari genere orationis atque a consuetudine communis
sensus abhorrere.' Ut me verum dixisse clarum sit: te rationem
dicendi, vel parte minima, non tenere. Sed in ulteriora quae, stultitia fretus tua, subicis penetremus.

the entire citizenry to put an end to tribute and levies — which indeed are grave evils of our time — hoping by this to easily gather popular favor. He rallied the people, indeed, but they met him with silence, and the two factions set aside their feuds and joined together; arming themselves, they surrounded the palace and — at the very moment he was calling his own for help and promising big things to the rest — attacked him with bold shouts, torches and arms, setting fire to the palace bridge and gate. He dismissed a part of his allies and escaped by a back door.

Free of that conspirator and out of danger, happy and delirious 65 with joy, all thanked the gods above; after which they reported what had happened to their governors, from whom they were used to receiving aid. And in the midst of that coup attempt, was there anyone out of that large population who did not use every effort to suppress the traitor, who did not remain loyal to their governors and did not rejoice to see the traitor shut out, who was not grieved to see him escape unharmed? Things being so (and the facts are clear as day) what was, indeed, what could be the "happy conquest of San Miniato" to use your words, if not the first event that I have just narrated in minute detail? And what, still using your words, would be "the sudden revolt," since the episode did not in fact lead to a revolt and cannot be so defined? For if by the reconquest of San Miniato you mean the resistance made against that infamous traitor and if you wish to pass off that attempt as a sudden revolt, why do you use words that disagree with the ideas and deeds you speak of? Nothing is further from eloquence than to use words that are unclear or that have a sense different from your meaning. The sibyls and the oracles may speak in this way, not orators, whose worst vice, as the greatest orator Cicero tells us, is to "distance oneself from daily speech and the customary practices of common sense."[90] That confirms my earlier statement that you know little or naught of the rules of rhetoric. But come, let us see what else you write in your madness.

66   *Age, postquam ad hunc locum pedetemptim fluxit oratio, ut in quem*
formidabilem casum prolapsi sitis et in quam praecipitem foveam incideri-
tis, si adeo estis dementes ac caeci ut non videatis, ostendat. Respondere vos
cupio quibus e locis quibusve de horreis inediae vestrae subveniendum iri
existimatis, cum ager hic omnis quem aratis suapte natura sit Cereri adver-
sus, ut pace integra atque secura ad victum urbis ipse non suppetat; hostili-
bus flammis ardebit et undique belli clade vastabitur, nisi forte Siciliam,
horreum populi Romani vestrumque frumentarium, hac aetate praesidium
subventuram esse putetis. Sed videte eo vos portu esse privatos quo vitam et
spiritum ducere solebatis et per Alpium iuga, ex agro Flaminio, quomodo
satisfieri possit tantae multitudini iudicate, cum sit transitus ipse difficilis
etiam omni carens molestia belli. At si ad difficultatem viarum accesserit
itinerum infesta turbatio, quae cessare in bello longe lateque diffuso non
potest, cogitare non possum, nisi Iuppiter ipse vobis de caelo pluat fruges,
vos vel fame sola non esse perituros.

67   Et quoniam satis est tua verba scripsisse, non resumam aliter
quae subnectis; respondebo tamen ad id quod quaeris, quibus videlicet e locis et quibus ex horreis inediae nostrae subveniendum
existimemus. Respondebo quidem tibi nos subventuros victui nostro ex horreis nostris, ex agro Florentino et ex illa Italiae parte
quam T. Livius, historicorum nobilissimus, ut verba sua referam,
dicit quod 'regio sit in primis Italiae fertilis, Etrusci campi, qui
Faesulas inter Arretiumque iacent, frumenti ac pecoris et omni
copia rerum opulenti.' Qui postquam in dicionem venerunt nostram, Dei gratia, nobis ad affluentiam suffecerunt. Nec hostiles
flammas bellicaeque cladis vastationem mineris precor; experti
quidem omnia sumus scimusque quid soleant quidque possint
ista nocere. Dimitte nobis curam hanc, nec portum, quem acco-
modatissimum nobis fateor, ablatum nobis obicias. Bella quidem

Come then! My discourse has arrived step by step to the point where it 66
should show you — if you are not so insane and blind that you don't see it
yourselves — the fearful collapse that is upon you, the steep pit into which
you have fallen. I would like you to tell me where and what supplies of
grain you will draw upon in order to feed the population, since your terri-
tory is by nature infertile, too poor to meet the needs of the city even in
times of peace. Your enemies will set fires and make raids everywhere, un-
less you think Sicily, granary of the Roman people and your main source of
cereals, will help you this time. But you need to recall that you may no
longer count on the port from which you used to draw life and breath, and
consider how difficult it would be to transport grain for so great a multitude
from Emilia Romagna across the Apennines, a difficult track even without
the obstacles caused by a war. But if to the difficulty of transport you add
the hostile disturbance of travel typical of a war waged over a wide terri-
tory, I really don't know how you can help dying just from famine, unless
Jupiter in person delivers grain from the skies.

Since it is sufficient to have transcribed your very words, I shall 67
not rehearse what you add to them; I will limit myself to replying
to your question, where and from what storehouses we think to
find grain enough to feed ourselves. My reply is that we shall sup-
ply our need for victuals from our own granaries, from the Florentine countryside and from that part of Italy which the greatest
historian, Livy, termed "a region among Italy's most fertile, those
Etruscan fields that extend between Fiesole and Arezzo, rich in
grain, livestock and all the products of the earth."[91] Thanks be to
God, from the time these lands have entered our jurisdiction they
have more than satisfied our needs. And please do without threatening us with enemy fires and raids; we have already been through
all that. We know about the things that are usually do harm and
that can harm. Don't concern yourself on our account, and don't
throw up against us the loss of the port, which I admit is a highly
convenient one. We have fought a great many wars against the
Pisans and our not having that port has always been of more harm

plurima gessimus cum Pisanis plusque nocuit eis nos portum illum non habere quam nobis. Nam quod de Flaminia dicis (adde, si placet, Umbriam et Picenum) non potest, ut autumas, impediri, nec adhuc bellum, quod nobis illatum fuerit, fame nos affecit, licet aliquando pretio res venierint cariori; meminerisque quod cui pecunia suppetit nihil desit, et impossibile prorsus esse quod urbem nostram possit aliquis, vel tuus dominus, obsidere. Nec metuas Iovem frumenta nobis de caelo pluiturum; satis erit si mediocriter nobis terra nostra respondeat.

68   Sed quid hoc disputo? Transactum est bellum illud, quod nec famem intulit nec caritudinem nobis fecit. Tantum quidem soli tuentur urbis nostrae moenia tuenturque civitates et oppida quae tenemus, tuentur montes et flumina, tuentur inaccessibilia loca, tuebitur et nostra potentia, quod frustra tu et alii talem nobiscum reputabitis rationem, sicut hactenus experientia docuit et per Dei gratiam edocebit. Et ut Iovem omittam tuum, quem scimus nihil esse nisi stultitiam gentium quae manuum suarum opera, veluti divinum aliquid, adorabant, scio quod Deus atque natura mortalibus invisibiliter pluit et efficit unde vivant. Et sicut solet et potest Deus uno anno populo suo, licet maximo, non victum solum sed ubertatem et copiam inextimabilem dare, sic et poterit multis annis. Et sicut Israel suum longo tractu temporis in deserto sine frugibus pavit, sic per misericordiam suam populum pascet suum medioque bellorum fremitu dabit et tuebitur nobis fruges retribuetque nobis misericordiam quam numquam huius populi benignitas pauperibus suis negavit et nedum suis, sed etiam alienis.

69   Et quis in orbe terrarum populus qui sumptu publico, cum penuria vel fames saevit, subveniat impotentium paupertati sicut populus Florentinus? Satis est ceteris horrea habere, de quibus

to them than to us. In fact, what you say about the impossibility of transport between us and Emilia Romagna (and add Umbria and the Marches, if you like) is untrue, and furthermore, until now no war started against us has ever reduced us to starvation, although some wars have raised prices; and don't forget that whoever has money in abundance will never be wanting for anything, and that no one (your lord included) will ever succeed in besieging our city. You need have no fear that Jupiter will have to rain down grain from the skies; it's quite enough that our fields produce an average harvest.

But why am I even debating the subject? That war took place 68 and it ended without our being reduced to famine or shortages. Great is the space embraced by the walls of Florence, that the fortified cities and towns we control embrace, that our mountains and rivers embrace, that the most remote areas embrace, that our power embraces; it is so great that you and others will reckon up accounts like that with us in vain, as experience has hitherto taught us and, please God, will continue to teach us. And to leave aside your Jupiter — who exists only as the foolishness of the pagans, who adored the work of their own hands as though it were something divine — I know that God and nature invisibly bring down rain upon us mortals and give us the sources of life. And just as God can (and usually does) grant his people, though many, enough to eat in a year and even much more than needed, so he will be able to do the same for multiple years. And just as He long fed his Israel in the desert without help of crops,[92] so too by his mercy He will bestow crops upon us and protect them, and he will pay us back for the mercy that the loving-kindness of this people has never denied to the poor — and not only our own poor, but that of foreign peoples.

Does any other people in the world relieve the poverty of the 69 powerless like the Florentine people do when famine and scarcity are raging? The rest are satisfied with maintaining granaries from

257

alimenta tali pretio depromantur quod rei publicae non sint damno. Pietas autem Florentina, considerans quod magnitudinem pretii ferre non possent inopes, quotidianum panem ordinat multisque locis urbis velut penora statuit, ubi panis vili pretio pauperibus, iuxta familiae numerum, dispensatur. Stat et farina publica semper in foro tali pretio quod non possunt divites, quibus venalia frumenta sunt, pauperes obsidere, talique diligentia res frumentaria disponitur quod illa, qua premuntur vicini, caritudo intra nostra moenia non sentitur. Quae quidem provisio, nostra memoria, solius anni spatio plus exhausit quam centum et quinquaginta milia florenorum; nec umquam incubuit tam gravis et acerba fames quod etiam forenses pauperes pellerentur urbe, qui venerant, vel prohiberentur introitu qui venirent.

70   Et quando credis Deum tantae misericordiae meritis defuturum? Cogitaverunt iam officiales ecclesiae fame nos opprimere, cum Sicilia simul et Apulia caritudine laborarent, et ferme quicquid erat in Italia frumenti, totum in manibus eorum esset. Sed aperuit Deus nobis insulas et horrea paganorum ministravitque nobis Mauritania, ministravit et Teucria quantum oportuit, ut noster populus aleretur. Et tu sperabas nos fame perituros, quos numquam Deus deseruit sed ubertatem maximam, illius belli tempore, sua benignitate concessit? Et quoniam rerum exitus docuit te penitus, cum illa scriberes, somniasse, satis sit quod proxime dictum est et articulum qui sequitur fideliter rescribamus.

71   Procedens igitur inquis: *An fortasse fines vestros tueri posse confiditis? Ego sane non video tantum virium vobis esse ut quattuor equitum legionibus, tot enim contra vos armantur, possitis obstare. 'At socii ferent opem rebus afflictis.' Digna quidem res in summo periculo auxilia*

which sustenance is handed out at a price that doesn't cause a loss to the state. The Florentines' sense of religious duty, recognizing that those without resources cannot sustain inflated prices, has organized a daily distribution of bread and has established storehouses in many places of the city where bread is made available inexpensively to the poor, in proportion to the size of their families. The market is never short of grain ground by the state at a price which prevents rich merchants from speculating upon the poor, and great pains are taken to store enough grain so that any famine in neighboring lands is not felt within our city walls. This provision has cost us, within living memory, over one hundred fifty thousand florins in a given year, nor has there ever been a famine so harsh and heavy that poor outsiders who have taken refuge in the city have been driven out, nor have those who have come to our gates been refused entry.

Do you perhaps think that one day God will cease to repay   70
such good actions? Already once before the officials of the Church hoped to take us by famine, in a period when Sicily and Apulia were suffering dearth and the officials controlled practically all the wheat to be had in Italy. But God put at our disposal the islands and the granaries of the pagans, so that Mauretania and even the Turks furnished us with what was needed to feed our people.[93] And you were hoping we would die of hunger, we whom God has never abandoned and to whom He granted of his goodwill the greatest abundance during that conflict? But since the outcome of events has taught us that you were dreaming when you were writing that, it will be enough just to faithfully transcribe what was said next and the section following.

Going on, then, you say: *Are you perhaps confident you can protect*   71
your borders? I don't think you quite have sufficient forces to be able to resist four legions of horse, for those are the forces being armed against you. "But the allies will reinforce us when we are in dire straits." Nothing forbids

implorare sociorum. Sed quis umquam vobis socius fuit cui vestra superbia non invisa sit? Quem non tergiversationum vestrarum fastidia satiarint? Qui non vos oderit? Qui non vestra calamitate laetetur, ut si sine suo periculo fieri possit, vos deleri funditus atque ex orbe terrarum exturbari non optet? An inania fortassis et falsa fingo? Bononienses velim hac in parte respondeant, qui iam annos novem vobiscum societate et foedere sunt coniuncti, qui primo, cum inter eos ducemque Liguriae dissensio nulla esset, vestram societatem amicitiamque secuti, priori sese bello non necessario implicuerunt, et cum pace in summa possent spectatores esse alienae fortunae, suam pro salute vestra in discrimen adducere maluerunt et eo in bello cuius molem paene totam suis humeris sustinendam esse viderent. Quam enim aliam offensionem dux iste Ligusticus, cum bellum indiceret, illis obiecit nisi quod aequo nimis vestram amicitiam foventes sese vestros omnino sequaces effecissent? Qua re dubitandum est nemini, si sese a vestris foederibus abscidissent, illius belli onus sibi nequaquam fuisse subeundum. Sed valuit sociorum integritas, valuit amor, valuit opinio. Itaque in rebus duris atque asperis vos, contra quod dignum erat, praepotenti et vicino domino, magno cum suo periculo, praetulerunt.

72   *Vos vero contra hos amicos et socios tam propitios, tam constantes, tam veteres, tam probatos, quales deinde in media pace fueritis ipsi norunt et omnis, non sine stupore quodam, vidit Italia. Hoc mihi, quamquam sitis impudentissimi, non negaturos esse confido: vos cum his tam fidelibus sociis non mediocrem controversiam habuisse vestra culpa susceptam, parumque abfuisse quin bello atque armis totam eam causam decerneretis, neque ullum amicitiae vetus officium, non communium fortunarum laborumque memoriam, quae una in coniungendis animis hominum valeat plurimum,*

invoking the help of allies when the situation is desperate. But have you ever had an ally that did not begrudge you your arrogance? Is there perhaps a single one that is not disgusted by your continual hesitations? That does not hate you? That does not rejoice at your misadventures, that would not want to see you defeated once for all and chased off the face of the earth, if it could happen without danger to themselves? Are they falsehoods and pure inventions, these words of mine? I would like to hear the reply of the Bolognese, who for these nine years now have been tied to you in a pact of alliance. By the mere fact of having united themselves with you and become your friends, they found themselves involved in that first conflict, against their will and without there having been any reason for discord with the Duke of Liguria; indeed they could well have stood aside as peaceful spectators but chose instead to risk their security for the sake of yours, and that in a war where the greater burden was clearly to be their own. In fact, what accusation did the said Duke of Liguria make against them in declaring war, but that of having shown excessive friendship for you, more than was fair, and so becoming your followers entirely? Truly no one doubts that if they had dissolved the alliance made with you they would never have been forced to uphold that burdensome war. But their integrity as an ally prevailed, their affection prevailed, their concern for reputation prevailed. And so, in dire and stressful circumstances, they preferred you to a most powerful lord and near neighbor, contrary to what was the appropriate course and exposing themselves to a grave threat.

On the other hand, how you have behaved in times of peace toward 72 *these friends and allies — so benevolent, so faithful, of such long standing and trustworthiness! — they well know and all Italy, not without astonishment, has seen. I trust that, despite your incredible effrontery, you will not deny what I am about to say: with these faithful allies you engaged in a controversy of no little moment through your own fault, and you were nearly at the point of resolving the question by armed warfare. But you were held back, not by any sense of duty toward old friendship, not by the memory of shared successes and labors — that which does the most to unite the hearts of men — not by the desire for harmony, not by any special favor*

non concordiae curam, non ullius gratiam societatis, non denique religio-
nem foederum tenuisse sed metum. Hic unus vobis contra socios, contra fi-
dem, contra divina et humana iura furentibus extorsit arma de manibus.

73   *Hi ergo nunc socii humeros suos ruinae vestrae subiciant? Non sunt*
adeo, ut opinor, insani ut pro his, quos non sine ratione deletos atque deper-
ditos velint, arma suscipiant. 'Sed accurrent,' dicet aliquis, 'ad commune
periculum repellendum, ad commune incendium restinguendum.' Primum
quidem intelligunt neque periculum neque hoc bellum esse commune quod
vos propriis furoribus accendistis, atque ideo vobis solis sustinendum non
iniuria existimabunt. Deinde, si qua suspicio occupabit animos et fueritis in
ea fingenda fortunati quod sine ulla intermissione temptatis efficere, profecto
magis erit eis curae pro suis defendendis finibus, quam pro vestris liberan-
dis, praesidia comparare.

74   *A tribus vero tyrannis quid auxilii sit sperandum non satis intelligo;*
alterius enim tenues atque afflictae sunt, alterius nondum reintegratae for-
tunae, ut hi ope aliena magis indigeant. A tertio vero tantum abest ut
quicquam exspectetis auxilii, ut cum ipse circumsaeptus undique in medio
belli flagrabit incendio, Florentinam opem ac fidem frustra imploraturus
esse videatur. Qua re desinite vobis spes vanas et inutiles conflare de sociis,
sed cogitate potius qua ratione, qua spe, quo denique fato atque fortuna vos
soli tantam belli magnitudinem subeatis.

75   *'An fortasse fines vestros tueri posse confiditis?'* Tune hoc, Lom-
barde, nos interrogas? Et qua nos potes ob hoc coniectura quove
exemplo terrere? Florentinusne vigor et huius populi magnanimi-
tas defendendaeque libertatis studium an forte defecit? Crede
mihi, longe maiore nos animo dispositos esse libertatem nostram
asserere tuerique quam vos—ignavia pusillanimitateque vestra,
qua nulla maior in orbe terrarum est—assuetos pati foedissimam

owed to the alliance, still less by the sacred bond of treaties, but simply by fear. It was this alone that tore the arms from your furious hands, keeping you from war against your allies, against your oath, and against all law, human and divine.

And these allies are now to lift you on their shoulders and save you from 73 *ruin? I do not consider them so foolish as to take up arms to help the very ones they should want to see, not without reason, defeated and destroyed. "But they will come running," someone will say, "to repel a common danger and extinguish a fire that threatens them as well." In the first place they understand that neither the danger nor this war is a matter of common concern: it was something your own furies ignited, and they will reckon, not without justice, that you alone should wage it. Then, if they start to harbor doubts and you turn out to be lucky in the plots you are continually trying to bring off, they will surely be much more concerned to guard their own borders than to liberate yours.*

In addition, I fail to understand what help you expect to get from three 74 *tyrants, one of whom is weak and ruined in his fortunes, while another has yet to recover from his misfortunes, so that both stand themselves in need of help. From the third there is so little hope of assistance that it will likely be he, trapped on all sides amid the fires of war, who will beg for Florentine aid and loyalty—and in vain. So leave off concocting these great and useless hopes about your allies and think rather in what way, with what likelihood of success, and with what fate and fortune you may endure a war on so large a scale.*

Are you perhaps confident you can protect your borders? You, a 75 Lombard, put this question to us? And by what inference, with what example could you make us afraid on this account? Has it ever happened that the Florentine people lacked the energy, greatness of soul or the determination to defend its own liberty? Heed me: we are much more ready to proclaim our liberty and to protect it than you—with your baseness and cowardice, unequaled in all the world—are accustomed to submit to foul

servitutem. 'Assuetos' dixi, non 'dispositos,' ne videar (sicut tu) de occultis alieni cordis temere iudicare. Forte quidem, quoniam quandoque redit in praecordia virtus, poterit aliquando spiritus Italicus — si prorsus Guinulorum, id est Longobardorum, sanguis posteritasque non estis — in vobis etiam excitari; poteritis adhuc forte vos animi vigore sicut et lege liberos appellare civesque Romanos poteritisque turpe, si Deus vult, excutere iugum vosque Galliam Cisalpinam et Gallorum genus gloriosissimum reminisci, cuius proprium est regia libertate frui, tyrannos odisse ac velut horrendum aliquid abominari vel levissimam servitutem.

76   Et ut ad nos redeam, cum perstet animus, suppetant vires, adsit et virtus, fines nostros confidimus nos sine dubio defensum ire. Et licet, ut subdis, tu sane non videas tantum virium nobis esse ut quattuor equitum legionibus — tot enim, ut inquis, contra nos armantur — possimus obstare, videmus et sentimus nos, qui scimus audaciam in bello pro muro haberi, qui novimus victoriam non in exercitus multitudine sed in manibus Dei esse, qui scimus pro nobis esse iustitiam, qui recordamur, quod tu negas, nos genus esse Romanum, qui legimus maiores nostros contra vim maximam hostium saepissime restitisse parvaque manu non solum defendisse res suas, sed insperatam habuisse victoriam. Videmus et sentimus, inquam, nos, qui prioris belli fortunam et exitum recordamur, et scimus nos de domini tui manibus Paduam et quicquid circa montes tenebat Euganeos eruisse.

77   Scimus et inclitum marchionem Estensem — qui sibi demens adhaeserat, ab eo contra foedera derelictum et, ardente belli turbine, de statu proprio laborantem — nos sibi socium ademisse, quique secum contra nos bellum hostis noster inceperat, nobiscum et pro parte nostra, nondum etiam socius, foedera pacis inivit.

slavery. I said "habituated," not "disposed," so as to avoid the impression, unlike you, of expressing reckless judgments about the hidden places of another person's heart. Perhaps, since virtue sometimes can be reignited in a heart, the Italic spirit will burn in you again,[94] provided you are not wholly and completely the blood and branch of the Guinoli, that is the Lombards; perhaps you may yet by strength of mind and by law come to call yourselves free and Roman citizens; perhaps you may, if God wills it, shake off the shameful yoke and remember Cisalpine Gaul and the glorious race of the Gauls, to whom it belongs to enjoy a royal liberty, to hate tyrants, and to regard with revulsion even the slightest servitude.[95]

But to return to us, since our spirit is steadfast, strength is not 76 lacking and valor assists us, we are confident that we will defend our frontier. And although you affirm that we haven't enough strength to resist four legions of cavalry such as, you claim, are ready to advance upon us, we see and we feel that strength: we, who know that in war courage is the true defense, certain that victory lies not in the number of soldiers but in the hands of God;[96] and we know that justice is on our side, mindful of our Roman origins (which you deny); we, who read how our ancestors have resisted huge enemy forces so many times, and how with few soldiers they not only defended the country but won unhoped-for victories. We see and we feel that strength, I say, mindful of the favorable outcome of the last war and aware that we have torn from your lord's hands Padua and all his possessions around the Euganean Hills.

We know also that the noble marquis of Este—who foolishly 77 made alliance with your lord only to discover himself left alone (in defiance of treaties) and in grave danger in the midst of the raging storm of war—was drawn away from this alliance by us, passing from our enemy at the start of war to our side at the signing of peace, even prior to becoming our formal ally. We know how your

Scimus eum—cum inter Lolium et Abduam invictum exercitum nostrum, fines vastantem suos, magno periculo gravique clade sustinuerit ultra mensem vix octo diebus—extremam sociorum nostrorum oram tumidis Arminiaca victoria copiis insedisse, tandemque, sicut notum est, amisso peditatu magnaque exercitus sui parte, non recessisse solummodo sed fugisse, qua quidem clade milia hominum perierunt. Scimus ab illa fuga victum illum eius exercitum ad dexteram Arni ripam in Pisanorum agris habuisse castra continua, nec umquam fines nostros, cum bellaciter Senensium et Perusinorum territoria quotidianis irruptionibus quateremus, ausos intrare.

78   Sed antequam hinc discedentes ulterius procedamus, dic, obsecro, vir oratorie, quibus historiis invenisti legiones equestres? Quem umquam delectum, a quo lingua rituque Romano 'legio' dicta est, ex equitibus factum esse legisti? Descriptus erat et certus equestris ordo, quibus equi cum stipendiis decreto perpetuo assignati erant, qui iussum non lectum dabant pro qualitate temporis equitatum. Peditum est delectus, et legio, quam aciei portionem Macedones 'phalangem,' Galli autem 'catervam' vocant, nostri vero, tam proprio quam appropriato nomine, 'legionem'; equitum autem 'manum,' 'turmam' aut 'alam' consuevimus appellare. Quae quidem adeo vera sunt, ut nullum diligentem historicum vel poetam egregium invenies qui consueverit ista confundere quique non inveniatur diligenter ista servare; distinguuntur enim haec ab invicem, opposita quadam et specifica ratione, qua non liceat alterutrum commutare.

79   Sed ut hinc discedam, ad ironiam confugiens inquis: "'At socii ferent opem rebus afflictis." Digna quidem res in summo periculo auxilia implorare sociorum. Sed quis umquam socius fuit cui vestra superbia non sit invisa? Quem non tergiversationum vestrarum

lord spent a month and a week between the Oglio and Adda rivers
in dangerous and costly combat against our undefeated army raid-
ing his territory; and when he pushed his troops, exulting at the
time in the defeat of the count of Armagnac, to the farthest borders of our allies, the result was the one we are all familiar with:
he was forced to retreat and even to flee, incurring the loss of his
infantry and a large part of his forces, namely thousands of men,
in that defeat. We know how, after the retreat, his defeated army
made permanent camp on the right banks of the Arno in Pisan
territory, never daring to pass our borders, despite the strikes and
raids we made on a daily basis into Sienese and Perugian territory.

But before continuing, pray tell me, great orator, in what his-   78
tory book did you come upon "legions of cavalry"? Wherever did
you find it written that a military draft, which in the Roman language and custom is called a "legion," included cavalry (*equestres*)?
The equestrian order was defined by following fixed norms: by
perpetual decree a horse and a stipend were assigned to each of its
members, and thus the cavalry was mustered by summoning the
equites and not by conscription as the occasion warranted. Foot
soldiers were conscripted, and the selection (*legio*) — that part of
the line of battle called a phalanx by the Macedonians and a
caterva by the Gauls — we used to call by its proper and appropriate name, "legion"; while in the case of cavalry we usually speak of
a company, squadron, or wing.[97] These are things so well known
that you will never find any worthy historian or poet of high merit
in any confusion on the matter or who is not careful to observe the
correct usage; in fact these two bodies are quite distinct, indeed
opposite types of military formation; they are not interchangeable.

But enough of this point. You then take refuge in irony, saying: 79
*"But the allies will reinforce us when we are in dire straits." Nothing for-
bids invoking the help of allies when the situation is desperate. But have
you ever had an ally that did not begrudge you your arrogance? Is there
perhaps a single one that is not disgusted by your continual hesitations?*

fastidia satiarint? Qui non vos oderit? Qui non vestra calamitate laetetur, ut si sine suo periculo fieri possit, vos deleri funditus atque ex orbe terrarum exturbari non optet?' 'At socii ferent,' inquis, 'opem.' Ferent certe, si non fuerint foedifragi vel ingrati. Ferent, inquam, rebus non afflictis, ut ais, sed integris atque florentibus quaeve quotidie per Dei gratiam reflorebunt. Sed ais: 'Quis umquam socius fuit cui vestra superbia non sit invisa?' Immo quis sociorum nos superbos duxit aut umquam conquestus fuit? Non est vitium, quod omnem magis dirimat societatem, quam superbia. Et quis umquam nostram respuit societatem? Quis, ea finita, foedus non libentissime renovavit? Non sunt haec signa superbiae. Nullius magis societas fugitur quam superbi; nullius magis appetitur in Italia quam populi Florentini. Nihil magis domino tuo vel libertatis hostibus odiosum est quam nostra potentia, quam nostrae societates et foedera, quae tot dominorum et populorum quot nobis connexi sunt vera salus praesensque fuere subsidium, quae qui malitia vel errore deseruit cito debitas poenas dedit. Et quem, obsecro, tergiversationum nostrarum fastidia satiarunt? Quid per 'tergiversationem' intelligis? Non credo relinquere, verso tergo, causam institutam, ut iura diffiniunt, sed, ut arbitror, foedifragium, animi mutationem et calumniosam inobservantiam promissorum. Quae quidem quis, nisi falsa fingat, communi nostro potest obicere?

80   Sed adhuc de sociis loquens nostris addis: 'Quis est qui vos non oderit? Qui non vestra calamitate laetetur, ut si sine suo periculo[24] fieri possit, vos deleri funditus atque ex orbe terrarum exturbari

That does not hate you? That does not rejoice at your misadventures, that would not want to see you defeated once for all and chased off the face of the earth, if it could happen without danger to themselves? You write, "But the allies will reinforce us." Certainly they will, if they are not violators of treaties or ungrateful. And they will reinforce us — note well — not with our affairs in dire straits, as you state, but at a moment when our affairs are flourishing (and day by day they will, thank God, go better still). You say: *But have you ever had an ally that did not begrudge you your arrogance?* Let me rather ask you: has there ever been an ally of ours that has considered us arrogant or has complained? There is no greater vice than arrogance to ruin an alliance of any sort. And who has ever rejected an alliance with us? Or who has not been delighted to renew a treaty of alliance with us after it has expired? These are hardly signs of arrogant conduct [on our part]. No alliance is more avoided than one with the arrogant; no alliance is more sought after than one with the Florentine people. There is nothing more hateful to your lord and the enemies of liberty than our power, our alliances, and our treaties, which have always represented, for all lordships and peoples allied with us, a true source of security and a constant help, and those who have abandoned them due to malice or error have soon suffered condign penalties. And just who, pray, is disgusted by our continual hesitation? What do you mean by "hesitation" *(tergiversatio)*? Not, I think, abandoning, turning one's back *(verso tergo)* on, a case that one has undertaken, as the law defines it;[98] probably, if anything, you mean the breaking of treaties, changing one's mind, or a fraudulent failure to observe promises made. But who, inventing falsehoods, could accuse our commune of acts like these?

Still talking about our allies, you add: *Is there perhaps a single one* 80 *that [. . .] does not hate you? That does not rejoice at your misadventures, that would not want to see you defeated once and for all and chased off the face of the earth, if it could happen without danger to themselves?* Now,

non optet?' Sed ut de odio dimittamus, quod occultum esse solet
et potest, et hoc tibi, qui talia stulte soleas affirmare, sicut tibi rebus arrogas, relinquamus, quis non videt hunc nostrum populum
tueri communem causam libertatis Italiae? Qui non fateatur victo
populo Florentino libertatem stare non posse? Qui non agnoscat
nobis servitute subactis totam Italiam sine remedio, sine resistentia
et, ut aiunt, sine sudore et sanguine servam fore? Quae cum ita
sint, hominum stultissime, clariora quidem sunt quam ut negari
valeant, quis nos oderit? Quis nostra calamitate laetetur? Quis nos
deleri funditus atque ex orbe terrarum exturbari nos optet, nisi tu
vel tui similes, quibus nihil pensi nihilque vilius libertate?

81   Verum stultitiarum tuarum testimonium quaerens inaniaque et
falsa confingens, ais: 'Bononienses velim hac in parte respondeant,
qui iam annos novem vobiscum societate et foedere sunt coniuncti,
qui primo cum inter eos ducemque Liguriae dissensio nulla esset,
vestram societatem amicitiamque secuti, priori sese bello non necessario implicuerunt, et cum pace in summa possent spectatores
esse alienae fortunae, suam pro salute vestra in discrimen adducere
maluerunt, et in eo bello cuius molem paene totam suis humeris
sustinendam esse viderent. Quam enim aliam offensionem dux iste
Ligusticus, cum bellum indiceret, illis obiecit nisi quod aequo nimis vestram amicitiam foventes sese vestros omnino sequaces effecissent? Qua re dubitandum est nemini, si sese a vestris foederibus
abscidissent, illius belli onus sibi nequaquam fuisse subeundum.
Sed valuit sociorum integritas, valuit amor, valuit opinio. Itaque in

setting aside hate (which can and usually does remain hidden) and giving you leave to speak on the subject (accustomed as you are to make silly claims like these as if it were your prerogative), who does not realize that our people defend the common cause of liberty in Italy? Is there anyone who is not ready to admit that, should the Florentine people be defeated, there would be no more liberty? Is there anyone who is not ready to admit that if we were subdued all Italy would become a slave without any chance of escape, without any kind of resistance and, as they say, without sweat or blood?[99] This being so, most foolish of men, and being so obvious as to be undeniable, who is going to hate us? Who is going to rejoice at our misadventures? Who is going to wish to see us defeated once for all and chased off the face of the earth, apart from you and your kind, for whom nothing is more cheap and worthless than liberty?

In search of some witness for your outrageous statements, you   81
add falsehoods and pure inventions[100] when you write: *I would like to hear the reply of the Bolognese, who for these nine years now have been tied to you in a pact of alliance. By the mere fact of having united themselves with you and become your friends, they found themselves involved in that first conflict, against their will and without there having been any reason for discord with the Duke of Liguria; indeed they could well have stood aside as peaceful spectators but chose instead to risk their security for the sake of yours, and that in a war where the greater burden was clearly to be their own. In fact, what accusation did the said Duke of Liguria make against them in declaring war, but that of having shown excessive friendship for you, more than was fair, and so becoming your followers entirely? Truly, no one doubts that if they had dissolved the alliance made with you they would never have been forced to uphold that burdensome war. But their integrity as an ally prevailed, their affection prevailed, their concern for reputation prevailed. And so, in dire and stressful circumstances, they preferred you to a most powerful lord and near neighbor,*

rebus duris atque asperis vos, contra quod dignum erat, praepotenti et vicino domino, magno cum suo periculo, praetulerunt.'

82   Haec omnia, ni fallor, scribis ad litteram. Quibus quidem verbis tuis bellum, quod contra Bononienses dominus movit tuus, iniustum et sine legitima causa declaras illatum. Magna quidem domino tuo laus magnaque iustitia, qui, quod innocuus omnino populus noluerit veteres probatissimosque socios et amicos foedifraga pravitate deserere, quod facinus summum erat, bello statuit persequendos! Cui cum tam levis, immo prorsus nulla causa suffecerit ut bellum tunc indiceret, credisne fictam aliquam causam ei defuturam fuisse, quandocumque ruptae fidei contaminatos scelere bello persequi decrevisset? Scio quod ille dominus tuus de belli iustitia numquam curaverit aut voluerit disputare, qui numquam rebus repetitis vel veram et realiter illatam conquestus iniuriam bellum movit. Maxima sibi summaque iustitia fines ampliare suos semper fuit spesque sola vincendi. Numquam respexit causam sed occasionem et ipsam acquirendi facultatem. Numquam bella gessit, ut tutus sine iniuria posset vivere, qui pro potentiae magnitudine certus erat neminem posse vel praesumere, licet concupisceret, ei nocere. Tantum enim eminebat inter Italicos, ut stultitia iamdiu summa fuisset in eum rem etiam minimam attentare, cum plus quam satis esset omnibus non offendi summaque gratia vel solam opinionem suae benivolentiae meruisse.

83   Potuit nos et alios, crede mihi, favoribus et pace decipere qui bello fecit, insidiis et iniuriis ut quilibet addisceret eum cavere, credoque Dei providentia factum esse quod talem ambitionem dominandique libidinem cunctis ostenderet, quod quilibet ab eo

contrary to what was the appropriate course, and by so doing exposing
themselves to a grave threat.

These are, if I mistake not, literally your words. According to   82
your own words, you state that your lord started a war against the
Bolognese that was unjust and devoid of a legitimate cause. Great
praise indeed for your lord! A fine example of his justice! Because
a harmless people refused to abandon and break perversely a sol-
emn treaty with its ancient and most faithful allies and friends,
which would have been a serious misdeed, he decided to make war
on them! If so futile — actually so nonexistent — a reason were
enough to justify starting a war, do you think the same lord would
experience any difficulties in alleging a false reason had he chosen
to make war on someone guilty of faithlessness against allies? I am
well aware that your lord has never had any scruples about a war
being just or not, nor has he ever had any interest in discussing the
matter, never having made war to obtain payment for damages received or to respond to an offense actually suffered.[101] For him the
greatest and highest justice always lay in widening his own borders
and in an unalloyed hope of victory. He has never had scruples
about reasons but only considered what circumstances were most
favorable and what prospect there was for success.[102] He has never
waged war with the intention of living in security and free from
harm,[103] he who had such power that he could count on no one
being able to harm him or risk trying to, much as they might have
liked to. His superiority to all others in Italy would have made it
the height of foolishness to attempt anything against him; everyone thought it quite enough not to be attacked by him and felt
extremely thankful to deserve his good opinion and goodwill.

He was capable, believe me, of deceiving us and others with fa-   83
vors and promises of peace, he whose wars, threats and outrages
had made all learn to fear him; and I think it must have been by
divine providence that he revealed to everyone his high ambitions

vim semper et semper insidias exspectaret. Cumque contra vim eius praesens magnumque, ne solum dixerim, remedium esset in populo Florentino, plus quam scribi valeat, te demiror quomodo tam stulte dubitandum esse nemini dixeris Bononienses sine bellorum onere remansuros fuisse si se nostris a foederibus abscidissent. Tutiores ergone fuissent soli quam sociati? Tutioresne fuissent prodendo socios atque foedifragi quam in fide manentes, maxima cum integritate defensi? Cogitavit dominus tuus, cum simul commune nostrum et illos bello peteret, nos ab invicem tam defensione quam animis separare certissimeque nos eos, defensionis nostrae tam necessitate quam studio, deserturos.

84   Sed Florentinorum integritas et animi magnitudo, fide et prudentia solita, stultam fecit sapientiam eius. Vidit enim dominus ille tuus[25] nos, de defensione nostra securos, magnam partem copiarum nostrarum cum Iohanne Haukud, equitatus nostri praefecto, relicta Tuscia, Bononiam transmisisse. Vidit, etenim, et obstupuit prius exercitum suum fugatum quam illuc pervenisse nostra subsidia cognovisset, nosque — maiorum nostrorum exemplo, qui simul, post insignem Cannensis pugnae cladem, in Italia sustinebant Hannibalem et mittebant ad partes Hispaniae Scipionem — vidit et admiratus est furorem Senensium gentiumque suarum impetum finibus arcere nostris in Tuscia retundereque copias, quas Bononiam miserat, in Lombardia.

85   Quae cum ita fuerint, an credis eos umquam paenitentiam habuisse quod in fide mansissent qui se viderint tanta fide tantaque caritate defensos? Velim Bononienses interroges an ex praeteriti ratione ius habeant ut nos spe pacis — quam eos habere potuisse priore bello somnias atque fingis, vel hoc habituros fore promiseris — nos relinquant. An eis nostra superbia fuerit invisa, qui, priusquam societas inita finem acciperet, nobiscum aliam contraxerunt?

and desire to dominate, with the result that in any circumstance one always expected violence or danger from him. And as the constant, essential, not to say sole bastion against his violence was the Florentine people, more than words can say, I am surprised by your absurdly writing that the Bolognese would never have been involved in war if they had abandoned their alliance with us. So they would have been safer alone than allied? They would have been made safer, then, by betraying allies and despising agreements than by keeping their word and being assisted with the fullest integrity? Your lord thought that by attacking our commune and theirs at the same time he could provoke each to fight for itself, separately, assuming that in our fear and desire to protect only ourselves we would have abandoned them.

But the integrity of the Florentines, together with their customary magnanimity, loyalty and prudence, turned the wisdom of your lord into foolishness.[104] For he saw us, safe in our own defenses, send a large contingent of our troops, under our cavalry commander John Hawkwood, to Bologna. He saw, amazed, his army put to rout even before he knew our reinforcements had arrived, and he saw, astonished, how — on the pattern of our forefathers, who, after being heavily defeated at Cannae, resisted Hannibal in Italy and sent Scipio to Spain — we withstood the fury of the Sienese and the attack by their men at arms inside our Tuscan borders, while at the same time pushing the troops sent against Bologna back to Lombardy.

This being so, do you really think they ever regretted behaving loyally once they saw that they had been defended with so much loyalty and love? I would like you to ask the Bolognese whether, on the basis of past events, they have the right to break with us in hope of peace — a peace that you idly imagine and pretend they could have had in the previous war or, as you promise, could have in this one. So they hate our arrogance, the very people who accepted a new alliance with us before the previous one had elapsed?

84

85

An qui tam avide societatis nostrae foedera renovaverunt, tibi fuisse videntur nostris tergiversationibus satiati? Vel spem ponentes in domino tuo, cuius fraudes longe plus quam potentiam metuebant, credis vel cogitas nos[26] odisse, nostra calamitate laetatum iri? Vel, cum in strage nostra claram libertatis suae ruinam videant et praesens ac fidum in salute praesidium, nos ex orbe terrarum exturbari velint aut funditus cupiant nos deleri? Si non valuisset integritas, si non valuisset amor, si non valuisset nescio quae, ut inquis, opinio, nonne valeret illa necessitas communioque periculi quod illi, quos socios vocas, aut etiam alii, nisi desipiant, sicut tu, clarissime videant: si sternamur, se mox absque remedio perituros?

86 Ista, ista necessitas efficit quod et tu, licet minus oratorie — cum causam destruat tuam, credo cogente rerum potentissima veritate — fateris, ista necessitas, inquam, efficit ut quae contra nos de sociorum malivolentia tam multa connumeras, nihil sint nisi vana, nisi commenticia, nisi strepitus verborum inanes, ut mox cum ad huius veritatis fundamenta pervenerint, diruantur et velut fumus aut pulvis ante venti furentis faciem evanescant. Numquam mihi visum est oratoris esse, quem 'virum bonum dicendi peritum' Cato diffinit, vincendi studio pro veris falsa dicere vel comminisci, quoniam, cum viri boni non sit, contra materialem illius diffinitionis particulam certe facit; sed fateri dicereque quod noceat summa dicentis imperitia est, cum eius oppositum, quod in eadem diffinitione subicitur, sit formale. Qua re, susceptae vastator causae, non orator, te minus admiror unum — quod sine risu, vel derisu potius, inter haec quae scribis, legi — tam insulse dixisse, videlicet quod Bononienses potuissent priore bello summa in pace spectatores

276

So those who renewed the alliance with us with such eagerness are the same as those who have grown tired of our hesitations? Do you really believe that they trust your lord, whose traps they used to fear more than his power? Do you think they hate us, that they rejoice at our misadventures? Or that, even knowing that our defeat would surely bring the end of their liberty whereas our security ensures them reliable help, they would like to see us defeated once for all and driven off the face of earth? If a sense of loyalty had not prevailed, if affection had not prevailed, if I know not what "prejudice," as you call it, had not prevailed, would there not also prevail that necessity and that shared danger which all those whom you call our allies—but others as well, if they (unlike you) have sense—see only too well: if we are knocked down, they will be without remedy and will be the next to perish?

It is this, it is for this necessity that even you admit—though 86 with scant rhetorical ability, as you contradict your own thesis, probably forced to do so by the facts—it is for this necessity, I say, that all you assert against us and all you attribute to the allies' presumed hate of us amounts to nothing but a tissue of inventions, lies and gossip without sense that, at the first test against the facts, crumbles and vanishes like smoke or dust in the wind.[105] I have never believed it to be the mark of an orator—if with Cato the [true] orator is "an honest man skilled in speaking"—to pass off the false as true or confound the two in order to win a case, since to do so would surely contradict the material part of the definition, that he be an honest man; yet to disclose and assert things that damage your case reveals an outright ignorance of speaking, contradicting the formal aspect of the definition. For this reason it little surprises me when you, a destroyer rather than defender of your own case, foolishly declare the following—the one thing that doesn't arouse laughter or scorn in your composition—i.e., that during the late war the Bolognese could have enjoyed peace as spectators

esse alienae fortunae, si nos reliquissent. Quam enim aliam offensionem, cum dux ille Ligusticus eis bellum indixit, obiecit nisi
quod aequo nimis amicitiam foventes nostram se sequaces effecissent nostros? O rationem oratoriam! Appositam! Concludentem!
Ergo: quoniam ille praetenderit hanc causam, verum est quod
summa in pace spectatores fuissent alienae fortunae. Non vides
huius tuae rationis infirmitatem similem illi quam ex Plauto refert
Cicero: 'Amicum castigare immane est facinus; nam ego amicum
meum hodie non castigabo'? Siquidem, ut ille per id quod facturus sit propositum vult probare, sic tu ex eo quod dominus tuus
finxerit illos carituros fuisse bello niteris demonstrare.

87   Sed iam tuas ineptias dimittamus. Quod autem dicis Bononienses novem annis nobiscum fuisse foedere sociatos, forte non
plures propter aetatem recordaris. Sed longaevior fuit ista coniunctio, quae videlicet inceperit plus quam viginti sex annis ante maximam Bononiensium capitis deminutionem, quae servitute con-
trahitur, et in quam intestinis seditionibus quorumdamque, quibus
patria venalis fuit, sceleribus inciderunt. Viginti sex annis, inquam,
Bononienses — ut vetera dimittam, quae litterarum monimentis,
magis quam memoria cuiuspiam qui viderit, retinentur, ad quae si
voluerim me referre multorum saeculorum annales erunt et tempora recurrenda — socii nostri fuerunt. Quo mirari desinas si nostram perstare²⁷ tunc videris societatem, quam rescindere contra
naturam (quae similia similibus, populos populis liberosque liberis
conciliat) contraque longi temporis consuetudinem (quae quidem
altera sit natura) fuisset, praesertim cum ante oculos Bononiensibus cunctis forent ampla et officiosa subsidia nostra, quibus iam ex
tunc plus quam annis viginti suam defenderant libertatem. Conti-
nuatio quorum recensque memoria oblivionem contrahi non sine-
bant, cum, versa vice, nihil possent praeter amicitiam, nulla tamen

of another's misfortune had they simply broken their alliance with us. For what accusation did that Ligurian duke make against them upon declaring war but that unfairly favoring our friendship had made them into our supporters?[106] What a brilliant rhetorical argument! Right on the mark! Utterly conclusive! *Ergo*, since he alleged this to be the case, it was in fact true that they might have been left in peace as spectators of another's misfortune. Don't you see that your reasoning has the weakness mentioned by Cicero, citing a passage from Plautus: "To beat up a friend is a wicked deed; therefore, I shall not beat up my friend today."[107] Just as he tries to prove his intent by what he was about to do, so you try to demonstrate something by the fact that your lord was pretending that they were going to be free from war.

Let's move on from this foolishness. As regards the fact that, according to you, the Bolognese had supposedly been our allies for nine years, maybe you don't remember that it was longer because you are too young. We are speaking of a friendship of long standing; it goes back more than twenty-six years, before Bologna experienced servitude and forfeiture of civil rights,[108] falling victim to internal conflict and to venal criminality — I say then that for twenty-six years — leaving out earlier instances, to be sought in historical records rather than in living memory, and I might cite the annals of many centuries and recurring ages — the Bolognese have been in alliance with us. So cast off your surprise that our alliance stood firm at that time: for to break this alliance would have been against nature (that unites like with like, popular regimes with popular regimes, the free with the free) and against ancient custom (which is like a second nature),[109] especially having witnessed as they all did our many acts of assistance that for over twenty years had, by that time, defended their own liberty; this they could not forget, the examples being so many and so recent, while they were asked simply to take a friendly position (without

87

rerum experientia—quoniam necessitas, Dei gratia, non occurre-
rat—vestitam, praeter unionem foederum, consiliorum communi-
cationem et, in depellendis societatum periculis, participationem
moderatissimam expensarum.

88   Quod autem inquis, nos, licet impudentissimi simus, non negaturos cum ipsis non mediocrem controversiam habuisse nostra
culpa susceptam pauloque abfuisse quin bello atque armis totam
eam causam decerneremus—licet totam vidisse scribas Italiam—
tibi forte potuit esse creditum atque inaniter visum cuius aures
haec ficta, quae refers, relationibus falsis implebant. Numquam
tamen inter nos ulla contentio fuit quae dissidium faceret quaeve
non in ipsius exortus incunabulis mox extincta sit. Declarant hoc
castruncula Bruscolis et Castilionis Gattorum; quorum illud cum
multis iuribus et dominorum voluntate nostrum esset, noluimus,
quod facillimum nobis erat, Bononienses expellere, sed ipsis nullum ius habentibus potentiores cessimus, quoniam eis situ circum-
viciniaque convenientius adhaerebat. Alterum vero, quo petra
scandali tolleretur, dirui maluimus quam tueri. Credo quod magna
spes et ingens harum rerum fama, domini tui permulcens aures,
patriam totam implevit vosque, paene coepta pro confectis assu-
mentes, in exspectationem maximam erexisse.

89   Quid autem aliud, quod illi suum praetenderent aut vellent,
potes fingere de quo potuerit inter nos vel minimum aliquid excitari? Discurre per viginti sex annorum spatia—quibus societas
nostra, renovis foederibus, viguit—et si potes invenias aliud quicquam in quo dici possit nos ipsorum coeptis (iustis aut iniustis)
vel leviter occurrisse. Ut, cum nihil recensere possis, pudeat pude-
reque debeat, si non fueris omnino frontis attritae, stultitiam tuam
tam largis habenis, licentiam tot mendaciis totque falsitatibus indulsisse. Sciasque nihil eorum[28] quae futura dicis, si quid valet

any concrete action, such being, thank heaven, unneeded), to respect the alliance, to report decisions taken, and to pay a very small portion of the expenses necessary to avert the dangers threatening all the parties so joined.

Yet you say that, despite our incredible shamelessness, we could 88 not deny being responsible for a conflict of some weight with the Bolognese that almost came to resolution by open warfare;[110] and you write that, despite this being known to all of Italy, it is *you* [whose version of events] could be trusted and (vainly) relied upon — you whose ears were filled with the falsehoods you mention, based on false reports. In fact, no controversy ever caused disagreement between us and any that arose was resolved at once. To this the towns of Bruscoli and Castiglione de' Pepoli stand witness. Regarding the first, though it was our right and the wish of the local lords, so far from expelling the Bolognese — an easy matter given our superior power — we ceded it to them, not because they had any right to it but because it was so close to their borders. Regarding the second, instead, we preferred to destroy it than keep it, in order to remove the thorn of contention.[111] Probably your great hopes and the many discussions about these events have tickled your lord's ear and stirred your entire country to who knows what expectations, mistaking harbingers for events.

Would you like to fabricate other episodes of even slight fric- 89 tion between us and them, in which they ostensibly demanded or laid claim to something we owed them? Consider these twenty-six years during which our alliance has stood firm through renewed treaties and see if you can find an instance in which we opposed, even slightly, their initiatives, whether just or unjust. As you shall find none, you should be ashamed (and you would have to be ashamed, were you not too brazen-faced[112] to blush) for having given free rein to your stupidity and indulged your uncontrollable propensity for telling lies. Know that none of your predictions, if reason has any worth, shall come to pass. Indeed our allies have

ratio, debere contingere, sed socios nostros—utpote numquam a nobis offensos quique nihil spei possint habere libertatis et status retinendi nisi nos viderint incolumes atque salvos—cognoscere periculum hoc et bellum esse commune; certique sunt illud nos nostris non accendisse furoribus, quos sciunt semper fugisse bellum, sed ducem tuum, incensum dominandi cupidine, nobis et aliis intulisse.

90   Sed inquis: 'Si qua suspicio occupabit animos et fueritis in ea fingenda fortunati, quod sine ulla intermissione temptatis efficere, profecto magis erit eis curae pro suis defendendis finibus, quam pro vestris liberandis, praesidia comparare.' Scio quemlibet magis suarum rerum curam habere quam sociorum; sed cum omnes sciant nostram ruinam suam fore et defendere nos nihil aliud esse quam pro suamet libertate pugnare, credisne eos rem quam propriam esse cognoscunt tua dementia neglecturos? Nimium tibi fidis, nimium de ea quam profiteris eloquentia, quisquis sis, tibimet tuo cum errore blandiris, qui putes socios nostros vel spe vanissima bonitatis tui domini, quam nullus, vel odio nostro, quod nullus habet, a nostrae defensionis proposito deterrere. Iacta quantum vis sesquipedalia verba, speciosa vocabula sublimesque sententias; credisne tua sic vestire mendacia quod fides tibi vel tuo domino tribuatur, quod conceptum longa rerum experientia metum excutias, quod id quod perspicacissimi viri velut ante oculos positum intuentur, ratione concluditur experientiaque probatur capti Sirenum cantibus valeant oblivisci?

91   Nam quod dicis: 'A tribus vero tyrannis quid auxilii sit sperandum non satis intelligo; alterius enim tenues atque afflictae sunt, alterius nondum redintegratae fortunae. A tertio vero tantum abest ut quicquam expectetis auxilii, ut cum ipse circumsaeptus undique in medio belli flagrabit incendio, Florentinam opem ac

never received any offense from us and they place all hope for the freedom and security of their states in our safety and salvation; they know that we are both equally affected by this danger and by this war; they do not doubt that we, who have always avoided war, were not driven to it by our own furies, but that it was your duke, burning with the lust of domination, who attacked us and others.[113]

But you add: *If they start to harbor doubts and you turn out to be* 90 *lucky in the plots you are continually trying to bring off, they will surely be much more concerned to guard their own borders than to liberate yours.* I know that it is more usual to attend to one's own interest than to that of one's allies, but since all know that our ruin would bring about their own ruin, and that defending us means defending their own liberty, do you perhaps think that your madness will induce them to neglect that which they are quite aware belongs to them? You rely too much on yourself and you are too pleased with your self-professed eloquence (whoever you may be): you flatter yourself with your own error if you believe that our allies will abstain from defending us, whether the reason be an utterly misplaced trust in your lord's goodness, which no one feels, or a feeling of hate toward us, which no one has. You can throw out all the sesquipedalian words, the flashy phrases, the lofty sentiments you want,[114] but do you really suppose you can cloak your lies enough to make others trust you and your lord, letting go fears based on long, sad experience—or, like sailors dazed by siren music,[115] losing their sturdy wits and ignoring something they know so very well that they seem to have it before their eyes?

For example, when you say: *In addition, I fail to understand what* 91 *help you expect to get from three tyrants, one of whom is weak and ruined in his fortunes, while another has yet to recover from his misfortunes. [. . .] From the third there is so little hope of assistance that it will likely be he, trapped on all sides amid the fires of war, who will beg for Florentine aid*

fidem frustra imploraturus esse videatur. Qua re desinite vobis spes vanas et inutiles conflare de sociis, sed cogitate potius qua ratione, qua spe, quo denique fato atque fortuna vos soli tantam belli magnitudinem subeatis.' Hoc totum quod dicis quis non irrideat, quis non stultissimum esse dicat? Tune praesumis Florentinos admonere quid non sperent, excitare quod cogitent qua ratione soli sint tanti belli magnitudinem subituri? Num te forte consulent vel ab eis, qui nesciunt nisi misera ratione servire, hoc est servili condicione subesse, capient monita vel exemplum?

92   Et quoniam de fato nos interrogas et fortuna, numquid haec vel illud in manibus mortalium sita sunt? Quae cum supra nos sint nec in nostra potestate versentur, quid aliud possumus respondere nisi constanter illa necessitate fatali, quae summi Dei voluntas est, illaque fortuna, quam eius dispositio ministrabit, huius belli turbine nos usuros? Unum autem, Dei benignitate, non deerit: animus scilicet integer, animus rectus, animus liber, animus ad cuncta quae Deus vult invictus, animus constans et impavidus et qui numquam defleturus sit se quicquam quod pro libertate fieri potuerit omisisse. Et ut videas, vir divine, quanto qualique tenearis errore, dic, obsecro, cum fatum necessitas quaedam sit, quot fatis et necessitatibus autumas nos subesse? Possuntne, fare precor, unius rei plures esse necessitates? Nescio si tam stultus eris ut plures audeas affirmare; quod si feceris, quae necessitas necessitati possit accedere fac assignes.

93   Quod cum fieri non possit—necessitas enim non fuisset si quid forsitan defuisset, nec accedens necessitas esse potest (posset si necessitatem aliam invenires[29])—nescio si videas aut intelligas quid nos mones. Possunt ad aliquem effectum plura requiri;

and loyalty — and in vain. So leave off concocting these great and useless hopes about your allies and think rather in what way, with what likelihood of success, and with what fate and fortune you may endure a war on so large a scale.[116] Who could ever keep from laughing this whole argument to scorn, who could ever think of it as anything other than utter foolishness? You have the impudence to warn the Florentines against aid they do not expect to get, while calling on them to consider how they might engage in such a major war by themselves? In short, they ought ask for your counsel or turn to those who only know how to act with pathetic servility, to enslave themselves, for suggestions and examples?

And seeing that you ask us to speak of fate and fortune, are these really matters in the hands of human beings?[117] Being above us and beyond our control, what else can we reply except that, in the whirlwind of war, we always seek to make use of the circumstances set by fatal necessity, that is by the will of our Lord God, and that fortune which He may put at our disposal? Truly, one thing will never be missing (and we thank divine goodness for it), and that is a strong spirit, an upright spirit, a free spirit, a spirit ready to sustain all that God may demand, a certain and fearless spirit, and a spirit that will never bewail not having done everything possible for the cause of liberty. And to make you understand the kind and degree of your error, prophet that you are, please tell me: since fate is a kind of necessity, just how many fates and destinies do you suppose we are subject to? Pray tell, can there be multiple necessities governing the same event? I don't know if you will be so foolish as to reply in the affirmative, but if so, go on and specify the necessity than can be added to necessity.

But since that is impossible — it would not be necessity if something should happen to be missing, nor can there be a supervenient necessity (there might be if you were to find a second necessity) — I doubt that you really know or understand your own advice. It can happen that different causes are required to bring

92

93

necessitatem autem unam esse necesse est, ut cum una solum unius rei necessitas sit, unum etiam esse fatum oporteat et non plura. Qua ratione, qua scientia quaeris, igitur, quo fato putemus illo bello resistere, cum cuiuslibet rei fatum simpliciter unum sit? Et ut pudendum et puerilem errorem tuum videas, qua grammaticae ratione dicis 'A tribus vero tyrannis quid auxilii sit sperandum non satis intelligo' moxque dividens ais 'alterius enim tenues et afflictae sunt, alterius nondum redintegratae fortunae. A tertio vero tantum abest' etc.? Quis grammaticam vel mediocriter doctus tria dividit per partitivum hoc nomen 'alter,' cui non convenit dividere, nisi solummodo circa duo?

94   Stulte nimis et inconsiderate loqueris ac imperite, qui nec quid dicas intelligis, nec quo modo loquaris advertis. Et tamen audes os in caelum apponere, nec solum tecum male sentire vel loqui, sed in publicum etiam egredi non vereris. Nam cum de fortuna simul etiam interroges, quae sit inopinatus rei eventus rationali creaturae contingens, tu respondeas velim, qui rem quae sciri non potest, cum occulta sit et inopinata, nos interrogas, qui non intelligas stultitiam tuam, qui subditorum nostrorum mentes agnoscis, qui sociorum nostrorum futura consilia stultitia praesentis tua, qui praesupponis alios esse facturos quod summa stultitia foret solummodo cogitare, qui, cum nihil eorum quae tam stulte praesagire de nobis et nostris ausus es videas evenisse, has stultitias[30] tamen in animum induxeris publicare.

95   Cur autem, cum pro tyranno — maximoque truculentissimoque tyranno — domino tuo loquaris, ipsum 'ducem Ligusticum et Ausoniae principem' vocas, contra vero antiquissimum principem

about some effect, but there is necessarily only one necessity, so that there is only one necessity for any one event; so too fate must be one, not several. For what reason, according to what theory, then, do you ask us "with what fate" we think to resist in that war, given that for everything there is just one fate? And to show you what coarse and childish errors you commit, tell me now, according to what rule of grammar do you say *I fail to understand what help you expect to get from three tyrants*, and then splitting the phrase you add, *one of whom is weak and ruined in his fortunes, while another has yet to recover from his misfortunes. [. . .] From the third there is so little [hope of assistance]* and so forth? Would anyone with even a minimal grasp of grammar have used the disjunctive word "the other" (*alter*), which is used to contrast two things, when speaking of three subjects?

In brief you express yourself so foolishly, carelessly and igno- 94 rantly that you realize neither what you are saying nor how. And yet you have the effrontery to raise yourself to high heaven, and aren't ashamed merely to think and express yourself badly at home, but even to go about doing it in public. In fact you ask for information about fortune, but as this is an unexpected event that befalls a creature endowed with reason, I would rather *you* reply, *you* who ask us for notice of something that cannot be known, that is inscrutable and unexpected: *you*, who have no idea of your own stupidity, but say you know the most hidden thoughts of our subjects, *you* who foresee in your stupidity the decisions that our allies shall take, *you* who expect others to do things that would be stupid enough just as thoughts, *you* who, despite seeing that none of your senseless predictions about us and our allies has come to pass, have still decided to make this stupidity public.

And then why, speaking on behalf of a tyrant — and one of the 95 greatest and most violent of tyrants at that — do you style your lord "Duke of Liguria and Prince of Ausonia," while you label

287

tam dominatu quam sanguine, Nicolaum illustrem marchionem
Estensem, maiores cuius iam nona generatione late dominati sunt
quique ante Frederici Secundi tempora claruerunt, quorum cele-
britas atque fama trium saeculorum longitudinem ferme com-
plent,[31] 'tyrannum' appellas? Cur eius commemoras afflictas esse
fortunas, quod quidem et machinatio domini tui fuit? Cur inclitum heroa Patavinae civitatis, multa iam successione moderatorem
et dominum tam dilectum suis tamque formidabilem aliis tamque
cunctis suis virtutibus et animi magnitudine celebratum, tyranni
denominatione denigras? Qui per dominum tuum, infidelissimum
socium, patria spoliatus atque dominio pulsus et extorris, solum
auxilii nostri spe, tam audacter, tam constanter et tam alto animo
domino tuo Paduam abstulit et in maximam dominii sui partem
semet ipse reposuit.

96   An talis civium suorum amor, qui tunc patuit, an tanta virtus,
quantam in ipso totus mundus obstupuit, meretur ut foeda tyrannidis appellatione depravetur? Cur istos et inclitum dominum
Mantuanum, quem tertium intelligis, tyrannos vocas, quos dux ille
tuus appellat dominos, dicit filios atque fratres? Quo fit ut vel tu
vel tuus dominus mentiatur. Si verum dixeris, dominus mendax
tuus; si verus sit sermo suus, quod te negaturum esse non credo,
clarum efficies quod mentiris. Nec dicas dominicos illos sermones
urbanitatis esse, non veritatis; quaenam urbanitas, quae virtus quidem est, in mendacio potest esse? Si falsum est quod urbane dicitur, et assentatio et mendacium est. Quid malis dominum tuum
esse: mendacem et assentatorem, an veridicum et urbanum? Tu
vero cur domini tui non imitaris exemplum? Cur urbane non loqueris sicut ille? Cur plus potest in te metus quam veritas, cum
dominum tuum appellas ducem, qui verissime sit tyrannus?

"tyrant" that prince of ancient stock and power—the illustrious
Marquis Niccolò d'Este, whose ancestors began nine generations
ago to extend their broad dominion and who won glory even before the time of Frederick II, so that the fame of their deeds spans
three centuries? Why do you allude to his economic difficulties—
which, by the way, are entirely due to your lord's intrigues? Why,
by calling him a tyrant, do you denigrate the celebrated hero of the
city of Padua—last in the line of an ancient family of rulers and
lords so loved by his people, so feared by others and so celebrated
by all for his virtues and magnanimity? It was he who, after being
despoiled of his country, expelled from his lordship and made an
exile by your lord, the most faithless of allies, was able—thanks
only to our help—to remove Padua with such bold and noble
resolution from your lord's rule and to retake control of almost his
entire original dominion.

Does such love on the part of his fellow citizens, shown so   96
clearly at that time, does that great virtue which struck the world
with awe, deserve to be dirtied with the ignominious label of tyranny? Why do you call "tyrants" these two, as well as the illustrious lord of Mantua (the third to whom you mean to allude), while
your own lord addresses them as lords and calls them sons and
brothers? It follows that either you or your lord is lying. If you are
telling the truth, your lord is lying; if his words are truthful (and I
don't think you are going to deny it), then you've made it clear that
you are lying. And don't say that your lord's speech is molded by
courtesy rather than truth: for what courtesy (which is a virtue)
can there be in lies? If something said with courtesy is false, that is
to flatter and lie. What is your preference: do you want your lord
to be false and flattering or honest and courteous? So then, why
not follow his example? Why not speak courteously as he does?
Why does fear rule you more than truth, so that you call your lord
a "duke" when in reality he is a tyrant?

97   Sed dices: 'Nonne caesareae maiestatis auctoritate dux factus est Mediolani comesque Papiae?' Factus est, fateor, si comites atque duces inter spumantes pateras titubantemque vino procerum nobiliumque coronam, in imperii praeiudicium atque damnum, turpi pecunia—non genere, non virtute, non meritis—procreantur; si possit, qui tyrannidem praescripserit tyrannusque continuo vivat, nisi prius[32] desierit esse tyrannus, in comitem vel ducem legitimum commutari; si titulus atque verba sufficiunt, non ad hoc etiam mores et merita requiruntur. Sed haec in aliud tempus (sunt enim amplissima) reservemus, et ad speranda sociorum subsidia veniamus.

98   Credisne quod oblitus sit illustris dominus marchio—licet, ut secundum tempora quibus loqueris nos loquamur, adhuc puer sit—credisne, inquam, quod non agnoscat et non recordetur cuius favoribus consanguineus eius fines suos invaserit et Sancti Georgii rebellaverit mediamnem quam 'Pullesinum' vocant, et quibus fautoribus ipsam recuperaverit atque confirmaverit statum suum et totam illam oppresserit pestem, qua facile poterat interire? Crede mihi: recordabitur, et gratitudine mutua, tam praesentis maximique beneficii stante memoria, non deseret socios praesentes suos. Non dabitur, crede mihi, heros inclitus Patavinus in tam reprobum sensum quod eos—a quibus principium habuerunt dominationis et status maiores sui quosque nuper sensit sibi tam propitios et amicos,[33] quod eorum favoribus quicquid possidet recuperaverit atque defenderit—periculo suo relinquens expertae perfidiae se domini tui committat.

99   Nec circumspectissimus dominus Mantuanus—qui novit dominum tuum quod dicat ('qui mecum non est contra me est') et quod tot laboribus et[34] expensis cogitaverit, ponte mirabilis fabricae, quem aedificari fecit apud Valesium,[35] rerum mutare naturam

You will reply to me: "Was he not elected Duke of Milan and   97
Count of Pavia by decision of His Majesty the emperor?" That he
was, if counts or dukes may be created amid brimming chalices
and crowds of dignitaries and notables tipsy with wine, to the
prejudice and loss of the empire, and thanks to bribes rather than
lineage, virtue or merit; if someone commanding a tyrannous regime and living continuously like a tyrant can be transformed into
a legitimate count or duke without ceasing to be a tyrant; if titles
and words suffice without good morals and worthy deeds.[118] But
of this another time (the topic is large); let us turn again to the
hoped-for assistance of allies.

Do you perhaps believe that the illustrious marquess and lord   98
has forgotten, although only a child at the time you write of[119] — I
say, do you perhaps believe that he does not know and does not
remember who it was that helped his relative to break across his
borders and sow rebellion in that river-bound part of the lands of
San Giorgio known as "Polesine"? Has he forgotten thanks to
whom was he able to regain control, strengthen his own state, and
defeat this terrible threat which had bidden fair to undo him?
Believe me: he will remember, and by way of returning the favor,
mindful of such important and active assistance, he will not abandon his active allies. Believe me, the celebrated Paduan hero will
not behave so abjectly as to abandon, to his own peril, the very
allies thanks to whom his ancestors were able to found their dominion and their estate, and who have lately given proof of kindness and friendship toward him, it being through their action that
he was able to recover and then defend all that he has[120] — in order
to commit himself to your lord, whose treachery he has experienced.

The most prudent lord of Mantua knows what your lord says   99
("he who is not with me is against me"),[121] and knows what he is
plotting to do with such expense and effort by means of the dike
of marvelous construction which he is having built near Valeggio:

sibique finibusque suis auferre saluberrimum flumen Mincii, quod
civitatem et paludem irrigat Mantuanam—adeo demens erit quod
se deserat vel sociorum defensionem, quae sua sit, omittat. Et licet
medio belli sit flagraturus incendio, non implorabit frustra Florentinam opem, qui noverunt et solent, etiam suae defensionis anxii,
oppressis sociis subvenire, sicut olim patuit subventione Bononiensium primo bello, et sicut effectus docuit hoc secundo. Talia
quidem auxilia per nos et alios missa sunt ad dominum Mantuanum, quod fuso ducis exercitu ac copiis omnibus profligatis, si
ceterae gentes, sicut nostrae, victoria voluissent uti, non frui,
successusque urgere communes, tam modicum reliquiarium fuisset
quod pace tutissima, Dei gratia, laetaremur. Nunc autem, quoniam ultima pars maliloquii tui restat, residuum totum simul
continenter in sequentibus describemus.

100   *Nisi forte vobis ferociores animos facit Gallicanum foedus. Miror in ho-*
minibus, qui se haberi volunt et prudentes et callidos, tantam insedisse de-
mentiam ut spes omnes suas in gente levissima collocarint. Mirarer in Italis
tantam perversitatem exstitisse naturae ut de Gallis bene sperare possent,
nisi vos venenum ac faecem Italorum, iam diu inimicos salutis Italiae,
cognovissem. Sed per Deum immortalem, cum pollens et fortis exercitus
agrum vestrum populetur, cum castra hostium in vestris finibus habeatis,
cum iam denique pro tectis ac moenibus patriae dimicaturi paene de muris
armorum strepitum sentiatis, quid auditis e Gallia illa Transalpina? Af-
feruntur, credo, quotidie rumores ac litterae; cuius, quaeso, sententiae? Le-
gati regiam regemque sollicitant, opem ex foedere debitam, cadentibus
paene rebus, implorant, ne a summo rege—quem sibi unum defensorem et

he is planning to change the regular order of nature and to divert for himself and into his borders that most vital of rivers, the Mincio, which flows into the city of Mantua and its lake. The lord of Mantua has not taken leave of his senses and will not fail to take care of his own interests or neglect the defense of his allies, which is his own defense as well. And though he is about to be engulfed in the fires of war, he shall not ask in vain aid from the Florentines,[122] who are aware of his situation and are accustomed to help their allies even at times when they are under attack themselves, as was clear before from the help they lent to the Bolognese in the first war, and as is now clear from the outcome of this second war. The help sent to Mantua by us and others was enough to throw the duke's army into turmoil and rout all his troops; and had the other peoples shared our wish to make the most of that victory and assure a happy result for all, not just reap its fruits, with God's help little would have been needed to acquire that stable peace we so desired.[123] But now, since the last section of your defamatory accusations remains, I give it here in its entirety.

Unless, perhaps, it is a treaty with the French that is making your 100 *hearts more fierce. I'm surprised that such insanity should take hold of men who wish to be thought prudent and astute, so that they place their hopes in a people so fickle. I would be surprised to find Italians so enormously wrongheaded as to trust the French if I hadn't long since recognized that you are the poison, the dregs of the Italians, the enemies of the security of Italy. But — by the immortal God! — when a strong and powerful army devastates your territory, when enemies are encamped inside your borders, when you are close to the point of having to defend your very homes, hearing from the walls the clangor of arms, what news arrives from the muchsung Transalpine Gaul? Words and letters arrive every day, I imagine, but of what tenor? The ambassadors supplicate the court and the king, beg for the help owed them by treaty, and, when the situation deteriorates, demand that the high king not desert them in their clear and present danger — the king whom they longed to have as their sole defender and lord, disdaining*

dominum, spreto caesare, neglecta Romana ecclesia, concupiverunt — in tanto et tam propinquo periculo deserantur expostulant. In armis hostem esse popularique iam fines eius; nisi succurratur, omnia brevi esse ruitura significant; esse eum regem in terris, qui saluti suae consulere possit, praeter eum neminem. Obsecrant obtestanturque per sacratissimi diadematis maiestatem ne desertos ac destitutos ludibrio dedat inimici; eius, addunt, inimici qui eis ob hoc maxime infensus sit, quod se et fortunas suas maiestati regiae, summa cum devotione, commiserint.

101   Miris deinde modis animos Gallorum, suapte natura leves ac tumidos, inflare student, miris suasionibus adhortari, si anniti parum velint, venisse tempus et apertam esse occasionem non solum Italiae capiendae sed ad manum suam imperii transferendi et ad nutum ecclesiae redigendae; sese cum Ianua, cum magna Italiae parte esse iam suos; nihil reliquum, oppresso duce Liguriae, quod terra marique suae magnitudini possit obstare; ducem autem ipsum, quamquam magnum aliquid videatur, primo belli impetu esse casurum. Itaque quibus parum est spei parumve consilii ad solum patriae defendendum, liberam possessionem Italiae atque orbis terrae imperium pollicentur.

102   Non sum dubius ad haec omnia benigna et grata responsa suscipiunt: regi salutem amicorum esse cordi et foedera nuper icta memoriae; bono se illos animo esse iubere, nequaquam eorum necessitati maiestatem regiam defuturam. Et fortasse, cum armatis legionibus egeatis, Galli legationibus prius pro vestra salute intercedendum putant, quod etiam si impetratis est maximum. Interim stabunt illi suis occupati deliciis, fruentur opima in pace opibus suis, dum vos miseri in tanto bellorum incendio conflagratis. Sed age: tueri velint non solum nuda auctoritate sed armis! Ut omittam qualis animus caesaris totiusque Germaniae futurus sit, si quis Gallorum motus ad Italiam fiat, cum sibi pro dignitate imperii — cuius in Italia caput est — viderit subeundum esse certamen; ut, inquam, omittam hoc, quod vero propius est omnem Gallorum impetum non solum posse tardare sed

*his imperial majesty and ignoring the holy Roman Church. The enemy—
they cry—has taken to arms and lays waste to his lands; if help is not
given soon, all will be lost. He is the only king in the world who can save
them, there is no other. They pray and implore the king, in the name of his
most holy crown, not to leave them alone and defenseless at the mercy of the
enemy, that enemy who (they add) is particularly hostile to them because
they have entrusted themselves and their fates to his royal majesty, with the
greatest devotion.*

Next they seek in wondrous ways to stir up the hearts of the French, a 101
*people by nature frivolous and conceited, to exhort them with wondrous
rhetoric. If they but exert themselves a little, the time is ripe and the moment propitious not only to take Italy captive but also to transfer the Empire into their own hands and to remake the Church at their command;
Genoa and a great part of Italy is already theirs; with the Duke of Liguria
defeated, no force by land or by sea could oppose his power; that duke,
strong as he may seem, will fall at the first attack. Thus, to precisely those
who have little hope and few means of defending the soil of their own country, the Florentines promise complete control of Italy and world dominion.*

I do not doubt that all this may provoke friendly and pleased replies, 102
*such as: the king has at heart the security of his friends and does not forget
pacts recently signed; he urges them not to lose heart, for His Majesty the
king will never fail to come in their aid. It may even be the case, although
you need armored legions, that the French decide to intervene for your security by first sending legations, which is the most you will get for your entreaties. In the meantime they will stand around, taken up with their
pleasures, enjoying their wealth in plentiful peace, whilst you wretches burn
in the conflagrations of war. But come: they may [after all] want to protect
you with their arms as well as their mere authority. I won't say how the
emperor and all Germany would take it if the French were to make any
move against Italy; they would have to contest any invasion to defend the
prestige of the empire, whose capital is in Italy. I don't say it, but this fact
alone could go far, not only to delay any French invasion, but to eliminate*

tollere atque cohibere. Veniant certe Galli et affletur vobis ab Occidente aura illa salutaris, per quam in summa malorum anxietate respirare possitis; venient tamen eo tempore ut non ad defendendam vestram salutem sed ad deplorandum casum et exsequias celebrandas venisse videantur.

103 *Quae tamen est ista dementia tanta, tam abhorrens ab omni sensu rationeque perversitas, ut cogitare possitis amplissimum regem—officiorum plurimorum, sanctissimae societatis atque affinitatis immemorem—ita Florentinas opes tuendas ampliandasque suo periculo suscepisse ut, ceterarum rerum omnium negligens, vestrae tantum salutis et gloriae studiosissimus videatur? Quod si tantam levitatem in eo rege putatis exsistere, ut pro hoste eum ducat, quem avus quondam suus dignitate decoravit et regia sibi affinitate coniunxit, quem ipse paulo ante socium atque amicum habuit, cui denique illustre singularis benivolentiae monimentum regalia dedit insignia ad generis et sanguinis Vicecomitum laudem sempiternam, si regem hunc, inquam, tam leviter, tam repente mutatum esse putatis, ut hunc—sibi sanguine et recenti admodum societate coniunctum, nulla prorsus ad id impellente causa nisi ut avertat a capitibus vestris impendens malum—bello temptet invadere, videte ne nimis magno errore ducamini.*

104 *Potuit fortasse vestra calliditas et illa immoderata fingendi mentiendique licentia, qua in rebus omnibus privatis ac publicis praeter ceteras gentes utimini, in mente regia aliquid suspicionis affigere, quo ipsum abalienatum aliquantulum a duce Ligustico redderetis. Sed absit ut tantum vestrae temeritati atque impudentiae datum sit ut ad libidinem mentis vestrae arma rex moveat bellumque suscipiat. Erit sibi ante oculos recens foedus quod pro utriusque principis dignitate, ad nullius iniuriam atque perniciem, ictum fuit. Obversabitur avi imago, gravissimi illius quondam et sapientissimi regis, cui olim, in rebus difficillimis adversisque temporibus, pater huius, Galeaz ille magnanimus, liberrima voluntate se obtulit et qua potuit ope*

and suppress it. Let's allow that the French come; let's allow that salutary Western wind to blow toward you. It might let you breathe amid your great anxieties; yet they will likely come at a time when they will not be safeguarding you but weeping for your downfall and celebrating your funeral.

What sort of madness is this, an obstinacy devoid of any sense or rea-   103
son, that should lead you to think that so important a king—a man forgetful of so many of his duties, of the bonds of holy religion and the ties of
blood—should undertake at his own peril to protect and enlarge the resources of the Florentines, to the point where he becomes utterly committed
to your security and glory alone, neglecting all his other affairs? And if you
think this king can be so fickle that he deems as his enemy a man upon
whom his grandfather once conferred a title of nobility and with whom he
made a marriage alliance, one whom he himself not long ago held to be his
ally and friend, to whom he gave royal insignia [for his coat of arms] as a
noble pledge of special affection to the eternal honor of the Visconti line—if
indeed you think this king so fickle, so suddenly changeable, as to try to
make war upon one to whom he is tied by marriage and a recent pact—
and for no other reason than to keep an impending doom from falling on
your heads—then watch out that you don't commit an irretrievable error.

It may be that your craftiness and ungovernable license to lie and engage   104
in conspiracies—of which you make use in all matters public and private,
more than any other people—have succeeded in fixing a shade of doubt in
that sovereign's mind and alienating him in some small measure from the
Duke of Liguria. But may God avert it that your temerity and impudence
should succeed in the king's taking arms and starting a war at your pleasure! He will be well aware of the pact only recently agreed to in defense of
the dignities of both princes, without seeking to offend or harm the interests
of anyone. There will arise before his mind's eye his forebear, that king in
his time most noble and wise, whom the present duke, the magnanimous
Giangaleazzo, volunteered to help in very difficult and uncertain circumstances, and whom he aided in every way possible. He will think of the

non defuit. Redibit in mentem cum regio sanguine bina coniunctio. Subibit animum, quem putatis vestris mendaciis obsedisse, veteris amicitiae recordatio aliquandoque etiam recognoscet vestras insidias et intelliget vos pro vestra libidine tam multa de duce optimo et principe clarissimo fuisse mentitos.

105   *Qua re non modo suis copiis vos non defendendos esse non existimabit, sed omni dignos supplicio iudicabit tantumque aberit ut vobis corruentibus manum det ut etiam optet assurgentes opprimere. Quod si in regia illa Transalpina vestra fraus plus quam amplissimi ducis integritas fidesque valuerit poteruntque vestra praestigia omnium officiorum et necessitudinum memoriam obscurare, mihi credite, nobis est animus sic Gallis obsistere, ut intelligant quod maiores sui saepissime experti sunt: perfacile Gallis Italiam petere, victores redire difficile. Unde proverbium illud a nostris hominibus usurpatum scimus: 'Italiam sepulcrum esse Gallorum.' Non exigit locus hic ut ad priscas historias et Romanae virtutis exempla vos revocem; quae ipsi nudius tertius vidimus, proferamus in medium. Venit in Italiam dux Andegavensis ille, quem non solum patris regis nomen ornabat, sed qui multos per annos regia fretus potestate tantis thesauris atque opibus abundabat, ut a ceteris Galliarum principibus formidabilis videretur; et venit tanto cum equitatu Gallico, tam valido et florenti exercitu, ut non modo de regno ad quod properabat spem haberet, sed de universae Italiae dominatu. Neque enim facile intelligebant homines quisnam tot armatis legionibus, tanto splendori nominis, tantis opibus auderet obstare. Contra erat qui animo et virtute sua maius praesidium non habebat: Carolus ille rex optimus, regum decus eximium, quo nihil umquam sol in terris vidit illustrius. Et erat novus in regno, nec eo quidem integro, sed intestinis factionibus procerumque discordiis iam diviso; auri praeterea inops, sed ingentis animi*

double marriage alliance that ties that man to his royal line. The memory of this ancient friendship will come over his mind, which you think to have besieged with your lies, and eventually he will realize what you are plotting and he will recognize for what they are all the lies you have told, for your own depraved purposes, about that excellent duke and most illustrious prince.

On this account he will not only reckon that you must not be defended 105 *by his troops, but he will judge you worthy of every punishment, and so far from helping you prevent your ruin, he will rather choose to suppress any who might rise up to do so. And if the fraud you are perpetrating in that transalpine royal palace should prevail over the upright and loyal behavior of the most noble duke, and if your deceptions should succeed in darkening the memory of all the obligations and affections that tie one to the other, believe me, we are resolved to oppose the French, so that they may understand what their ancestors have experienced many times, that it is very easy for the French to enter Italy, but difficult to return thence victorious. Whence our popular proverb: Italy is the tomb of the French. No need to recall to you the ancient stories and exemplars of Roman prowess; I limit myself to note those which we have ourselves witnessed recently. There came to Italy the famous Duke of Anjou, remarkable for his father's royal title but also because, after many years of support from the royal power, he boasted of such riches and treasure that the other French princes regarded him as formidable; and he came with so large a troop of French knights and such a famous and strong army that he hoped to establish lordship, not only over the lands of the Kingdom he was marching upon, but all Italy. In fact men could not think of anyone who would dare resist so many armed legions, such an illustrious name, and so many resources. On the other side was a man who had no greater protection than his own courage and strength: Charles, best of kings, the glory of royalty, than whom the sun has seen none on earth more illustrious. At the time he had but recently come into his kingdom and lacked full control of it, as it was torn by internal conflict and disagreement between dignitaries; poor in gold but rich indeed*

virtute ditissimus. Hic paucis admodum Italorum copiis fretus, ita saepe Gallos afflixit, ita ad extremum contudit ac dissipavit, ut ex tanta multitudine pauci in patriam redire potuerint, plerique ferro caesi, multi laboribus inediaque consumpti. In quibus ipse dux periit, hoc uno felix, ne tantae vivus ignominiae dedecorique restaret.

106   *Vos etiam priore bello, quod cum duce gessistis, egregiam Gallorum in Italiam manum nobilissimumque et fortissimum Arminiacensem equitatum, pretio et pollicitationibus, conduxistis, eoque freti praesidio spes animo vanas insulsasque capiebatis. Sed cum iam superbiam vestram Italia tota non caperet, sparsit in auras Deus cogitationes inanes atque impias. Vidistis ut repente vir belli atque pacis artibus illustris, Iacobus de Verme, quem honoris causa nomino, et quo, pace ceterorum dicam, clarius militiae iubar non habet Italia, et hostium ducem cepit et, luce altera, reliquum fugientem subsecutus exercitum, ubi primum attigit, dissipavit ac vicit. Illa, illa fuit insignis salutarisque victoria per quam non solum Cisalpina haec Gallia, sed omnis Italia ab ignominia et vastitate liberata est, quae principis huius Ausonii in omnibus terris ac nationibus clarum, vobis etiam formidabile, nomen fecit, in qua denique, si quid haberetis sanitatis, nisi vos caecos et miseros in praecipitium ageret infinita temeritas, praesentissimo potuissetis exemplo cognoscere quam vanum quamque ridiculum sit Gallicanis auxiliis contra Italos sperare victoriam.*

107   *At vos furor et rabies et impatientia quaedam pacis oblivisci faciunt omnium salutarium exemplorum; non tenetis ista memoriae nihilque —
nisi imperium crudele, nefarium —* [36] *mente cogitationibusque versatis. Potuistis quidem soli, et in vestris manibus situm erat, Italiae pacem dare, sedare tumultus, auferre discordias, res denique Italas tanta tranquillitate componere quanta non fuerant patrum avorumque memoria. Nam cum in Italia vos post Liguriae principem scire multa, posse omnia videremini*

in virtue and greatness of spirit. Although supported by very few Italian troops, he so often harassed the French, he so blunted and scattered their forces, that in the end only a few of that great multitude were able to return home; most were cut down by the sword, worn down by fatigue and hunger. Among the dead was the duke himself, fortunate only in this: that he did not survive to witness his own shame and ignominy.

Already in the last war you Florentines fought against the duke, you 106 *hired, using both pay and promises of pay, a noteworthy force of the French and the famous and powerful cavalry of Armagnac to come to Italy, and supported by their protection, you acquired empty and foolish hopes. But now, since all of Italy has not been won over by your arrogance, God has thrown to the winds your vain and impious plans. You have seen how suddenly that man celebrated for the arts of peace and war, Jacopo dal Verme, whom I mention here for honor's sake — than whom, with all due respect to the rest, Italy has no more brilliant military light — captured the enemy commander; the day after he pursued the remainder of the fleeing army and no sooner did he catch up with it than he scattered and defeated it. This, this was the victory, famous and blessed, that saved our Cisalpine Gaul and all Italy from shame and devastation, which made celebrated (though for you terrifying) the name of this Ausonian leader in every nation and place of the globe! This victory could have furnished the clearest possible example — if you had any sense, if your limitless rashness not did drive you, blind and wretched, to the precipice — of how ridiculous and vain it is to hope to defeat Italians by reliance on French aid.*

But the fury, rage and intolerance of peace that afflict you make you 107 *forget all salutary examples. The latter you forget, while you turn over in your mind and thoughts nothing but a cruel, wicked rule. You alone — and the choice lay in your hands — could have brought peace to Italy, quelled uprisings, erased conflicts, and in short, brought back the kind of tranquility to Italian affairs of state such as only our fathers and grandfathers remember. Since, next to the prince of Liguria, you seemed the most well-informed and the most effective power in Italy, and since he was more eager*

essetque ille etiam quam dignitati et splendori sui nominis conveniret pacis
avidior (propter quam non sine amicorum suorum stomacho ita se haberet
humiliter, ita et quaedam indigna quotidie patientissime toleraret, ut et vobis cervices erigeret, qui paci eratis adversi) et eorum, qui melius sentiebant,
corda posset inflectere, nil prohibebat, si vobis pacis studium placuisset, pacem perpetuam esse futuram. Sed abhorrebant curiae vestrae a consilio
quietis, et animos vestros urgebant conceptorum scelerum stimuli et aures
vestras sanioribus monitis obstruebant atque oculos occaecabant Furiae illae
pestiferae quas peccata vestra de sedibus Tartareis excitarant.

108   Itaque semper contra salutem Italiae, contra pacem, contra bonorum
consilia, contra patriae vestrae statum ac requiem sic fuistis accensi ut sine
dubitatione videremini non pro cura et conservatione vestrae rei publicae
vigilare, quod unum volebatis intelligi, sed ad civitatis et libertatis voluntarium interitum festinare. Qui quidem ita iam proximus est ut et vos iam
iam impendentis ruinae terrore concutiat et universam Italiam ad spectaculum vestrae calamitatis attollat.

109   Ventum est tandem ad illam invectionis tuae stultitiam, quae
calci tui tam inepti sermonis praecedentique discursui debebatur.
Coepisti quidem in nos furere; nunc in auctores nostros, Francorum regem nationemque Gallicam, debaccharis. Principio tamen,
nos illosque coniungens, postquam nos cogitare qua ratione, qua
spe, quo denique fato atque fortuna soli tantam belli magnitudinem subeamus, veluti desperare cuncta nobis necesse sit, ad-
monuisti, subinfers: 'Nisi forte vobis ferociores animos facit Gallicanum foedus,' moxque, velut anguis quem pressit forte viator,
'attollens iras et caerula colla tumens,' addis: 'Miror in hominibus,
qui se haberi volunt et prudentes et callidos, tantam insedisse dementiam ut spes omnes suas in gente levissima collocarint. Mirarer in Italis tantam perversitatem exstitisse naturae ut de Gallis

for peace than befitted his title and his resounding fame — so much so that his conciliatory attitude irritated his allies, and he would bear each day with the greatest patience charges he did not deserve, for example, that he had stiffened your stubborn hostility to peace — and since he was able to influence the hearts of right-thinking people, nothing stood in the way of a durable peace, had your desire for peace been genuine. But your Signoria shrank from counsels of quiet, and the thought of the crimes you had planned goaded you on, deafening you to wiser advice, and your eyes were blinded by the plague-ridden Furies whom your sins had aroused from their Tartarean homes.

In brief, you have always been so hostile to the welfare of Italy, so op- 108 *posed to peace, so deaf to the counsels of good men, so indifferent to the prestige and tranquility of your fatherland, that you are not standing guard out of concern for the preservation of your commonwealth, as you wish to have believed, but you are hastening toward the voluntary destruction of your city and your liberty. This fate is now nigh, so much so that you are already stricken with terror at your impending collapse, and you are raising up all of Italy to watch the spectacle of your undoing.*

Your invective has finally arrived at the very essence of stupidity, 109 the debt of stupidity that its earlier part owed to its end. You began by inveighing against us, now you continue by throwing yourself like a madman against our founders, the king of the Franks and the Gallic nation.[124] At first you joined us together with them, and then you warn us to consider by what plan, with what chance of success, and with what fate and fortune we might enter so great a war by ourselves, as though it was necessarily a desperate act; then you add *Unless, perhaps, it is a treaty with the French that is making your hearts more fierce.* At this point, like a serpent under a wayfarer's foot, "rising up, and puffing out its dusky coils,"[125] you assert: *I'm surprised that such insanity should take hold of men who wish to be thought prudent and astute, so that they place their hopes in a people so fickle. I would be surprised to find Italians so enormously wrongheaded*

bene sperare possent, nisi vos venenum ac faecem Italorum, iam diu inimicos salutis Italiae, cognovissem.'

110   'Nisi forte vobis,' inquis, 'ferociores animos facit Gallicanum foedus.' Si 'ferociores' intelligis id est 'magis feros,' cave: ferocitatem hanc unde somnies provenire posse? Mitissima quidem regis illius et omnium Gallicorum natura est, benignum etiam Florentinorum ingenium, ut contra rationem sit congregatis atque[37] coniunctis, qui natura mites et benigni sint, nasci feritatem ex eis vel in feroces ex benignis et mitibus commutari. Sin autem 'ferociores' hoc est fortiores velis, sicut dicimus 'ferocem militem,' id est manu fortem, sensum hunc, qui virtutis esse soleat, non recuso. Quis autem mundi princeps aut tantae potentiae populus umquam fuit, nec Romanum excipio, qui potentissimi Christianorum principis illius societate receptus se non reputet et ducere debeat fortiorem?

111   Sed prosequeris: 'Miror in hominibus, qui se haberi volunt prudentes et callidos, tantam insedisse dementiam ut spes omnes suas in gente levissima collocarint.' Et dic, obsecro, numquamne legisti *Synonyma* Ciceronis? Lege, si placet, et invenies: 'Callidus, veterator, vafer, versutus, astutus, subdolus, insidiosus.' Quis autem est intellectus tam obtusi qui se velit callidum — quod maximum et evitabile vitium, immo vitia, sicut vides, sonat — ab aliquo reputari? Qui non calliditatem occultet et dissimulet quantum potest? Profecto nihil magis calliditati contrarium quam calliditatem quam habeas aperire, nisi forte qui callidus sit cupiat fugi, calliditate metui neve decipere valeat evitari. Prudentes esse cupimus et videri; parum autem astutos nos apparere volumus talique moderatione quod malitiae suspicio penitus auferatur, ut cum Florentini maxime velint et soleant cum hominibus conversari,

as to trust the French if I hadn't long since recognized that you are the
poison, the dregs of the Italians, the enemies of the security of Italy.

Unless, perhaps, you say, *it is a treaty with the French that is making*   110
your hearts more fierce. If by "fierce" you mean "more savage," beware:
whence comes this savagery you are dreaming of? That king and
all the Gauls are most calm by nature, just as the Florentines are
of a peaceful cast of mind; hence it would be illogical if, when the
two were conjoined, men who were naturally gentle and kind
should give birth to savagery, or if kind and gentle men should be
utterly changed and become ferocious. If, however, by "more fierce"
you mean "more valiant" as in the expression "the valiant soldier,"
that is to say, brave in combat, I won't say no to that meaning of
the word, which refers to a virtue. Where in the world has there
ever been a prince or a popular regime, including the Roman, of
such enormous power that it does not think itself, and ought not
to regard itself as rendered more valiant by an alliance to the most
powerful of Christian princes?

You go on, however: *I'm surprised that such insanity should take*   111
hold of men who wish to be thought prudent and astute (callidos), *so that*
they place their hopes in a people so fickle. Pray tell me whether you
have ever consulted Cicero's *Synonyms*? Read it, please, and you will
find: "astute *(callidos):* intriguing, cunning, malicious, artful, con-
niving, insidious."[126] Who would be so dense as to want to be
considered *callidus* by someone, a term indicating a grave and
avoidable vice to be shunned, or rather multiple vices, as you see?
Who is there who will not hide and dissemble his "astuteness" *(cal-*
liditas) as much as he can? Nothing, then, is further from "astuteness" than revealing one's own "astuteness," unless the astute person wishes to be shunned, feared for his cunning, or avoided for
his ability to deceive. What *we* wish is both to seem wise and to
be wise[127]; we have small desire to appear *callidi*, and only to a
moderate degree, so that suspicion of malice may be entirely removed. When Florentines would hold converse with mankind,

nolint, etiam si fors[38] esse cupiant, callidi apparere,[39] veteratores
atque tales qui merito fugiantur.

112   Denique quid miraris? 'Hominibus,' inquis, 'qui se velint haberi
prudentes et callidos, tantam insedisse dementiam ut spes omnes
suas in gente levissima collocarint.' Et quis te ferat maiestati tanti
regis nominique tam celebris nationis adeo turpi sugillatione detrahere celsitudinemque summi principis et tam validae gentis
tamque gloriosae nomen levitatis infamia maculare? Semel nomen
Christi tam rex Francorum quam universae Galliae receperunt. Et
qui reges, quae gentes aut provinciae tenacius huic fundamento
verae certaeque salutis vel constantius inhaeserunt? Quis umquam
audivit et locum et gentem in his, quae sunt fidei, vel leviter vacillare? Quonam in loco vel imperiosius vel vehementius errores extincti notatique sunt? Ubi fides sincerior, ubi clarior, ubi perfectior
atque constantior est? Ut hac sola ratione turpe sit tibi turpeque
cuilibet hanc constantiam levitatis, quam imponis, infamia depravare. Nam, ut et pietatem erga Deum dimittam, quae gens regi fi-
delior quaeve perseverantior atque paratior animam ponere pro
rege suo, pro honore suo, pro iure, veritate et iustitia sua? Nescio
quibus in rebus aliis constantiam desideres, cum in his, quae
summa et gravia sunt, in eis plus constantiae quam in ceteris com-
perias gentibus.

113   Gens est iucunda, fateor, laeta, cuique nefas sit parcere parto vel
cogitare de crastino. Has naturae bonitates damnas crimine levitatis, quasi tristis aspectus, horrida supercilia ceteraque, quibus Stoi-
corum gaudebat austeritas et disciplina immo tumebat, talia sint
quod nihil aliud rectum possit aut debeat iudicari. Sciunt Galli in
his, in quibus decet esse graves, esse severi, sciunt in aliis esse faciles, esse laeti, ut maior requiratur auctoritas quam tua, vel Lom-
bardi cuiuspiam, quae possit de tantae gentis moribus iudicare.

they do not will, even if they might perhaps wish, to appear *call-idi* — crafty folk and the kind of men who deserved to be shunned.

And what are you "surprised at"? "At such insanity" "by men who wish to be thought prudent and astute," that is, "who place their hopes in a people so fickle." But who can bear your offending with such a shameful insult the dignity of so great a king and the name of so illustrious a nation, and staining with the infamous charge of fickleness the august person of such a high prince and the name of this powerful and glorious people? The king of the Franks and all the Gallic peoples alike once accepted the name of Christ. And what king, people or province has held as tenaciously or with greater conviction this, the basis of true and certain salvation? Who has ever heard of this nation and people showing the slightest vacillation in its faith? Is there another region where heresies have been denounced and extirpated with greater conviction and force? Where else can be found a faith more sincere, clear, exemplary and firm? This alone suffices to explain why it is vile on your or anyone else's part to defame such steadfastness as inconstant. Apart from their devotion to God, is there perhaps a people more faithful to its king or greater in abnegation and readiness to sacrifice itself for its king, for its honor, for right, truth and justice? I know not what constancy you find wanting in them in other matters, since in these, the most important and essential matters, you may find them the most constant of all peoples.

They are, I admit, a delightful and happy people that dislikes tight spending or having regard for the future. But for these pleasant traits of character you call them inconstant, as if the severe looks, forbidding bristly brow, and such-like marks of Stoic austerity (or inflated pride) were to be thought the only correct attitude. The Gauls know how to be serious about things that call for gravity, but they also know how to be relaxed and happy in other things; an authority greater than yours or another Langobard's is wanted to judge the manners and ways of such a great nation.

112

113

Genus enim hominum est apertum, innocuum, benignum, amica-
bile cuique sit duplicitas inimica, ut quanto magis cogito bonitatem totius illius generis[40] et naturam, minus videam cur debeat de
levitate damnari; ut etiam si spes nostras omnes in gente tot virtutibus conspicua poneremus, nec nos temeritatis possis aut debeas
criminari.

114   Verum serenissimus ille rex sic voluit nos sibi coniunctos et socios esse, quod in illa foederum unitate curaverit atque voluerit
non se solum sed etiam propinquos nostros et socios aggregare.
Verum in conceptae levitatis accusatione perstans, quam te vides
petulanter et iniquissime cavillari, subdis: 'Mirarer in Italis tantam
perversitatem exstitisse naturae ut de Gallis bene sperare possent,
nisi vos venenum ac faecem Italorum, iam diu inimicos salutis
Italiae, cognovissem.' O verba pulchra, verba vera, verba digna
quae tu solus, incomparabilis artifex maliloquii mendacissimusque,
promulges. Pulchrumne, licet hostis sis, cum falsum dicas, hosti
detrahere minuereque, licet hostium, notam omnibus dignitatem?
Quanto melius hic, qui nil molitur inepte, de Teucro loquens ait:
'Ipse hostis Teucros insigni laude ferebat.' Nonne laus quam feceris
hostium, sive viceris sive victus fueris, laus est commendatioque
laudantis? Estne decus domini tui, cuius potentiam tantam iactas,
quod cum Italiae faecibus bellum gerat?

115   Tune—turpis foetidaque sentina, sterquilinium et sordium
sordes—audes Florentinos faecem Italiae nominare? Faecis hac
appellatione quid intelligis? Urbem an cives? Non credam Antonium Luscum meum, qui Florentiam vidit, nec aliquem alium,
quisquis fuerit, si Florentiam[41] viderit urbem, istam esse vere flo-
rem et electissimam Italiae portionem, nisi prorsus desipiat,
negaturum. Quaenam urbs, non in Italia solum sed in universo

Truly, they are a forthright, peaceful, goodwilled and lovable people, and one that despises hypocrisy; and the more I think of the goodness and character of this people, the less reason I see to blame it for inconstancy; indeed, were we to repose all our hopes in a people with as many admirable virtues as this, you neither could nor should charge us with imprudence.

In fact that most severe king wanted to build a relationship of 114 friendship and alliance, and took pains to unify the league by including also our neighbors and allies in its terms.[128] And yet you persist in your accusation of inconstancy, a (perceived) trait you jeer at with ill-humor and great injustice, adding *I would be surprised to find Italians so enormously wrongheaded as to trust the French if I hadn't long since recognized that you are the poison, the dregs of the Italians, the enemies of the security of Italy.* What fine words! Holy words, words worthy of the incomparable calumniator and incorrigible liar that you are! Do you think it a fine thing to discredit and belittle an enemy — even if you are their enemy when saying something false — although the worthiness of your enemies is something known to everyone? How different the words of the great author, who does nothing without good reason, about the Trojans: "Even the enemy paid the tribute of great praise to the Trojans."[129] Isn't it true that when you praise an enemy, whether you be victor or vanquished, you also praise yourself? Is it a mark of honor for your lord, whose great power you boast of, that he wages war upon the dregs of Italy?

And *you*, you foul and vile being, you disgusting filth, offspring 115 of filth, how dare you call Florence the dregs of Italy! What do you mean by the name "dregs"? The city or its citizens? I cannot believe that my Antonio Loschi, who has been to Florence, or anyone else who has visited this city, can deny that it is the flower of Italy and its finest part, unless he is an utter fool. What other city, not only in Italy but in the whole world, can boast of

terrarum orbe, est moenibus tutior, superbior palatiis, ornatior
templis, formosior aedificiis? Quae porticu clarior, platea specio-
sior, viarum amplitudine laetior? Quae populo maior, gloriosior
civibus, inexhaustior divitiis, cultior agris? Quae gratior situ, salu-
brior caelo, mundior caeno? Quae puteis crebrior, aquis suavior,
operosior artibus, admirabilior omnibus? Quaenam aedificatior
villis, potentior oppidis, municipibus numerosior, agricolis abun-
dantior? Quae civitas portu carens tot invehit, tot emittit?

116   Ubi mercatura maior, varietate rerum copiosior ingeniisque
subtilioribus exercitatior? Ubinam viri clariores? Et — ut infinitos
omittam quos recensere taedium foret rebus gestis insignes, armis
strenuos, potentes iustis dominationibus et famosos — ubi Dantes?
Ubi Petrarcha? Ubi Boccaccius? Dic, precor, ubinam summum
Italiae loco virisque, foedissima belua, poteris assignare, si Florentini sique Florentia faex Italiae dici possunt? Vellet Deus quod,
stante gloria stanteque re publica Florentina in eo quod est libertatis atque potentiae, talis esset, si tamen esse potest, reliqua mediae
nominationis Italia, quod comparati ceteris Florentini faex Italiae
dici possent. Verum quia tantus excessus rebus his corruptibilibus
impossibilis prorsus est, pudeat te — spurcissimorum spurcissime,
stercus et egeries Lombardorum, vel potius Longobardorum —
Florentinos, verum et unicum Italiae decus, faecem Italiae nominare!

117   Nam quod venenum etiam nos Italiae vocitas, adeo falsum est,
quod Ianuenses et Veneti, Maris Inferi Superique principes ac domini, Florentinorum incolatum multi faciant et cum eis libentissime
conversentur et vivant, non fugiant ut venenum; quod similiter

stronger walls, more imposing palaces, wealthier churches, more elegant homes? Which has more splendid porticoes, more beautiful squares, streets more pleasant in their breadth? Or a population more numerous, citizens more illustrious, inheritances more substantial, fields better cultivated? Or a situation more delightful, a climate more salubrious, greater cleanliness? Or springs more plentiful, waters sweeter, craftsmen more industrious, more admirable than any others? What city has a countryside more checkered with villas, more powerful towns, more numerous villages, a greater population of country folk? What other city without a port receives and sends so many goods?

What city has commerce more prosperous, boasting a greater 116 variety of goods, and practiced by more subtle minds? And where have there been more illustrious men? To pass over the infinite number — it would be tedious to list them singly — who have made a name for their actions, who have shown valor in war, who have become powerful and famous in just lordships, where will you find another Dante, another Petrarch, another Boccaccio? Pray tell, you filthy beast, what would you designate as the best part of Italy in terms of place and people if Florence and the Florentines are to be called "the dregs of Italy"? Would to heaven that Florence as it now is — glorious and well governed[130] — might, *per impossibile*, stand in comparison to the average state in Italy, with respect to freedom and power, such that Florence *could* be called the "dregs of Italy"! But as such greatness is impossible in this world of corruptible things, you should be ashamed of yourself — you who are the lowest of the low, the filth and excrement of the Lombards, or rather Longobards[131] — for calling the Florentines, true and sole pride of Italy, the "dregs of Italy."

Just how false it is to term us the "stain" (*venenum*) of Italy 117 (which you also do) is reflected in the way that the Genoese and the Venetians, lords and commanders of the Tyrrhenian and Adriatic seas, treasure the Florentine colony in their cities, happy to trade

tota facit Italia, faciunt et omnes orbis undique nationes. Quod adeo verum est, quod artificiose non 'virus,' non 'toxicum' dixeris, sed polysema locutione 'venenum,' quod vocabulum exprimere tincturae soleat ornamentum, sicut apud Severinum legitur: 'Nec lucida vellera Serum Tyrio miscere veneno.' Cum enim nec vere nec aliqua ratione dici possit Florentinos esse virus, sed ornatum potius et non parvum decus Italiae, quis novit an sub obtentu convicii verum, quod omnibus clarum sit, occulte licet, curaveris designare? Vel potius omnipotens ipse Deus, qui vera germanaque veritas est, inter verba intentionemque mendacii, quae tua sunt, hanc intenderit veritatem; ut cum tu mendax atque maledicus Florentini nominis infamiam vel potius iniuriam, cum infamare nequeas, senseris, Deus per 'faecem' 'reliquias,' per 'venenum' 'decus' et 'ornamentum' Italiae dederit agnoscendum.

118   Et ut ad tuas ineptias redeamus, quae naturae perversitas est Italos posse bene sperare de Gallis? Ego vero de cunctis cunctos bene sperare posse (nedum de Gallis Italos)[42] credo, contraque naturam esse non posse sperare. Siquidem cum sperare sit voluntatis actus, quae semper ad utramque partem contradictionis se habeat libere, dic, obsecro: quando, stante voluntate, verum erit quem non posse sperare? Nimia foret naturae perversio si nobis sperandi potentia tolleretur! Sperare quidem, non sperare vel etiam desperare voluntatis est, cui rerum huiusmodi facultatem adimere nihil aliud esset quam tollere nobis arbitrii libertatem et ipsam extinguere vim et potentiam voluntatis, quae sine libertate foret necessitas, non voluntas; ut cum involutum cerebrum et intellectum maliloquiis habeas, sic ea que scribis intexas quod ex

and live with them, in nowise avoiding them as if fearing a "stain": and so the rest of Italy and the nations of all the world. The truth of this appears in your choice of metaphor: not "venom" or "poison" but a word that lends itself to various interpretations. Take Boethius, who writes "Do not beautify the shining fabrics of the East / with Tyrian stains (*veneno*)."[132] Since it is untrue and indefensible to say that the Florentines infect or stain Italy, since they render it more precious and give it not a little luster instead, who knows but that you weren't taking pains to signify in cryptic fashion, under the cloak of your insulting talk, the truth that everybody knows? Or else God Almighty himself, who is true and actual Truth, wished to insert this veracious statement in the midst of the many lies you have invented, with the effect that while you, deceitful liar, thought you were defaming the good name of the Florentines (or rather doing an injustice to what you cannot defame), at the same time God brought it about that "dregs" would be understood as "holy treasure," and "the stain" as "the splendor" and "pride" of Italy.

But to return to your nonsense, what would be so unnatural 118 about Italians placing their hopes in the Gauls? I rather hold the view that anyone can hope in anyone, not just the Italians in the Gauls; what is unnatural is not to be able to hope. Since hope is an act of the will that can freely orient itself to either side of a contradictory, pray tell: when exactly, so long as our will remains unchanged, will it be impossible to hope in something that is true? It really would be a perversion of nature if our power of hoping were taken away from us! To hope, not to hope, to lose any hope—all these acts belong to the will; to deprive us of this faculty would be tantamount to depriving us of free choice and quenching the very force and power of the will. Without liberty there would only be necessity, not free will. But just as you keep your brain and mind wrapped up in evil speech, so you interweave what you write with meanings that are not only different from

ipsis non alius solum sed oppositus elici possit sensus. Sic naturae perversitatem admiraris, quod si non adsit quod perversum putas naturalia tolli necesse sit nec intellectus hebetudine potentiam ab actu noveris segregare.

119   Totiens autem in hoc erras ut mihi visum sit dignissimum fuisse tot et tantis ineptiis, quibus ignorantia videatur tua, minime respondere, nisi primus verborum tuorum intuitus — ornatu quodam et strepitu, licet inani, verborum — mereri nescio quid auctoritatis et gratiae videretur. Et quoniam huic particulae satis, immo plus aequo, sumus immorati, iam hinc ad alia procedamus, si tamen unum quod dicis, ne fugere vel fateri videar, absolvamus. Arguis enim quod salutis Italiae iamdiu nos cognoveris inimicos. O virum perspicacis intellectus et admirabilis cognitionis! Si tamen probabile sit eum, qui nesciat ea quae sunt, sic explorata ratione tenere quae non sint quod super alios cognoscere videatur, unde cognoscis, obsecro, nos salutis Italiae, sicut asseris, inimicos? An quoniam tyrannidi domini tui totam Italiam ambienti restitimus, quoniam cupienti libertatem extinguere nos constantius atque potentius quam cogitaret obiecimus, salutis Italiae nos cognoscis — cum alii dicant athletas et pugiles, ab omnibus dissentiens — inimicos? Hanc autem ignorantiam tibi soli — credo quidem te nullos in hoc habere socios — relinquamus, ut videre possimus qualiter in sequentibus debaccheris.

120   'Sed per Deum immortalem,' inquis, 'cum pollens et fortis exercitus agrum vestrum populetur, cum castra hostium in vestris finibus habeatis, cum iam denique pro tectis et moenibus patriae dimicaturi paene de muris armorum strepitum sentiatis, quid auditis

what you intend, but the opposite of it. Thus we find you expressing surprise at something unnatural, but if what you deem unnatural were not present, natural things would necessarily be abolished, and the weakened intellect would not be able to distinguish
potentiality from act.

These are errors you commit so often that my initial impulse 119
would have been not to reply at all to such a series of absurdities,
a clear sign of your ignorance, were it not that the first impression
made by the elegant alarums (however misplaced) of your prose
seemed to grant it some authority and favor. But as we have dedicated enough time, indeed more time than it is worth, to this part
of your discourse, let's get on with the rest. First, though, let me
acquit myself of another affirmation of yours, lest it seem that I
wish to avoid the question or to agree with you. You declare that
you know we have been for some time the enemies of Italian security. What a marvelously penetrating intellect this fellow has, what
wonderful depth of understanding! Yet if it is likely that a man
who doesn't know what exists clings with such utter certainty to
what doesn't exist that he appears [to himself] to enjoy superior
understanding, how on earth do you know that we are the "enemies of Italian security," as you claim? Is it because we stood up to
the tyranny of your lord, who aimed at subjugating all Italy? Or
because the man who intended to suppress liberty found in us a
resistance stronger and more tenacious than he expected? Is that
how you know that we are enemies of the security of Italy, while
everyone else — unlike you — considers us its heroes and champi-
ons? We shall happily leave you alone (I think on this point quite
alone) to your ignorance so we can take a look at the madness in
the rest of your remarks.

But — by the immortal God!, you add, when a strong and powerful 120
army devastates your territory, when enemies are encamped inside your
borders, when you are close to the point of having to defend your very
homes, hearing from the walls the clangor of arms, what news arrives from

e Gallia illa Transalpina?' Interroga, quod propius est, quid faciamus. Resistimus, viriliterque resistimus, hostes propulsamus, sociorum vestrorum moenia quotidianis terremus aggressibus, duces pollentis illius et fortis exercitus cum ipsorum copiis temptamus ad servitia nostra traducere, minuere vestras et nostras augere copias. Socio nostro domino Mantuano magnam et validam exercitus nostri manum et auxilia sociorum, quae iam ad nos pervenerant quaeque fideliter veniebant, ne se desertum sentiat, destinamus. Iam videbis, finitis domini tui stipendiis, strenuum virum Paulum Ursinum, Romani generis Guelfaeque dignitatis et fidei memorem, castra vestra relinquere et pro nobis, Romanis et Guelfis, contra vestra signa pugnare. Iam videbis et alium gentium multarum ducem, Biordum de Michiloctis, merito discedentem a vobis in foedera nostra transire. Iam videbis et senties gentes vestras et copias in nostrum territorium redeuntes, amissis discursoribus rorariorumque acie dissipata, turpiter aufugisse. Iam audies universum illum vestrum exercitum obsidebundum oppidulum nostrum, Rincinis, circumdare tandemque, turpi discessione, coepta liquisse sua. Videbis etiam incomparabilem ducem Carolum Malatestam, nostris et aliorum sociorum congregatis auxiliis, inclita Venetorum manu fluvialem domini tui classem victoria plenissima dissipare, nec non et terrestrem exercitum apud Governum castrum illud, tormentorum ictibus dissipatis moenibus, expugnantem, duce viro illo, belli atque pacis artibus illustri, Iacobo de Verme, quem celebrande victoriae nostrae[43] gratia nomino—licet clarius habere militiae iubar neges Italiam—viriliter fugavisse.

121   Procul tunc artes militarisque peritia et illa pollentis exercitus fortitudo dominique tui infinita potentia! Et ut verum non

the much-sung Transalpine Gaul? Ask us what *we* are doing—that would be more to the point. We resist, and we resist manfully, we repel our enemies, we attack each day the walls of your allies, we attempt to bring to our side the mercenaries of that strong, powerful army and its troops, we weaken your forces and strengthen ours. We assigned a large detachment of our best soldiers and the reinforcements of our allies, both those on hand and those due by pact, to the lord of Mantua, our ally, lest he feel himself abandoned. Soon you shall see, when the purse of your lord for troops has been drained, the valiant Paolo Orsini, remembering his Roman origins, his good name as a Guelf, and his faith, leaving your camp to fight for us—who are Romans and Guelfs—against your standards. Soon you shall see as well another captain of numerous armed men, Biordo de' Michelotti, leaving you, as is just, and joining our alliance.[133] Soon you shall see and hear tell of your men and troops who, passing the borders of our territory, have been shamefully put to flight after losing their skirmishers and seeing their light infantry defeated. Soon you shall have report of how your whole army—after besieging our small town of Rincine— has suffered the dishonor of abandoning the field without completing its mission.[134] And you shall see that remarkable commander, Carlo Malatesta, having deployed the reinforcements sent by us and other allies, use the help of renowned Venetian troops to rout completely the river fleet of your lord; and you shall also see his land army—under the great captain Jacopo Dal Verme, celebrated for his prowess in war and peace, whom I mention for the sake of honoring our own victory (and to refute your claim that Italy has no brighter beacon of military virtue[135])—which had broken down the walls of that town with catapults and was on the point of taking it, heroically put to flight near Governolo.[136]

So enough of the prowess, military experience and the cele- 121 brated boldness of that strongest of armies, and enough of the infinite power of your lord! And so as not to pass over the truth in

taceam, nisi fuisset occultum foedus, quod quidam Bononiensium—magnis corrupti pecuniis—cum domino tuo percusserant,
quo non permiserunt illi victores uti victoria, si quid potest de talibus affirmari, dies illa beati doctoris et praesulis Augustini potuit
afferre maximam domino tuo cladem, multosque miseros de iugi
sui servitudine liberare. Sed nondum dies advenerat positura tyrannidi tantae finem; erit tamen, erit, crede mihi, quando Deus
vult, qui nihil in humanis rebus corporeum, cum ea omnia trans-
eant, fecit aeternum. Dic tu, quid tanta fecerit domini tui potentia
etsi repperit nos spem omnem nostram, ut arguis, in aliquo posuisse? Posuimus, fateor, magnam spem in serenissimo Francorum
rege, quantique momenti fuisset—nisi, sicut Deo placuit, proh
dolor, eius principis fuisset infirmitas—crede mihi dominus tuus
sensisset. Sed nimis verum est poeticum illud: 'Heu nihil invitis
fas quemquam fidere divis.'

122   Non potuit enim—ut debebat, ut decreverat, ut optabat—inclitus ille princeps ferre sociis opem, succurrere filiis et amicis
auxiliari. Siquidem non concessit id divinitas, quae gravis morbi
regem aegritudine detineri permisit nimis longo temporis spatio;
continuit et oratores nostros ne tantum principem mox tempta-
rent, ut extra periculum sanus fuit, offensionum nostrarum querimonia perturbare, ne recens sospitati redditum tam molestae rei
laederent aporia. Quam rem postquam rex ex oratoribus nostris
agnovit, tam graviter tulit quod ipsos paenituit; nos autem pertae-
sum fuit rem ipsam in eius notitiam perduxisse, dubitantibus omnibus (tanta fuit benignitas et animi sui commotio) recidivationis
periculum, scientibus hunc eventum tibi forte, certissime vero fore
tuo domino nimis gratum.

silence, if it had not been for that secret pact between your lord and some Bolognese who had allowed themselves to be corrupted with large sums of money, preventing the victors from taking full advantage of their victory, if one may state one's views about this, on the day of the blessed doctor and bishop Augustine[137] this event could have brought the final ruin of your lord and the liberation of many unfortunates from the yoke of slavery. But that day had not yet come when the last word had been said of that great tyranny; it shall come, all the same, believe me, it shall come when such shall be the will of God,[138] who has created nothing destined to last in eternity among the physical trappings of the life of men, but that sooner or later must vanish. And then, tell me, what would the great power of your lord have done even if he had discovered that we had put all our hopes (as you claim) in a certain person? We had placed great hopes, I confess, in the most serene king of the Franks, and what that might have meant your lord would soon have discovered, if God had not, alas, intended that sovereign to become ill. That poetic tag is all too true: "It is not right, alas, to place hope in any individual if the gods will otherwise."[139]

The illustrious sovereign was unable to help his allies, his sons 122 and his friends, as he was obliged to, as he had decided to, as he had hoped to. It was God, that is, who did not allow it, letting a serious malady weaken the king over an excessively long time; and He kept our ambassadors from seeking to disturb so great a sovereign with complaints about the insults suffered until he was wholly cured and out of danger, so that such unfortunate news would not fill him with anxiety when he had only recently regained his health. Informed at last by our ambassadors, his displeasure made our ambassadors regret the delay. It displeased us to have to apprise him of the news, since all, knowing his great affection for us, feared a relapse, and were aware that such an event would no doubt have pleased your lord and probably yourself.

123   Non defuit tamen Dei bonitas, quae mentem regis et constantiam gentis nobis ostenderet et linguis obloquentium obviaret.
Siquidem stetit, Dei dono, regia valetudo, quo factum est ut eius
ordinatione validus exercitus pararetur, cum quo comes inclitus
Arminiaci in fratris ultionem tuique ducis exitium, praesidium
nobis, in honorem Gallici nominis et in testimonium fidei regiae
satisfactionemque foederum in Cisalpinam Galliam se transferret,
vexillis regalia ferens signa. Quae, cum praeter conceptam ex regis
infirmitate spem calliditas domini tui vidisset realiter praeparata,
causa fuerunt ut proelio fractus apud Governum, maiora metuens
per Venetorum colligatorum nostrorum manus, indutias moxque
pacem, qualem habere potuit, consentiret. Quique miserat in Tusciam quattuor, ut iactas et ineptissime scribis, equitum legiones
(vere tamen rectiorique locutione 'maximum equitatum') Florentinam gloriam et libertatem sub iugum suae tyrannidis redacturus,
spe sua frustratus, in Tuscia bello fractus turpiterque fugatus in
Lombardia, superbe bellum intulit et humiliter pacem fecit; credoque singulari Dei providentia factum esse quod hostibus, quos
habebat potentia sua contemptui, non se superiorem bello, non
etiam aequalem, quod nobis non mediocris gloria foret, sed in-
feriorem, ut Deo placuit, se videret.

124   Haec scio bello secundo, quod nobis intulit, facta fuisse; haec
scio te negare non posse. Quid autem audiremus e Gallia quidque
per oratores ibidem ageretur nostros et quid eis responderetur et
peterent, ut sciri possit te velim, qui propinquior eras quique cuncta
refers et non alium audiamus. Dicis ergo: 'Afferuntur, credo, quotidie rumores ac litterae cuius, quaeso, sententiae? Legati regiam regemque sollicitant, opem ex foedere debitam ⟨concupiverunt⟩,⁴⁴

However, divine goodness did not fail, and it revealed the king's   123
mind to us as well as the resolution of his people, and stopped the
tongues of naysayers. Restored to complete health, thanks be to
God, the king ordered a strong army to be gathered under the illustrious Count d'Armagnac, and to cross the border of Cisalpine
Gaul, bearing the royal arms on its banners, to revenge his brother,
defeat conclusively your duke, succor us, honor the good name of
the Gauls, show the king's loyalty, and respect agreements.[140] In
the circumstances your astute lord, having become aware that the
king really was preparing for war (notwithstanding the illness that
had given him hope), upon suffering defeat at Governolo, fearing
further defeats at the hand of our Venetian allies, first agreed to a
truce and then to a peace under such conditions as he could obtain. And thus the one who had sent "four legions of cavalry" in
your boastful and botched phrase (it were better to have said "a
great cavalry") in order to subject the glory and liberty of Florence
to the yoke of his tyranny, finding himself checked in his hopes,
defeated on a Tuscan field of battle and shamefully forced to flee
back to Lombardy, started by arrogantly declaring war and ended
by humbly signing a peace. I believe it was brought about by a
special providence of God that to the enemies whom his power
had held in contempt he saw himself made not superior, not even
equal — which would have been no small source of glory for us —
but (by God's good pleasure) actually inferior.

These I know to be events in the second war he made on us;   124
these I know you cannot deny. What news we would hear from
Gaul, what our ambassadors would do, what answers were given
and what questions were asked in response, are things I wish it
were possible for you to learn, who were closer to the events. We
have heard that it was you and none other who reported them all.
Thus you say: *Words and letters arrive every day, I imagine, but of what
tenor? The ambassadors supplicate the court and the king, beg for the help
owed them by treaty, and, when the situation deteriorates, demand that the*

cadentibus paene rebus implorant ne a summo rege, quem sibi
unum defensorem et dominum, spreto caesare neglectaque Romana ecclesia, in tanto tamque propinquo periculo deserantur,
expostulant. In armis hostem esse popularique iam fines eius; nisi
succurratur, omnia brevi esse ruitura significant; esse eum regem
in terris, qui saluti suae consulere possit, praeter eum neminem.
Obsecrant obtestanturque per sacratissimi diadematis maiestatem
ne desertos ac destitutos ludibrio dedat inimici; eius, addunt, inimici qui eis maxime ob hoc infensus sit, quod se et fortunas suas
maiestati regiae, summa cum devotione, commiserint. Miris deinde modis animos Gallorum, suapte natura leves ac tumidos, inflare student, miris suasionibus adhortari, si anniti parum velint,
venisse tempus et apertam esse occasionem non solum Italiae capiendae sed ad manum suam imperii transferendi et ad nutum ecclesiae redigendae; sese cum Ianua, cum maxima[45] Italiae parte
esse iam suos; nihil reliquum, oppresso duce Liguriae, quod terra
marique suae magnitudini possit obstare; ducem autem ipsum,
quamquam magnum aliquid videatur, primo belli impetu esse casurum. Itaque quibus parum est spei parumve consilii ad solum
patriae defendendum, liberam possessionem Italiae atque orbis
terrae imperium pollicentur.'

125   Mirari satis non possum, foedissima belua,[46] temeritatem et
stultitiam tuam, qui scias nos tunc habuisse legatos in Francia (qui
non erant), qui tibi fingas legationis nostrae formam, quid orent
legati nostri, quid enarrent, quid afferant, quidque polliceantur et
petant, et nedum fingas, sed pueriliter et stultissime fingas. Tune
putas acumine mentis, experientia rerum vel ingenii bonitate ad
consiliorum nostrorum rationem attingere, vel quid dicere fac-
ereque decernat Florentinorum prudentia divinare? Nescis, stultissime, nescis quam brevi temporis hora, quam parva rerum varietas
prudentum consilia, maximeque nostra, commutet, quibus proprium, immo proprie proprium est vel minima momenta rerum et
temporum ponderare, quibus numquam fixum determinatumque

high king not desert them in their clear and present danger — the king
whom they longed to have as their sole defender and lord, disdaining his
imperial majesty and ignoring the Holy Roman Church. The enemy —
they cry — has taken to arms and lays waste to his lands; if help is not
given soon, all will be lost. He is the only king in the world who can save
them, there is no other. They pray and implore the king, in the name of his
most holy crown, not to leave them alone and defenseless at the mercy of the
enemy, that enemy who (they add) is particularly hostile to them because
they have entrusted themselves and their fates to his royal majesty, with the
greatest devotion. Next they seek in wondrous ways to stir up the hearts of
the French, a people by nature frivolous and conceited, to exhort them with
wondrous rhetoric. If they but exert themselves a little, the time is ripe and
the moment propitious not only to take Italy captive but also to transfer the
Empire into their own hands and to remake the Church at their command;
Genoa and the greatest part of Italy is already theirs; with the Duke of
Liguria defeated, no force by land or by sea could oppose his power;
that duke, strong as he may seem, will fall at the first attack. Thus, to
precisely those who have little hope and few means of defending the soil of
their own country, the Florentines promise complete control of Italy and
world dominion.

Your insolence and stupidity, you foulest of beasts, continue to   125
surprise me: you "know" that at that time we had ambassadors in
France (but we did not); you invent the kind of mission that they
carried out, what our ambassadors supposedly asked, related, decided, and sought to obtain; you not only make it up, you do so in
a childish and utterly stupid way. Do you really think you are intelligent, experienced and ingenious enough to deduce the reasons
behind our counsels or to guess at what the prudence of the Florentines decided to say and to do? Don't you know, you fool, that a
single hour or a small variation in events will change the counsels
of the prudent, especially in our case? For us it is proper — and
properly so — to weigh the slightest variations in events and circumstances; for us a decision is never fixed and settled for good

consilium est nisi cum agitur nisique, rebus ipsis instantibus, ex tempore consulatur.

126   Oratores autem nostri, post duos menses et ultra cum in Franciam appulerunt, quam opem, quibus rebus cadentibus implorabant? Stabant, Dei gratia, res steteruntque, licet strepitus illius tempestatis instaret, nec cessere loco sed obviam se fecere periculis Deique gratia sine periculo periculum oppresserunt. Erras, demens vesaneque vates et, ut superius dixi, vemens, hoc est sine mente vates; erras, profecto, qui divinas nos per oratores—quos diu post aggressum, firmatis rebus tutique periculo, in Franciam misimus—opem *rebus cadentibus* implorasse expostulasseque, *tanto tamque propinquo periculo, non deseri* ceteraque quibus, veluti consiliorum nostrorum conscius, stultissime spatiaris. Erras siquidem nec nosti Florentinorum magnanimitatem, cuius virtutis non est suppliciter petere quod debetur, nec illa fingere quibus sua dignitas minuatur.

127   Non requirebamus, igitur, opem ut perituri, sed ut quibus ex foedere debebatur, dicentes oculos totius Italiae sociosque suos atque nostros ad haec notanter esse conversos; hinc omnes coniecturam assumpturos quidnam possit ex regia colligatione sperari, quantum in Gallis possit esse praesidii, famam et gloriam regis et gentis in optima mundi parte ex hac subventione fideique observatione pendere. Antiquissimos filios, devotissimos servitores novosque colligatos et socios offensos esse—improperantibus gentibus suis atque dicentibus: 'Videamus si forte rex veniat atque galli, et liberent eos'—maiestatemque suam in sociis eius offensam esse reputationemque Gallorum vilipendio habitam. Nos pro nostris iniuriis, Dei gratia, dignam assumpturos ultionem, sed ad

until it is acted upon and unless counsel is taken directly under the pressure of events.

Our ambassadors, then: after more than two months in France, just what kind of help would they have appealed for on behalf of a cause that was [you say] on the point of collapse? Our cause was solid, thank God, and would remain so despite the murmur of the approaching storm; so far from giving way, we faced dangers squarely, and, thank God, we subdued the dangers that threatened without danger. You are mistaken—a crazy and demented soothsayer, and, as I called you above, a mindless *(vemens)* soothsayer, i.e., one who is utterly lacking in sense[141]—you are badly mistaken to divine that we sent ambassadors *when the situation had deteriorated*, when in fact we sent them to France long after the start of hostilities, when our cause was strong and we were not in danger, in order to demand that *the high king not desert them in their clear and present danger* and the other things you expatiate upon, as if you had been a party to our decisions. You are greatly mistaken and you do not know the greatness of spirit of the Florentines: it is not in keeping with their virtue at all to plead for what is due them— or to invent things that might diminish their good name.

We asked for help not as one in straits but as one who asks for his due according to agreements, noting that all Italy and her allies were watching with great attention, for this would show what degree of trust could be given to a future alliance with the king, what help could be forthcoming from the Gauls, how the fame and glory of the king and his people depended in the principal part of the world[142] on his aid and respect he showed for loyalty. We further added that those who from time immemorial were their children and devoted servants, lately allied with him by a pact, were offended by the voices of those taunting them with the shout of "Let's see if the king and his Gauls come in to free them," offending His Majesty before his allies and denigrating the repute of the Gauls.[143] We set about taking due vengeance for our own injuries,

altitudinem iniuriae regalis culminis ulciscendam nos et nostros socios non sufficere; nisi funditus extirpetur serpens ille Ligusticus manuque regia potentiaque Gallici nominis exstirpetur, numquam expiatum erit scelus illud iniuriae, quo tam contumeliose non est veritus in sociis regiae maiestatis, regem et nationem Gallicam violare.

128 His et his similibus—quae decus Italicum, Romanum genus et Florentinorum decebant gloriam et, quod prius honoris gratia dici debuit, mentem animosi principis gentisque Martiae poterant commovere—debita repetebamus auxilia, non ploratu vel imploratu, sicut fingis, sed vera, sed mascula ratione. Procul a nobis et dignitate nostra quiritatus illi serviles atque plebeii, vel illae lacrimae tristesque querelae, quae quidem te forte decent et tibi similes, et quas de nobis incongrua ratione commentus es. Cur autem, inter alia quae nobis imponis, dixisti—quodque stultius est, nos dixisse confingis—nos sprevisse caesarem et Romanam ecclesiam neglexisse? Nosne regiae gravitati diceremus ob ipsum et eius foedera naturalem dominum nostrum caesarem contempsisse, qui sibi sit sanguine proximus, liga iunctus, cunctisque respectibus benivolus et amicus? Nosne Christianissimo principe devotissimoque sanctae matris ecclesiae diceremus nos Romanam ecclesiam neglexisse? An adhaerere maiestati suae est ambo vel alterum praedictorum? Numquid dominus tuus, cum longi temporis instantia miraque largitate curavit regi praefato foedere iunctus esse, vel sprevit caesarem vel neglexit ecclesiae dignitatem? Si non ipse, cur de nobis extimas atque fingis?

129 Unum scio: quod dominus tuus neglexit nos specialiter curavisse. Dominum quidem nostrum summum pontificem et Romanam ecclesiam expresse fecimus excipi, quod benignitas regia, schismate non obstante, iussit—sicut petivimus—annotari.

by the grace of God, but we and our allies were not enough to avenge the insults to his sovereign highness; only complete elimination of the Ligurian snake[144] by means of the royal hand and the power of the Gallic name could fully avenge him for the enormity of that injury, wherein your lord had the effrontery to insult and dishonor the king, the Gallic nation and the allies of his royal majesty.

With these and other words — befitting the good name of Italians, our Roman descent and the glory of the Florentines, and, more importantly, suited to stir the soul of a bold sovereign and a warrior people — we asked for the help due to us, without weeping or imploring, as you pretend, but with true and masculine reasoning. Far from us and our honor be those slavish and plebeian wailings, the tears and plaints! These may be well for you and yours, but you ascribe them wrongly to us. And why, among the many things you say we did, do you say (and still more foolishly, pretend that *we* said) that we despised the emperor and ignored the Church of Rome? We are supposed to have said to His Majesty the king that we despised the emperor, our natural lord in his own person and by mutual agreement, he who is a relation of the king, his ally and in everything favors and befriends him? We supposedly said to the most Christian king, most devoted to Holy Mother Church, that we would disregard the Church of Rome? Is it required to adopt one or both of the aforesaid attitudes to be allied to His Majesty? Surely your own lord, during the entire time he worked (and spent) mightily in order to come to an alliance with the said king, did not despise the emperor or neglect the authority of the Church?[145] If *he* did not, why do you reckon and pretend that *we* did? 128

I know this for certain: that which your lord neglected, we cultivated with particular care. In fact we expressly strove to support the supreme pontiff our lord and the Church of Rome, as ordered by the king in his generosity, despite the schism, and as we 129

327

Et tu, inconsideratissima belua, nos mentiris Romanam ecclesiam neglexisse, fingis oratores nostros dicere 'hostem in armis esse, popularique fines eius'? Qua grammaticae[47] ratione potest antecendenti vel substantivo pluralis numeri relativum aut adiectivum construi singulare? Cui coniungitur, obsecro, pronomen illud 'eius,' quod est numeri singularis? Numquid oratoribus, qui loquuntur, an finibus, de quibus est sermo? Recognosce, puer, recognosce tuos errores, in quos incidisse, cum turpe sit grammatico, turpius est logico, sed turpissimum oratori. Nec fugias, ut intelligendum sit per illud relativum 'eius' personam regis. Sciebat enim rex sociorum fines — quos popularetur hostis — suos non esse populationesque illas immediate non esse regni vel regis damnum, iniuriam vel offensionem, sed sociorum, quas ulcisci prohibereque deberet, ad quod, ut dictum est, validum exercitum destinabat. Incommodum esse, non dedecus sociorum in illis offensionibus rex videbat, cum turpe non sit pari vel maiori potentia bello premi; turpissimum autem et inexpiabile dedecus esse vastari vel invadi praesumptione vel temeritate minoris, quod tu [nos] fingis non solum nos excellentiae regis imponere sed ex tua persona conaris in regiam iniuriam persuadere.

130   Non est modestiae circumspectionisque Florentinae, quod sibi turpe non fuerit, falso praesertim in alterius contumeliam dedecusque transferre, nec, quod omnino non sit, improperare celsitudini tanti regis et eius mentem mendaciis perturbare. Vide circumspiceque, stultissima belua, qualiter ignorantiae culpam atque notam effugias. Hinc, si verum dixeris, grammaticam offendis; inde vero, si falsum senseris, oratoriam diligentiam artisque rhetoricae instituta perturbas, nobis attribuens quod non decet vel

requested. And you, thoughtless beast, *you* spread the lie that we neglected the Church of Rome, and you put the following words in the mouth of our ambassadors: *The enemy has taken up arms and lays waste to his lands.* And what law of grammar permits agreement between an antecedent or substantive in the plural with a singular pronoun or adjective? To whom, if you please, does that "his," in the singular, refer? Perhaps to the ambassadors who are speaking, or else to the lands which the phrase mentions? Admit, my boy, admit your errors, which would bring shame to a grammarian, even more to a logician, and most of all to an orator. And don't try to get off the hook by saying that the "his" agrees with "king." The king well knew that the lands of the allies being devastated at the time by his enemy were not his and that the sacks did more damage, outrage and insult to his allies than to him; his duty was to take revenge for them and interdict them, to which end he had gathered an army, as was said. The king saw the offenses his allies had suffered, not as a mark of shame, but only as a setback, since it is not dishonorable to be pressed hard by a power equal to or greater than one's own, while it is dishonorable and a source of inexpiable shame to be invaded or devastated by the rashness or audacity of a less powerful enemy — a disgrace you pretend that we laid upon the king's excellence, but which [in fact] *you* in your own person[146] tried to argue, to the detriment of the king.

It ill accords with Florentine modesty and prudence to falsely 130 attribute events which would hold no disgrace for us in order to insult and disgrace another person [i.e., the king], or to reproach His Highness for acts which were entirely free of dishonor and to trouble his mind with lies. Be careful and look about you, you stupid creature, how you go about escaping guilt and disrepute for your ignorance. On the one hand, if you've said the truth, you've committed an error of grammar; on the other hand, if you've lied, you lack the precision expected of an orator and you violate the rules of rhetoric, attributing to us implausible behavior and

splendori regiae maiestatis imponens quod eidem cedat ad dedecus et ruborem quodque nimis debeat iracundiam tanti regis contra tuum dominum provocare. Nam licet nos id fingas dicere, tu
tamen es qui dicis proque domino tuo dicis, et sicut alia multa
contra dictam maiestatem et in eius contumeliam ista dicis, ut dignissimum sit serenitatem eius et universos regni proceres contra
dominum tuum, cuius beneplacita non transires, sine dubio com-
moveri.

131   Verum, ad mendacia rediens tua, comminisceris atque fingis
quod miris modis animos Gallorum, ut inquis, suapte natura leves et tumidos, oratores nostri conentur inflare. Nondum satur
maledictis es! Hactenus Gallos leves dixisti, nunc leves et tumidos
criminaris. Quis tantae procacitati tuae, digna vicissitudine, valeat
respondere? Nimis erat hoc eis vel semel obiecisse, licet iudicio
meo falsum sit. Equidem eos video, sicubi gravitas requiratur,
talem praestare constantiam quod adici nihil possit. Si sint con-
versatione laeti, convivatione iocundi, collationibus placidi, cum
pietate in Deum tum fidelitate in regem, fide in reliquis non
constantes solum sed constantissimi sint, cur ipsos levitatis accu-
sas? Hoc unum scio quod si semel in dominum insurgent tuum,
tibi videbuntur et eidem maxima nimis firmitate constantes. Pro-
pinqua sunt virtutibus vitia facilique depravatione potest medium
ad extrema reduci. Rigidus et crudelis iustitiae custos dicitur,
misericors vero remissus; frugalitas avaritia vocatur, et licet liberalitas sit medium prodigalitatis, facile trahitur ad extremum. Sic
tu frontis hilaritatem, laetitiam cordis et iocunditatem mentis levitatem vocas, quae deberes appellare virtutem. Tumidos autem ela-
tos atque superbos ducis,[48] quod animi sint alti, quod indignan-
tis, quamvis non sine ratione, naturae. Potes in haec facillima

ascribing to His Majesty's splendor things that would result in his shame or embarrassment—and likely provoking the anger of this great king against your lord into the bargain. In fact, although you pretend we made these statements, it's really you who make them, and you are speaking on behalf of your lord; as in so many other cases, your statements are contrary to his interests and insult him. Doubtless it would be a most worthy thing for His Highness and all the peers of his realm to be provoked to action against your lord, whose approval you would not trespass.

For example, to go back to your lies, you feign and pretend 131 that our ambassadors tried in every conceivable way to flatter the Gauls, who (you say) by nature are fickle and proud. You just can't stop using offensive language: before the Gauls were "fickle" and now they are accused of being "fickle and proud." You are so shameless, who could reply to you in kind and as you deserve? It was bad enough to make the former charge, one that I think is unjust. As far as I can see, in matters requiring the greatest seriousness, they act with complete constancy. If they are affable in conversation, lively at banquets, peaceful in discussion, showing both piety toward God and loyalty to the king, and in other things reliable and wholly reliable, why do you accuse them of inconstancy? I'm certain of one thing: if they ever attacked your lord, you and he would find them all too resolute in their constancy. Not very much separates virtue from vice and a little corruption is enough to pass from the right mean to excess. The guardian of justice may be called unbending and cruel; the indulgent man compassionate. Parsimony passes for avarice and although liberality is the right mean with respect to prodigality it is easily taken for an excess. Thus you label as fickle a jovial temper, cordiality and good humor, which you ought to call virtues. At the same time you consider them arrogant and proud because they are magnanimous and naturally, but not without reason, inclined to indignation. You can slip into these vices very easily. But that innate

declinatione transire. Sed illa naturae bonitas innata Gallis, benignitas humanitasque cogunt omnes illa, quae vitiosa videntur in eis, veras virtutes, non vitia, reputare.

132   Quod autem mendacissime fingis, nos ipsos adhortari venisse tempus et apertam occasionem non solum Italiae capiundae, sed ad manus suas imperii transferendi, forte verisimile tibi videri potest, qui secundum stultitiae tuae nutum quid dicamus quidque gens illa respondeat—quasi mandatorum nostrorum testis et eorum quae gerantur in Francia conscius—vanissima relatione designas; quae num vera sint nolo quod alius quam tu ipse respondeas. Dicis enim sicuti mirus orator qui diligenter narrata mox destruat et causam dedat suam. Itaque quibus parum est spei parumve consilii ad solum patriae defendendum, liberam possessionem Italiae atque orbis terrae imperium pollicentur ut—stante verborum tuorum hac verissima, quod et ego fateor, ironia—nec vera sint nec verisimilia quae praemittis. Concedere solemus et possumus quae sunt in nostra potestate, licet aliquando defendere nequeamus, ut potentioris interpositione personae saltem in hostis non veniant dicionem. Quis autem, nisi stultus, cum de suarum rerum defensione laboret, maiora quae sua non sint nec ab eius pendeant potestate solet offerre? Talis autem et tam vanus oblator apud quos, nisi stultissimos, inveniret auditum?

133   Sed veniamus ad reliqua. 'Non sum dubius,' inquis, 'ad haec omnia benigna et grata responsa suscipiunt: regi salutem amicorum esse cordi et foedera nuper icta memoriae; bono se illos animo esse iubere, nequaquam eorum necessitati maiestatem regiam defuturam. Et fortasse, cum armatis legionibus egeatis, prius pro vestra salute intercedendum putant, quod etiam si impetratis est maximum. Interim stabunt illi suis occupati deliciis, fruentur opima in pace opibus suis, dum vos miseri in tanto incendio

cordiality peculiar to the Gauls, their generosity and courtesy compel everyone to consider characteristics that could seem negative as unquestionable virtues, not vices.

The bald-faced lies you deal out—that we would have attempted to convince them with the claim that the occasion was ripe to conquer Italy and for the empire to be transferred into his hands[147]—might well seem likely to you, guided as you are by stupidity, who make empty reports about our words and that nation's replies as if you had witnessed our embassies and followed events in France. I want you to respond personally as to whether these charges are true. What a wondrous orator you are: you build up a narrative, then destroy it and surrender the case. Thus, in line with the highly veracious irony of your discourse—which I agree is ironic[148]—your premise is neither veracious nor probable: that the very persons who have few hopes of and few measures for defending their country are promised the complete control of Italy and of the entire world. We are accustomed and able to cede our possessions on occasion when we are unable to defend them, in order that—thanks to the intervention of a greater power—they do not fall under enemy jurisdiction. Who except a dolt would, while struggling to protect his own possessions, offer greater things that are neither his nor dependent on his power? What man who made such empty offers would find any apart from complete idiots to give him a hearing?

But let us carry on to the remainder. *I do not doubt,* you say, *that all this may provoke friendly and pleased replies, such as: the king has at heart the security of his friends and does not forget pacts recently signed; he urges them not to lose heart, for His Majesty the king will never fail to come in their aid. It may even be the case, although you need armored legions, that the French decide to intervene for your security by first sending legations, which is the most you will get for your entreaties. In the meantime they will stand around, taken up with their pleasures, enjoying their wealth in plentiful peace, whilst you wretches burn in the*

132

133

conflagratis. Sed age: tueri velint non solum nuda auctoritate sed
armis! Ut omittam qualis animus caesaris totiusque Germaniae
futurus, si quis ad Italiam Gallorum motus fiat, cum sibi pro dignitate imperii—cuius in Italia caput est—viderit subeundum esse
certamen; ut, inquam, omittam hoc, quod vero propius est, omnem Gallorum impetum non solum posse tardare sed tollere atque
cohibere. Veniant certe Galli et affletur vobis ab Occidente aura
illa salutaris, per quam in summa malorum anxietate respirare
possitis; venient tamen eo tempore ut non ad defendendam
vestram salutem, sed ad deplorandum casum et exsequias celebrandas venisse videantur.'

134   Bona verba satisque, ni fallor, apposita praemisisti! Cum autem
Gallos ego alti animi, tu vero tumidos esse velis, quomodo congruit quod pro sociis, quos iuvare debeant et in quorum offensionibus offensi sint, intercedere se disponant? Quod honorare
dignentur hostem, ut legatione regia dominum tuum[49] moneant,
rogent, vel requirant ut ab armis discedat et regis socios ulterius
non offendat? Tamne vanus es tu et alii, ne dominum vestrum dicam, adeoque vobis nescio quid de principatu totius Italiae persua-
sistis ut dignissimum reputetis, etiam debere, principum principes
vestrum hunc ducem verbis et factis, velut summum aliquid, honorare? Sed absit quod qui tyrannice subditos opprimit quique vi,
pecunia dolisque super omnes tyrannidem extendere semper quaerit a legitimis verisque principibus cultu talis honorificentiae cele-
bretur.

135   Quid autem de caesare vel Germania somnias, quibus in Italia
nihil inimicitius quam tuus dominus esse debet, qui iustum sacro-
sancti imperii dominatum, sub caesarei vicariatus obtentu, crude-
lem in tyrannidem commutavit? Debitum caesaris est et obtinen-
tium imperii principatum succurrere populis, opprimere violentos,

conflagrations of war. But come: they may [after all] want to protect
you with their arms as well as their mere authority. I won't say how the
emperor and all Germany would take it were the French to make any
move against Italy; they would have to contest any invasion to defend the
prestige of the Empire, whose capital is in Italy. I don't say it, but this fact
alone could go far, not only to delay any French invasion, but to eliminate
and suppress it. Let's allow that the French come; suppose that salutary
Western wind should blow toward you. It might let you breathe amid your
great anxieties; yet they will likely come at a time when they will not
be safeguarding you but weeping for your downfall and celebrating your
funeral.[149]

You've begun with fine words and quite apposite ones, if I mis-   134
take not! Since, however, I believe the Gauls to be noble and you
think them arrogant, how is it in keeping [with your view] that
they would be disposed to intercede on behalf of allies whom they
are duty-bound to help, allies by offending whom they too are offended? How is it possible that such arrogant folk would deign to
show honor to an enemy and send him an embassy to advise, request or require him to lay down arms and renounce further trou-
bling the king's allies? Are you really so deluded? Have you and
the others, not to say your lord, such illusions about one day
controlling all Italy as to think it right — no a duty! — that the
greatest sovereigns show homage in word and fact to this your
duke, as if he were some kind of supreme authority? May one who
oppresses his subjects under a tyrannical regime and attempts
(with force, gold and deceit) to extend that tyranny over all never
receive such homage from legitimate and true sovereigns!

And then what nonsense do you spout about the emperor and   135
Germany, whose greatest enemy in Italy is none other than your
lord, he who, under the cover of an imperial vicariate, has transformed the just lordship of the Holy Roman Empire into a cruel
tyranny?[150] It is the duty of the emperor and of any obtaining imperial rulership to help the people, defeat the violent, extirpate

335

tyrannidem exstinguere et ne nomen adulteretur imperii providere. Sed his et aliis quae proxime rettuli respondeat tibi stultitia tua, respondeat eventus rerum, respondeat constantissima tot laborum tolerantia nostra et illa Florentinorum bello paceque felicitas, quam Deus dignatus est nobis offensis per iniuriam indulgere.

136 Subdis autem, ut nos a debiti subsidii spe deterreas vanitate solita, multa, quibus tibi persuadere videris regem illum, tam divinae quam humanae fidei specimen, percussorum nobiscum foederum oblitum iri. Dicis etenim: 'Quae tamen est ista dementia tanta, tam abhorrens ab omni sensu rationeque perversitas, ut cogitare possitis amplissimum regem officiorum plurimorum, sanctissimae societatis atque affinitatis immemorem, ita Florentinas opes tuendas ampliandasque suo periculo suscepisse ut, ceterarum rerum omnium negligens, vestrae tantum salutis et gloriae studiosissimus videatur?' Et ne per cuncta trahar neque singula sed rerum summam referam, tu dignitatem domino tuo concessam, tu affinitatem regiam, tu societatem et amicitiam, tu regalia signa commemoras, quae quantum coget respondendi necessitas verbis referam tuis.

137 Nunc autem, ut ad verborum tuorum principium redeam, nonne maxima teneris stultitia qui audeas affirmare nos esse tam fatuos quod cogitare possimus amplissimum regem, ceterarum rerum omnium negligentem, fore nostrae salutis et gloriae tantummodo studiosum? Quibus hanc dementiam, obsecro, vel — ut usitatius loquar — amentiam obicis? Nonne Florentinis — quorum circumspectio nota est, qui rerum agibilium, sicut sunt, expertissimi reputantur, quique administratione maximae rei publicae, cui praesunt, abunde docti sunt — nullum populum nullumque dominum aut principem esse quem simul non oporteat rebus plurimis providere? Discunt bello, discunt pace Florentini quotidie sibi sociis, sibi subditis sibique propriis civibus multotiensque extraneis

tyranny and protect the good name of the empire. But to these and other obligations I have just mentioned let an answer be given by your stupidity, let an answer be given by the outcome of events, and let an answer be given by the staunch tenacity of our efforts, and by the good fortune in peace and war that God has seen fit to give us Florentines, who have suffered so much injustice.

To contrive that we give up hope for the aid due to us, you add 136 in your empty chatter many other things which seem to persuade you that this king—a model of constancy toward God and men— has forgotten the pact signed with us. In fact you say: *What sort of madness is this, an obstinacy devoid of any sense or reason, that should lead you to think that so important a king—a man forgetful of so many of his duties, of the bonds of holy religion and the ties of blood—should undertake at his own peril to protect and enlarge the resources of the Florentines, to the point where he becomes utterly committed to your security and glory alone, neglecting all his other affairs?*[151] To save words and discuss only the essential issues, you recall the concession of the title of nobility, then the relation by marriage with the royal house, then alliance and friendship, then the king's coat of arms; about which things I shall quote you when necessary.

But coming back to the start of your discourse: Aren't you in 137 the grip of the utmost stupidity when you dare affirm that we are foolish enough to believe a king of such importance could be occupied exclusively with our security and our glory? To whom do you impute such madness, or (to use the commoner word), such nonsense? Do you mean to remind the Florentines—celebrated for their circumspection, who are regarded as experts in the conduct of practical affairs, and who have learned abundantly how to administer the greatest of republics, over which they preside— that there is not a single people, lord, or prince but has to follow many affairs at the same time? Every day the Florentines learn, in war and in peace, that they must consult the interests simultaneously of their allies, their subjects, their own citizens, and many

eodem tempore consulendum. Ergo quod diuturnis experientiis in
se vident, nec possunt continuo non sentire, possunt in aliis igno-
rare? Cum quot diebus te necesse sit comedere quo vivas, credes
alios posse subsistere si non edant?

138   Quo videre potes quam stulta sit cogitatio tua. Numquamne
putavimus regem—infinitis gentibus imperantem cuiusque sit, pro
magnitudine rerum suarum, scire meditarique quicquid in orbis
ambitu praeparetur—una solum posse cogitatione, cura providen-
tiaque teneri? Semper tamen cogitavimus, etiam si sibi maiora
forsan incumberent, ipsum, summae constantiae regem, numquam
nos, si molesti quicquam urgeret, filios devotos fidelesque socios
deserturum. Nec nos fefellit opinio; quam primum, enim, per va-
letudinem potuit, ducem et exercitum venturum in Italiam praepa-
ravit, ut illum dominum, qui ligam et societatem regiam non
ignorans socios tanti principis fuit ausus offendere, castigaret. Non
reputavit amicum, non socium, non affinem, non etiam consangui-
nem illum, qui nulla iusta causa—immo qui solum praetendit in
causa foedus regium vel, ut tu nominas, Gallicanum—socios suos
invasit acrique bello sibi statuit persequendos. Cumque quem felicis memoriae regis avus affinitate dignatus, externum licet, ornarit
in comitem cuique rex ipse sacratissima lilia sua concesserit ex
media saltem parte monstro virulentae viperae subicienda (quam
rem maximi facerent non dedisse, faciunt et male dimittere, peius
non repetere, pessime non auferre), cum inquam videant ex hac
offensione nostra contra dominum nostrum regem, cum tot cumu-
latis beneficiis, tot honoribus totque gratiis non immemorem
solummodo sed ingratum, dignum non putarunt cui parcendum
foret tamque manifestae scelus iniuriae remittendum.

times foreigners as well. So could they really be ignorant that what they have experienced each day, and cannot avoid being aware of continually, applies to others? If you need to eat each day in order to live, could you really believe that others can survive without meals?

So you can see just how foolish your line of reasoning is. Could 138 we ever really have thought that the king, sovereign of countless peoples and held accountable for keeping abreast of what happens across the world, can take up only a single problem, concern or action at a time? All the same, we have always supposed that a king of the most sterling loyalty as he, even when pressed by duties perhaps greater, would never abandon us in our time of need, us his devoted sons and loyal allies. And we were not mistaken, for as soon as his health allowed, he chose a leader and an army to send to Italy to punish the ruler who, despite knowing of their league and alliance with the king, dared offend allies of so great a sovereign. The latter did not reckon as a friend, ally, nor even as a relation by marriage or blood anyone who invaded the territory of his allies without just cause — or rather parading a royal (or, as you prefer, Gallican) treaty as an excuse — and who decided to wage cruel war upon those allies. But when your lord, whom the king's grandfather of happy memory thought worthy, though a foreigner, of the title of count, and whom the king himself allowed to add to his arms the most sacred lily (in the middle, at least, beneath his own monstrous, poisonous viper — they would have done best not to allow that, they did badly to forsake the lilies, worse not to ask for them back, worst of all not to take them back) — then, I say, once the French saw from the insult to us (and thus to the king) that this man was not only forgetful but also ungrateful to the king our lord, who had heaped benefits, honors and privileges upon him, they did not consider him worthy of pardon and forgiveness for a crime of such manifest injustice.

139   Velim autem tecum, si placet, intelligere: cum neges regem suo
periculo suscepisse Florentinas opes tuendas ampliandasque, quod
periculum tanto regi posset ex his, quae numeras, provenire?
Numquid forsitan, sicut quondam Romani, Caesare duce, nunc
dominus tuus transibit Alpes et montes penetrans Gebennenses[50]
contra regem in Galliis bellum geret? Vel quod aliud sentis regi
periculum imminere? Quid per opes Florentinas intelligis: divitias
an potentiam? Divitiae vero nostrae, licet rex et omnis Gallia ferant nobis in hostes opem, quid recipient incrementi? Quid exter-
nae defensionis nobis opus est, ut eas a tui domini violentia
tueamur? Ad potentiae vero nostrae vel divitiarum ampliationem
tuitionemque decetne nos tantum principem forte requirere quem
et eius auxilia debeamus sequi, non praecedere, cuique deceat nos
servire? Non ad defensionem nostram sed ad opprimendum hostem, quo sospite securi fore non possumus, et ad ulciscendas suas
iniurias observationem foederum petebamus, quo sibi nos possemus (non haberet ipse nobis, non enim id decuit) militare.

140   Sed oportet in hoc detegere quod sentimus, quo videas tu et alii
sciant, sciat et ipse dux tuus, sciant et omnes, nos ad defensionem
nostram—cui per Dei gratiam in nobis fuit, sicut experientia notum fecit, abunde praesidii—numquam regem voluisse requirere,
sed solum ad delendum hostem suam potentiam excitare. Scie-
bamus inclitum illum regem non coniecturis solum, quae multae
sunt, sed certissima ratione tenere se ducis tui machinationibus,
magica nescio qualiter arte confusum, in id morbi, quo laborabat,
arreptum esse. Qua quidem re gaudebamus causae tam urgenti
tamque gravi legitimam et apertam (offensione nostra, immo regia) causam accessisse. Sed nondum dies venerat sua, nonque regi
longeque minus et nobis concessum erat illud opprimere posse

Please explain your thinking to me: Since you deny that the   139
king would have undertaken at his own peril to protect and extend
the resources of the Florentines, what peril could have come to so
great a king from the sources you enumerate?[152] Could the danger
be such, as in Roman days under the general Caesar, that your lord
will cross the Alps near Geneva to make war upon a king in Gaul?
Or what other danger do you think threatens the king? And what
do you mean by "the resources [opes] of the Florentines" — wealth
or power? Touching our wealth, even if the king and all Gaul came
to help us against the enemy, what increase would this give? Of
what outside help do we have need in order to defend our wealth
from your lord? To increase and protect our power or our riches
would it really be seemly for us to turn to so great a sovereign,
whom we would have to follow as supporting troops, not precede
him, and on whom decorum would require us to dance atten-
dance? We asked for our agreements to be respected, not in order
to defend ourselves, but to eliminate an enemy whose safety was
our insecurity, and to take revenge for his insults. We did it so
that we could fight on his side, not so that he would have to fight
in our stead, which would have been unseemly.

But it were best to clarify our intentions, in order for you to   140
realize and others to know, including your duke and everyone else,
that we never asked the king's help for the sake of defending ourselves — having, thanks be to God, more than adequate means to
the task, as events showed — but only asked him to spur his forces
to destroy the enemy. We knew that illustrious sovereign harbored
not a few suspicions and was convinced by certain proofs that the
evil he suffered was the work of your duke's plots, the unlucky results of I know not what magical skill. It pleased us that so
weighty and important grounds for action were added to our legitimate and manifest one, i.e., the offense given to us and therefore to the king. But his time had not yet come, and it was not
vouchsafed either to us or to the king to suppress that monster,

341

monstrum quod, sicut eventus probat, certi sumus ab aeterno fuisse divino numini reservatum. Sed haec omittamus; adeo quidem in praeteritum transierunt, quod vanum sit ea, nisi solum ad reprehensionem mendacii, recensere. Volo tamen advertas regium periculum te non inaniter solum sed stultissime nominasse et amplitudinem tutelamque nostrarum opum ineptissime posuisse, quas tuendas et ampliandas tam indecens esset et ineptum gloriosum illum regem suscipere quam stultissimum nos vel alios postulare.

141 'Potuit fortasse,' dicis, 'vestra calliditas et illa immoderata fingendi mentiendique licentia, qua in rebus omnibus privatis et publicis praeter ceteras gentes utimini, in mente regia aliquid suspicionis affigere, quo ipsum abalienatum aliquantulum a duce Ligustico redderetis.' Quid est immoderata fingendi mentiendique licentia? Dic: a quo vel a quibus hoc Florentinis concessum est? Daturne nobis, ut inquis, praeter ceteras gentes fingendi mentiendique licentia, qua rebus omnibus privatis et publicis uteremur? Si dari potuit, quid reprehendis? Numquid nefas est nos uti vel aliquem alium iure suo? Si vero data non est aut dari non potuit, quid 'licentiam' vocas quae de concedentis auctoritate dependeat? Videsne quam inepte, immo quam absurde vocabulum istud 'licentia' ponas? Videsne te prorsus non intelligere quid vel quo modo dicas? Verum nec fingendo nec mentiendo, non etiam, quod proprie nostrum est, verissima recensendo quae multa dicere poteramus a duce tuo regem benignissimum alienavimus.

142 Scio, nec me potes in hoc decipere, quid et qualiter regem illum in indignationem adduxerit. Cupiens enim dux tuus, perpetua ambitione succensus et Gebellina factione permotus, civitatem Ianuensium occupare—sicut stultae sunt cogitationes hominum— invidia nostra cogitavit hoc posse perficere misitque suos oratores

which, events showed, was destined to happen through divine intervention.[153] But enough, these events belong to the past; and the
only point in reviewing them would be to censure your lies. However, I still want to have you see why your reference to the peril
run by the king was not only beside the point but totally witless,
and your mention of enlarging and preserving our resources was
utterly irrelevant. To have preserved and extended our resources
would have been as unseemly and unnecessary for that glorious
king as it would have been foolish for us to request his doing so.

It may be, you say, *that your craftiness and ungovernable license to lie*   141
and engage in conspiracies — of which you make use in all matters public
and private, more than any other people — have succeeded in fixing a shade
of doubt in that sovereign's mind and alienating him in some small measure
from the Duke of Liguria. Now what is this ungovernable license to
plot and lie? Do tell me, who ever granted this license[154] to the
Florentines? Was it one person or many? Is it really the case, as
you say, that license has been granted us to plot and lie in all affairs public and private more than to other peoples? If license was
granted us, why censure us? Surely it's not wicked for us or anyone else to exercise what is our right? And if this was not or could
not have been granted to us, why say "license," as of a thing dependent upon the authority which grants it? Don't you see how misleading and absurd your use of the term "license" is? Do you realize that you understand neither what you say nor how you say it?
Verily it was neither by plotting nor by lying nor even by reviewing the numerous facts we could have alleged (which is more our
style) that we distanced the beloved king from your duke.

I know well (and about this you cannot deceive us) why and   142
how he angered the king. Motivated by his own unsleeping ambition and by the Ghibelline faction, your duke wished to take
over the city of the Genoese — such are the foolish thoughts
of mankind — and he thought he could bring it off by exploit-
ing the envy that existed toward us. He sent his ambassadors

in Franciam, qui persuaderent puritati regiae nos solo obsistere, etiam ligae nostrae societate, quam numquam tamen contraximus, ne civitate Ianuae, quae se iam regi obtulerat, potiretur, tractans et intendens artibus solitis atque pecuniis illam a rege vicariatu vel censu vel alio modo quolibet obtinere. Sensimus hoc et mirati sumus hominis impudentiam et per oratorem nostrum obiecta, quorum copiam habueramus,[51] curavimus expurgare. Quo plane factum est ut ipse rex manu tangeret oculoque videret quicquid ibidem habebat obstaculi de domini tui machinationibus derivari, nosque non obsistere regi sed tyranno, quem sentiebamus satagere modis omnibus ut urbem illam per fas et nefas sub suae tyrannidis redigeret dominatum.

143   Haec prima labes indignationisque principium, quibus accessit nescio quis rescitus quo maleficii et aegritudinis regiae culpabilis factus est; accessit dixi, nescio quidem si praecessit. Hoc unum scio: Deum testor aeternamque salutem, technam hanc, si techna fuit, vel veritatem, si verum aut repertum fuerit, a nobis nullo modo fidem (illud enim asserere nequibamus) vel principium habuisse. Gavisi sumus, fateor, hanc opinionem esse conceptam, et cum rem ipsam esse cordialiter doleremus et culpam domini tui vehementissime miraremur, optabamus tamen opinionem tanti sceleris tenaciter regis, procerum et etiam populorum mentibus inhaerere et eos pro veritate facinoris in ultionem debitam inflammari. Nec nunc volo discutere numquid infandis artis magicae fraudibus sive carminibus arreptas detur alicui

to France in order to persuade his Royal Blamelessness to block us from his soil and to prevent our treaty alliance (which in fact we never signed) from getting control of the city of Genoa, which had already offered itself to the king, since the duke himself was negotiating (by means of his usual arts and bribes) to keep control of it by means of royal vicar or by tribute or by some other means.[155] We were aware of all this and, shocked at his impudence, tried to rebut the accusations (of which we had a copy) through our ambassadors. And so it came to pass that the king had direct experience of how all the difficulties of that situation derived from the machinations of your lord, and knew that we were opposing, not the king, but the tyrant, whom we knew was doing everything he could, by fair means and foul, to bring that city under his tyrannical lordship.

This was the first debacle, the original motive of our indigna-   143 tion, and then somehow there was added the news that your lord was guilty of sorcery and the king's sickness. I say "added," but in fact I don't know which came first. Of this alone I am certain: I swear by God and the salvation of my soul that we have never given credence to this piece of trickery, if it existed, or to this truth, if it is ever revealed to be truth, being unable to verify it; nor did we initiate the story. It pleased us, I admit, that the story got started, and although the circumstance itself deeply pained us and the guiltiness of your lord much surprised us, at all events we hoped that word of so great a crime might strike root in the minds of king, dignitaries and common people, and push them to mete out a proper punishment in proportion to the truth of the offense. I don't really want at this point to discuss whether with the unspeakable deceptions of the art of magic or with spells it is given to anyone to seize or

solvere mentes
quas velit atque aliis duras immittere curas,
sistere aquam fluviis et vertere sidera retro,

ut ait ille. Nolo nunc, inquam, hoc discutere; nimia quidem cernimus quotidianis experientiis, multa etiam legimus, quibus hoc posse fieri facillime persuaderem. Nec id etiam volo disserere quidnam esset quo culpa tui domini videretur, postquam naturae solvens debitum de medio sublatus est, ne forsan in filios paterna scelera puniantur; licet, si veritas audita fuisset et adhuc forent qui vellent audire, clara posset fide perpendi quod, rebus indiscussis, in dubitationem potuit a quolibet revocari.

144   Verum, ut ad verba redeam tua, Florentinine praeter ceteras gentes immoderate mentiuntur et fingunt? Ipsine soli? Unde ergo verum est propheticum illud: 'Dixi in excessu meo: "omnis homo mendax"'? Quid autem significat apud te praepositio illa 'praeter'? Nonne ponitur exceptive? Sed dices: 'Exclusivam illam dictionem apposui propter id, quod dixeram "immoderate"' (quasi dicas: 'mentiuntur et fingunt omnes, sed immoderatius vos'). Sed unde, precor, hoc exploratum habes? Numquid testis es omnium gentium et nationum? Numquid cum hostem te profitearis, tibi credi putas fidemque deberi? Non es gentium omnium si mentiantur vel non vel an fingere soleant informatus. Cunctas enim gentes non nosti, nec cum omnibus conversatus es, nec quam effrene cuncti mentiantur et fingant. Nullum igitur huius rei tuum testimonium esse potest; verum facillimum hostibus tutumque mendacium cunctis est, quod non possit vel difficillime valeat reprobari.

set free whatever souls he wants,
plunge others into torment, stop
the flux of water or make stars
turn backward in the sky.[156]

I don't want to discuss this now; we see enough instances every day and we also read of many cases which might very easily persuade me that this could have happened. And I prefer not to enter into why your lord might seem guilty of the deed, since he has now passed away, and the sons who survive him risk paying for the misdeeds of their father. In all this, if the truth had been heard and if there were still those interested in hearing it, one could confidently judge a matter which anyone could call into doubt in the absence of an inquiry.

Returning to your words — is it supposed to be the case that the   144 Florentines misrepresent and lie wildly, more than any other people? Are they the only ones? How then could the prophecy be true: "In my rashness I said: 'Every man is a liar'"?[157] What do you understand here by "more than"? Are you using the preposition in the exceptive sense?[158] You may reply "I used the expression to modify 'unbridled,'" as if to say "all plot and lie, but you do so in a specially unbridled fashion." But please, how can you be certain of that statement? Surely you haven't seen in person all peoples and nations? Perhaps, though openly our enemy, you think we should believe and trust you? You cannot know if all peoples lie or if it is or is not their habit to misrepresent things. In fact you don't know all peoples, nor have you had occasion to speak with representatives of each one, nor do you know the extent to which they all lie and misrepresent. Hence your testimony on this matter is worthless; but it is extremely easy and safe for enemies to lie to everyone, because they can't be condemned for that, or only with the greatest difficulty.

145   Sed quid in hoc diutius moror? Scio tibi durius fore quod
obicis posse probare quam mihi, si veniatur in periculum, repro-
bare. Unum tamen scio: quicquid delatreris, nullum in orbe terrarum dominum nullumque populum quem nobis possis de fidei
integritate praeferre. Cuius quidem rei sunt plurima documenta,
quorum unum evidens et invincibile signum est: reiteratio foederum, quae qui nobiscum contraxit, ad tempus libentissime refir-
mavit. Sed cur amplius insto? Clarum est, et privatim et publice,
Florentinos cum omnibus mundi gentibus conversari, mercari con-
trahereque, quod profecto non esset, si tam immoderate fingerent
et mentirentur. Coutuntur Florentinis, qui nec fallere cupiunt nec
falli; coutuntur siquidem et eis summa complacentia delectantur,
circumspicientes subtilitatem in lucro, cautionem in pacto, sinceritatem in observando.

146   Sed iam haec satis. Quod autem, dominum referens tuum,
inquis 'a duce Ligustico' reminisci me fecit eius quod inconsiderate
praemiseras. Appellasti quidem eum supra 'ducem Liguriae,' nunc
vero 'Ligusticum.' Illud autem cum falsissimum sit, hoc non prohibet esse verissimum. Equidem credo non incongrue dici posse de
quocumque, parvo licet, principe quod mundanus sit princeps;
mundi principem vero nullum esse, nisi toti mundo principetur.
Unde vocas, igitur, dominum tuum 'Liguriae ducem,' qui nescio
quo titulo dux sit solummodo Mediolani? Absit per Dei clementiam nomen istud, nec umquam possit ipse vel alius, qui tyrannus fuerit, 'dux Liguriae' nominari. Tibi vero reprehensibile nimis
est, licet magnam Liguriae partem tyrannide premat sua, cum
institutus fuerit in ducem—licet magnae, licet nobilis—civitatis
illius provinciae, ducem propterea Liguriae nominare. Nam, ut
cetera sileam, cum Liguria proxima sit Tusciae finibus solumque
Macra fluvio dirimatur extendaturque per Tyrrheni Maris littora

But why do I dwell on the point? I know that it would be   145
harder for you to prove your accusation against us than for us to
refute it, if it were to be put to the proof. At any rate, of this I am
certain: you may bark all you like but you cannot find in all the
world a sovereign or people more loyal than we are. The proofs of
this are countless, beginning with a clear and indisputable fact: the
renewal of alliances, made on time and to the greatest satisfaction
of the stipulators. Why insist? All know how the Florentines, on
the public as well as the private level, maintain relations with all
the world's peoples, doing business and making agreements, which
could not happen were they to lie and deceive in an unbridled way.
They associate with the Florentines, who wish neither to deceive
nor to be deceived; they associate with them, in fact, and with the
greatest pleasure, because they recognize the Florentine skill in
turning a profit, prudence in fashioning agreements, and honesty
in keeping them.

But I have spoken enough of this. Now, when speaking of your   146
lord you call him "Ligurian duke" which reminds me of an earlier
careless statement of yours. A bit before you refer to him as the
"Duke of Liguria," now as "Ligurian." The first claim is absolutely
false but nothing prevents the second from being perfectly true. As
far as I am concerned, it is not wrong to say of any ruler, however
petty, that he is an earthly ruler, while one cannot call a person
"lord of the earth" unless he rules over the whole earth. Why then
do you refer to your lord as "the duke of Liguria" when he is only
the Duke of Milan (and by what title I know not)?[159] May the
good Lord not grant him this title, and may it never happen that
he or any other tyrant be called "the duke of Liguria." It is deplorable for you to call him "duke of Liguria" on account of his being
made duke of the provincial capital (though great, though noble),
however much he oppresses large part of Liguria. After all, since
(for one thing) Liguria borders Tuscany, separated only by the
river Magra, and runs along the coast of the Tyrrhenian Sea as far

Varum usque—qui sit Narbonensis provinciae limes per Anti[no]
polis⁵² et Niciensis urbis agros fluens—quae regio Genuam, Sao-
nam, Albinganam, Vintimilium, Naulensem civitatem et Niciam
multosque populos et oppida ⟨amplectitur⟩⁵³ quae, per Dei gratiam, domini tui nondum occupavit nec occupabit ambitio, quomodo vocas eum 'Liguriae ducem,' cui tantum deficiat ut illi provinciae dominetur?

147   Dimitto plura, quae maliloquio tuo repetens eadem insulse
prosequeris quibus iam antea fuit responsum. Et ut ad ultimum
huius tuae particulae veniamus, de circumspectione quidem regia
loquens ais: 'Aliquando recognoscet vestra insidias et intelliget vos
pro vestra libidine tam multa de duce optimo et principe clarissimo fuisse mentitos. Qua re non modo suis copiis vos non defendendos esse non existimabit, sed omni dignos supplicio iudicabit tantumque aberit ut vobis corruentibus manum det, ut etiam
optet assurgentes opprimere.'

148   O ducem optimum, qui tyrannus sit, tyrannice semper vixerit,
tyrannica crudelitate saeviat et debacchetur in subditos, occupare-
que vicinos plus quam tyrannice moliatur! O clarissimum principem, qui vere sit princeps omnium tyrannorum! Vere quidem
etiam princeps in subditos, qui scilicet primus ante alios et omnium prima capiat! Testantur hoc agri, domus, vestes, equi ceteraque non pretio sed iniuria capta; testantur famulae, testantur et
concubinae, in quibus obviaverunt iniuriis contumeliae. Vis et
iniustitia deosculatae sunt se! Quae cum sentias et verissima quadam tuae orationis particula conquestus sis, non pudet tamen
(quod honestissime taceri potuit, immo debuit) dicere 'ducem optimum principemque clarissimum' qui sit saevissimus tyrannorum,
quod quam vere dicas omnium iudicium sit.

as the river Var (which borders on the province of Narbonne), passing through the territories of Antibes to Nice, and is a region that ⟨includes⟩ Genoa, Savona, Albenga, Ventimiglia, Noli, and Nice, and many peoples and cities which thank God your power-hungry lord has not yet conquered and never will—how can you call him "duke of Liguria" when he does not control large portions of that province?[160]

I leave aside other parts of your discourse, in which you repeat   147
the absurd and evil accusations that I have already replied to. I come then to the end of this passage where, speaking of the king's prudence, you affirm: *eventually he will realize what you are plotting and he will recognize for what they are all the lies you have told, for your own depraved purposes, about that excellent duke and most illustrious prince. On this account he will not only reckon that you must not be defended by his troops, but he will judge you worthy of every punishment, and so far from helping you prevent your ruin, he will rather choose to suppress any who might rise up to do so.*

O excellent duke, he who is a tyrant, has always lived tyran-   148
nously and inflicts and vents forth upon his subjects his tyrannical cruelty, besides trying to invade his neighbors with his more than tyrannical plots! O illustrious prince—truly the prince of all tyrants! And truly a *prince* to his subjects is this man who holds *primacy* over others and takes their *principal* goods![161] The fields, the houses, the clothes, the horses and other sorts of things taken by force and not by payment, they all bear witness to his tyranny. The serving maids bear witness, as do the concubines, in whom insult meets with injury! Violence and injustice meet and kiss![162] But even if you are aware of his character—and in the truest part of your oration you complained about it—aren't you ashamed to call a cruel tyrant an "excellent duke and most illustrious prince"? It would have been perfectly honorable, indeed it was obligatory, to keep silence about his character; but everyone can judge for himself how true your statements are.

149   Cum autem rex inclitus ille cognoverit insidias domini tui super negotio Ianuensi intellexeritque pro libidine sua contra sinceritatem et innocentiam nostram eum tam multa fuisse mentitum, memor foederum et offensionum nostrarum, quae suae sunt, dignissimos existimabit non defensione, qua non egemus,[54] sed ultione, quam de domino sumat tuo. Dic, tamen, artifex egregie florentis eloquii, quid intelligere voluisti cum scriberes: 'Qua re non modo suis copiis vos non defendendos esse non existimabit, sed omni dignos supplicio iudicabit'? Quid est 'non existimabit non defendendos esse' nisi quod dicere non vis: 'defendendos ducet'? Quod cum ita sit, pudeat, pudeat cum nugis istis in publicum prodiisse, quibus fias, ponderantibus dicta tua, ridiculo postquam in ipsis vide⟨nte⟩s tam multa contra vim rationemque dicendi te, supina nimis ignorantia, posuisse.

150   Sed iam in reliqua transeamus. Inquis ergo: 'Quod si in regia illa Transalpina vestra fraus plus quam amplissimi ducis integritas fidesque valuerit poteruntque vestra praestigia omnium officiorum et necessitudinum memoriam obscurare, mihi credite, nobis est animus sic Gallis obsistere, ut intelligant quod maiores sui saepissime experti sunt: perfacile Gallis Italiam petere, victores redire difficile. Unde proverbium illud a nostris hominibus usurpatum scimus: 'Italiam sepulcrum esse Gallorum,' etc. Longo quidem tractu discurrens si Galli descenderint in Italiam, incliti regis Ludovici quondam ducis Andegavensis exemplo nec non et Iohannis Arminiaci comitis, quorum flendos potius quam gloriandos Italiae recenses interitus, tibi dominoque tuo spem victoriae polliceris. Quae quidem verba nolo repetere; satis enim est ea semel ultimo loco tui maliloquii notavisse. Respondebo tamen summae rerum,

Besides, as soon as that exceptional sovereign heard of the de-   149
ceptions of your lord about the Genoa question and learned that
the latter had told so many capricious falsehoods against our honesty and innocence, and — mindful of agreements and of the offenses against us, which are also against him — he believed us certainly worthy of help, not for our defense (no need) but in order
to punish your lord for his mistake. So now tell me, master of eloquence sublime, what you meant to say when you wrote: *On this*
account he will not only not reckon that you must be defended by his troops,
but he will judge you worthy of every punishment. What does "he will
not reckon that you ought not to be defended" mean if not the
exact contrary of what you write, that is, "he will decide that you
ought to be defended"?[163] This being the case, shame on you for
having published this foolishness, such as to make you ridiculous
in the eyes of anyone who gives it the slightest attention, and looks
at all you have written there, all too heedless in your ignorance,
that is contrary to reason and eloquence.

But let us continue. *And if the fraud you are perpetrating in that*   150
transalpine royal palace should prevail over the upright and loyal behavior
of the most noble duke, and if your deceptions should succeed in darkening
the memory of all the obligations and affections that tie one to the other,
believe me, we are resolved to oppose the French, so that they may under-
stand what their ancestors have experienced many times, that it is very easy
for the French to enter Italy, but difficult to return thence victorious.
Whence our popular proverb: Italy is the tomb of the French, and the
rest.[164] Speaking at length of the possibility of a descent of the
Gauls into Italy, citing the examples of the celebrated King Louis,
onetime duke of Anjou, and of Jean, count of Armagnac, whose
deaths (even more tragic than glorious) in Italy you pass in review,
you raise hope in yourself and in your lord of victory. I do not
wish to repeat the words; it is enough to have once cited them,
along with the last part of your inflammatory accusations. I will

quaeque carpenda singulariter videbuntur, postquam id fecerim, explicabo.

151   Spem capis, igitur, obtinendae victoriae contra Gallos propter duo quae nostris temporis recenses exempla, quasi sis oblitus quam instabilis quamque mutabilis sit fortuna, illis praesertim[55] quibus videtur arrisisse. Nonne meministi Virgilianum illud:

multa dies variusque labor mutabilis aevi
rettulit in melius, multosque alterna revisens
lusit et in solido rursus Fortuna locavit?[56]

Sed ipsam Dei dispositionem, quam quia praeter intentum nostrum agat et occulta sit 'fortunam' dicimus,[57] potesne de praeteriti ratione praesumere quid actura sit, quae sic agat ut ab aeterno sancitum est praeviderique non possit antequam agat nec postquam egerit pervideri? Et si vobis est animus sic Gallis obsistere quod quae minaris eveniant, cum in manibus Dei sint, noli gloriari tamquam ventura sint, sed opta potius metueque quod possit contrarium evenire.

152   Nec exempla sumas ex his quae placent sed ex his quae multotiens acciderunt cogitaque quod in libris veritatis scriptum fuerit: undecim tribus Israel contra Beniamin, consulto Domino, pugnavisse bisque notabili clade victos, tertio congressu fuisse victores et tribum illam adeo delevisse quod fleverit Rachel filios suos nec voluerit consolari quia non essent. Vide quotiens vicerint Macchabei; aliquando tamen victi sunt. Vicit Pyrrhus gemino congressu Romanos, contusus tertio, quarto profligatus est. Hannibal etiam Poenus, collatis signis, quinquies victor, Marcello duce ferme victus, vincendus Africano Maiori tandem reservatus est.

now address the general sense of your writing and, after having
done so, I shall respond to your seeming slanders individually.

You harbor the hope, we said, of defeating the French on the   151
basis of two recent events that you mention, as if you knew not
the instability and mutability of fortune, especially toward those
she seems first to have smiled upon. Do you not remember Vergil's
lines:

> the many days and varied labors of this changeable age
> improve many things; by turns Fortune laughs at men
> and sets them back upon their feet?[165]

But can you presume to know God's plan — which we call "Fortune" since the divine will acts independently of our aims and we
cannot know it — can you really understand what will happen
from the pattern of past events? Can you know God's will, who
acts from all eternity and whose actions can neither be predicted
nor whose motives, even after the fact, perceived? And if your intention is really to oppose the French in order to carry out your
threat, since all is in the hands of God, don't boast as if all that
were destined to happen; rather, wish for it to happen, and at the
same time be fearful lest the contrary occur.

Don't just take as examples the instances you like but those that   152
have occurred many times, and attend to what is written in the
Book of Truth. Eleven tribes of Israel, after having besought the
Lord, fought against Benjamin and were twice defeated, but came
away victorious from the third encounter and inflicted so resounding a defeat upon that tribe that Rachel mourned her sons and
found no consolation for their loss.[166] Think of how many times
the Maccabees won; yet sometimes they were defeated. Pyrrhus
defeated the Romans in two battles, suffered heavy losses in the
third, and was defeated in the fourth.[167] Hannibal of Carthage won
five times in pitched battles before being nearly defeated by Marcellus and his definitive defeat at the hands of Scipio Africanus.

153   Nullis in rebus minus quam in bellis exempla praeterita, spes vel cogitationes humanae respondent. Sed, per immortalis Dei maiestatem, unde tibi tantus de Gallica natione contemptus? Nonne, si priscas consideremus historias, Romanos iam tunc florentes apud Alliam flumen Galli Senones acie fusos turpiter fugaverunt et Urbe tota, praeter solum Capitolium, sunt potiti? Nonne, licet postea, duce Camillo, pulsi, caesi fusique sint tandemque etiam in Etruria, Dolobella Romano quidem duce, deleti fuerint, tamen aliquando Romanos vicerant, Urbem afflixerant, et, ut aliqui volunt, Capitolinae redemptionis aurum exportarunt? Sed ut Senones omittamus, nonne Gallorum gens Ticinum sive Papiam, Mediolanum, Brixiam Veronamque civitates aedificaverunt et a Rubicone, supra qua discurrit et flectitur Appenninus, quicquid intra montes et circa Padum est ad extremum usque Venetiae angulum multis saeculis imperio Galliaeque nomine tenuerunt? Nolo comparare Gallos invicem et Latinos. Utraque quidem gens laudibus pollet suis; nunc hi, nunc illi leguntur fuisse victores. Nam et utriusque gentis ingentem fuisse potentiam testis est Plinius, qui tertio ex *Naturalis Historiae* libris refert, 'nuntiato Gallico tumultu, solam Italiam, etiam sine Transpadanis, id est Foroiuliensibus, et externis auxiliis, armavisse equitum octingenta milia, peditum septingenta milia,' qua incredibilis apparatus magnitudine licet Gallorum etiam potentiam extimare. Et cum terrarum orbis in Romanorum monarchiam cessit, auctore imperialis principatus Caesare, post omnem Italiam, Africam, Hispaniam Graeciamque, Iudaeam et alias plurimas Orientis gentes in Romanam venerunt Transalpinae Galliae dicionem.

154   Non dicas igitur ita vos paratos Gallis resistere quod intelligant, ut sui maiores, perfacile Gallis Italiam petere, victores redire difficile. Venerunt aliquando viceruntque, et Italiae partem non re

356

In no sphere of activity are examples from the past, and men's   153
hopes and plans, of so little value as they are in war.[168] But whence,
almighty God, all this disdain for the Gallic people? Is it not the
case, if you look at early histories, that at a time when the Romans
were already a successful nation, the Galli Senones at the Battle of
the Allia River broke their line, put them to flight, and took control
over all of Rome save the Capitol? In later times too, despite their
rout under Camillus, with loss and defeat, and the dispersion into
Etruria when Dolabella was the Roman leader — did they not still
beat the Romans from time to time, threaten Rome and, according
to some, take away as ransom the gold of the Capitoline?[169] But
apart from the Senones, isn't it the case that the Gallic people
founded the cities of Ticino, to wit Pavia, Milan, Brescia and Verona, and for many centuries dominated the whole region of the Po
valley to the furthest corner of Venetia, that whole region beyond
the Rubicon north of the Apennine ridge, calling it "Gallia"? I do
not wish to compare the Latin and the Gaul. Both are peoples worthy of praise. We read that now the first won, now the second.
Pliny is witness to the might of both peoples, narrating (in Book
Three of the *Natural History*) that "upon news of the Gallic uprising,
Italy alone, without the Transpadani (that is inhabitants of Cividale
del Friuli) and the outside auxiliary army, armed eight hundred
thousand knights and four hundred thousand infantry,"[170] and the
size of this exceptional war machine allows us to deduce the power
of the Gauls. And only after the whole world had submitted to the
monarchy of the Romans under the empire created by Caesar, after
all Italy, Africa, Spain, Greece, Judaea and many other Oriental
peoples, did Transalpine Gallia come under Roman authority.

So don't say that you are ready to put up resistance against the   154
Gauls because they understand that, like their ancestors, it is very
easy for Gauls to enter Italy, difficult to return as victors. They
have come at various times and at various times they have won,
not merely conquering part of Italy but stamping it with their

solum, sed etiam nomine, suam fecerunt. Galli vero sic a Romanis victi sunt quod, licet non amiserint Galliae nomen, nihil tamen Galliarum remanserit quod victum profligatumque non fuerit sub imperiumque non venerit Romanorum. Nulla vero gens umquam fuit quae totam tenuerit Italiam. Verum quid rationis est genti victoriam, quae solummodo Dei munus est, ad gloriam imputare? Si Romani vicerunt Italiam, cum qua quingentis annis continuis pugnaverunt, si postea ducentis annis Romani cum Italis universum orbem subegerunt, plane Dei donum dici debet; nec expers talis gloriae fuit, etiam cum Comatae Galliae victae sunt, Gallia nostra Togata, sed simul cum Romanis reliquaque Italia Romanum imperium armis infinitisque victoriis pepererunt. Nulla tamen natio totius orbis imperium praeter Italiam, Dei dono, meruit obtinere, et meruit, credo equidem, quoniam Deus dedit; donum enim non fuisset si pro meritis, non dantis gratia, datum esset, sed iustitiae debitum, quod Deum reddere non potuit obligatum.

155   Si qua tamen ea gloria est, Romanorum et Italiae est. Primum quidem Assyriorum imperium, quod et Babylonicum dictum est, a Nino Beli filio sumpsit auspicium totamque tenuit Asiam, quae medium terrarum orbem creditur obtinere, donec ad effeminatum traducitur Sardanapalum, a quo per Arbacen transfertur in Medos, quod, sicut Deo placuit, ad Graecos, Alexandri Magni virtute fortunaque, pervenit. Tandem vero multo sanguine multisque victoriis transiit ad Romanos et Italos, sub eisque tres mundi partes in unius monarchiae titulo convenerunt, quod alias numquam legitur accidisse.

156   Sed ad Gallias, quas adeo reprimis, redeamus. Et unde tibi quod Gallis ad Italiam venire sit facile dicas, difficile vero redire victores? Et de Gallis quidem, qui tot urbes vestras condiderunt,

name. But [thereafter] the Gauls were so thoroughly defeated by the Romans that if the name "Gallia" survived, still there was no part of the [two] Gauls themselves[171] that was not defeated, dispersed and annexed by Roman dominion. No people has ever governed over the whole of Italy. Indeed, what reason is there to treat a victory as the glory of a people if it is simply a gift of God? If the Romans defeated Italy, against which they fought for a full five hundred years, and if the Romans, with the Italic peoples, conquered the entire world, this must be viewed as a gift of God. And even when Long-haired Gaul was defeated, our Toga-wearing Gaul was part of that glory; indeed, it together with the Romans and the rest of Italy created the Roman Empire through their arms and countless victories. At all events no nation except Italy has had the merit, by divine gift, of conquering the whole world, and I believe it earned this precisely because God gave it; it would not have been a gift if it had been given in proportion to Rome's merits rather than by the free grace of the giver; it would rather have been a debt of justice, that it could not have been binding on God to reward.[172]

Still, if there is any glory in her empire it belongs to the Ro- 155 mans and to Italy. The most ancient empire, the Assyrian or Babylonian, began with Nilus, son of Belus, and it extended across all Asia, believed to be the center of dry land, finally reaching the effeminate Sardanapalus: when, thanks to Arbax, it passed to the Medes[173] and then, as God willed, owing to the force and fortune of Alexander the Great, it passed to the Greeks. Eventually, after much loss of blood and many victories, it came into the possession of the Romans and the Italians, under whom the three parts of the globe[174] were gathered under a single government, which (according to all written sources) had never happened before.

But let us return to the [two] Gauls, which you are keeping 156 so much in check. Why ever do you say that it is easy for the Gauls to enter Italy, but difficult to return as victors? Enough

satis dictum sit. Venerunt enim in Italiam et vicerunt, pulsisque exinde Tuscis, quos legimus ea tempestate qua se tractus Maris Inferi, quod et Tuscum dicitur, ac Superi, quod et Adriaticum nuncupatur (ab Adria, Tuscorum colonia) protenditur imperium obtinebant. Nec vicerunt solum sed totam illam patriam tenuerunt. Senones autem, a quibus Romanos victos et Urbem captam diximus, vicerunt et victi sunt et ad internicionem taliter, Dolobella duce, deleti quod nullus ex ea gente remanserit, ut scribit Seneca, qui incensam a se Romanam urbem gloriaretur.

157   Et ut ad Robertum Guiscardum, quem Normandum fuisse fama est, qui tam multa gessit in Apulia atque Samnio, transeam, nonne venit in Italiam rex Pipinus domitoque Aistulpho, Longobardorum rege, quicquid iuris sanctae matris ecclesiae per violentiam occupaverat reddere compulit victorque suam remeavit in Franciam? Nonne filius eius, inclitae famae felicisque memoriae Carolus Magnus, lacrimis et conquestu requisitus ecclesiae, contra Desiderium, filium et successorem Aistulphi, de Galliis venit obsessaque Papia perfidum regem cepit, captivum misit in Galliam et omni regno Longobardorum in suam dicionem redacto statum et honorem suum ecclesiae reddidit, Romamque veniens primo patricius et paulo post eligitur imperator? Quique rex venit in Italiam, imperator et victor redivit in Galliam et pluribus annis per se et filios ac nepotes et pronepotes suos omnem illam Italiae tenuit portionem quae nunc dicitur Lombardia.

158   Nec unum velim omittere, quod hic gloriosisimus imperator in Tusciam veniens, inter Lucam et Pistoriam in honorem Beati Petri Apostoli, sub promontorio quod Montecatinum ab indigenis dicebatur, aedem sacram construi fecit; quae postea loci plebes facta est in provincia de qua natus sum, ad dexteram Nevolae ripam,

has already been said of the Gauls who founded so many of your cities. Indeed they came to Italy and they conquered, expelling the Etruscans who (we read) at the time ruled over the Lower Sea, also called the Tuscan Sea, and the Upper Sea, also called the Adriatic after Adria, colony of the Etruscans. Not only did they win, they took control of the whole region. But the Galli Senones, as we saw, first defeated the Romans at an early time and were then defeated and routed in turn by Dolabella, with the result that of a people which (as Seneca writes) could boast of setting fire to Rome, naught was left.[175]

But to pass over Robert Guiscard, said to be a Norman, author 157 of so many campaigns in Apulia and Samnium, did not King Pippin enter Italy, subdue Astolfus king of the Lombards, force him to restore everything belonging to Holy Mother Church and illegally taken by him, and return as a victor to France? Did not his son, that Charlemagne of clarion fame and happy memory, invoked by the Church with tears and wails, come out from the Gauls to fight against Desiderius, son and successor of Astolfus, and in the siege of Pavia take the perfidious sovereign and send him to Gaul a captive, and, after taking possession of the whole Longobard kingdom, restore the status and honor that were due to the Church; and on arriving in Rome, was he not elected, first patrician, and soon after emperor? Therefore he came to Italy as king, returned victor and emperor to France, and for a great many years held for his self, sons, nephews and great-nephews all that part of Italy now called Lombardy.

I would like to recall that when this most glorious emperor was 158 in Tuscany, on the promontory known locally as Montecatini between Pistoia and Lucca, he had a church built in honor of St. Peter the Apostle. This became the parish church of the province where I was born, on the right bank of the river Nievole, which

qui fluvius toti patriae nomen dedit, qui locus, Ptolemaeo teste, 'Lucus Feronis' antea dicebatur. Unde et nobilior pars terrae Pisciae 'Ferraria'—corrupto, sicut arbitror, vocabulo—pro 'Feronia' vulgo dicta est. Qui princeps reliquias Florentinorum—quas Totila, Dei flagellum, urbe diruta, dissipaverat—colligens, Romanis supplentibus cives, quos illa vastitas perdidit, urbem nostram restituit. Cuius rei, post celebrem famam et chronicas nostras, monumentum est quod ad dexteram Arni ripam antiquam ecclesiam sanctis dedicatam apostolis vel restituit vel aedificavit dotavitque; repertaeque sunt in arcula aenea, paucis annis elapsis, sub altariolo S. Iohannis Baptistae sanctorum pretiosae reliquiae, quas clerus et populus ignorabat, et quas, ut antiquissimae litterae testabantur, donum Caroli Magni, Romanorum imperatoris, esse constabat. Quo desinas admirari Florentinorum devotionem ad sanctissimam domum Franciae sicque gloriosissimus ille sanguis peculiarem curam huius sui populi semper gessit.

159   Et ut prisca illa, licet verissima, dimittamus, nonne felicis recordationis gloriosaeque memoriae Carolus Primus, Hierusalem et Siciliae rex, tunc Provinciae et Folchalcherii comes, ordinatione Urbani Quarti deposito Manfredo, qui tunc Siciliae regnum per tyrannidem occupabat, venit in Italiam, rex factus est, pugnavit et vicit? Siquidem Carolus ipse magna classe venit ad urbem et rex inunctus est cumque fortissimus suus terrestris exercitus propter Gebellinorum congregationem in Lombardia clausis aditibus moraretur, invicta Florentinorum Guelforum manus, qui iam annis ferme septem extorres patria gloriose in Lombardia militabant, se novi regis exercitui coniunxerunt. Quae res causa fuit ut, Lombardis cedentibus, exercitus transiret incolumis tandemque, expugnato

gives its name to the whole area I come from, once called "Lucus Feronis," as Ptolemy states.[176] Indeed the nether part of the town of Pescia is popularly called "Ferraria," which I think is a corrupted survival of the original name "Feronia." That sovereign [Charlemagne] next gathered the surviving Florentines, dispersed by Totila "scourge of God" after the destruction of the city — and with the help of Roman citizens, themselves victims of the disaster, he reconstructed our city. This is shown by the celebrity of this fact and by our chronicles, furthermore by the existence of an ancient church dedicated to the Holy Apostles on the right bank of the Arno, which he reconstructed or perhaps built, and enriched with his donations. Here, a few years ago, a small bronze casket came to light under the little altar of Saint John the Baptist, containing precious relics of saints, hitherto unknown to the clergy and the parishioners: the earliest inscriptions identified them as a gift of Charlemagne, emperor of the Romans.[177] So, shed your surprise at the Florentine devotion to the royal house of France, and at the special affection of that very glorious house has consequently borne toward this people.

And, leaving aside such ancient episodes, incontestable though they are, is it not true that when Charles I, he of happy repute and glorious memory, king of Jerusalem and Sicily, at that time count of Provence and Forcalquier — the one who deposed Manfred, tyrannical occupant of the kingdom of Sicily, according to the wishes of Urban IV — first came into Italy, he was elected king, fought, and won? Since indeed Charles came in person to Rome with a large fleet and was anointed king, and since his powerful land army was delayed by the Ghibelline blockage of the access route in Lombardy, the intrepid Florentine Guelf forces that had then been fighting as exiles with renown for seven years in Lombardy in due course joined the army of the new king. So it was that, the resistance of the Lombards broken, the army passed unharmed and, eventually, the king and all his troops took and

159

captoque oppido Sancti Germani, rex cum omnibus copiis, supe-
ratis saltibus asperrimisque Brutiorum montibus, in Samnium venit, ubi Manfredum offendit apud Beneventum cum maximo sui
exercitus comitatu; qui sicut erat ingenio ferox, optimum factu ratus fessum exercitum aggredi, cum omnibus copiis suis pugnae
praebuit facultatem.

160   Rex autem, ut hostes adesse sensit, locum castris delegerat quo
cogi non posset invitus ad pugnam. Hortantur sui quod viris
equisque, aspero fatigatis itinere, requiem donet; periculum fessos
integris congredi. Florentinorum consiliosiores aderant; quid sentiant quaerit. Festinandum esse respondent ne gentibus augeatur
hostis aut forte, consilium mutans, pugnam detractet, quo nihil
regi posset esse calamitosius. Rex, ut erat alti animi conficiendae-
que rei avidus, ignominiosum reputans ad pugnam venientibus
cedere, statuit experiri proeliandi fortunam, confisus suorum virtuti, quam putat etiam lassitudinis incommodo plus valere.

161   Dat ergo pugnae signum. Primi steterunt in ordine Florentini,
fortissima quidem acies et expertissimorum in armis. Septingenti
fuisse traduntur, hastati omnes, tectis et armatis equis, sub galeis
cuncti cristatis, multi galeis tecti capita papaeque signis ornati,
quod adhuc, in illius felicis diei memoriam, Guelforum nostrae
civitatis universitas tenet. Admiratus eos Manfredus interrogasse
traditur quinam essent; responsoque Florentinos exules esse Guelfos, tunc suos requisivit ex Florentia Gebellinos, qui cum admodum paucissimi (duos quidem affuisse memoriae traditur) respon-
dissent aliosque esse custodia civitatis occupatos, 'Hodie,' dixit ille,
'Guelfi Florentini non possunt non esse victores. Si vicero quidem

conquered the town of San Germano, passed through the defile and rigid peaks of the Abruzzi, and reached the region of Samnium, where near Benevento he encountered Manfred at the head of an immense number of soldiers.[178] Manfred, being aggressive by nature and thinking it the best choice to attack a tired army, offered battle with all his troops.

The king, for his part, realizing the enemy was at hand, chose a   160
place for encampment from which he could not be compelled unwillingly to give battle. His officers exhorted him to rest his men and horses after the tiring and difficult passage, it being dangerous to set tired soldiers against soldiers in the full of their energy. The most authoritative in counsel of the Florentines were present, and he asks them what they think.[179] They reply that his response must be rapid lest new troops join the enemy or else the enemy choose not to fight, which would be the worst outcome for the king. Bold and eager to have the matter decided, reckoning that it would be dishonorable to give way before the enemy's advance, the king makes the decision to test the fortune of battle, trusting in the valor of his men, whom he believes would prevail in spite of their fatigue.

Thus he gives the signal for battle. In the first line were the   161
Florentines, a mighty company of soldiers and among the most experienced in battle. Seven hundred, it is said, all with lances, the horses in battle armor, each with a crested helmet and many with the pope's arms, as the Guelf party still today bears in memory of this happy event. It is said that Manfred saw them with admiration and asked who they were; learning that they were the exiled Florentine Guelfs, he then besought his own Ghibellines from Florence, who, being extremely few in numbers (it seems there were just two of them) replied that the others were occupied with guarding their own city. "Today," he said, "the Florentine Guelfs cannot fail to win. If I win, I will bring them over to my side, and

eos, faciam meos: urbe, bonis dignitatibusque restituam. Si vicerint, scient uti victoria.' Rex pugnaturus primum Florentinis impetus concessit honorem. Irruunt igitur acieque tota miscentur. Irruunt et Galli hostesque, suis signo notissimis mixtos, caedunt et Manfredum ipsum acriter pugnantem conficiunt. Galli victores totum regnum occupant.

162   Huic Carolo Primo Carolus tuus Tertius, quem meritis verisque laudibus celebras, sanguine Quintus, gratia Dei successit. Contra quem, cum et ipse sanguine Gallus esset, quod inclitus rex Ludovicus, dux Andegavensis, parum profecerit tam magnifico, sicut memoras, apparatu, non ignavia gentis, crede mihi, sed hominis infelicitas fuit; invictus enim armis, morbo confectus est. Nusquam victor nec victus, peste, proh dolor, absumptus est absumptusque clarissimus princeps Sabaudiae comes absumptusque maxima parte exercitus, ut omnia haec felicitati regis Caroli, non victoriae suae vel Italicae gentis gloriae, dignum sit, si recte sentire voluerimus, imputare. Nam et victoriam quam Deus concessit domino tuo contra deflendae memoriae Iohannem Arminiaci comitem, scis tu, scimus et omnes, altitudine magis animi et audacia, quae solet obesse consilio ducis et gentis, quam vestrarum copiarum fortitudine contigisse.

163   Crede mihi quod si Deus dedisset duces et gentes nostras, Paduanae victoriae superbas gloria, Gallorum castris castra coniungere, dies ille sudores maximos domino tuo graviaque pericula magnamque cladem verisimiliter attulisset. Verum exercituum Deus Sabaoth, iuxta suae praeordinationis seriem cuncta perficiens, victorias[58] statuit sicut bonum est in oculis suis. Quicquid autem sit, hoc unum scio quod nostra non potes damnare consilia. Consilia quidem non eventus, sed praeparatio probat. Si feceris

restore the city and their property and public offices to them. If they win, they shall know how to make good use of the victory."[180] When the battle was about to begin the king granted the Florentines the honor of the first charge. Our side hurls itself against the enemy and the whole line fights hand-to-hand. The French charge too and cut down the enemy amid the mêlée, killing Manfred himself, who fought with great ardor. The French were victorious and took over the whole realm.

This Charles I was succeeded by the grace of God by your   162 Charles III (V of the line) whom you extol with just and deserved praises. The fact that the famous Louis duke of Anjou, another of Gallic descent, could do little against him despite a great array of forces (as you recall yourself) was not due to the baseness of that people, believe me, but to the man's own ill fortune: though invincible in battle, he was stricken down by disease. Neither victor nor vanquished, he succumbed at last to the plague, as did the famous prince count of Savoy and the greatest part of the army. All this is best imputed to the good fortune of King Charles, if we wish to view the event in the correct light, and not to any victory by him or to the glorious deeds of the Italian people.[181] And even the victory which God granted to your lord against the late Jean, count of Armagnac, of mournful memory — as you know, as all know — was due more to his pride and recklessness, usually a hindrance to wise counsel for captains and peoples, than to the courage of your own army.

Believe me, if God had permitted our commanders and men,   163 proud in their splendid victory at Padua, to join the troops of the French, that day would have brought your lord great struggle, heavy damage and probably a memorable defeat. Yet the God of Hosts, who acts according to his preordained plan, decided victories as it seemed good in his eyes.[182] But I am certain of this at all events: you cannot criticize our decisions. Preparedness, not outcomes, are the test of good counsel. If you have done all that you

enim quantum in te fuerit, quod debes et humana coniectura capit, exitus infelicitas defleri, non damnari consilii quod praecessit gravitas et ratio debet. Nec pendet vel colligi potest ab eventu temeritas, sed ab ordinatione rerum, ut nisi factum vel omissum fuerit aliquid quod fieri non debuit vel omitti iudicio sapientum, temere susceptum dici non possit, licet felicitas aliquando defuerit, quae quidem solius divinitatis donum, non humanitatis opus est.

164   Etenim sicut Deus, qui prima causa rerum omnium est, invisibiliter praeoperatur in omnibus, sic scit quem exitum cunctis, quae per nos efficit, sit daturus. Credo tamen dominum tuum et (si qui possunt esse de tyrannorum salute solliciti) multos suos nihil magis illius primi belli tempore timuisse quam descensum ducis Bavariae—qui sibi Paduam abstulit Veronamque, iussu domini tui vastatam, ad rebellionem usque concussit—et adventum incliti comitis Arminiaci, qui somnos illos suos altissimos et suaves urgentissimis curarum stimulis saepe rupit. Parique ratione, cum sensit secundo bello regium praeparatum exercitum, adeo perterritus est quod bello sicut erat fractus in manibus incliti dominii Venetorum, cuius fuimus illo tempore colligati, temporales indutias primo pacemque postremo consensit. Nec puduit dominum tantae potentiae non ulcisci contumeliam aquatici terrestrisque exercitus sui, turpiter apud Governum fusi, sed velut necessitati cedens et tempori, manus dedit, et non aliter quam se victum fatens, quas potuit condiciones pacis accepit.

165   Vade nunc, stulte, iacta potentiam domini tui et quattuor equitum legiones! Divina subditos nostros mirabilia temptaturos! Sperne Gallos! Quid a nobis audiant quidque respondeant, amentia

could, all that you ought and all that is within the power of human foresight, the unhappy outcome should be mourned, but the gravity and rationality of the counsel taken previously ought not to be condemned. Rashness does not depend on, nor can it be inferred from the outcome, but only from the design: unless an action was carried out or omitted that was not supposed to be carried out or omitted in accordance with the counsels of the wise, it can't be said that something has been done rashly, even though it may not be attended by success. The latter is the gift of divinity alone, not the work of mankind.

Just as God is the prime cause of all things and always acts be- 164 forehand but unseen, so He knows what result He will assign to all that He causes to happen through us. Still, I think that your lord and many of his followers (if there really can be those who care about a tyrant's welfare) feared nothing more in that first conflict than the descent of the Duke of Bavaria — who took Padua from him and spurred Verona to revolt after it had been devastated at your lord's command[183] — and the arrival of the celebrated Count of Armagnac, a man who often disturbed his most deep and pleasant slumber with the sharpest goads of anxiety. In the same way, during the second conflict, on hearing that the king had got up an army, he was so terrified, because at that point he had been beaten and was at the mercy of our then ally Venice, that he agreed to a truce and then to peace. Nor did so powerful a lord feel shame at his inability to avenge the humiliation of his army's ignominious loss on both water and land, put to flight as they were at Governolo, but he gave in to the inevitability of circumstance and yielded, just like someone confessing himself beaten, and accepted the best conditions he could get.

So go now, fool, and boast of your lord's power, of those four 165 legions of horse! Prophesy how our subjects will be put to the test by marvelous deeds! Despise the Gauls! Let your madness dictate

designa tua. Dic nos ad civitatis et libertatis interitum festinare, dic totam erectam Italiam ad spectaculum nostrae calamitatis et has ineptias tuas cum exitu rerum compara. Sique tantum tibi datur prudentiae, saltem disce tam magna iactantibus raro fortunam et cogitationum exitus respondere, foreque parcior in obloquendo disce, si tamen poteris frenum tuae petulantiae, quo vanitatis crimen effugias, adhibere.

166 Quod autem dicis in proverbium versum esse ('Italiam sepulcrum esse Gallorum'), non ex eo factum est quod in Italia Gallici periclitentur exercitus, quod de Senonibus quondam legimus et nostro tempore semel tantum, dicere possumus contigisse rarissimeque possit, si percurras historias, recenseri. Bella namque quae cum Cisalpinis Gallis fuere Romanis, non 'Gallica' sed 'Italica' dici debent. Non exercituum periclitatio, quod rarissimum fuit, sed alia ratio fuit quae tale proverbium usurpavit. Etenim temporibus meis erat quod nulli domini nullaque communitas gentes equestres unius idiomatis per totam Italiam ad stipendia retinerent; duarum vel trium linguarum gentes delectabantur habere, putantes cum id esse praestantius oboedientiae promptitudine quam certatim geniti diversis orbis partibus exhibebant, tum tutius conspirationum difficultate, quas propter aemulationem reputabant impossibile posse conflari. Quin etiam, cum res deducebatur ad pugnam, omnibus studium erat honoris proprii gloriaeque etiam atque famae gentis suae, quo magis animosi certamini miscebantur. Et cum ea tempestate Gallis altissima pax esset, veniebant in Italiam, quae semper bellis scatuit, nobiles eius gentis, studio gloriaque pugnandi. Cumque naturale sit eis lucem pro laude pacisci, quotiens pugnabatur, plures ex Gallis quam ex exercitu toto fundentes sanguinem moriebantur, ut loco miraculi foret Gallorum aliquem decennalis militiae periculis superesse; cumque

what they hear from us and what they reply. Go ahead and say that we are hurtling toward the ruin of our city and our freedom; say too that all Italy is watching to see the spectacle of our defeat — and then compare this nonsense with the outcome of events. And if you have a whit of prudence, learn once for all that those who boast of their own greatness this way rarely get the good fortune and the outcome they expect; and learn to be more cautious when maligning someone, if you are still capable of bridling your insolence, and flee from the reproach of vainglory.

As regards the reason for what you say has become proverbial, that Italy is the tomb of the Gauls, that is not because it is risky for French armies to be in Italy, because (we read) that was on one occasion the case for the Galli Senones, and once also in our times. But if you read the history books you will find these are very rare episodes. Indeed, the wars of the Romans against the Cisalpine Gauls should be called the "Italic," not the "Gallic" Wars. It was not the risks (very rare) run by Gaulish armies but something else which explains the employment of that proverb. In my day no overlord or commune in all Italy practiced hiring knights of one single tongue. They preferred instead to have men who spoke two or three different languages, reasoning that (on the one hand) competing to show the worth of their nations of origin they could be relied upon to be obedient, and that (on the other hand) the same rivalries excluded the hatching of any conspiracies. And so it happened that in the clash of battle all showed they cared for personal honor and for the glory and fame of their respective nations, with the result that they fought with greater courage. There being at the time perfect peace in lands of Gaul, the nobles of that nation flocked to Italy, ever the hotbed of conflict, fired by the desire for combat and glory. Since it is normal for them to sacrifice life for glory,[184] every combat left more Gauls dead on the field than the rest of the army lost, and so it was thought miraculous if a Gaul survived ten years of fighting; and when a soldier returned

166

contingeret aliquem famosum hominem post decennium, ex quo
stipendia meruisset in Italia, sospitem redire in patriam, carissi-
mus apud suos et honoratissimus habebatur. Hinc quod virtutis
testimonium erat inolevit ut proverbialiter diceretur 'Italiam sepulcrum esse Gallorum.' Et tu, si Lombardus es, cum antiquissimi
generis Gallorum aliquis esse debeas, in maiorum tuorum dedecus
et in ignominiam Lombardiae, quam tu ipse Galliam Cisalpinam
vocas, quae sunt gloria gentis illius, ignorantia rerum detrahen-
dique libidine, turpi nimis ratione depravas.

167   Sed de Gallis satis. Nunc ad illa quae de nobis concludens
obloqueris veniamus. Dimissis ergo Gallis, ad nos redis et inquis:
'At vos furor et rabies et impatientia quaedam pacis oblivisci faciunt omnium salutarium exemplorum; non tenetis ista memoriae
nihilque—nisi imperium crudele, nefarium—mente cogitationibusque versatis. Potuistis quidem soli, et in vestris manibus situm
erat, Italiae pacem dare, sedare tumultus, auferre discordias, res
denique Italas tanta tranquillitate componere quanta non fuerant
patrum avorumque memoria. Nam cum in Italia vos post Liguriae
principem scire multa, posse omnia videremini essetque ille etiam
quam dignitati et splendori sui nominis conveniret pacis avidior
(propter quam non sine amicorum suorum stomacho ita se haberet humiliter, ita et quaedam indigna quotidie patientissime toleraret, ut et vobis cervices erigeret, qui paci eratis adversi) et eorum,
qui melius sentiebant, corda posset inflectere, nil prohibebat, si
vobis pacis studium placuisset, pacem perpetuam esse futuram.
Sed abhorrebant curiae vestrae a consilio quietis, animos vestros
urgebant conceptorum scelerum stimuli et aures vestras sanioribus
monitis obstruebant atque oculos occaecabant Furiae illae pestiferae quas peccata vestra de sedibus Tartareis excitarant. Itaque
semper contra salutem Italiae, contra pacem, contra bonorum consilia, contra patriae vestrae statum ac requiem sic fuistis accensi ut
sine dubitatione videremini non pro cura et conservatione vestrae
rei publicae vigilare, quod unum volebatis intelligi, sed ad civitatis

home after a decade of military service in Italy he was received with the greatest affection and the greatest honor. Indeed, as this was seen as a mark of great valor, a sort of proverb began to go around: "Italy is the tomb of the Gauls." And though descending perforce (if you are a Lombard) from the ancient Gallic race, you in your ignorance and your lust to give insults, disfigure in all too shameful a way the glories of that people, to the disgrace of your own ancestors and the ignominy of Lombardy, a land you yourself call Cisalpine Gaul.*

Enough has been said of the Gauls. Let us turn to what you 167 say in the last part of your harangue against us. Having dealt with the Gauls you return to us: *But the fury, rage and intolerance of peace that afflict you make you forget all salutary examples. The latter you forget, while you turn over in your mind and thoughts nothing but a cruel, wicked rule. You alone — and the choice lay in your hands — could have brought peace to Italy, quelled uprisings, erased conflicts, and in short, brought back the kind of tranquility to Italian affairs of state such as only our fathers and grandfathers remember. Since, next to the prince of Liguria, you seemed the most well-informed and the most effective power in Italy, and since he was more eager for peace than befitted his title and his resounding fame — so much so that his conciliatory attitude irritated his allies, and he would bear each day with the greatest patience charges he did not deserve, for example, that he had stiffened your stubborn hostility to peace — and since he was able to influence the hearts of right-thinking people, nothing stood in the way of a durable peace, had your desire for peace been genuine. But your Signoria shrank from counsels of quiet, and the thought of the crimes you had planned goaded you on, deafening you to wiser advice, and your eyes were blinded by the plague-ridden Furies whom your sins had aroused from their Tartarean homes. In brief, you have always been so hostile to the welfare of Italy, so opposed to peace, so deaf to the counsels of good men, so indifferent to the prestige and tranquility of your fatherland, that you are not standing guard out of concern for the preservation of your commonwealth, as you wish to have believed, but you*

et libertatis voluntarium interitum festinare. Qui quidem ita iam proximus est ut et vos iam iam impendentis ruinae terrore concutiat et universam Italiam ad spectaculum vestrae calamitatis attollat.'

168 Haec ultima verba tua sunt, plena fellis quaeve a solito mendaciorum tuorum more non abhorreant; facileque possem omnia sine responsione dimittere, nisi me movissent verba tua, quibus dicis illum dominum tuum ad Italiae pacem tam obnixe dispositum et nos, versa vice, fuisse semper pacis affectu, consilio et operibus inimicos. Promptum est libereque potest quilibet haec et maiora proferre. Verum populi decernere non possunt bella moveri sine multorum assensu, quod adeo difficile semper fuit et praesertim in hac nostra re publica, quod durum fuerit etiam pro defensione libertatis et status popularem habere consensum, sine quo pace vel bello nihil esse potest efficaciter constitutum, ut moribus nostris arduum semper fuerit necessarium etiam bellum suscipi, nedum quod moveatur voluntarium obtineri. Nec mirum; quicquid enim bella nostra deglutiunt, sola tributorum praestatione persolvitur. Tributorum, inquam, quae, sicut urget necessitas, consensus omnium praecipit et de bursis nostrorum civium haurienda disponit. Quo fit ut nisi summa necessitudo compellat, quae nulla nobis est nisi defensio libertatis, numquam bellum fieri vel suscipi decernatur. Adde quod nostra civitas non ingenita nobilibus ambitione regitur, sed bonitate mercatoria gubernatur; cumque nihil inimicitius esse possit mercatoribus quodque mercimoniis ac artibus plus afferat detrimenti quam strepitus turbatioque bellorum, certum omnibus esse debet mercatores et artifices, in quorum manibus nostrae rei publicae gubernacula sunt, pacem diligere vastitatemque bellicam abhorrere.

169 Tu vero contra naturam rerum, contra mores et consuetudinem hominum, contra veritatem et evidentiam agibilium, Florentinos esse dicis pacis hostes bellique cupidissimos sectatores, et illum

are hastening toward the voluntary destruction of your city and your lib-
erty. This fate is now nigh, so much so that you are already stricken with
terror at your impending collapse, and you are raising up all of Italy to
watch the spectacle of your undoing.[185]

You conclude with these words, as spiteful and as stupid as was   168
to be expected from your customary practice of mendacity. I might
easily just let it go without responding, but I am struck by your
claim that your overlord was dedicated in all ways to bringing
peace to Italy while we, on the contrary, have always been enemies
to any disposition, proposal and attempt to have peace. An individual, if he wishes peace, may easily say such things and more.
But peoples cannot decide to wage war without the assent of the
many, a thing always difficult, notably in our republic, where it is
hard to attain consensus — necessary for any effective decision in
war or in peace — even in defense of liberty and of the state itself.
Because of these practices it has always been difficult for us to
sustain a war, even a war of necessity, let alone start one of our
own free initiative.[186] Nor is that surprising, for whatever costs
our wars swallow up are paid for by the proceeds of taxation alone.
Taxes, I may add, levied of necessity by consensus and raised by
emptying the pockets of our citizens. Therefore, unless in a situation of the utmost urgency, which in our case means only the defense of our liberty, there is never a decision to declare war or to
enter war. It should be added that our city is not ruled by nobles,
prey to congenital ambition, but governed by honest merchants.[187]
And since nothing can be more hateful to merchants and more
harmful to commerce and manufacture than war's confusion and
disorder, everyone understands that the merchants and craftsmen,
in whose hands the government of our republic is placed, love
peace and detest the devastations of war.

You, however, in contradiction of the natural course of things,   169
against the habits and manners of men, against truth and the evidence of facts, say that the Florentines are enemies of peace and

dominum tuum avidiorem pacis quam dignitati et splendori sui
nominis conveniret. Quae quam vera sint declaraverunt litterae
suae, per quas sponte nobis, post insultationem nostrorum finium,
bellum velut hostis indixit, praefatus se pacem Italicam optavisse.
Pacemne cupit qui nulla ratione bellum infert, bellum denuntiat
et minatur? Pacemne diligit qui bello, quod inter Paduanum et
Veronensem dominos gerebatur, se permiscens, malum quod iam
tepescebat integrans dividensque cum socio spolia pactionibus
quas servaturus non esset, ambitione sola, sicut pactum docebat et
declaravit exitus, bellum gessit? Pacemne diligit qui socii portionem, contra fidem et foedus, per coniugem occupans, mox in socium foedifragium iustissime conquerentem sceleratissime bello
surgit, ipsumque, iuncto cum communibus inimicis foedere, de
socio inimicum, de domino servum, de divite pauperem, de felice
miserrimum bello facit? Quid est hoc nisi ponere ius in armis, nisi
velle tantum praestare causa quantum se sentit antistare potentia?

170   Nobiscum autem cum ligam et concordiam firmasset in civitate
Pisana, cuius primum et principale capitulum erat ad se mutuo
nullatenus offendendos, nonne mox, concluso foedere, omnibus
terris suis velut hostes prohibuit Florentinos vanissimaque fingens
et falsa cavillatus est nos eum decrevisse, miro pecuniarum effluvio, de medio tollere quocumque modo fieri posset, quod nihil
aliud inferre poterat nisi scelus gladii vel veneni? Cumque nostra
sinceritas respondisset hoc impossibile nobis esse, nisi tam horrendum facinus cum ministris suis fidissimis tractaremus, quod

incorrigible warmongers, while that lord of yours is more desirous of peace than comports with his rank and the splendor of his reputation. How true all that may be is shown by the letter with which, of his own initiative, after having attacked our borders, he declared war on us, proving himself an enemy, despite his preliminary words auguring peace in Italy.[188] Does a man want peace who for no reason starts, declares, and threatens a war? Does he love peace who, intervening in the war underway between the lords of Padua and Verona, stirring up a source of friction that was dying down and dividing the booty with an ally by secret agreements he had no intention of respecting, fought a war out of purely personal ambition, as, after all, the pact let one surmise and the end showed so clearly? Does the man love peace who uses his wife to take hold of the portion due to his ally, against his word given and the accords made; and then, when the ally with perfect justice protests this treaty violation, with the utmost wickedness makes war upon him; and, then, having entered into a pact with their common enemies, by means of war turns an ally into an enemy, a lord a servant, a rich man a poor man, a happy man a wretch? What is this if not making right depend upon arms,[189] if not wishing to distinguish oneself in a cause to the degree that one feels oneself superior in power?

Regarding us, is it not true that, directly upon signing the 170 league and the peace accord of Pisa — the first and main article of which prevents one side from harming the other — he expelled all Florentines from his lands like enemies, adducing a whole set of concocted lies and falsehoods, to the effect that we had decided to remove him in one way or another, as much as to say by the dagger or by poison?[190] And when we replied in all honesty that such a thing would have been quite impossible for us, unless we had colluded with his most trusted ministers to carry out so horrible a crime, that such a plot would have been foolish and risky to

stultum et temerarium foret aliquo modo temptare et quod hoc non a nobis vel Florentinorum aliquo sed a suis stipatoribus formidaret, cognoscens se non posse tam falsa defendere, novum aliquid non minus impossibile commentus est. Finxit enim nos decrevisse percussores immittere qui eum, iuxta morem suum aucupio vel venationibus occupatum, gladio, iaculis, arcu vel balista conficerent et intra fines custoditissimos sui nemoris temeritate stultissima trucidarent, quasi posset exploratum nobis esse tempus et locus vel exeuntis ad talia comitatus aut possibile nobis foret aliquos reperire Lombardos vel Tuscos tam vitae propriae contemptores quod ad mortem certissimam, incerti commissa perficere, se conferrent.

171 Erantne forte nobis Hesperii fratres qui solvenda parentibus centum milia florenorum, ut ille fingebat, pro tam pulchro scelere paciscerentur? Quibus cum pacem irritam facere cogitaret, Iohannem Ubaldinum, valida latronum societate stipatum, Senas misit, per quos nobis bellum, nil tale verentibus, antequam denuntiaret inferret; experientiaque didicimus totaque vidit Italia ipsum vel turbatis rebus, ruptis foederibus et pace violata bellum gerere, vel pace foederibusque firmatis nihil aliud quam bellacia cogitare. Dicas aliis quam Italicis dominum illum tuum avidiorem pacis esse quam splendori suae dignitatis et nominis conveniret; nobiscum talia, si placet, noli iactare mendacia. Difficile nimis suadere verbis aliquid, cuius oppositum rerum evidentia cognoscatur. Et quod bellum post captum, depositum et occisum ab ipso patruum socerumque fuit in Italia quod ipse non gesserit, iuverit, foverit, moverit? Quis umquam in ipsum (dic, obsecro) bellum fecit? Quis etiam contra statum suum aliquid attentavit aut ausus fuit pro magnitudine potentiae cogitare? Et quis adeo stultus qui bello

attempt in any case, and that he should fear such an attack less from us or any Florentines than from his own bodyguard—on seeing that he could no longer sustain affirmations so patently false, he went and invented another no less improbable. For he then put it about that we had planned to hire some assassins who would have killed him while he was out hunting or fowling, as was his wont, by sword, javelin or arrow shot from a bow or crossbow; we would have designed to murder him from within his heavily-guarded estate, with unheard-of boldness—as if we could be in a position to discover (let's say) where, when and with whom he set out to hunt, and as if it were easy to find a few Lombards or Tuscans so careless of their lives that they would betake themselves to certain death to carry out a plan with such uncertain results.[191]

Did we perhaps have in our employ, as he pretended, those   171 Spanish brothers who for one hundred thousand florins, to be paid to their parents, had contracted to carry out this fine misdeed? And all the while he was trying in this way to destroy the peace, he was sending Giovanni Ubaldini and a band of thugs to Siena to make war on us indirectly, something we had no reason to fear until the ruse was exposed.[192] Thus we learned from experience, and all Italy saw, that he either makes war by sowing dissension, scorning agreements, and violating peace, or else in peace-time and with peace treaties signed, he can only plot acts of war. Go tell the others, not the Italians, that that lord of yours desires peace more than befits the splendor of his rank and reputation;[193] with us, please just avoid a mouthful of lies like that. Words cannot be convincing when the facts show the exact contrary of one's words. Has there ever been a war—since the time he imprisoned, deposed, and killed the man who was both his uncle and father-in-law—which he has not either waged, supported, fostered, or actually caused? Who, pray tell, made war on him? And who has made any attempt against his state or has dared even to think of such, given his enormous power? Who is so stupid as to challenge

provocet potentiorem? Quis in Italia dominatus, qui contra potentiam suam auderet bella movere?

172   Unum scimus quod et te, licet insanias, negatum ire non arbitror, quod numquam necessarium bellum intulit vel suscepit. Voluntaria semper arma movit, voluntaria, eaque ipsa nefaria, bella
gessit. Rupta fide, violata pace calcatisque foederibus bellaciter
semper cuncta turbavit. Poterat omne bellum quod insurgeret,
poterat omne scandalum pullulans ante nativitatem et in ipso
conceptu contundere totamque, si voluisset, Italiam bonitate et
humanitate sua summa pacis dulcedine continere. Qualiter hoc
fecerit tribus bellis, quae nobis intulit, duobusque, quibus Veronensem et Paduanum confecit dominos, declaravit. Ducem semper habuit ambitionem; hanc secutus, omni fide et honestate foe-
data, divina humanaque turbavit. Quo dominandi spes et flatus
impulit, pedem tulit; unde reppulit, pedem traxit. Hanc Arcton,
hoc sidus, sedens et ambulans, dormiens atque vigilans, semper
sibi proposuit, semper velis remisque secutus est. Ibi fas, ubi vel
minima spes augendae dominationis effluxit.

173   Hac de causa bella gessit, hac intentione—pactus sibi Veronam
dominoque Paduano Vicentiam—bellum Veronense suscepit. Hac
rabie Vicentiam, ruptis foederibus, per coniugem suam cepit. His
actus stimulis, deceptum socium adortus bello, sociis Venetis Tar-
visium linquens, pro se, sicut pepigerat, Paduam occupavit. Hac
eadem siti civilia bella Ianuensium et miras eiusdem gentis ducum
alternationes semper fovit. Hoc (proh dolor!) scelere levitatem
Bononiensium ad invicem civica dissensione concussit. Hac eadem

a more powerful adversary to a war? What government in Italy is there that would dare start a war against his power?

We know one thing that not even you, mad though you be, are going to deny: he never started or engaged in a war that was necessary. When he took up arms it was always voluntary; the wars he engaged in were always voluntary — and always wicked.[194] Betraying trust, violating peace and trampling upon treaties, his warmongering has always been a source of disturbance. He could have quieted any war that broke out, blunted every burgeoning cause of offense in its cradle; had he so intended, he could have employed goodness and humanity to maintain Italy in the ultimate sweetness of peace.[195] How he actually behaved was shown in the three wars that he waged against us and the two in which he swept away the lords of Verona and Padua. His guide has always been his ambition: following it, defiling all trust and honor, he threw everything human or divine into confusion. Where hunger for power and pride pushed him, there he went, and when they were absent he stood aside. That has been his cynosure, that his polestar, which seated or afoot, asleep or awake, he has always kept before him; that is the goal he has always pursued with sails and oars. Anything was licit as long as it held out a glimmer of getting more power. 172

The was the cause that drove him to war; it was with this intention that he started the War of Verona, after having made a pact that Verona was to be his and Vicenza the lord of Padua's. Because of this mad lust he took control of Vicenza by means of his wife's family, breaking accords. Spurred by this ambition he made war on his deceived ally, leaving Treviso to his Venetian allies while, as agreed, he took Padua for himself.[196] Because of this thirst he has always fostered the internal conflicts of the Genoese and engineered the surprising coups and countercoups in the line of Genoese doges.[197] Because of this criminal objective, alas, he has afflicted the fickle Bolognese with civil strife. Using the same 173

fraude nunc Astorgium, nunc inclitum comitem Albericum, astu variae ludificationis, adiuvit.[59] Hoc proposito Bononiensibus civilis dominationis caput erexit moxque coepit erectum mille machinationibus agitare; tandemque stultum et infelicem illum populum, cum in libertatem vana credulitate se putat asseri, iugo suae tyrannidis fecit miserabiliter occupari.

174   Dic nunc, quicumque sis, hunc Liguriae principem avidiorem pacis fuisse quam splendori suae dignitatis et nominis conveniret! Dic nos—quibus nihil gravius quam bellum gerere, nihil difficilius quam bella, licet necessaria, deliberare, nihil optabilius amoenitate tranquillitatis et pacis, nihil incommodius privatim et publice bellica vastitate—a quietis et pacis consiliis abhorruisse et exorna, si placet, verbis! Auge vel honesta sententiis! Crede mihi: nihil fidei penes bonos et graves—et facta, non verba, ponderantes—poteris promereri. Verum, inconsideratissima belua, cum nos post Liguriae principem scire multa, posse omnia dicis, quomodo nos 'faecem Italiae' tam alte de nobis sentiens appellasti? Si faex Italiae sumus, quomodo potuimus nos soli, et in nostris manibus situm erat, Italiae pacem dare? Hoc opus non extremae faecis sed summi capitis esse solet. Si pacem Italiae, sicut forsan intelligis, esse ducis sub uno capite convenire idque tribuis duci tuo, pacem hanc fateor in manibus nostris esse. Sed absit a nobis ut dominum habeamus perdita libertate, pro qua maiores nostri nosque etiam tam longo tempore, tanto sanguine totque laboribus, tot expensis, tanta cum gloria dimicavimus!

175   Absit, inquam, et opto. Video equidem quod, si manus dederimus, cuncti cederent et, ut iam praefatus sum, sine sudore vel

trick, he first helped Astorre and then the great Count Alberico, adroitly playing the one off the other. With this as his aim, he set up a chief magistrate, then began to agitate against his own creation using a thousand plots; in the end he caused that foolish and unhappy people, who credulously believed themselves to have been made free, to be placed wretchedly under the yoke of his tyranny.[198]

Say now, whoever you are, that this prince of Liguria desired 174 peace more than befitted the splendor of his rank and reputation! Say that we — for whom nothing is more burdensome than waging war, nothing harder than deciding upon a war, however necessary, nothing more pleasant than tranquility and peace, nothing more damaging either privately or publicly than the destruction of war — say that *we* were the ones who drew back in horror from the counsels of quiet and peace, and embroider your lie with fine words, if you like! Build up your argument with noble sentiments! Believe me, you will never earn respect from upstanding men, serious men who look to facts and not words. After all, thoughtless animal that you are, how can you say we are the most well-informed and powerful state after the prince of Liguria, then call us, having rated us so highly, the "dregs of Italy"? If we were the dregs of Italy how could we alone — and it fell entirely to us — have brought peace to Italy? A task like that is usually worthy not of the dregs of Italy but of the highest authority. If for you peace in Italy signifies, as perhaps you meant to say, being under a sole authority, which furthermore you identify with your lord, I admit that a peace of that sort *does* depend entirely upon us. But may we never submit to a ruler and lose that liberty for which our ancestors and we ourselves have battled for so long, at the price of so much blood lost and so many sacrifices, at so much expense, and earning so much glory!

Never may it come to pass, I say, and that is my hope. It's clear 175 that if we had given in, everyone would have ended up giving in,

sanguine foedissimam subiret Italia servitutem. Nos obiex, nos
obstaculum soli sumus ne cursum perficiat per omnem Italiam ille
tyrannicus dominatus, qui tot urbes, tot castra totque oppida
miserrima condicione subegit. Hanc pacem dominus tuus optabat,
hanc cupit, et inaniter semper cupiat — oro — tali patre digna
posteritas. Sed mihi vel tellus optem prius ima dehiscat omnia vel
medium fiant mare redeatque cataclysmus transcendens triginta
cubitis omnes montes quam talis videatur abominatio super ter-
ram. Huius autem pacis quam dominus tuus optabat, fateor, Florentinos semper hostes et obstaculum exstitisse. Vera vero pax,
quae bellum omne sopiret, quae conservaret statum et tranquilli-
tatem Italiae, in manibus eius erat. Ipse, ipse concutiebat omnia
cupiditate regnandi. Ipse solus, si manus abstinuisset ab aliis, si
turbantibus alios, ut poterat, obstitisset, solo verbo cuncta sedas-
set. Ipse solus potuit pacem serere totamque simul Italiam, nobis
etiam faventibus, in pacis dulcedine continere. Cumque posset
deberetque, cum nullum videret par stare caput nullumque tale
quod formidinem sibi posset inferre, de statu suo super omnes
esse securus, debuit et alios reddere pari ratione securos, non omnes bello, minis, nutu secretisque proditionibus exterrere. Quievisset terra ante faciem eius et moriens de se verum et aeternis cele-
brandum laudibus nomen — velut auctor pacis, non perpetuus belli
fomes — ac deflendum omnibus reliquisset.

176   Credo satis tuis maliloquiis, quisquis sis, tam abunde quam
rationabiliter et, quod nullos negaturos arbitror, verissime respondisse. Nec quicquam remansisse puto quod non fuerit diligentissime confutatum. Si potes alicubi te tueri, si potes nostra

and, as I said, Italy would have been reduced, without blood or sweat, to the most loathsome slavery. We were the only bulwark, the only barrier against the spread of his tyrannical lordship all across Italy, a lordship that has immiserated so many cities, so many towns and so many villages. This is the peace that your lord has been wishing for, this is the peace he desired, and I hope his offspring, who are worthy of such a father, may continue to wish for it—in vain. For myself, may the earth swallow me up, the sea cover everything and a second deluge rise thirty cubits above the highest peaks before an abomination of this kind may be seen upon the earth again![199] The Florentines, I agree, have always opposed and been contrary to the peace that your lord wishes. But the truth is that true peace, of a kind that composes any conflict and preserves the peace and good standing of Italy, depended entirely upon him. It was he who disrupted everything with his hunger for power. He alone, had he kept his hands off other states, had he blocked, as he could have, all those who were creating turmoil for other states, could have brought quiet everywhere with a single word.[200] He alone could have sown peace and preserved Italy whole, with our full support, in a state of blessed peace. Indeed, since he had no equals to his power and nothing to fear, he could and ought to have been both completely secure in his own state and able to make all others safe, rather than terrifying them with war, threats, commands, and secret betrayals. The land would have fallen quiet before his face and at his death he would have left behind a justly famous name, worthy of eternal praise, that of a peacekeeper, not a tireless warmonger, a name to be mourned by all.[201]

I believe these words of mine are reply enough to your defamatory accusations, whoever you be, many enough, consistent enough and (no one dare deny it) intrinsically true enough. Nor do I think there remains anything else that I have not refuted with the utmost care. If you can protect yourself somehow, if you can

176

reprehendere, fac audacter; vel disces tu vel, quod semper mihi placuit, discam ego. Fac tamen tali tam certa, tam valida ratione respondeas vel reprehendas quod iterum invehendi non tribuas occasionem, materiam et necessitatem. Dimitte patriam, oro, dimitte, si placet, et Gallos, quos non expedit in tuum dominum, cuius placita sequeris, provocare. Mihi tecum sit, obsecro, de dictis hinc inde certamen; nec dicamus solum, sed probemus persuadeamusque. Dicendi quidem latissima facultas est, nec minus possumus falsa fictaque dicere, et ornate[60] dicere, quam vera compertaque. Cum in periculum probationis aut improbationis venerimus, iudicium aliquod esse poterit de veritate, de vi ratione dicendi. Quove tibi viam aperiam, dixi multa pro patria, dixi contra dominum tuum pauca quaedam, sicut respondendi necessitas compulit; ex libidine quidem maledicendi, Deum testor, me penitus nil dixisse. In quo velim haec nostra legentes boni consulant; exigerem hoc etiam a temet ipso, si tibi foret aliquod de dicendi ratione iudicium.

177   Dixi multa respondique pro Gallis; dixi plurima contra te, maledicta tua et imperitiam tuam. Conare, si potes, ut ad ista respondeas, adducta, sicut decet, in medium ratione. Non obiurgeris et ego non obiurgabor. Possum te dicere (quis enim vetat?) assentatione Gnatonem, crudelitate Sullam, nec Sullam solummodo sed Marium, Cinnam, Neronem sive Caligulam; possum et Domitianum possumque Munatium, possum luxuria te dicere Sardanapalum, voluptate Xerxem, qui novae delectationis auctori edicto publico constituit praemia. Possum libidine te vocare Priapum atque Silenum et, ut ad historias transeam, Antonium triumvirum et qui in hac re cuncta Veneris monstra vicit: nequitiae foedissimae spurcissimum Varium Antoninum, qui et Heliogabalus dictus est.

criticize what I have said, be bold to do so: either you will learn something, or I will, and I've always liked learning.[202] But this time I ask you to reply or criticize with reasoning that is well-founded and solid enough to leave no room, ground or need for another dispute. And please, I beg you, leave our fatherland out of it and the Gauls too; it avails you but little to provoke them against the lord whose opinions you follow. Let's keep the contest between me and you, and limit it henceforward to words; and not mere words, but words that prove and persuade.[203] The power of speech is extremely broad, and we are no less able to make false and fictitious statements, and in an elegant way, than to make true and evident ones. Once we risk proof or disproof, it is possible to make a judgment about truth and about rhetorical skill. To show you how to go about it, I have spoken much in favor of my country, a little against your lord (and only what necessity required), and nothing at all, as God is my witness, for the pure pleasure of defamation. I wish that those who read these writings of ours will approve of this course, and I should make this same requirement of you yourself as well, if you possess any critical judgment about the art of rhetoric.

I have said much in this reply in defense of the Gauls, and much more against you, your lies and your ignorance. Try, if you can, to respond to my criticisms, setting out your reasons, as is only proper. You won't be blaming me and I won't feel blamed. I could call you (who is to prevent me?)[204] a Gnathon for your fawning, a Sulla for your cruelty, and not only a Sulla but a Marius, a Cinna, a Nero or a Caligula, even a Domitian or a Munatius, to boot; I could call you a Sardanapalus of sensuality, a Xerxes of pleasure — he who set up a public prize for the invention of new forms of pleasure. For lust I can call you Priapus or Silenus or (turning to the historians) the triumvir Antony, and that champion of venereal monstrosity, that wretched example of the worst perversion that was Varius Antoninus, known as Heliogabalus.

177

Possum etiam te P. Clodium appellare, incestu sordidum in soro-
rem, infamem pollutis caeremoniis, sacrilego concubitu corruptis-
que iudicibus pecunia, nec non et prostitutis infandorum iudicum
nequitiae per venale nefas scelusque nocturnum pueris ingenuis
nobilibusque matronis, prout quisque pro suae voluptatis libidine
cupiebat, turpiter absolutum. Possum et invidia te dicere Mucium
vel Aglauron, iracundia Magnum Alexandrum Plutarchicumque
Fundanum; superbia Tarquinium, qui septimus regnavit in urbe;
avaritia L. Septimulum, Q. Cassium, Midam aut Tantalum; rapa-
citate Verrem, perfidia Ptolemaeum aut Iudam, inanis gloriae iac-
tatione Thrasonem, curiosa temeritate Bladudem Anglorum regem, qui nexis alis, affectato volatu, dum aviculas imitari satagit,
super Apollinis templum ruens in urbe quae dicitur Trinovantum,
ut scribitur, miserabiliter extinctus est.

178   Possum per historias poemataque discurrens te vitio quolibet
aliquibusque notare vocareque cuiusvis nomine vitiosi. Potes et tu
me sugillatione simili, si volueris, afficere, et nunc hunc nunc illum
pro criminationis differentia nominare. Possumus et ambo pari ratione quemcumque placuerit lacessere maledictis et laudibus etiam
exornare. Cavenda tamen sunt hinc inde mendacia, praesertim si
maledixerimus. Reprehensibile quidem nimis est alium corripere si
non fiat debita ratione. Mentiri vero falsoque cuipiam — etiam
inimico, quem privatim odio habeas, vel hosti patriae, quem publice detesteris — crimen imponere non inhonestum solummodo
sed turpe, sed abominabile scelusque quod nulla ratione valeat ex-
piari.

179   Si veritate, si ratione viceris, dabo manus nec in aliquo refraga-
bor. Si pergas et errores fovens tuos pervicacia putes vincere, referam tibi quae scripsit Hieronymus Augustino, ut aetatem non
contemnas meam: 'Memento Daretis et Entelli et vulgaris prover-
bii quod 'bos lassus fortius figat pedem' .' Durius quam putes est
iuveni senem dicendo vincere. Cum enim iuventae senectus ferme

I could call you Publius Clodius, stained with incest committed with his sister, he who profaned sacred rites, committed adultery, corrupted judges with money and sold to them, pandering to their various sick tastes, boys of good family and Roman noblewomen, in return for release from charges. I can call you in envy a Mucius or Aglaurus, in anger an Alexander the Great or Plutarch's Fundanus, in pride Tarquin, seventh king of Rome, in avarice Lucius Settimulus, Quintus Cassius, Midas or Tantalus, in avidity Verres, in perfidy Ptolemy or Judas, in vainglory Trason, in foolish curiosity a Bladud, that English king who stupidly donned a pair of wings and tried to fly like a little bird, only to crash down upon a temple of Trinovantum and meet his end.[205]

Leafing through the histories and poems I can well accuse you 178 of any vice and call you by the name of any vicious personage I please. You too, if you wish, may insult me in the same coin and call me one thing or another to set my faults in relief. For that matter we can each heap insults or any sort of praise on whomever we please. But on either side one must avoid speaking falsely of others, especially if we insult them. It is highly reprehensible to attack someone without just cause. To lie, indeed to accuse anyone unjustly — whether a personal enemy whom you hate for private reasons, or an enemy of your country whom you despise publicly — is not only dishonest but vile and abject: it is a crime that cannot be expiated.[206]

If you should win because truth and reason are on your side, I 179 will submit and make no objection.[207] If you go on and keep warming over those same old errors, thinking you can win a contest of stubbornness, I will reply with Jerome's words to Augustine, inviting you to not look down on me because of my age: "Remember Dares and Entellus, and the popular proverb that 'The tired bull digs in deeper its hoof.' "[208] When it comes to speech it is harder than you may suppose for a young man to best an old one. Although age gives way to youth in all physical

cedat in omnibus quae corporibus exercemus, quoniam loquacior
tamen vetustas est, dicendo solet facile superare. Haec enim aetas
tot audivit, tot didicit atque vidit, quod in tanta rerum copia difficile nimis ei sit multiloquio modum ponere. De ceteris contendat
cum senibus iuventus, de vincendo secura; consilio vero pugnaque
dicendi moneo non decertet.

180   Sum armatus notitia rerum, veritate negotiorum et iustitia causae. Scio foedera, scio societates, scio violationes et foedifragia;
scio quid contra nos factum novique similiter et in multis quid in
nos, fide pessumdata, sit tentatum. Uberrimam habeo materiam
pro libero principeque populo contra tyrannidis impotentiam atque iugum, pro fide contra perfidiam, pro iustitia contra iniquitatem, pro veritate contra mendacia, pro rebus solidis contra vana
figmenta. Velit Deus, si periculum fecerimus in dicendo, quod pro
medietate materiae sit mihi satis oris mediocrisque facundiae.
Non vereor, si concesserit hoc Deus, non habere victoriam quoti-
dieque me fortius quam ut resisti valeat[61] certaturum.

181   Quando posset enim contra talia deficere quid dicatur? Quando
dicenti pro talibus non abundantissime suppetet quod assensu
cunctorum perspicue concludatur? Quis ita segnis atque tepentis
eloquii qui causam agens istam excitante materia non calescat?
Qui rem tam claram perspicue docere non possit? Qui, cum pro
parte quam tueor stet certissima veritas atque prompta, non debeat etiam pervicacibus perorare? Qui non possit interrogationum
vehementia pungere, immo confodere, ex opposito disputantem?
Qui non possit exclamationibus rem augere? Qui non possit permovere crebris indignationibus animos auditorum moderataque

exercises, it usually surpasses it easily in speech, as old age is more loquacious.[209] At my age I have heard, learned and seen so many things and have such an abundance of material that it is surpassingly hard to place bounds on the ocean of my chattering. Let the young compete with the old in other matters, secure in their victory, but when it comes to giving advice and verbal knockabout I advise them to stand aside.

I stand armed with knowledge of facts, the truth behind events, and a just cause. I know the treaties, I know the alliances, I know the violations and betrayals: I know what has been done against us and I know just as well what has been attempted many times in bad faith. I am not wanting for examples to set a free sovereign people against the arrogance and yoke of a tyranny, fidelity against perfidy, justice against iniquity, truth against lying, certain facts against mere inventions. May God will, if we dare enter a contest of words, that I may have the modicum of eloquence and boldness proportionate to half of the material at my disposal. If God will allow me these, I shall have no fear of losing and I shall fight every day with a strength greater than he will be able to resist. 180

Indeed, when could one ever run out of things to say about such matters? When would the person speaking on behalf of such themes not be abundantly supplied with proofs clear enough to end in universal consent? Does there exist an orator so lazy or tired who in defense of this cause would not warm up to so rousing a theme? Who would not be able to expound convincingly a question so clear? Who, with the truth so palpably and undeniably on his side, would not feel a duty to prove it even to the most obstinate? Who would not know how to puncture, indeed transfix his adversary with the vehemence of his cross-examination? Who could not amplify his speech with emotional outbursts?[210] Who would not know how to stir the public with his indignation and use dignified remonstrance to win their sympathy for persons and 181

conquestione taliter afficere quod in commiserationem personarum et temporum inclinati sibi faveant et adversariis irascantur?

182   Sed quid moror? Exeat e latebris haec vipera, quae tot dicendi
reflexibus pro vipera declamavit. Efficiam, ni fallor, quod sibilare
desistat. Nunc autem, si dignum sique tibi videtur hominis ratione
degentis esse nullum laudabilem finem in re tanti ponderis quanta
sit maledicere Florentinis, tibi proponere quem intendas nisi maledixisse, nisi famam tantae gentis voluisse tot exquisitis mendaciis
obscurare, nisi, sicut dixi, malitia frui tua; sique pulchrum, oratorium et artificiosum est orationis initio fidei, si quam assequi debeas, abrogare culpa tua et procacitate tua; sique quod adversariis
optandum est velut crimen aliquod obicere dignum putas; si mendaciis eos, in quos dixeris, insectari, quae cunctis aperta sint, ex
arte rationeque dicendi iudicas esse posse; si divinare, quove rectius loquar affirmare, quae videris ex praeteritis, quae sunt argumentum et coniectatio futurorum, nedum non speranda fore sed
potius desperanda; si tam multa polite dicere, quae non arguas nec
probes (probari quidem non possunt) pulchrum ducis, resume,
responde, proba, dic ut appellantium est: 'Quod non dixi, dicam,
quod non probavi, probabo.'

183   Dic et fac, ut libet; mendaciis tamen abstineas moneo. Parmenonis verbis, ut ille inquit, 'hac lege tibi fidem abstringo meam.
Quae vera audivi taceo et contineo optime. Sin falsum aut vanum
aut fictum est, continuo palam est: plenus rimarum sum, hac atque illac perfluo. Proin tu, taceri si vis, vera dicito.' Tacebo quidem, immo fatebor et assentiam quae vera dixeris. Si redibis ad
falsa, non patiar; mox in conflictationem descendemus. Nec credo
te mendaciis obtinere quae voles, nec falsitati succumbere veritatem. Fac etiam quod saltem de grammatica non offendas aures

circumstances, getting them to favor his side and be outraged at his opponents?[211]

But what is stopping you? Let this viper, who has spoken on 182 behalf of the Visconti viper with all sorts of twists of its tongue, stop hiding in its lair. I will manage, I think, to stop its hissing. If, however, it seems to you worthy and right for a reasonable creature that you propose to achieve no goal in so important a matter as insulting the Florentines except slander, no goal in blackening a great people's name with carefully wrought lies except (as I've said)[212] indulging your own malice — if it is fine, eloquent and artful for an orator, at beginning of his speech, to destroy all his credibility (if you deserve any) through your own fault and your own impudence — if it seems a fine thing to fling out as a misdeed something which adversaries ought to wish for — if you think it proper for an orator to unload upon an opponent affirmations that no one finds true and then to prophesy (or I should more correctly say "assert as true") things for which past events (source of the future) give one no right to hope, let alone expect — if you think it a fine thing to say all that in a fancy style but without a shred of proof (and indeed they couldn't be proven) — well, then start over, reply, prove, and declare, like someone appealing a decision: "What I have not yet said, I shall say; what I have not proven, I shall prove."

Say and do what you like; I advise you only not to lie. In the 183 words of Parmeno: "I give you my word, but on this condition: if what I hear is true, I will keep quiet and calm; if instead it is false, if it is a flat-out lie, it will be immediately evident. I am full of holes and leak on all sides. So if you want me to be quiet, tell the truth."[213] I shall be silent; indeed I shall admit and give assent to the true things you will say. If you start to lie again, I'll not stand for it and I'll return to the fray. I don't believe that you can get what you want with lies, nor will truth yield to untruth. And be careful at least not to offend my ears with more grammatical

393

meas, in quam rem puduit vicem tuam te totiens incidisse. Nec artis rhetoricae rationem laedas, memor quod non satis sit dicere nisi probes, et quod probare non sufficit nisi persuadeas. Haec satis; multa quidem secundo congressu, si perrexeris, reservare decrevi. Vetus enim proverbium est remanere vacuum atque nudum qui quicquid habet expenderit et dixerit quicquid novit.

errors, of which you have already made a disgraceful number. And have respect for the rules of rhetoric, remembering that talk without proof is not enough, and that proof alone is not enough if you cannot convince. But let us stop here; there are many things which I have decided to set aside for our second encounter, if you want to try again. As the old proverb has it, naked and empty-handed is he who spends all that he has and says all that he knows.

Note on the Texts and Translations

अ९ఇఠ

In 1976 Ronald Witt estimated that Salutati had penned some eight thousand missives in more than thirty years of service as chancellor of Florence.[1] Armando Nuzzo has recently offered a complete census of the surviving letters and a list of their *incipits*, dating from 7 April 1375 to 30 April 1406, for a total of 7,479 missives.[2] A first major contribution to their knowledge was the anthology published by Hermann Langkabel in 1981.[3] The texts included in the present anthology follow Langkabel's edition, to which Rolf Bagemihl and I are indebted for some explanatory notes as well. We refer readers to the opening section of Langkabel's volume for a discussion of the editorial criteria he employed.[4]

In the case of *De tyranno*, our starting point has been Ercole's 1914 critical edition, mentioned above in the Introduction. There are six known manuscript witnesses to Salutati's *De tyranno*:

G   Florence, Biblioteca Medicea Laurenziana, MS. Gadd. 90 sup. 41.2

M   ——, MS. Laur. 78.12

P   Paris, Bibliothèque Nationale de France, MS. Lat. 8573

S   Rome, Biblioteca Vittorio Emanuele II, MS. Sess. 167 (1443)

V   Vatican City, Biblioteca Apostolica Vaticana, MS. Reg. lat. 1391

Z   Siena, Biblioteca Comunale, MS G VII 44.

Ercole described at length the first five witnesses listed above, but his codicological expertise left much to be desired and, as we shall see, it also prejudiced his *constitutio textus*.[5] A much more detailed and accurate description of three of them is now in *Catalogo*.[6] For clarity's sake, I have decided to indicate these witnesses with the same sigla that Ercole used for his edition. MS Z, in-

397

stead, is not to be found either in Ercole's edition or in *Catalogo*. It was brought to my attention by James Hankins, for which I thank him. This codex is briefly described in both *Iter Italicum* and the recent online *Inventario dei manoscritti medievali della Toscana*, although with some inaccuracies in both cases.[7] Miscellaneous and composite, this text only reports chapters 1 to 4 of *De tyranno* (ff. 66r–82v), breaking off right before the beginning of the last section, the one concerned with Dante's "condemnation" of Brutus and Cassius to hell. As suggested both by the speech immediately following *De tyranno* in this manuscript (ff. 82v–84r) and by several other features, the scribe must have been a young Paduan student (and not a very gifted one, at least to judge from the many mistakes he makes in copying these two texts). The main importance of this witness lies in its reporting of an anonymous oration (titled *Pro populo paduano Ad Antonium generalem ministrum ordinis minorum salutatio atque obl . . .* [page damaged] *. . . me boni artium et legum doctoris*), which was delivered sometime in 1405–6.[8] The cleric praised in this anonymous oration was Antonio Vinitti (better known as "Antonius de Pereto"), as reported on f. 84v.[9] Since Pereto is a village near Aquila, it is possible (although far from certain) that this Antonio should be identified with the dedicatee of Salutati's treatise. Antonio Vinitti of Pereto was minister general of the Franciscans from 1405 to 1408 and again from 1415 to 1420,[10] thus shortly after Salutati's *De tyranno* started circulating and during the pontificate of Innocent VII, who died on 6 November 1406.

In regard to the relationships between the *De tyranno* witnesses mentioned above, Ercole — who, it is worth remembering, was primarily an expert on legal history — considered S to be the closest exemplar to the archetype and probably the oldest too. By contrast, in his entry on *De tyranno* for the 2008–9 manuscript exhibition, Quaglioni holds that the earliest surviving copy of Salutati's treatise is certainly V.[11] As first shown by Ullman and

later confirmed by other scholars, V was copied by one of Salutati's scribes.[12] Manuscripts M and P, though not put together
within Salutati's circle, date from around the same time as V.[13] In
regard to their accuracy, S is far from correct, as shown in the apparatus reporting its many errors and omissions. Z (which, as said
above, breaks off at the end of chapter 4) is marred by an impres-
sive series of omissions, *sautes de même au même*, and banal mistakes.[14] Though less flawed, V is not immune from significant inaccuracies either. The same is true of M, though to a lesser extent,
whereas P stands out as the most accurate exemplar.[15] Finally,
G — the most recent exemplar of *De tyranno* — is of little value in
reconstructing the text, as is also the case with the more recent
exemplars of *Contra maledicum et obiurgatorem*.[16] A characteristic
feature of that manuscript — as clearly shown in the apparatus — is
its frequent offering of a different *ordo verborum* dictated by a classicizing taste that is certainly not Salutati's.[17]

What led Ercole astray in the first place was his hasty assump-
tion that since all witnesses but S report three works of Salutati
(*De tyranno*, *De verecundia*, and the *Tractatus super primam epistolam
Senecae ad Lucilium*), they must be closely connected to one another.[18] Not surprisingly, this thesis has turned out to be false also
in regard to two manuscripts of *Contra maledicum et obiurgatorem*, as
we shall soon see. In view of the methodological flaws evident in
Ercole's philological note on *De tyranno*,[19] I decided to collate all
witnesses again and compare my results with his. In doing so I
have found that his collation is accurate. Consequently, my apparatus is largely similar to his, except for the presence of Z. The
main differences occur when he adopts in the text readings that
are typical of S against the other exemplars. Since I disagree with
him regarding the reliability of S,[20] I have done the opposite in
a number of instances, thus relegating S to the apparatus and
adopting the form transmitted by G, M, P, V, and Z instead. Another significant difference is that Ercole's apparatus reports banal

discrepancies in spelling, whereas mine does not. All this, however, has led me to propose a *stemma codicum* very similar to his. I simply hold — as said above — that there is no reason to consider S closer than the other witnesses to the archetype, whose existence is shown by a number of cases reported in the apparatus. I thus believe that the relationships between the extant manuscripts of *De tyranno* can be schematized as follows:

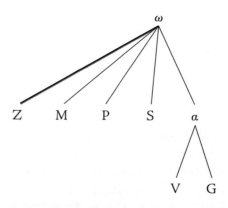

The situation is different with the *Contra maledicum et obiurgatorem*. In this case one can rely on a very precise (almost perfect) exemplar, which was most likely composed under Salutati's own supervision. I am speaking of O, whose importance I have already highlighted in the catalog of the 2008–9 Salutati manuscript exhibition.[21] Before briefly discussing the main philological features of the present edition of *Contra maledicum et obiurgatorem*, it is necessary to provide a list of witnesses. For consistency's sake, I have decided to use the same sigla as used in my edition of this text in *La vipera e il giglio*. The *Contra maledicum et obiurgatorem* is preserved in the following five manuscripts:

L   Florence, Biblioteca Medicea Laurenziana, MS. 90 sup. 41.2
N   Florence, Biblioteca Nazionale Centrale, MS. Naz. II IV 165
O   Oxford, All Souls College, MS. 94
P   Paris, Bibliothèque Nationale, MS. Lat. 8573
V   Vatican City, Biblioteca Apostolica Vaticana, MS. Vat. lat. 3134

In *La vipera e il giglio* I discuss at length the manuscript tradition of *Contra maledicum et obiurgatorem*. The collation shows that L and N derive from a lost copy (α), while the other three witnesses — stemming in turn from an archetype — are all on the same level. The outstanding accuracy of O, which was made under Salutati's supervision, and its use of punctuation like that expounded in the author's *Ratio punctandi*, make it a witness of the utmost importance. Yet no manuscript of *Contra maledicum et obiurgatorem* derives from it directly. The thorough collation of all the manuscripts listed above in *La vipera e il giglio*[22] demonstrates that the *stemma codicum* of this work is as follows:

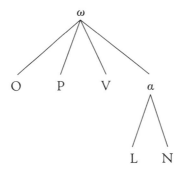

Finally, a few words on the only text that is not by Salutati included in this anthology: Antonio Loschi's *Invectiva in Florentinos*, whose tradition consists of the following six manuscripts, here too indicated with the same sigla as used in *La vipera e il giglio*:

B   Oxford, Bodleian Library, MS. Bywater 38
LU   Lucca, Biblioteca Statale, MS. 1436
MA   Florence, Biblioteca Marucelliana, MS. A CCXXIII
R   Ravenna. Biblioteca Classense, MS. 271
T   Milan, Biblioteca Trivulziana, MS. 751
V   Vatican City, Biblioteca Apostolica Vaticana, MS. Vat. lat. 3134

The philological analysis of these witnesses[23] leads to the following *stemma codicum*:

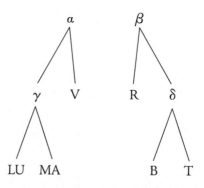

For a detailed analysis of the relationships between these witnesses, I refer readers to *La vipera e il giglio*.[24] A few things, however, are worth repeating here. First of all, V is the only manuscript containing both Loschi's invective and Salutati's reply. Since the former immediately precedes the latter, as one would expect, the text of *Contra maledicum et obiurgatorem* in V does not report Loschi's statements in full, but is limited to the first few words in each citation. As such, V stands out as a unique exemplar of this work of Salutati's. Also, the two main branches making up the *stemma codicum* of Loschi's invective (α and β) could be called "Apennine" and "northern Italian," respectively. The reason is that while witnesses pertaining to α come from Emilia-Romagna or

northern Tuscany (a Malatesta chancery for V, the areas of Pisa-Lucca for LU and Florence for MA), thus placing themselves — as it were — on the mountain border separating these two regions, those of *β* were copied in northern Italy (B originated in the Veneto, T in Lombardy, and, finally, R in the Po Valley). A case separates these two branches: whereas at the beginning of §18 of Loschi's invective, *β* offers the *tricolon* "non tenetis ista memoriae nihilque — *nisi impium, crudele, nefarium* — mente cogitationibusque versatis" (italics mine), *α* reports the less convincing "nisi impe-rium crudele, nefarium." All manuscripts of *Contra maledicum et obiurgatorem* transmit the formula as we find it in *α*, thus showing that Salutati used a copy of Loschi's *Invectiva in Florentinos* belong-ing to this branch of the *stemma codicum* above. Finally, I take this opportunity to do justice, once again, to Loschi's Latin prose. In his reply to the Visconti secretary, Salutati accuses him (or, rather, the author of this invective, since he argues that so distinguished and knowledgeable a humanist as Loschi could not be the author of this heinous slander) of having said the very opposite of what he must have meant when he wrote as follows (§§105 and 149 of *Contra maledicum et obiurgatorem*, quoting *Invectiva in Florentinos* §16): "Qua re non modo suis copiis vos non defendendos esse *non* exis-timabit sed omni dignos supplicio iudicabit" (italics mine). As discussed in *La vipera e il giglio*,[25] this reading is marred by a mis-take that occurred independently both in *α* and in *β*, then passed down to all witnesses of Loschi's writing. The scribes simply did not recognize the second *non* in the phrase mentioned above as having an emphatic, rhetorical function, so that the text should be reported as follows: "Qua re non modo suis copiis vos non defen-dendos esse existimabit *(non!)* sed omni dignos supplicio iudicabit" (again, italics mine). Interestingly enough, a very similar case oc-curs in the manuscript tradition of another text of the time closely linked with Loschi's invective and Salutati's reply: Bruni's *Lauda-tio florentinae urbis*.[26] Evidently, the "link" connecting these three

works, as Tanturli calls it in a recent essay, proves to be true also in regard to philological issues.[27]

S. U. B.

I have based my translation of *On Tyranny* on the one published by Emerton but have updated it in terms of language and corrected it on a number of points. Baldassarri's sensitive Italian translations of all texts have been of invaluable help.

R. B.

NOTES

1. Witt, *Public Letters*, p. 3.

2. A. Nuzzo, *Lettere di stato di Coluccio Salutati. Cancellierato fiorentino (1375–1406). Censimento delle fonti e indice degli 'incipit' della tradizione archivistico-documentaria*, 2 vols. (Rome: Istituto Storico Italiano per il Medio Evo, 2008). See also, by the same scholar, the essay "L'epistolario del Salutati. Una presentazione," in *Coluccio Salutati e l'invenzione*, pp. 225–30.

3. See p. 422, below, in the list of abbreviations for the full title.

4. See Langkabel, pp. 24–26.

5. For Ercole's description of these five witnesses, see his 1914 edition, pp. 185–94.

6. See *Catalogo*, pp. 168–69 (P), 169–70 (V), and 213–14 (G). Important information on M and S is offered ibid., 167–69. For a close description of G and P, see also *La vipera e il giglio*, pp. 91–92 and 94–96, respectively.

7. See P. O. Kristeller, *Iter Italicum*, 7 vols. (Leiden: Brill, 1963–96), 2:162–63, and the *Inventario dei manoscritti medievali della Toscana*, online at http://codex.signum.sns.it.

8. As attested by the following passage (f. 83v): "Hec quidem cum vera sint et haberi semper debeant verissima tamen etate nostra efficit summus atque beatissimus noster pontifex VII Innocentius." The *incipit* and *explicit* of this speech read, "Video preses inclite universi⟨tatis⟩ cives

vosque . . ." and ". . . vestra pietate vestraque gratia nobis videre condonastis," respectively.

9. There one reads as follows in regard to the minister general and his many praiseworthy qualities: "Itaque religiosissime Antoniii [sic] Peretree inviolenter hos cunctos possides quos tuis amplissimis virtutibus tuaque mira humanitate comparasti."

10. And then, again, in 1415–20.

11. See *Catalogo*, p. 167.

12. See Ullman, pp. 268–72 (where he identifies what he calls "Salutati's fifth scribe" as the one who copied this and other manuscripts belonging to the chancellor's library). Ullman's opinion has been confirmed by S. Zamponi, "Nello scrittoio di Coluccio Salutati: il Lattanzio Placido Forteguerriano," in *Tra libri e carte. Studi in onore di Luciana Mosici*, ed. T. De Robertis and G. Savino (Florence: Cesati, 1998), pp. 549–92, at 572. See also M. Marchiaro's description of MS. V in *Catalogo*, pp. 168–70.

13. See M. Marchiaro's description of V, *Catalogo*, p. 170: "Per il testo del *De tyranno*, il Reg. lat. 1391 risulta il più antico testimone insieme al Laur. 78.12 e al Parigino lat. 8573."

14. Since Ercole did not include Z in his critical edition, I have listed a number of its mistakes and omissions in my apparatus, so as to show its poor level of accuracy. As for its variants, at least one is worthy of attention, i.e., the formula found on p. 132: "hanc optabant, hanc sperabant, hanc intendebant." Z is the only witness reporting this *tricolon*, whereas all other manuscripts read, "hanc optabant, hanc intendebant."

15. On P's reliability for the text of *De tyranno*, see Piacentini, *Catalogo*, p. 169. P has also shown to preserve an accurate copy of *Contra maledicum et obiurgatorem*, though to a lesser extent; see below, p. 401, within this same philological note.

16. See below, p. 401.

17. Limiting ourselves to the opening paragraphs, see notes 24, 26, 28, 30, and 31 to the Latin text.

18. See Ercole's 1914 edition, p. 194, where, after comparing the contents of G, M, P, and V, he writes, "nur bei S wird der Traktat de Tyranno von

Schriften begleitet, die mit Coluccio gar nichts zu tun haben. Daraus ergibt sich die ganz natürliche Voraussetzung, dass unter den ersten vier Hdss. ein enges Verhältnis besteht." The other works transcribed in S are all religious in content; see ibid., p. 193.

19. See ibid., pp. 193–205.

20. I am not alone in disagreeing with Ercole's rationale for establishing the text of *De tyranno*. In *Catalogo*, p. 169, A. Piacentini expresses some puzzlement at Ercole's philological decisions: "Qualche spunto è stato fornito dall'edizione data da Francesco Ercole del *De tyranno*, per quanto in più punti discutibile nella valutazione delle varianti."

21. See the entry on this work of Salutati's in *Catalogo*, pp. 171–73, as well as pp. 174–75 for a description of MS. O by the present writer and C. Dondi.

22. See *La vipera e il giglio*, pp. 103–13.

23. See ibid., pp. 81–89, and my preliminary essay "La *Invectiva in Florentinos* di Antonio Loschi," *Esperienze Letterarie*, 35.1 (2010): 3–28.

24. *La vipera e il giglio*, pp. 81–89.

25. See ibid., pp. 87–89, where I also refer to other cases of similar mistakes caused by the rhetorical doubling of *non* in humanist texts of the time.

26. See ibid., pp. 88–89, and my edition of Bruni's *Laudatio*, p. lxxx.

27. See Tanturli, "Un nodo."

Notes to the Texts

❧❧❧

SALUTATI, DE TYRANNO

1. Patavi *om.* Z

2. vir *om.* G

3. erudite] vir erudite G

4. diligere] non diligere G M P V Z

5. non denegare] denegare G M P V Z

6. communionem humanam] humanam communionem G

7. homine libero] libero homine S

8. abundare] abunde G

9. quo cunctis] quotiens Z

10. Tu meas episolas quasdam *om.* Z

11. dici solet] solet dici Z

12. dixeris accidens] accidens dixerim S

13. illa] ea S

14. efficiens *om.* Z

15. a me] me G

16. Dominus mihi] mihi Dominus Z

17. detegatur mea] mea detegatur G

18. infimum] infirmum Z

19. dedignabor te] te dedignabor G

20. plus de me] de me plus Z

21. tyrannus] tyrannus sit G

22. adiciendo quotuplex sit tyrannus *om.* S

23. numerari] nominari Z

24. reppererim] repperim *P*

25. etiam *om.* G

26. habebat] habebant *Z*

27. fors] sors *GSV*

28. inserta est] est insita G

29. graece *om.* S

30. vassileus] baxilleos G; vassilleus *M*

31. vassileuo] baxilleo G; vassileo S

32. idem est] est idem G

33. haec *om.* S

34. ponam textum] textum ponam G

35. librorum moralium] moralium libro G

36. exponens illa verba] illa verba exponens G

37. tyrannum non diffinivit solum] tyrannum solum non diffinivit G

38. alius in . . . alius in *om.* Z

39. Deus quantum . . . apud se *om.* Z

40. dominatur intus] intus dominatur G

41. non affligat proximos] proximos non affligat G

42. habere potestatem] potestatem habere G

43. nequitia] iniquitia *Z*

44. scrutatur renes] renes scrutatur G

45. intuetur *om.* G

46. facere valeat] faceret vellet S

47. voluntatis liberae] liberae voluntatis G

48. restricta legibus] legibus restricta G

49. pessundare leges] leges pessundare G

50. facultatesque proprias] propriasque facultates G

51. congruit] convenit *Z*

52. vel si . . . re publica *om.* Z

53. *Modern texts of Seneca read* regamque.

54. et cetera . . . legum metu' *om.* Z

55. servat] observat G

56. vel, ut expressius loquar, singulum *om.* Z

57. scribentes Theodoro] Theodoro scribentes G

58. invadenti principatum] principatum invadenti G

59. cum caede vel sanguine] cum sanguine vel caede M

60. defendat] defendit G

61. praefecto praetorio] papae G M P S V Z

62. scripserunt] rescripserunt Z

63. provincialibus] provincialibus resistendi S

64. resistendi *om.* S

65. permissa *om.* Z

66. vocatus ad iudicium] ad iudicium vocatus G

67. plebei] plebeia G

68. Exstat] Est M

69. proiectus est] est proiectus G

70. interrogatus *om.* G M P S V Z

71. quisnam Scipio [. . .] auctor fuerit *om.* S

72. cum fratre in Hispania caesus] cum fratre per Scipionem in Hispania caesus S

73. susceperit] suscepit P S V

74. advecta] adducta Z

75. multitudo *om.* S

76. debere videri] videri debere G

77. colligendis] colligendis omnibus M *(not reported in Ercole's apparatus);* omnibus colligendis Z

78. Curiatio] Curiato G M P S V Z

79. et *om.* G M P S V Z

80. clarissimum historicorum] historicorum clarissimus G

81. P.] Publium M (*not reported in Ercole's apparatus*) *and* Z

82. tueantur auctore] auctore tueantur G

83. Quam si nequeant *om.* Z

84. in clara] inclara *Ercole's 1942 edition*

85. emisset agrum] agrum emisset G

86. Asina] Asinae G

87. plus auctoritatis et fidei praebere] auctoritatis et fidei plus praebere G

88. velit] velint M

89. resisti posse] posse resisti G

90. momentum naturae] naturae momentum G

91. incumbat] incumbit M

92. rerum praesentium] praesentium rerum G

93. recognoscat principem] principem recognoscat G

94. coeperit] coepit G V Z

95. titulum iustum] iustum titulum G Z

96. est *om.* M

97. iudicatus hostis] hostis iudicatus G

98. *Modern texts of Juvenal read* vulnere.

99. non concludit quod iustae *om.* Z

100. eruditissimus] evidentissimus M

101. librorum illorum] illorum librorum G

102. et *om. Ercole (who, however, refers in his apparatus to the reading* et quasi *transmitted by all manuscripts)*

103. tertii *om.* Z

104. omnium] hominum G

105. autem *om.* M

106. reverentiam sacramenti] sacramenti reverentiam G

107. sententia] sententiam *M*

108. liberatis] libertatis *G M S Z*

109. et celebrandus *om. Z*

110. quilibet patriae] patriae quilibet *M*

111. auctoritatis rei publicae] rei publicae auctoritatis *G*

112. remansisset in exercitu] in exercitu remansisset *G*

113. pugnare] pugnasse *M*

114. insurgat] et insurgat *S*

115. aut populi *om. G*

116. numerari] enumerari *G*; nominari *Z*

117. tamen] enim *Z*

118. C.] Gaii *S*

119. *In the best manuscripts this passage from Cicero's* On Duties *reads* obsistere. *See next note.*

120. *On this (corrupt) passage from Cicero's* On Duties *(2.7.23), see note 73 to the English translation. In most manuscripts the Latin reads:* Multorum autem odiis nullas opes posse obsistere, si antea fuit ignotum, nuper est cognitum. Nec vero huius tyranni solum, quem armis oppressa pertulit civitas, † apparet cuius maxime portui interitus declarat † quantum odium hominum valet ad pestem, sed reliquorum similes exitus tyrannorum. *Ercole edits it as follows:* Multorum tamen odiis nullas opes posse obsistere, si antea fuit ignotum, nuper est cognitum. Nec vero huius tyranni solum, quem armis oppressa pertulit civitas ac paret cum maxime mortuo, interitus declarat, quantum odium hominum valet ad pestem, sed reliquorum similes exitus tyrannorum.

121. bella quidem] quidem bella *M*

122. nos quibuscumque] quibuscumque nos *M*

123. cunctis temporibus reddidit] reddidit cunctis temporibus *G*

124. querelam temporum] temporum querelam *G*

125. haberet] habent *Ercole (who puts in the apparatus the reading shared here by all MSS:* haberet)

126. pauca om. *Z*

127. aut tam . . . ipse deficerem *om. Z*

128. tamen umquam] umquam tantum *M*

129. invenies apud Ciceronem] apud Ciceronem invenies *G*

130. orationes eius] eius orationes *G*

131. reviviscentis] reviviscentes *Ercole (who erroneously claims in the apparatus that all MSS, except G, read* reviviscentes *instead of* reviviscentis)*

132. egit] agit *S*

133. gratias egit Caesari] Caesari gratias egit *G*

134. condicionem rerum] rerum condicionem *G Z*

135. futurarum] futuram *α (not in Ercole's apparatus)*

136. scribat] scribit *M*

137. meliores] meliorem *M*

138. conatibusque cunctis] cunctisque conatibus *G*

139. imperaret] imperarent *G V Z;* imperare *M*

140. crudelius] crudelis *Ercole's 1942 edition*

141. inflammaret odium] caelum inflammaret *G*

142. Martis vis] vis Martis *S*

143. debeat nemo] nemo debeat *G*

144. Faustum] Iaustum *Ercole*

145. Sullam] Sulla *M*

146. docuerat generos timere Pompeius] docuerat generum timere *α (not in Ercole's apparatus);* didicerat generum timere *P S V Z (also G and M according to Ercole). In this case we have adopted Ercole's reading, which follows the correct form of Florus's citation, so as to make this passage intelligible.*

147. patruelibus] parvulis *in Ercole's edition, where — as said above — this whole passage from Florus is quoted in its correct form.*

148. in principem] in principe *α (Ercole's apparatus only reports G, not M)*

149. hoc] haec *G V*

150. usus] visus *Ercole and Ercole 1942*

151. redegisset in actis] in actis redegisset G

152. confirmatos ab eo] ab eo confirmatos G

153. concessos] conceptos V

154. C.] Gaius S

155. revocatus a Corsica] a Corsica revocatus G

156. Tiberio *om.* Z

157. L.] Lucius S

158. delatos] unde latos S

159. recusasset] recusasse G M P S V Z

160. non *om.* S

161. mortem eius] eius mortem G

162. optasse votis] votis optasse G

163. disceptans cum Antonio] cum Antonio disceptans G

164. facibus] faucibus *both Ercole and Ercole 1942*

165. percussores] percuossores *Ercole*

166. rogalibus] regalibus G

167. probarint] probaverint α. *In his apparatus Ercole fails to report that* M (α), *too, reads* probaverint.

168. odio Caesaris] Caesaris odio G

169. licentiam contra Caesarem] contra Caesarem licentiam M

170. obloquendi] loquendi Z

171. superi] superius G V

172. coniuraverunt in eum] in eum coniuraverunt G

173. quod] quod ut P S V Z. *In his apparatus Ercole fails to report that* G (α), *too, reads* quod.

174. Brutus] Bruti P S V Z. *Contrary to Ercole's apparatus, also* M (α) *reads* Brutus.

175. magnanimitatem eorum] eorum magnanimitatem G

176. in excusationem eius] in eius excusationem G

177. mentes] vires G

178. potest accidere] accidere potest G

179. satiari] saturari M

180. loquar vocabulo] vocabulo loquar G

181. reliquos] aliquos G

182. fuerit cruenta] cruenta fuerit G

183. alicui] alicuius G M P S V Z

184. C.] Gaii S

185. curanda] sananda α

186. verba tua] tua verba M

187. plebes] plebs S Z

188. adhibere poterat] poterat adhibere S

189. cursum tenentem suum] suum cursum tenentem G

190. obtemperem et pare0am] pareamque et obtemperem G

190. obtemperem et pareT et pareamque G

191. est tua] tua est G

192. trudenda] trahenda S

193. quam] quam quod S

194. conveniat multitudo] multitudo conveniat G. *In his apparatus Ercole erroneously attributes to G as well the reading* conveniat multitudo *transmitted by all the other witnesses instead.*

195. Quid] Quid autem G

196. hoc] haec G V

197. quoad] quo G M P S V Z. *We thus adopt Ercole's correction to the text.*

198. principatus] principatum V

199. difficulter] difficiliter G

200. monarchici] monarchia α

201. devenire *om.* Z

202. devenire principem] principem devenire G

203. numquam romana . . . numquam fuisset *om.* Z

204. fuisset finis malis] malis fuisset finis G

205. reperitur vocabulum istud 'fraus'] vocabulum istud 'fraus' reperitur G

206. patrem patriae] patriae patrem G

207. potest esse] esse potest G

208. hanc optabant, hanc intendebant] hanc optabant, hanc sperabant, hanc intendebant Z

209. intendebant gloriam] gloriam intendebant G

210. Caesar *om.* M (*not listed in Ercole's apparatus*)

211. tria illa capita] tres illas facies P

212. coloris rubei] rubei coloris G

213. creatorem omnium] omnium creatorem G

214. patrem patriae] patriae patrem G

215. capitibusque] vultibusque P

216. nigredo] nigredo ex parte S

217. confitentis est] est confitentis G

218. primo rubeoque capite] ore primo rubeoque P

219. C. Cassio] Antonio G V S

220. superatum videret Cassium] Cassium videret superatum G

221. maior *om.* S

222. Caesaris filius] filius Caesaris M S

223. nigro capiti] vultui nigro P

224. ad *om.* G V

225. occidendo proditorie Caesarem] proditorie Caesarem occidendo G

226. ponendi finem malis] malis ponendi finem G

227. bella civilia] civilia bella G

228. Cassius atque Brutus] Brutus atque Cassius G

229. orbantes patriam] patriam orbantes G

415

230. poetico artificio res pertractant] poeticas artificio res tractant G. S, *too, reads* poeticas.

231. celebrare viros] viros celebrare G

232. tandem *om.* G

233. conservatos a Graecis] a Graecis conservatos G

234. reputati ab] deputati a G

235. Dareteque] Daretaque M

236. potes *om.* G

237. Daretem] Dareta M

238. Sin] Si G

239. accusa meam] meam accusa G

240. sum enim [. . .] quam docere *om.* G

241. felix et [. . .] omnibus carus *om.* G; carus. M *adds:* Amen

LOSCHI, INVECTIVA IN FLORENTINOS

1. servituti] servienti V (α), B (δ)

2. nisi impium, crudele, nefarium] nisi imperium crudele, nefarium α

SALUTATI, EPISTULA AD PETRUM TURCUM

1. diu *om. in Novati's edition* (Salutati, Epistolario, III, ep. 13.10, pp. 634–40, *on 636*), *but included in the MSS of Salutati's* Contra maledicum et obiurgatorem, *where the letter appears separately as a letter of transmission.*

SALUTATI, CONTRA MALEDICUM ET OBIURGATOREM

1. verba videlicet] verba diffundere P

2. vere vel idonee] vera vel idonee N O

3. amiserant] amiserat *in modern texts of Sallust*

4. quas ego . . . sentio] quas ego universas civium esse optimorum et fortissimorum virorum sentio *in Cicero,* Catilinarian Orations *2.9.20*

5. breviloque] breviloquio *a*

6. notabilem] nobilem *N O*

7. aliquosque torrentes] aliosque torrentes *a O*

8. *Corrected;* ratione *MSS*

9. talis nominis sonum] talem nominis sonum *a*

10. ais] inquis *V*

11. opibus] operibus *V*

12. prorsus et impossibile] prorsus impossibile *V*

13. probari] probari possit *V*

14. Ludovicus] Ludovicus ipse *V*

15. *The text of Loschi's pamphlet employed by Salutati reads* servienti — *reported in B V only among the surviving MSS of the* Invectiva in Florentinos — *instead of* servituti.

16. pedem] pedes *P V. Of the MSS of Loschi's* Invectiva, *only the late codex MA reads* pedem.

17. ipsorum] eorum *P*

18. arbitrio] ab arbritrio *O*

19. mutatio] mutatis *P*

20. ibi *omitted in V*

21. tantus plausus] tantusque plausus *P*

22. confecissent] confecisset *a*

23. animos audientium] animum audientium *V*

24. si sine suo periculo] si sine periculo *O*

25. dominus ille tuus] dominus tuus *O*

26. non *MSS; but compare cap. 79*

27. perstare] praestare *V*

28. eorum] horum *V*

29. inveniret *MSS*

30. has stulticias] has stulticias tuas *P V*

31. complent] complet *P*

32. nisi prius] nec prius *N V*

33. propitios et amicos] propitios amicos *P*

34. et] ac *P V*

35. Valesium] Valegium *V*

36. *The* α *branch of the* Invectiva's *stemma codicum, the one followed by Salu-tati, reads* imperium crudele, nefarium, *whereas* β *reports the correct reading* nisi impium, crudele, nefarium; *see Cicero,* Philippics *3.1.3, and idem,* De domo sua *47.*

37. atque] ac *O*

38. fors] forte *V*

39. callidi apparere] apparere callidi *P V*

40. generis] gentis α *V*

41. Florentiam] Florentinam α *P*

42. Italos] Italicos *O*

43. *omitted in O*

44. *Compare* §100, *where Loschi's* concupiverunt, *omitted in all witnesses to the present passage, is supplied.*

45. maxima] magna *at* §101

46. belua] bestia *V*

47. grammaticae] grammatica *P*

48. ducis] dicis *L V*

49. tuum] vestrum *V*

50. montes . . . Gebennenses] *sc.* Genava; *see Caesar,* Gallic War *1.6.*

51. copiam habueramus] habueramus copiam *O*

52. Antipolis *instead of* Antinopolis *is probably a mistake to be attributed to the archetype rather than to Salutati.*

53. *Supplied: missing in all MSS.*

54. egemus] egeamus *O*

55. illis praesertim] praesertim illis *O*

56. *Modern texts of Vergil read* variique *and omit* -que *after* multos.

57. dicimus] ducimus *O V*

58. victorias] victoriam *V*

59. adiuvit] adivit *α V*

60. ornate] ordinate *V*

61. *Possibly* valeat *should be emended to* valeas.

Notes to the Translations

ꙮ

ABBREVIATIONS

Bruni, *Historiae* — L. Bruni, *Historiae Florentini populi*, 3 vols., ed. and trans. J. Hankins, (Cambridge, MA: Harvard University Press, 2001–7).

Bruni, *Laudatio* — L. Bruni, *Laudatio florentine urbis*, ed. S. U. Baldassarri (Florence: SISMEL-Edizioni del Galluzzo, 2000).

Bueno de Mesquita — D. M. Bueno de Mesquita, *Giangaleazzo Visconti Duke of Milan (1351–1402). A Study in the Political Career of an Italian Despot* (Cambridge: Cambridge University Press, 1941).

Catalogo — *Coluccio Salutati e l'invenzione dell'Umanesimo. Catalogo della mostra tenutasi a Firenze, Biblioteca Medicea Laurenziana, 2 novembre 2008–30 gennaio 2009*, eds. T. De Robertis, G. Tanturli, and S. Zamponi (Florence: Mandragora, 2008).

Cognasso, *Il ducato* — F. Cognasso, *Il ducato visconteo da Gian Galeazzo a Filippo Maria*, in *Storia di Milano, VI, Il ducato visconteo e la Repubblica ambrosiana (1392–1450)* (Milan: Fondazione Treccani, 1955), pp. 1–76.

Cognasso, *L'unificazione* — F. Cognasso, *L'unificazione della Lombardia sotto Milano*, in *Storia di Milano, V, La signoria dei Visconti (1310–92)* (Milan: Fondazione Treccani, 1955), pp. 3–567.

Coluccio Salutati e Firenze — *Coluccio Salutati e Firenze. Ideologia e formazione dello Stato*, eds. R. Cardini and P. Viti (Florence: Pagliai, 2008).

De Rosa   D. De Rosa, *Coluccio Salutati. Il cancelliere e il pensatore politico* (Florence: La Nuova Italia, 1980).

Ercole   C. Salutati, *Tractatus de Tyranno*, ed. F. Ercole (Berlin-Leipzig: Walther Rothschild, 1914).

Ercole 1942   C. Salutati, *Il Trattato "De tyranno" e lettere scelte*, ed. F. Ercole (Bologna: Zanichelli, 1942).

Faraone   G. Faraone, *Antonio Loschi e Antonio da Romagno* (Messina: Centro Interdipartimentale di Studi Umanistici, 2006).

Galli   G. Galli, "La dominazione viscontea a Verona," *Archivio Storico Lombardo* ser. VI, 54.4 (1927): 475–541.

Langkabel   H. Langkabel, *Die Staatsbriefe Coluccio Salutatis. Untersuchungen zum Frühhumanismus in der Florentiner Staatskanzlei und Auswahledition* (Cologne-Vienna: Böhlau, 1981).

McCormick   A. P. McCormick, "Freedom of Speech in Early Renaissance Florence: Salutati's *Questio Est Coram Decemviris*," *Rinascimento* s. II, 19 (1979): 235–40.

Pastine   L. Pastine, "Antonio Loschi umanista vicentino," *Rivista d'Italia* 18.1 (1915): 831–79.

PL   J. P. Migne, *Patrologiae cursus completus, series Latina*, 221 vols. (Paris: Migne, 1844–64).

Pseudo-Minerbetti *Cronica volgare di anonimo fiorentino dall'anno 1385 al 1409 già attribuita a Piero di Giovanni Minerbetti*, a cura di E. Bellondi (*Rerum Italicarum Scriptores*, s. II, 28.2–3) (Città di Castello-Bologna: Lapi-Zanichelli, 1915–17).

Salutati, *Epistolario*	C. Salutati, *Epistolario*, 4 vols., ed. F. Novati (Rome: Istituto Storico Italiano per il Medio Evo, 1891–1911).
Salutati, *De fato*	C. Salutati, *De fato et fortuna*, ed. C. Bianca (Florence: Olschki, 1985).
Salutati, *De laboribus*	C. Salutati, *De laboribus Herculis*, 2 vols., ed. B. L. Ullman (Zürich: Thesaurus Mundi, 1951).
Salutati, *De nobilitate*	C. Salutati, *De nobilitate legum et medicinae. De verecundia*, ed. E. Garin (Florence: Vallecchi, 1947).
Salutati, *De seculo*	C. Salutati, *De seculo et religione*, ed. B. L. Ullman (Florence: Olschki, 1957).
Stefani	Marchionne di Coppo Stefani, *Cronaca fiorentina*, ed. N. Rodolico (*Rerum Italicarum Scriptores*, s. II, 30.1) (Città di Castello: Lapi, 1903–13).
Ullman	B. L. Ullman, *The Humanism of Coluccio Salutati* (Padua: Antenore, 1963).
Villani	G. Villani, *Nuova cronica*, 3 vols., ed. G. Porta (Parma: Fondazione Pietro Bembo-Guanda, 1990–91).
La vipera e il giglio	S. U. Baldassarri, *La vipera e il giglio. Lo scontro tra Milano e Firenze nelle invettive di Antonio Loschi e Coluccio Salutati* (Rome: Aracne, 2012).
Viti	P. Viti, "Loschi, Antonio," in *Dizionario biografico degli Italiani* 66 (Rome: Istituto della Enciclopedia Italiana, 2006), pp. 154–60.
Witt, *Hercules*	R. G. Witt, *Hercules at the Crossroads. The Life, Works, and Thought of Coluccio Salutati* (Durham, NC: Duke University Press, 1983).

Witt, *Public Letters*   R. G. Witt, *Coluccio Salutati and His Public Letters* (Geneva: Droz, 1976).

Zaccaria   V. Zaccaria, "Le epistole e i carmi di Antonio Loschi durante il cancellierato visconteo (con tredici inediti)," *Atti della Accademia Nazionale dei Lincei. Memorie. Classe di scienze morali, storiche e filologiche* s. VIII, 18.5 (1975): 367–443.

Zaccaria, *Loschi e Salutati*   V. Zaccaria, "Antonio Loschi e Coluccio Salutati (con quattro epistole inedite del Loschi)," *Atti dell'Istituto Veneto di Scienze, Lettere ed Arti. Classe di scienze morali, lettere ed arti* 129 (1970–71): 345–87.

Zaggia   M. Zaggia, "Linee per una storia della cultura in Lombardia dall'età di Coluccio Salutati a quella del Valla," in *Le strade di Ercole. Itinerari umanistici e altri percorsi. Seminario internazionale per i centenari di Coluccio Salutati e Lorenzo Valla (Bergamo, 25–26 ottobre 2007)*, ed. L. C. Rossi (Florence: SISMEL, 2010), pp. 3–125.

SALUTATI, SELECTED STATE LETTERS

1. Livy 1.57–60 (Lucretia), 3.44–51 (Virginia), 2.10, (Horatius Cocles), 8.9 (Mucius Scaevola), 10.28 (the Decii).

2. For this common formula, see Cicero, *On His Own House* 90, and Ovid, *Fasti* 6.359.

3. In keeping with many classical texts, "Latium" stands as a synecdoche for the Italian peninsula.

4. Pope Urban VI (reigned 1362–70).

5. That is, the region of the old Etruscan empire, which traditionally extended as far south as the north bank of the Tiber.

6. *Libido dominandi* (lust for domination) is an Augustinian phrase describing a perversion of the soul's basic desire for God as it appears in unredeemed mankind.

7. Seneca, *Epistles* 3.24.7.

8. See, respectively, Jeremiah 4:22, Psalms 139:4 and 58:8. Most of the biblical quotations in this letter show variations from the text of the Vulgate.

9. See, respectively, Jeremiah 15:4 and 5:15.

10. Jeremiah 5:17.

11. Jeremiah 22:17.

12. See Genesis 4:13.

13. Henry VI and VII, Frederick II, his sons Manfred and Conradin, and Louis of Bavaria.

14. Jeremiah 15:5.

15. Jeremiah 4:3.

16. Jeremiah 23:1.

17. The whole paragraph refers to the account of Sodom in Genesis 18:20–33, esp. 24–26.

18. A reference to the story of Lot in Genesis 19.

19. For the three quotations, see Jeremiah 10:24, Psalms 129:3, and Jeremiah 10:25.

20. In the original, 1375; the Florentine year began on the Feast of the Annunciation, 25 March.

21. Charles V, "the Wise" (1338–80, reigned 1364–80). The letter cited immediately below is the first in the present collection.

22. See Letter 1, §§5 and 6, above.

23. Caesar, *On the Gallic Wars* 1.1.

24. Probably sodomy, a common charge against Florentines.

25. For the sack of Faenza in the Romagna (March 1376), see ep. 29 in Langkabel, pp. 121–24, and William Caferro, *John Hawkwood: An English*

Mercenary in Fourteenth-century Italy (Baltimore: Johns Hopkins University Press, 2006), pp. 182–86.

26. See below, Epistle 6, §6 and note.

27. Urban VI had crowned Charles III of Durazzo, "the Short" (1345–96), king of Naples and Sicily on 1 June 1381, in Rome. See David Abulafia, "The Italian south," in *The New Cambridge Medieval History*, VI, ed. M. Jones (Cambridge: Cambridge University Press, 2000), pp. 512–13. In using the word *filius*, Salutati means that Charles III was Urban's son in Christ, not his natural son.

28. Vergil, *Aeneid* 10.501.

29. In December 1385 Charles III of Durazzo received the crown of Hungary (as Charles II), with the approval of most of the people and the nobles, in the process dethroning Mary, daughter of Louis I of Hungary (d. September 1382). Louis's widow, Elizabeth, headed the plot against Charles, who died in the prison of Visegrad (probably poisoned) on 24 February 1386.

30. For the central phrase, echoed in other works of Salutati, see Lucan, *Pharsalia* 8.16–17.

31. Charles III of Durazzo was the great-grandson of Charles II of Anjou, king of Naples (reigned 1285–1309). The son of Charles III was Ladislas I of Durazzo.

32. See Lucan, *Pharsalia* 1.281.

33. The viper is Giangaleazzo Visconti. Since the time of the Crusades (according to legend), the Visconti had borne on their arms an image of a snake devouring a child.

34. Giangaleazzo Visconti was known as the Count of Virtue thanks to his inheritance, via his wife's dowry, of the county of Vertus in Champagne; see Bueno de Mesquita, p. 10; Cognasso, *L'unificazione*, pp. 409–10. In mockery Salutati refers to him in this and many other chancery documents as *Virtutum comes* (the count of the virtues).

35. Despite preliminary agreements on 19 April 1387, between Giangaleazzo Visconti and Francesco da Carrara (lord of Padua) for the division of the territories of Alberto della Scala (lord of Verona and Vicenza),

three days after the Milanese conquest of Verona, Giangaleazzo turned it over to the control of his wife, Caterina Visconti (21 October 1387). See Bueno de Mesquita, pp. 74–78.

36. For the League of Pisa, signed on 9 October 1389, see Bueno de Mesquita, pp. 108–10. See also the *Reply* §170. For the present letter, see Langkabel, ep. 114 (p. 261), and A. Barlucchi in *Coluccio Salutati e Firenze*, pp. 147–48, with bibliography.

37. For the order of expulsion, issued soon after the League of Pisa in October 1389, see Bueno de Mesquita, pp. 111–12.

38. For the mediatory role of Pietro Gambacorta (lord of Pisa), see Bueno de Mesquita, pp. 104–10. For the relations in this period between Hawkwood, the celebrated English condottiere, and the Florentine republic that he served (though not exclusively) from 1378, see Caferro, *John Hawkwood*, pp. 191–208.

39. The day after signing the League of Pisa with Milan, Florence stipulated a further agreement with Bologna, Lucca, Perugia, and Pisa for the maintenance of peace in Tuscany, the Romagna, and the Papal States: see Bueno de Mesquita, p. 110. The contract mentioned above is that between Florence and Hawkwood.

40. For the May 1390 attack on the territory of Montepulciano, see Bueno de Mesquita, pp. 114–15, 121–22. The lord of Cortona mentioned in the following sentence was Uguccio Casali.

41. For this attempt of the Visconti to take control of San Miniato, a town strategically located between Pisa and Florence, see Bueno de Mesquita, p. 113, with further sources.

42. That is, Boniface IX (1389–1404), pope of the Italian obedience. Salutati's diplomatic language reflects the politics of the Great Schism: Charles V did not recognize Boniface as the legitimate pope but rather Clement VII of the French obedience. The Florentines themselves recognized Boniface. By the phrase "the successor of the first elected," Salutati indicates only that Boniface was elected in succession to the first pope of the Italian obedience but leaves open the question of consecration, i.e., whether he was the true pope.

43. See §6 below for further allusions to the supposed victory. The battle in question is that of Alessandria (25 July 1391), in which Count Jean III of Armagnac (and Count of Comines by marriage from 1378), fighting for Florence, was defeated by the Milanese under Jacopo Dal Verme; see Bueno de Mesquita, pp. 131–32, and *Reply* §120 and note.

44. John 11:33.

45. A reference to the notorious imprisonment of Bernabò Visconti by his nephew and son-in-law (6 May 1385): see Bueno de Mesquita, pp. 31–34. Regarding Visconti relations with France, on 17 July of the same year, Bernabò's niece, Isabella of Bavaria, was married to King Charles VI of France.

46. Giangaleazzo's letter mimics here the inflated, quasi-biblical style of papal breves.

47. For the legendary Carolingian reconstruction of Florence, see *Reply* §158, and S. U. Baldassarri, "Like Fathers, like Sons: Theories on the Origins of the City in Late Medieval Florence," *Modern Language Notes* 124.1 (2009): 23–44, with further references.

48. For Charles I Anjou's expedition in Italy, see *Reply* §§159–61 and notes. Charles de Valois (1270–1325) was the son of Philip III and the brother of Philip IV "le Bel"; for his autumn 1301 visit to Florence and his decisive action on behalf of the Black Guelfs, see Villani, 9.49.

49. The rulers mentioned are Manfred of Swabia, defeated at Benevento in 1266 (see *Reply* §§159–61 and notes); Manfred's father, Emperor Frederick II; Frederick I Barbarossa; Henry IV, emperor during the Investiture Conflict with Pope Gregory VII in the twelfth century; Louis the Bavarian; and his ally the antipope Nicholas V (reigned 1328–30).

50. Another reference to the viper on the Visconti coat of arms.

51. The archbishop Giovanni Visconti was created a cardinal in 1329 by the antipope Nicholas V, favorable to Louis, only to renounce the title later in the same year. For his occupation of Bologna, a city that was part of the Papal States, see A. Sorbelli, *La signoria di Giovanni Visconti a Bologna e le sue relazioni con la Toscana* (Bologna: Zanichelli, 1901), pp. 81–177,

and F. Baldasseroni, "La guerra tra Firenze e Giovanni Visconti," *Studi storici* 11 (1902): 361–407; 12 (1903): 4–94.

52. Carlo Malatesta (1368–1429), lord of Rimini, Fano, and Cesena, was named by Urban VI rector of Romagna in 1385 and standard-bearer of the Church in 1386.

53. Horace, *Epistles* 1.18.84.

54. On relations between Florence and Francesco Novello da Carrara III, lord of Padua, during the wars with Giangaleazzo, see *Reply* §98 and note. The area of Italy alluded to in the previous sentence is Milan and northern Italy.

SALUTATI, ON TYRANNY

1. On Antonio of Aquila, see the Introduction, p. xiv, and p. 398.

2. Genesis 2:18.

3. Aegidius Romanus, *On the Rule of Princes* 2.1.6, 3.2.32; Marsilius of Padua, *The Defender of Peace* 1.3.

4. Salutati, *Epistolario* 7.10.

5. 1 Corinthians 4:7, 10.

6. Salutati employs Aristotelian terms, meaning approximately: "Whatever I am, whether [we consider] the essential and nonessential elements of my being." Aristotle's books on logic and natural philosophy were the backbone of the curriculum in arts at the University of Padua.

7. Augustine, *Commentary on the Psalms* 99.15. Salutati again signals his familiarity with Aristotelian analysis of causation.

8. Augustine, *Enchiridion* 1.1, 23.8; idem, *On the Catholic and Manichean Ways of Life* 1.6.9ff. Salutati affirms the orthodox Catholic position on grace and merit, possibly with the implication that Antonio's excessive praise smacks of Pelagianism, a temptation to intellectual pride.

9. Matthew 10:8.

10. Justin, *Epitome* 2.1 (an epitome of a lost history by Pompeius Trogus).

11. Isidore, *Etymologies* 9.30; Augustine, *City of God* 5.19; Balbi, *Summa*, s.v. *tyrannus*; Papias, *Vocabularium*, s.v. *tyrannus*; Bartolus, *On Tyranny* 1.

12. Seneca, *On Clemency* 1.11–12; Isidore, *Etymologies* 9.30; John of Salisbury, *Policraticus* 4.1, 8.17.

13. Vergil, *Aeneid* 8.480–84.

14. Ibid., 7.266; Servius on *Aeneid* 8.266.

15. Gregory the Great, *Moralia* 12.38. See also Bartolus, *On Tyranny* 2 and note 23, below.

16. Gregory the Great, *Moralia* 12.38. See also Bartolus, *On Tyranny* 2.

17. Baldus de Ubaldis, *Commentary on the Codex* 1.2.16 [*Codex* 1.1].

18. Psalms 7:10; Apocalypse 2:23.

19. Aegidius Romanus (Egidio Colonna, Giles of Rome), *On the Rule of Princes* 2.2.3ff.; Thomas Aquinas, *On the Rule of Princes* 1.6, 2.8–9; William of Ockham, *Dialogue* 3.2.6.

20. Aegidius Romanus, *On the Rule of Princes* 2.2.3, for the articulation of this entire passage and also of §7.

21. That is, rule can be analyzed from the point of view of constitutions or by the types of rule naturally found in a household. This view is derived from Aristotle's *Politics*, books 1 and 3; see James M. Blythe, *Ideal Government and the Mixed Constitution in the Middle Ages* (Princeton: Princeton University Press, 1992), chapter 2, for its application in scholastic political theory.

22. William of Ockham, *Dialogue* 3.2.6. Salutati thus rejects the view of Aristotle that tyranny is a particular constitution, a corruption of monarchy: tyranny can beset all constitutions. See, for example, the tyrannical rule of the Decemvirs under the Roman republic (2.12 below).

23. Bartolus, *On Tyranny* 12; Salutati, *Epistolario* 5.6. The phrase *in communi re publica* distinguishes the government of a commune or city-state republic from a royal commonwealth. For the meaning of *respublica* in Salutati's time (which does not mean "nonmonarchical government," as today), see below, 4.16, and J. Hankins, "Exclusivist Republicanism and the Non-Monarchical Republic," *Political Theory* 38.4 (2010): 452–82.

24. Seneca, *Hercules Furens* 399–400.

25. John of Salisbury, *Policraticus* 8.17; Thomas Aquinas, *On the Rule of Princes* 1.6.

26. Salutati's relatively permissive view of tyrannicide follows in the tradition of John of Salisbury and Thomas Aquinas. Salutati knew John of Salisbury's *Policraticus* well; see below, 2.13 and 3.1. A few years after Salutati's death, a position close to his was articulated by the theologian Jehan Petit, but it was rejected as erroneous and heretical by the Council of Constance, Session 15 of 6 July 1415. Cicero describes the positive valuation of tyrannicide as a *factum pulcherrimum* (a glorious deed) as a traditional attitude of the Roman people in *Of Duties* 3.19.

27. *Corpus iuris civilis, Codex* 8.4.1.

28. *Corpus iuris civilis, Digest* 43.16 and *Digest* 1.1.3.

29. *Corpus iuris civilis, Digest* 4.2.

30. *Corpus iuris civilis, Codex* 3.27; *Corpus iuris civilis, Digest* 48.8.

31. *Corpus iuris civilis, Codex* 3.27.

32. Salutati, *Epistolario* 4.5.

33. Livy 4.13–15.

34. Livy 4.14.7.

35. Florus, *Epitome* 2.2; Valerius Maximus 3.2.17; Orosius, *Historiae adversus paganos* 1.9.1; Cicero, *Catiline* 1.3.

36. Valerius Maximus 6.2.3.

37. Livy 6.17–20.

38. Livy 6.20.13. See also Cicero, *Philippics* 1.32.

39. Livy 29.11ff.; Augustine, *City of God* 1.30.

40. Valerius Maximus 3.2.17.

41. Ibid. 9.13.3. See also Livy, *Periochae* 55.

42. Eutropius, *Breviarium* 4.26; Orosius, *Historiae adversus paganos* 5.9; Florus, *Epitome* 1.31.

43. Livy 30.44.1.

44. Valerius Maximus 7.5.2.

45. Ibid. 6.9.11.

46. Florus, *Epitome* 1.18.11; Eutropius 2.20.2; Orosius, *Historiae adversus paganos* 4.7.9. On the confusion between Florus and Seneca (both named Lucius Annaeus), frequent in Salutati's time, see in this volume Salutati's *Reply to Loschi* §32.

47. Macrobius, *Saturnalia* 6.29.

48. Valerius Maximus 7.5.2.

49. Thomas Aquinas, *Commentary on the Sentences of Peter Lombard* I Dist. 44 q. 2 a. 2; ibid., II Dist. 44 q. 2 a. 2.

50. Salutati, *Epistolario* 6.5.

51. *Digest (De vi et vi armorum)* 43.16. The idea is that an immediate response might be impossible owing to the lack of resources (for example), but that action should be taken as soon as possible after an act of tyrannical usurpation has been taken.

52. *Corpus iuris civilis, Digest* 44.1.137.

53. Ibid., 48.5.2ff.

54. Salutati, *Epistolario* 6.18. Salutati seems to be condoning conspiracy against a tyrant who has already established his power, but note the qualifications made at the end of the chapter.

55. Thomas Aquinas, *Commentary on the Sentences of Peter Lombard* II Dist. 44 q. 2 a. 2.

56. Bartolus, *On Tyranny* 15.

57. Ibid., 13.

58. Baldus de Ubaldis, *Commentary on the Codex* 1.2.16.

59. Thomas Aquinas, *On the Rule of Princes* 1.6; Bartolus, *On Tyranny* 31.

60. Thomas Aquinas, *On the Rule of Princes* 1.6; idem *Summa Theologiae* 2.2 q. 42 a. 3.

61. Livy 1.58–60.

62. Livy 2.44–48.

63. Juvenal, *Satires* 10.113–14. Juvenal was from the town of Aquino, hence is called "Aquinas" here.

64. John of Salisbury, *Policraticus* 8.19–21.

65. Ibid., 3.12.

66. Ibid., 3.15.

67. Ibid., 8.16 and 23.

68. Ibid., 8.18.

69. Ibid., 8.21.

70. Nero and Phalaris were famous ancient Roman and Greek tyrants, respectively. Ezzelino III da Romano (1194–1259), tyrant of Padua, was the eponymous subject of a well-known tragedy by Albertino Mussato (1261–1329), an early humanist: see *Humanist Tragedies*, tr. Gary Grund, ITRL 45 (Cambridge, Mass., 2011). Busiris was a mythological tyrant implicated in the Hercules legends, about whom Salutati writes in *The Labors of Hercules* 3.20.

71. Thomas Aquinas, *Commentary on the Sentences of Peter Lombard* II Dist. 44 q. 2 a. 2.

72. Cicero, *Of Duties* 1.1.36.

73. Thomas Aquinas, *On the Rule of Princes* 1.6.

74. John of Salisbury, *Policraticus* 8.19. See also Suetonius, *Caesar* 82.2.

75. John of Salisbury, *Policraticus* 8.19.

76. Cicero, *Of Duties* 1.8.26.

77. Ibid., 2.7.23.

78. Ibid., 1.14.43; 1.13.112; 2.8, 27. See also *Epistles to Atticus* 7.13.1 and 10.4.2.

79. Cicero, *Familiares* 1.9.18.

80. Cicero, *Epistles to Quintus* 3.1.9. See also ibid., 3.5.3, and *Epistles to Atticus* 4.16.13.

81. Cicero, *Pro Marcello* 5.14; *Familiares* 6.6.4ff.

82. Cicero, *Familiares* 2.16.1.

83. Ibid.

84. Ibid.

85. Cicero, *Epistles to Atticus* 4.19.2.

86. Cicero, *Familiares* 7.5 and 13.15–16. See also *Epistles to Atticus* 9.6, 16; 10.8.

87. Cicero, *Epistles to Atticus* 8.11.2.

88. Cicero, *Familiares* 6.6.8; *Epistles to Atticus* 8.15.1; *Pro rege Deiotaro* 13.35; *In Vatinium* 6.15; *Pro Sestio* 63.132.

89. Cicero, *Pro Marcello* 1.1ff.; *Pro Ligario* 1.1ff.

90. Cicero, *Familiares* 4.4.3.

91. Cicero, *Pro Marcello* 8.25.

92. Cicero, *Familiares* 4.9.2.

93. Ibid., 4.9.3.

94. Lucan, *Pharsalia* 1.6–7.

95. Ibid., 1.126–27.

96. Cicero, *Pro Marcello* 10.31.

97. Ibid., 6.17.

98. Florus, *Epitome* 2.13.90.

99. Cicero, *Philippics* 2.13.31.

100. Valerius Maximus 1.1.3; Cicero, *On Divination* 2.35.74.

101. Valerius Maximus 1.1.2.

102. Livy 3.21.

103. Cicero, *Philippics* 2.13.29. See also idem, *On Duties* 3.4.19.

104. Suetonius, *Caesar* 1.85.

105. Plutarch, *Caesar* 67; *Brutus* 18; Cicero, *Epistles to Atticus* 14.2; *Philippics* 2.89; Dio Cassius 44.21; Appian 2.119–20 (the last two works, however, were not available to Salutati).

106. Suetonius, *Caesar* 84.1.

107. Ibid., 84.2.

108. Ibid., 84.4.

109. Ibid., 84.5.

110. Ibid., 89.1.

111. Macrobius, *Saturnalia* 2.4.18. This "defense of Cato" is diplomatically ambiguous, since Augustus always claimed to be defending the traditional commonwealth (*respublica*) against its domination by a faction. That Salutati accepts this "Augustan" interpretation of the outcome of the Roman civil war is clear from 4.11–20. See Hankins, "Exclusivist Republicanism."

112. Lucan, *Pharsalia* 1.126ff.; Florus, *Epitome* 2.13.4; Orosius, *Historiae adversus paganos* 2.18.1; Augustine, *City of God* 3.14.

113. Cicero, *Pro Marcello* 8.23.

114. Cicero, *Pro Plancio* 39.94.

115. Horace, *Carmina* 1.14.1–3.

116. Suetonius, *Tiberius* 24.

117. For the monarchical commonwealth (*respublica*), see Cicero, *De re publica* 1.42 and 3.47, quoted in Augustine, *City of God* 2.21.

118. Salutati probably means Augustus and the "good" emperors of the second century such as Hadrian, Trajan, Antoninus Pius, and Marcus Aurelius; much less plausibly, one or more of the Holy Roman Emperors. *Princeps*, here translated as "principal citizen" to reflect the political reality of Caesar's time, from the time of Augustus onward comes to mean "emperor"; in the later Renaissance it typically refers to any individual with sovereign power over a state.

119. This was the dominant view in the Roman Empire and throughout the Middle Ages, championed (among others) by Petrarch: see his *Familiares* 3.7.

120. Salutati, *Epistolario* 1.1. But the saying, which bears a Senecan stamp, is proverbial.

121. Aristotle, *Politics* 1.2.3. See also Thomas Aquinas, *Summa Theologiae* 2.1 q. 105 a. 1; 2.1 q. 10 a. 11; *Summa against the Gentiles* 4.76; Aegidius

Romanus, *On the Rule of Princes* 3.2.3; Dante, *De monarchia* 1.5–14; idem, *Convivio* 4.5–14; William of Ockham, *Dialogue* 3.1.2.9–11.

122. *Politia vel aristocratia*: Aristotle's names for the virtuous popular regime and aristocracy (the best regime of the few) in *Politics* 3, respectively, as these terms were translated by William of Moerbeke in the thirteenth century; see Hankins, "Exclusivist Republicanism."

123. Suetonius, *Augustus* 28.

124. Vergil, *Eclogues* 4.31–35.

125. Suetonius, *Caesar* 86; Petrarch, *De gestis Caesaris*, 36.42 (ed. G. Crevatin [Pisa: Scuola Normale Superiore, 2003], p. 321).

126. Dante, *Inferno* 34.37–45 and 55–67.

127. Jerome, *De nominibus Hebraeis* 23.3.12; *Epistles* 1.39.

128. Matthew 27:34.

129. Florus, *Epitome* 2.17.12; Valerius Maximus 9.9.

130. Florus, *Epitome* 2.17.14.

131. Benvenuto da Imola, *Comento* (ed. Lacaita) 2:559; *Ottimo Comento* (Pisa, 1827), p. 583.

132. Suetonius, *Caesar* 50.2.

133. Ibid., 82.3.

134. Florus, *Epitome* 2.17.8.

135. Vergil, *Aeneid* 6.612.

136. Dares Phrygius, *History of the Fall of Troy* 39; ps. Dictys Cretensis, *Journal of the Trojan War* 4.18.22; Guido de Columnis, *History of the Destruction of Troy* 29. Ps.-Dictys was said to be from Knossos in Crete, hence the confused reference to him as Gnosius Dictys.

137. Lucius Cornelius Sisenna (120 BCE– 67 CE); Salutati's source is Servius, *Commentarium in Vergilii Aeneidem* 1.242.

138. Livy 1.1.

139. Dares Phrygius, *History of the Fall of Troy* 51–52; ps. Dictys Cretensis, *Journal of the Trojan War* 4.18.22.

ANTONIO LOSCHI, INVECTIVE AGAINST THE FLORENTINES

1. This is one of the key motifs developed by Loschi in his poem of August 1396, *Ad illustrem principem ducem Mediolani ut pacem cogitet per viam belli exortatio*, and the related letter to Antonio da Romagno (see Faraone, pp. 100–105, 94–99); for the relation between these texts and also Salutati's reply, see ibid., pp. 11–13, 39–44.

2. Loschi's chief model in this text is Cicero, starting from this impetuous beginning, structured as a series of interrogative propositions, an echo of the famous denunciation at the beginning of the first *Catilinarian Oration*. The accusation that the Florentines are hypocritical and constantly hatching plots is a recurring theme of Loschi's poem *Ut pacem cogitet per viam belli exhortatio* and its accompanying letter (Faraone, pp. 94–95).

3. See Loschi's *Ut pacem cogitet per viam belli exhortatio* (v. 57) for the accusation of *superbia*: Faraone, pp. 104–5. For its significance as a mark of tyranny, see Salutati's own *On Tyranny*, chapter 1, above.

4. A reference to Florence's recapture (9 January 1370) of San Miniato, which had rebelled in 1367; see Stefani, r. 716, p. 272, and r. 710, pp. 269–70.

5. For the failed revolt led by Benedetto Mangiadori on 21 February 1397, see Pseudo-Minerbetti, cap. 12, pp. 210–11; Bruni, *Historiae* 11.45–48. For another attempted revolt, probably aided by Giangaleazzo, see Bueno de Mesquita, p. 113.

6. Presumably Loschi alludes to a serious grain shortage that affected the Florentine territory in 1400.

7. For this conventional definition of Sicily, see Cicero, *Verrine Orations* 2.2.3, 2.2.5, 2.5.9, 2.5.123; Lucan, *Pharsalia* 3.67.

8. Giangaleazzo's acquisition of Pisa took place on 19 February 1399. On 21 October 1392, the Milanese ally Jacopo d'Appiano took Pisa from the pro-Florentine Pietro Gambacorta; see the poem of Giovanni Guazzaloti published in *Lamenti de' secoli XIV e XV*, ed. A. Medin (Florence: Libreria

di Dante, 1883), pp. 20–23, and Salutati's letter to the Bolognese of 22 October 1392 (Langkabel, ep. 136, pp. 298–99). Jacopo died in September 1398, and his son and successor made the 1399 sale to Milan, for which see Zaggia, pp. 26–27, and note 70, with references.

9. A reference to the agreements leading to the anti-Milanese league signed by Florence, Bologna, Alberto II d'Este, Francesco III Novello da Carrara (11 April 1392), and Francesco Gonzaga (1 September 1392): see Bueno de Mesquita, pp. 144–45, and Cognasso, *L'unificazione*, pp. 564–66. This reference helps to date the present text to 1401, and probably before October.

10. For the expression, see Cicero, *Pro Marcello* 27.

11. In response, Salutati (*Reply* §88) will minimize the importance of this episode and parry with the counter-example of Florence's concession to Bologna of two towns in the Apennines, Castiglione de' Pepoli and Bruscoli.

12. Niccolò III d'Este, Francesco III Novello da Carrara, and Francesco Gonzaga, allies of Florence in the second war against Milan, which began in March 1397.

13. A reference to the league between Florence and the French king signed on 29 September 1396, for which see Bueno de Mesquita, pp. 203–5, and Cognasso, *Il ducato*, p. 28. Among sources possibly used by Salutati, see Pseudo-Minerbetti, under 1396, cap. 7, p. 207. Loschi mentions it in his *Exhortatio* (v. 42): see Faraone, pp. 102–3, and note 1.

14. Among many sources for vices traditionally ascribed to the French, including vanity and inconstancy, Loschi and Salutati were certainly aware of Petrarch, *Bucolicum carmen*, Eclogue 12.

15. See Salutati's *Reply* §117. An analogous phrase applied to Florence appears in Loschi's poem of August 1396 (v. 27): see Faraone, p. 102.

16. The same formula occurs in the letter accompanying Loschi's poem of August 1396: see Faraone, p. 97, and note 6.

17. That is, their, the Florentines', lands. See *Reply* §129 for Salutati's criticism of this use of the possessive.

18. An allusion to French losses in the Hundred Years War.

19. Loschi uses the formula *opima pax* with reference to Florentine raids into Pisan territory in June 1396, in the letter to Antonio da Romagno cited in note 1: see Faraone, p. 97, and note 5.

20. By his first marriage to Isabelle de Valois, daughter of King John II of France, Giangaleazzo inherited the title of "Comte de Vertus"; see Selected State Letters, note 34, above.

21. The original concession of the privilege of including the French lilies on the Visconti coat of arms dates to 1387, in connection with agreements for the marriage of Valentina Visconti, Giangaleazzo's daughter, to Louis, duke of Orleans, brother of King Charles VI (1386). The lord of Milan's request to change the position of the lilies was made in 1392, granted in 1394, and confirmed in 1395. See Zaccaria, p. 382, with references.

22. See Salutati's criticism of this passage in *Reply* §141.

23. That is, the economic help given by Giangaleazzo's father, Galeazzo Visconti, to King John II of France, after his defeat and capture at the hands of the English: see Bueno de Mesquita, p. 10, and Cognasso, *L'unificazione*, pp. 409–10.

24. Loschi refers to two marriages: that between Giangaleazzo and Isabelle de Valois and that between Valentina Visconti and Louis of Orleans. For the second marriage and its context, see Bueno de Mesquita, pp. 63–68, and Cognasso, *L'unificazione*, pp. 525–27, 550–51.

25. See Salutati's criticism of the use of the double negative in this sentence (subsequently corrupted in other texts of the *Invective*) in *Reply* §147.

26. Loschi cited the proverb, but only to reject it, in his earlier rhymed letter of October 1394 addressed to Niccolò Spinelli and Cavallino Cavalli; see Zaccaria, pp. 382–83.

27. For these episodes concerning Louis I of Anjou and Charles III Durazzo (and Amedeo VI of Savoy), see Bueno de Mesquita, pp. 19–21, 28–29, and Cognasso, *L'unificazione*, pp. 501–13. As noted by Zaccaria, p. 374, one of Loschi's first poems (never completed) was in praise of Charles III. "The Kingdom" refers to the Kingdom of Naples in southern Italy.

28. Probably an echo of Wisdom 5:15; see also Job 21:18; Hosea 13:3; Psalms 1:4, 34:5; and Isaiah 17:13. A comparable formulation and image appear in the poem to Giangaleazzo cited in note 1; see Faraone, pp. 102–3 (vv. 37–38).

29. Among Loschi's many encomia to the condottiere Jacopo Dal Verme, the one in honor of the *militiae iubar Italiae*, in a letter from the summer of 1388, appears to be his first composition written at the Visconti court; a second, written the following December, belongs to the period of celebrations of Milan's conquest of Padua; see Pastine, p. 387, and Zaccaria, pp. 376–77. See also the essay by Angelo Piacentini, "Episodi della fortuna del carme *Maxime dux Ligurum* di Antonio Loschi," *Italia Medioevale e Umanistica* 53 (2012): 181–223.

30. Ausonian leader: a leader native to Italy, from the ancient poetic word for the autochthonous people of Italy. Loschi is contrasting the Italian patriotism of the Visconti with the Florentines, who seek mercenary alliances with the barbarian French (or "Gauls") from across the Alps.

31. Jean III, count of Armagnac, was defeated while in the service of Florence by Milanese forces (under Jacopo Dal Verme) at Alessandria on 25 July 1391; for this famous battle (mentioned even by Ariosto, *Orlando Furioso* 33.21–22), see Romanelli, *La calata di Giovanni III d'Armagnac in Italia e la disfatta di Alessandria* (Rome: Edizioni Museo, 1936), pp. 30–36; Bueno de Mesquita, pp. 131–32; and Cognasso, *L'unificazione*, pp. 559–62.

32. An analogous phrase (*aspera / Tuscorum rabies*) was adopted by Loschi in his hortatory poem to Giangaleazzo, cited in note 1; see Faraone, p. 100, vv. 2–3.

33. The Latin text recalls Cicero, *Philippics* 3.1.3.

34. This assertion is stressed in the letter to Antonio da Romagno and the poem to Giangaleazzo, *Ut pacem cogitet*, cited in note 1; see Faraone, pp. 94–105, esp. 96–98 (letter) and 104–5 (vv. 60–63 of the poem).

35. The imagery of the Furies driving Florence comes up in the same poem to Giangaleazzo, *Ut pacem cogitet*, cited in note 1; see Faraone, pp. 100–105, esp. 102–3 (vv. 26–36).

SALUTATI, LETTER TO PIETRO TURCHI

1. On Pietro Turchi, secretary to Carlo Malatesta of Rimini, see the Introduction, p. xxiii.

2. Compare Cicero, *On Duties* 1.17.58, and idem, *De legibus* 2.5. More broadly, here and in various parts of his *Reply*, Salutati adopts the commonplaces that are defined as *partes iustitiae* (arguments of justice) and *partes fortitudinis* (arguments of fortitude) in the pseudo-Ciceronian *Rhetorica ad Herennium* 3.3.4–5.

3. This draws upon the incipit of *In Quintum Caecilium divinatio* 1, Cicero's preliminary speech to his oration against Verres, as was already noted by Novati (Salutati, *Epistolario*, III, ep. 10, p. 637, note 2).

4. The passage has the character of a *topos* but seems to correlate to Cicero, *Pro Sestio* 7.

5. This is the accusation at the opening of the *Invective* (§1, corresponding to Salutati's *Reply*, §10). The chancellor's irony here is built around the Latin form of Loschi's family name, *Luscus*, which as an adjective has the primary sense of "blind in one eye/deprived of sight" and the secondary sense of "suspicious" (it is the root of the Italian *losco* and the French *louche*). It is also possible, as is pointed out by Novati (Salutati, *Epistolario*, III, ep. 10, p. 638, note 1), taking up a suggestion of Moreni, that the celebrated line in Dante about the Florentines of Fiesolan descent (*Inferno* 15.67, *Vecchia fama nel mondo li chiama orbi*) comes into play in this context.

6. As for the passage remarked in note 3 above, here again the commonplace seems charged with reference to a specific source, in this case Cicero, *Pro Murena* 86. For the expression *caritas patriae* adopted by Salutati, see Cicero, *Tusculan Disputations* 1.37.90, and idem, *On Duties* 3.27.100.

SALUTATI, REPLY TO A SLANDEROUS DETRACTOR OF FLORENCE

1. For *gratis* in the sense of "without pay," see Terence, *Phormio* 72, a favorite text of Salutati's.

2. Thus Loschi's opening qualifies as a typical *vitiosum exordium* (faulty exordium) of the *commutable* (interchangeable) category according to the definitions of the (pseudo-Ciceronian) *Rhetorica ad Herennium* 1.7.11, and Cicero, *De inventione* 1.18.26. Salutati develops his assertion in §11, below.

3. Here too Salutati models his content and form on Cicero, *Philippics* 2.4.9: *Quid enim est minus non dico oratoris sed hominis quam id obicere adversario quod ille si verbo negarit longius progredi non possit qui obiecerit?* (For what is more beneath, I don't say an orator but a man, than to make an objection to an adversary that the latter can overturn with a word, halting the prosecution's efforts?) The point made in the next sentence is also emphasized, in relation to law and medicine, by Salutati in his *De nobilitate*, 34 (ed. Garin, p. 238).

4. See *Rhetorica ad Herennium* 2.8.12: *Neque tamen ei rumori nos fidem habere dicemus, ideo quod quivis unus homo possit quamvis turpem de quolibet rumorem proferre et confictam fabulam dissipare.* (But we say that we do not trust in such a rumor, because any individual could circulate a foul rumor or made-up story about anyone.) See also §177, below.

5. According to the scheme of argumentation in Cicero's *De inventione* 1.49.92, Loschi's *Invective* falls into the category of *turpis argumentatio*, a defamatory attack upon a person of unstained honor. For the friendship between Salutati and Loschi and their mutual esteem, see S. U. Baldassarri, *Umanesimo e traduzione da Petrarca a Manetti* (Cassino: Università di Cassino, 2003), pp. 65–70, and Salutati's private letters, especially *Epistolario*, II, ep. 7.21 (pp. 340–42); II, ep. 8.4 (p. 380); II, ep. 7.23 (pp. 354–58); in the last he is addressed as *carissime fili* (dearest son).

6. See note 5 to Salutati's *Letter to Pietro Turchi*, above.

7. The expression *Spartam suscipere* or *accipere* (take on Sparta), later commented upon by Erasmus, *Adagia*, ed. S. Seidel Menchi (Turin: Einaudi, 1980), pp. 40–59, and indicating a troublesome task unwisely taken on, Salutati probably took from Cicero, *Letters to Atticus* 1.20.3 and 4.6.2.

8. That is, he has been deprived of the *ad hominem* attack. See Cicero, *De inventione* 2.9.28–29 and 32–34.

9. For the expression *os caelum apponere* (set your mouth against heaven), see Psalms 72:9. This verse is often taken up in medieval texts against *superbia*, or the sin of pride. See Salutati, *Epistolario*, II, ep. 6.7 (p. 163).

10. In the opening paragraphs Salutati passes from noting the *impudentia* of Loschi to noting his *amentia*. While impudence and madness are hardly unusual imputations in contexts of this kind, it is precisely these deficiencies as well as his *inhumanitas* that Cicero lays against Verres in famous orations, and also against Marc Antony in the *Philippics*. The same two men are among the negative moral exemplars Salutati lists at the end of his oration (below, §177). The common philosophical and rhetorical topos of *consensus omnium*, or universal consensus (e.g., Aristotle, *Nicomachean Ethics*, 10.2.1173A; Cicero, *On the Nature of the Gods* 2.4–5), to which Salutati naturally makes recourse several times in this *Reply*, returns in Salutati's *De nobilitate* 1 (ed. Garin, p. 10) and other works.

11. That is, salvation. Compare Salutati, *De nobilitate* 3 (ed. Garin, p. 14) and 19 (pp. 163–64); for the classical and Christian sources it is enough to mention Aristotle, *Nicomachean Ethics* 1094a, and Thomas Aquinas, *Summa theologiae* 2.1 q. 91 a. 2.

12. Salutati is invoking the theological distinction between the nature of beatitude, whose eternal nature we share in by participation, but which *quoad nos* (with respect to our own nature) is merely perpetual, since it has a beginning in the moment of the Christian's salvation. See C. Fabro, *La nozione metafisica di partecipazione secondo S. Tommaso d'Aquino* (Rome, 2005). Salutati's point may be that persons not yet saved still have a fundamental orientation toward their supernatural end of beatitude, whatever human ends they may adopt in this life.

13. Matthew 5:22. For the presence of Florentines in all nations, a commonplace of panegyrics of Florence before and after Salutati, see §§69, 168–69 below, with notes; see also §115 for other passages of a panegyric character.

14. That is, do they subserve the highest end of the contemplative or active lives?

15. For this classical commonplace, see Cicero, *Tusculan Disputations* 5.16.47 (citing Plato, *Republic* 400d), and Seneca, *Epistles* 75.4.

16. See the deuterocanonical or apocryphal Book of Judith 13:1–10. For Porsenna, see Livy 2.12, and Florus, *Epitome* 1.4.2. Salutati also used this celebrated episode in his rebuttal of Giangaleazzo's charge of a Florentine plot against his life (for which see below, §170): Langkabel, ep. 108 (p. 255, 16 December 1389).

17. Here and elsewhere in his oration (see above, *Letter to Pietro Turchi*, note 2) Salutati employs the rhetorical commonplaces known as *partes iustitiae* and *partes fortitudinis* (or, offices of justice and offices of strength) in *Rhetorica ad Herennium* 3.3.4–5; see also ibid. 4.42.54–55.

18. See Cicero, *Of Duties* 1.7.22, a celebrated passage that takes up the equally famous ninth epistle ascribed to Plato (358A). To speak in defense of one's own country counts as an appeal to natural right; see Cicero, *De inventione* 2.22.66.

19. See Aristotle, *Rhetoric* 2.3.16 (1380b): "Men are not angry with the dead." Salutati may have culled this reference from *In Aristotelis rhetorica* of Aegidius Romanus (Giles of Rome), of which he owned a manuscript (see *Catalogo*, p. 353, cat. 19).

20. Compare Salutati's *Questio est coram decemviris* in McCormick, p. 240 (with the sources there indicated by the editor).

21. Compare Cicero, *Pro Cluentio* 158–59.

22. This argument, suggested by Cicero, *De inventione* 149.94, is applied by Salutati in many missives defending Florence, especially during the War of the Eight Saints; see, e.g., Langkabel, ep. 25 (p. 116, to the College of Cardinals, 8 March 1376), Letter 2 in the present volume.

23. Salutati's celebration of the Florentine merchants is a major theme of his reply to Loschi, and furthermore one of the earliest in the encomiastic literature of the city. Here it may suffice to refer to a passage in praise of Florence in a poem close in date and culture to the chancellor: F. Sacchetti, *Il libro delle rime*, ed. F. Brambilla Ageno (Florence: Olschki-University of Western Australia Press, 1990), pp. 47–48, canzone 47 (*O gentil donna ornata di biltate*), vv. 14–21, and Salutati's letters including Langkabel, ep. 25 (p. 115, 8 September 1376); ep. 39 (p. 144, 5 September 1376), and ep. 114 (pp. 261–62, 25 May 1390). For late Trecento Florentine

political poetry against the Visconti, see L. Mancino in *Coluccio Salutati e Firenze*, pp. 204–10, cat. 78, with bibliography.

24. See Cicero, *In Quintum Caecilium divinatio* 39.

25. This concept is a topos of classical and medieval literature, naturally favored in texts of a moralizing or satirical nature.

26. Here Salutati accuses his opponent of adopting the *argumentatio controversa*, a captious attempt to sustain a doubtful proposition using still more doubtful assertions; see Cicero, *De inventione* 1.49.91.

27. Ovid, *Fasti* 6.771–72.

28. Acts 1:7, combined with a phrase from the Pater Noster.

29. The second verse of the final distich of Walter Map (Gualterius Anglicus), *De cane et lupo*, attributed to Aesop; see A. L. Hervieux, *Les fabulistes latins depuis le siècle d'Auguste jusq'à la fin du Moyen Âge*, 5 vols. (Paris: Firmin Didot, 1893–99; repr. New York: Franklin, 1965), 2:344; also ed. S. Boldrini as *Uomini e bestie: le favole dell'Aesopus latinus. Testo latino con una traduzione-rifacimento del '300 in volgare toscano* (Lecce: ARGO, 1994), p. 162. The first verse, *Non bene pro toto libertas venditur auro* (liberty is not well sold for all the gold in the world), was the signature tag of an as yet unidentified copyist in the Salutati circle (see G. Tanturli in *Catalogo*, pp. 75–78, 80–84, entries 11, 13). Another Map fable is cited in Salutati's famous letter to Andreolo Arese of 1385 about Giangaleazzo's capture of Bernabò Visconti (cited below, note 82).

30. Similar phrasing occurs in letters from throughout Salutati's political career: see Langkabel, ep. 14 (p. 101, 1375), ep. 99 (p. 241, 1389), ep. 110 (p. 258, 1390), and especially ep. 176 (p. 361, 30 June 1402, following the defeat of Bologna, when a direct attack on Florence seemed imminent). For the defense and price of liberty, see Cicero, *Of Duties* 1.23.81.

31. The passage surely reflects John of Salisbury, *Policraticus* 7.25. It may also reflect a passage about the early Romans in Livy 1.17. At the end of this paragraph, Salutati ironically adapts the traditional appellation of the pope, "servant of the servants of God."

32. Livy 2.3.2–3 (Loeb translation). Salutati refers to the same source in a letter to the Bolognese praising freedom: Langkabel, ep. 35 (p. 137, 1 July 1376).

33. For this biblical expression, see Genesis 2:23, 29:14, 37:27; Judges 9:23; 2 Samuel 5:1, 19:12; Ephesians 5:30. The same phrase is employed by Salutati in reference to Florence's Roman origins, in letters to the Roman people, e.g., Langkabel, ep. 41 (p. 149, 12 October 1376) and ep. 55 (p. 170, 27 May 1380).

34. For this uncertainty and also its application to other cities, see Isidore of Seville, *Etymologies* 15.1.1–2.

35. See Varro, *De lingua latina* 5.5.33. For Roma/Romula, see Servius, *Ad Vergilii Aeneidem* 1.273. For the Arcadi, see Ovid, *Fasti* 1.461–501; Vergil, *Aeneid* 8.51–54 and 337–41; Livy 1.5.1. For Valentia see Servius, *Ad Vergilii Aeneidem* 1.273, and Solinus 1.17.

36. Where the modern Piazza della Repubblica is located. The capitolium was slightly northwest of the forum, near the corner of via Vecchietti and via Campidoglio.

37. In Salutati's time the characteristic shape was visible in the area near the Via Torta, as it still is today.

38. Presumably near the modern via delle Terme.

39. The Florentines believed their Baptistery, in fact built around 1100, to have been a Roman temple dedicated to Mars.

40. For the statue, see L. Gatti, "Il mito di Marte a Firenze e la 'pietra scema,'" *Rinascimento*, s. II, 35 (1995): 210–30, and the entry by R. Chellini in his critical edition of the *Chronica de origine civitatis Florentiae* (Rome: Istituto Storico Italiano per il Medio Evo, 2009), pp. 171–79. For the event, see G. J. Schenk, "L'alluvione del 1333. Discorsi sopra un disastro naturale nella Firenze medievale," *Medioevo e Rinascimento* 21 (2007): 27–51, with references.

41. Salutati often insists on the Roman origins of Florence. See the letter to Pope Boniface IX in which he speaks of the Romans and Florentines as a "single people" (Langkabel, ep. 163, pp. 344–46, 17 November 1398). For Fiesole, see Florus, *Epitome* 3.18.11, and the notes to §§26 and 28.

42. Sallust, *Catilinarian Conspiracy* 28.4.

43. Cicero, *Catilinarian Orations* 2.9.20.

44. Ibid.

45. Modern authorities believe the foundation of Florence was planned by Julius Caesar and carried out under Augustus; see Colin Hardie, "The Origin and Plan of Roman Florence," *Journal of Roman Studies* 55.1 (1965): 122–40.

46. Ptolemy, *Geography* 3.1.43. In this quote Salutati omits the town of Roselle; he returns to Lucus Feronis below, §158.

47. Pliny, *Natural History* 3.5.52; in his critical edition ([Leipzig: Teubner, 1906], p. 252), K. Mayhoff reads *Florentini praefluenti Arno appositi,* as Salutati conjectured. See this edition for the variant readings referred to in Salutati's next clause.

48. Pliny, *Natural History* 3.5.52.

49. Ptolemy lived in the second century of our era, Saint Zenobius in the fourth, so if Salutati's first guess is correct, that the *Fluentini* in contemporary texts of Pliny is a corruption for *Florentini,* Florence's change of name cannot have occurred in the fourth century, as a pious tradition held.

50. See Paulinus of Nola, *Vita Ambrosii* 50.1 (*PL* 14.44), and Villani, 2.24.74–80.

51. See Jerome, *De nominibus Hebraeis* ad vocem (*PL* 23.845A).

52. Jerome, *De situ et nominibus locorum Hebraicorum* ad vocem (*PL* 23.914B). On Salutati and Jerome, see E. Antonucci in *Catalogo,* pp. 329–31, cat. 108.

53. Perhaps an allusion to "Doubting Thomas," the disciple of Christ who said he would not believe Christ had risen from the dead until he had touched his wounds with his finger; see John 20:25.

54. Florus, *Epitome* 2.9.27–28 (Loeb translation). Salutati's text is corrupt and therefore differs somewhat from that found in modern editions (see Notes to the Texts). On the early Renaissance confusion between Seneca and Florus, see the notes in this volume to *On Tyranny* 2.6, 3.11, as well as Novati's comment in Salutati, *Epistolario,* III, p. 298.

55. That is, Ferentino in the province of Frosinone, whose Latin name is Florentinum or Ferentinum.

56. However, no witness for this reading is given by P. Jal in the apparatus to his critical edition of Florus (Paris: Belles Lettres, 1967, 2:27). Salutati is arguing that the Florentia mentioned in Florus as a *municipium* in the 80s BCE is a different town in Campania.

57. That is, the traditional date for the passing of the Ordinances of Justice, a date seen by Florentines as the beginning of the guild regime that still governed the city in Salutati's day.

58. See Psalms 7:10, Apocalypse (Book of Revelation) 2:23, and Jeremiah 17:10 for the biblical expression, utilized frequently in Salutati's letters, e.g., Langkabel, ep. 152 (p. 320, 26 April 1395, to Giangaleazzo Visconti).

59. Cicero, *De re publica* 6.3. This is one of Salutati's favorite quotations, often repeated in his state correspondence, as noted by Langkabel, p. 29.

60. See Seneca, *Hercules Furens* 922–23. The humanist cites the same verses in his well-known 1385 letter to Andreolo Arese: see Salutati, *Epistolario*, II, ep. 6.5 (pp. 146–59, on 152).

61. Romans 9:19. See also Esther 13:9.

62. A role underscored by Salutati in numerous letters; see that to Boniface IX (13 September 1397: Langkabel, ep. 160, pp. 337–39), in which Salutati mentions Florence's many actions as *ecclesiae pugilem* (boxer of the Church).

63. Therefore (following Cicero, *De inventione* 1.29.45), a *simplex conclusio* in rhetorical theory, because the Florentines not only did not commit the fact they could not have done so.

64. A reference to the War of the Eight Saints (1375–78), during which the newly elected Salutati served as chancellor. See Witt, *Hercules*, pp. 126–32; the letters in Langkabel, pp. 88–170; the section edited by F. Sznura in *Coluccio Salutati e Firenze*, pp. 89–92; the entry by L. Mancino, ibid., pp. 159–60, cat. 68, with bibliography, to which may be added D. S. Peterson, "The War of the Eight Saints in Florentine Memory and

Oblivion," in *Society and Individual in Renaissance Florence*, ed. W. J. Connell (Berkeley: University of California Press, 2002), pp. 187–91.

65. Louis IV of Bavaria, or Louis the Bavarian (1282–1347), crowned emperor January 1328 by senator Sciarra Colonna in Rome, attempted to depose John XXII and replace him with the antipope Nicholas V in April of that year. Galeazzo was the chief supporter of Louis's descent into Italy, as noted also by Bruni, *Historiae* 5.125.

66. That is, persons living outside the walls of Florence on farms and in villages who recognized Florentine signory but were not members of guilds and therefore lacked political rights. See §45.

67. This passage helps to date Loschi's invective to early in 1401; see *La vipera e il giglio*, pp. 21–25.

68. *Antiquius* literally means "older" or "more ancient" (i.e., more venerable) and only in a transferred sense means "preferable," "better" or "more desirable."

69. The *topos* of *dulcedo libertatis* (sweet liberty), which comes from various classical and late-antique sources (Livy 1.17 and 2.9; Orosius, *Historiae adversus paganos* 6.12.4) is one of the commonest in Salutati's public letters (see, for instance, *To the Italians*, in this volume, Letter 5, §3), as noted by Witt, *Public Letters*, p. 39, and idem, *"In the Footsteps of the Ancients": The Origins of Humanism from Lovato to Bruni* (Leiden: Brill, 2000), pp. 308–9. The concept of *ius*, a right human order stemming from God or natural law, has no exact translation in modern English. Here the contrast is between the stable legal framework of Florentine rule over its subject population and the arbitrary rule of a tyrant.

70. Another common theme in Salutati's letters, e.g., Langkabel, ep. 163 (p. 345, to Boniface IX, 17 November 1398).

71. Making Loschi guilty of the *contraria argumentatio*, the self-contradictory argument, identified by Cicero, *De inventione* 1.49.93.

72. The *iocundum* is happiness in this life, not beatitude in the next; it includes corporeal goods such as pleasure and health, but also worldly goods like wealth, status, and security.

73. That is, the opposition between life in liberty and life under a tyrant, another frequent *topos* in Salutati's writings; see Langkabel, ep. 22 (p. 109, 28 January 1376), ep. 24 (p. 112, 13 February 1376), ep. 35 (p. 137, 1 July 1376); *On Tyranny* 1.7–9.

74. See John 1:14.

75. Therefore a case of *erronea dispositio* according to Cicero, *De inventione* 1.21.30.

76. Nation: translating *genus*, in the premodern sense of nation, i.e., an extended kinship group or race.

77. Hence an instance of *adversa argumentatio*, according to Cicero, *De inventione* 1.49.94.

78. That is, Florentine subjects already have liberty, so by definition they cannot hope for it. The argument would work only if liberty were a status that did not admit of degrees. In the earlier part of the paragraph, Salutati relies on the belief of ancient Greek philosophers that zero is not a number.

79. The Visconti claimed dominion over Genoa and its territory; hence Ligurian.

80. The Visconti attempt to take San Miniato took place in 1369–70; Loschi was probably born toward 1368 (Viti, p. 154).

81. See Stefani, p. 270, r. 711. The emperor in question was Charles IV (not III) of Luxemburg (1316–78), king of Bohemia from 1346, crowned emperor in 1355.

82. Salutati refers to the ruse by which Giangaleazzo imprisoned his uncle and father-in-law Bernabò Visconti on 6 May 1385, annexing the lands under his power. For this infamous episode, to which Salutati often alludes in the present text, and for Giangaleazzo's second marriage in 1380, to Bernabò's daughter Caterina, see Bueno de Mesquita, pp. 31–32, and Cognasso, *L'unificazione*, pp. 513–19. For an understandably different treatment of the episode, see the chancellor's 1385 epistle to Andreolo Arese (see note 29, above) in *Epistolario*, II, ep. 6.5 (pp. 146–59), edited with an Italian translation in Ercole 1942, pp. 119–27, 245–51.

83. Examples of this common *topos* familiar to Salutati include Caesar, *Gallic Wars* 6.30.2; Cicero, *Pro Marcello* 6; and Vegetius, *Epitome rei militaris* 3.26.4.

84. See Stefani, p. 272, r. 716, where the key to the conquest on 9 January 1369/70, is ascribed to *un pover'uomo, che si chiamava Luperello* (a poor man called Luperello).

85. For this celebrated episode see, of the sources best known to Salutati, Livy 33.32–33; he may also have known Plutarch, *Flamininus* 10.

86. See Pseudo-Minerbetti, pp. 210–11, cap. 12, under the 1396 (1397 in the modern style of dating), and Salutati's letter to King Charles IV (Langkabel, ep. 158, pp. 332–33, 2 April 1397).

87. Pseudo-Minerbetti, under 1396, cap. 12, p. 211.

88. A clear echo of the ancient commonplace that *nemo malus felix* (no evil man is happy), which is attested, for example, in Juvenal 13.236–42, and Cicero, *De legibus* 2.43–44; *Against Verres* 2.1.7 and 38.

89. Mangiadori's failed revolt dates to February 1396 (1397 in modern dating), or twenty-seven years after the Luperello episode of January 1369 (1370 in modern dating).

90. Cicero, *De oratore* 1.3.12. The same precept appears in a letter that sets out a kind of educational program (Salutati, *Epistolario*, III, ep. 13.3, p. 606, to Lodovico degli Alidosi). This letter is dated by Novati to 1402, but to 1397 by M. Martelli, "Schede per Coluccio Salutati," *Interpres* 9 (1989): 237–52, at 247–49.

91. Livy 22.3.

92. See Exodus 16:11–35.

93. In almost identical words, Salutati often mentions the failed attempt by officials of the Church to take Florence by starvation in 1375: see Langkabel, ep. 3 (p. 89, 20 September 1375); ep. 29 (pp. 121–22, 6 May 1376); ep. 34 (p. 133, 29 June 1376). For Florence's successful resistance (see the opening of §68, above), see Bueno de Mesquita, with references. *Teucria* was commonly used by humanists to indicate the lands in Asia Minor controlled by the Turks; the Teucri are the Turks: see Salutati, *Epistolario* III, 208.

94. Doubtless an allusion to Petrarch, *Italia mia* (*Rerum vulgarium fragmenta* 128.95–96); compare also Vergil, *Aeneid* 2.367.

95. See the discussion of this passage by P. Gilli, "Coluccio Salutati, chancellier de Florence, et la France," *Bibliothèque d'Humanisme et Renaissance* 55.3 (1993): 479–501, on 497–98.

96. This traditional phrase appears throughout Salutati's letters, public and private; for example several times in the letter to Charles III Durazzo that is a kind of unfinished "mirror of princes": *Epistolario*, II, ep. 5.6 (pp. 11–18), edited with an Italian translation in Ercole 1942, pp. 77–104, 215–34.

97. A nearly literal quote from Isidore of Seville, *Etymologies* 9.3.46. See ibid., 9.3.51 and 9.3.62 for the terms in Salutati's next clause. Salutati's information about the equestrian order probably derives from Livy 1.43; see also ibid. 1.13.8 and 5.7.13.

98. For the definition of *tergiversatio* (hesitation), see *Corpus iuris civilis*, *Digest* 48.16.1; Salutati may also have had in mind the discussion of the term's etymology in Isidore of Seville, *Etymologies* 10.271, *ad vocem*.

99. Florence as the unshaken bastion of resistance to the spread of Visconti tyranny is a familiar *topos* of the propaganda orchestrated by Salutati; see for example a letter of about the same time to Francesco Novello of Padua: Langkabel, ep. 178 (p. 363, 17 December 1403). For the classical phrase at the end of this line, see letters to Antonio di ser Chello (*Epistolario*, II, ep. 5.17, p. 87, 1383) and to the Perugians (Langkabel, ep. 21, p. 108, 1376).

100. Here Salutati replies to Loschi's rhetorical question (cited above, §71) using Loschi's own words.

101. The last two cases were considered legitimate grounds for a just war.

102. In this passage and more generally in the entire text of the *Reply*, the two classical models for Salutati's portrait of Giangaleazzo are Catiline (as pointed out in Bruni, *Laudatio*, p. 28; see Cicero, *Catilinarian Orations* 3.7.16–17, and Sallust, *Catilinarian Conspiracy* 5.1–6) and above all Caesar (see especially Lucan's *Pharsalia*, 1.143–50, 5.301–4).

103. Here Salutati alludes to the famous maxim of Cicero, *Of Duties* 1.11.35: *Quare suscipienda quidem bella sunt ob eam causam, ut sine iniuria in pace vivatur* (One must therefore undertake a war only in order to live in peace and without injustice), just as a few words earlier the notion of just war only following a formal request for compensation derives from ibid., 1.11.36. That definition of just war was widely accepted in the whole medieval era (see the sources cited in Salutati, *On Tyranny* 2.1) and is assumed by Salutati by the time of the military conflict with the papacy, whether in state missives (Langkabel, ep. 37, p. 140, 12 July 1376, to Henry II of Castile) or in private letters (*Epistolario*, I, ep. 3.23, p. 214, 5 November 1375, to fra Niccolò Casucchi).

104. A variation on 1 Corinthians 1:20.

105. The language reflects various biblical passages, especially Wisdom 5:15; see also Job 21:18; Hosea 13:3; Psalms 1:4, 34:5; and Isaiah 17:13. This imagery, also adopted by Loschi (see below, §106, corresponding to *Invective* §17), was not uncommon in political correspondence of the period; see Salutati's letter to Charles VI, which quotes a letter of the Milanese chancery (Letter 6, §5 in the present volume). See also Langkabel, p. 288. For the reference in the next sentence, see Marcus Porcius Cato the Censor, *Ad filium*, fr. 14; Seneca the Elder, *Controversiae* 1.9; Quintilian, *Institutio oratoria* 12.1.1; Apuleius, *Apologia* 94; as well as Isidore of Seville, *Etymologies* 2.3.1. Loschi mentions this precept in the preface to his commentary on Cicero's orations, edited by F. C. Begossi, *Antonio Loschi segretario pontificio: L' "Inquisitio artis in orationibus Ciceronis" e la corrispondenza politica di Martino V*, PhD diss. (Milan: Università Cattolica del Sacro Cuore, 2002), pp. 398–409, at 402.

106. An almost literal reprise of Loschi's words cited above at §71.12–13.

107. Salutati alludes to Cicero, *De inventione* 1.49.95, or more probably the pseudo-Ciceronian *Rhetorica ad Herennium* 2.23.35, both of which cite Plautus, *Trinummus* vv. 23–26 as an example of fallacious reasoning (*vitiosa ratio*), in the second case with the commentary *Ex eo quod ipse facturus est, non ex eo quod fieri convenit, utile quid sit ratiocinatur* (This is reasoning about the utility of a thing based on what he is going to do, not on what it is suitable to do). Salutati's quote actually departs from the text of the

playwright and of Cicero, who both have Megaronides assert that he will reprove his friend.

108. For *deminutio capitis*, here translated as "forfeiture of civil rights," see *Corpus iuris civilis, Digest* 4.5.11, and *Institutes* 1.16.4.

109. That custom is a second nature is a well-known philosophical dictum found in many authors, including Aristotle, Cicero, and Augustine. Above, Salutati refers to the acts of treason that brought Bologna, already defeated by Milan at the Battle of Casalecchio on 26 June 1402, into Visconti's power the following month; see Bueno de Mesquita, pp. 279–80, and Cognasso, *Il ducato*, pp. 59–64. Salutati also refers to the agreements between Bologna and Florence at the time of the War of the Eight Saints, for which see Salutati's contemporary letter to the Bolognese: Langkabel, ep. 26 (p. 117, 22 March 1376).

110. Here Salutati replies to Loschi's assertion reported in §72.

111. See 1 Corinthians 1:23, and the commentary of Isidore of Seville, *Etymologies* 7.2.40.

112. This formula appears in the satirists; see for instance Juvenal 13.242, and Martial 8.59.2.

113. By "others" Salutati refers to the principal parties that contracted the anti-Visconti alliance with Florence on 11 April 1392: Bologna, Alberto II d'Este, and Francesco III Novello da Carrara, followed on 1 September 1392 by Francesco Gonzaga; see Bueno de Mesquita, pp. 144–45, and Cognasso, *L'unificazione*, pp. 564–66.

114. Horace, *Art of Poetry* 97. At the start of the present paragraph, Salutati takes up a passage of Loschi's *Invectiva* already cited at §73.

115. The phrase is hardly rare, but its irony is probably reinforced by its place not only in Cicero, *De finibus* 5.18.49, but also in medieval *ars dictaminis* texts, notably of the school of Rinuccini, which developed Cicero's reference to the liberal arts: see G. Tanturli, "Cino Rinuccini e la scuola di Santa Maria in Campo," *Studi Medievali*, s. III, 17.2 (1976): 625–74, at pp. 667 and 670.

116. This passage agrees with §74 above (§10 of Loschi's invective) with a truncation of the first sentence.

117. This and the following paragraph clearly echo the treatment of the topic in Salutati, *De fato*, especially 3.5–7 (ed. Bianca, pp. 150–67).

118. This passage reveals that Salutati viewed Giangaleazzo as a tyrant both *ex defectu tituli* and *ex parte exercitii*, following his classification in *On Tyranny*, 1.8–9. See Witt, *Hercules*, p. 387: "While liberty had always been closely connected with law in Salutati's thought, in the last five years of his chancery the war of Florence and her allies against Milan was conceptualized as a battle between legitimate and illegitimate powers where the nature of the specific constitutional regime was ignored." Visconti was named duke by Emperor Wenceslaus (after payment of 100,000 florins) in May 1395, and in that year (5 September) the ceremony took place in the Basilica of Sant'Ambrogio. See F. Moly, "Rituale sacro e autorità ducale: La processione per l'incoronazione di Gian Galeazzo Visconti nel messale di sant'Ambrogio," in *I luoghi del sacro*, ed. F. Ricciardelli (Florence: Pagliai, 2008), pp. 63–81, with references.

119. Since Niccolò III d'Este succeeded his father in July 1393 at the age of nine, he was still a minor at the time when Loschi wrote his *Invective* (1401).

120. A reference to the recovery of Padua by Francesco Novello da Carrara, aided by Florence, in June 1390, after it had been taken by Giangaleazzo in December 1388: see Galli, p. 511; Bueno de Mesquita, pp. 122–23; Cognasso, *L'unificazione*, pp. 559–62; and ep. 97 and 110 in Langkabel, pp. 237–38, 256–58. See also a further letter of 1390 (Salutati, *Epistolario*, II, ep. 6.3, pp. 252–64), and letters of other dates (e.g., Langkabel, ep. 114 and 178, pp. 262 and 363) for the long-standing alliance between the Carraresi of Padua and Florence.

121. Matthew 12:30, the well-known expression attributed here to Giangaleazzo with a blasphemous connotation.

122. Here Salutati follows his pattern of adapting passages already cited by Loschi to polemical effect; see §74. For the Valeggio dike, see Pseudo-Minerbetti, pp. 174–75, under 1393, capp. 12–13; Bueno de Mesquita, pp. 165–66 (with sources); Cognasso, *Il ducato*, pp. 14–15.

123. Salutati refers to the victory of Florence and its allies over Visconti forces at Governolo (28 August 1397), four days after the latter had been

defeated by Carlo Malatesta in another riverbank battle, at Bondeno. On the inability of Florence and its allies to profit from these circumstances, see Bueno de Mesquita, pp. 211–12; Cognasso, *Il ducato*, pp. 34–35. The phrase "make the most of victory" in the previous clause is perhaps meant to recall Hannibal's lack of decision after his victory at Cannae; see Florus, *Epitome* 1.22.21, and also Livy 22.59.

124. In using the word *auctores* (founders) here Salutati refers to the Carolingian refoundation of Florence, for which see below, §158; see also Gilli, pp. 283–98, as well as an epigram of Salutati on a lost fresco, for which see A. T. Hankey, "Salutati's Epigrams for the Palazzo Vecchio at Florence," *Journal of the Warburg and Courtauld Institutes* 22 (1959): 363–65, at p. 365, and G. Tanturli in *Catalogo*, pp. 183–84.

125. Vergil, *Aeneid* 2.381. In the preceding sentence Salutati takes up with variations a passage of Loschi (above, §74), following his usual practice in this text. The next sentence takes up the quotation given in §100.

126. In classical Latin, *callidus* can have either a positive ("astute") or a negative ("cunning") connotation. Salutati insists that the negative sense is the correct, classical one, misled, it would seem, by a pseudo-Ciceronian text, the *Synonyma*, in fact a medieval Latin thesaurus. Salutati's text must have been similar to one like Florence, Biblioteca Riccardiana, MS. Ricc. 667, fol. 106r, which contains the same definition (*Callidus, veterator, vafer, versutus, astutus, subdolus, insidiosus*) and was copied from a manuscript owned by Salutati (see f. 105r). On this pseudo-Ciceronian work and Salutati's interest in it, see Ullman, p. 225.

127. *Esse quam videri* (it is better to be than to seem [virtuous]) is a Roman philosophical maxim (originally Greek), cited by Cicero, *De amicitia* 98; Sallust, *Catilinarian Conspiracy* 54.6; and many other authors.

128. Terms that, as noted by Cognasso, *Il ducato*, p. 28, had a duration of five years and allowed any ally of Florence to join within three months of its publication.

129. Vergil, *Aeneid* 1.625. The preceding sentence is closely echoed by the dislike of calumny and diminution of others expressed in Salutati, *Questio est coram decemviris*, in McCormick, p. 239.

130. For the phrase *stante re publica,* see Cicero, *Of Duties* 2.3, "when public affairs were in good condition," "when the commonwealth was still uncorrupted."

131. Salutati presumably prefers the original (Langobard) rather than the corrupted spelling (Lombard) so as to allude to early medieval history when the Longobards were a nation of invading barbarians.

132. Boethius, *Consolation of Philosophy* 2.carm5.8–9. In the original Latin, *venenum* carries a range of meanings, including drug, poison, venom, tinge, stain, scourge, and shame.

133. In May 1397: Bueno de Mesquita, pp. 207–09, 217. This section of the text returns to the events of the first months of the second Florence-Milan war. For the *condottiere* Biordo de' Michelotti, who died on 10 March 1398, see Salutati, *Epistolario,* III, ep. 10.13 (pp. 276–78) and ep. 10.25 (pp. 327–30). For Paolo Orsini, see Langkabel, ep. 176 (p. 361, to Boniface IX, 30 June 1402, with references).

134. See Pseudo-Minerbetti, p. 216, under 1397, cap. 6.

135. A reprise of Loschi's praise of the mercenary captain given above, §106.

136. See §99 and note 123 for the short-lived victory in 1397 of Carlo Malatesta and the Florentine forces over Milanese forces at Governolo and the incapacity of the anti-Visconti forces to take advantage of it, discussed also at §121.

137. 28 August.

138. The phrase *Deus vult* was famously the motto of the First Crusade.

139. Vergil, *Aeneid* 2.402. This paragraph continues to refer to the Florentine victory at Governolo.

140. On Bernard d'Armagnac's planned incursion into Italy in order to avenge his brother's death, consistent with the agreements between Charles VI and Florence of 29 September 1396, see Bueno de Mesquita, pp. 203–4, and Cognasso, *Il ducato,* pp. 32, 35. The peace alluded to below is the truce signed at Pavia on 11 May 1398: Bueno de Mesquita, p. 223; Cognasso, *Il ducato,* pp. 39–40; Pseudo-Minerbetti, under 1397, cap. 24 (this and other sources note that the peace was to have lasted ten years).

141. See the last sentence in §18. Salutati's wordplay relies on a common false etymology of *vemens* (= *vehemens*) from *vis* (violence) and *mens* (mind); the word is more plausibly derived from *veho*.

142. That is, Italy.

143. Here Salutati plays upon the twin meanings of "Gallus": "Gaul" or "rooster," as our adoption of lowercase for the Latin word underscores.

144. A negative reading of the serpent of the Visconti arms, a kind of leitmotif present from §15 to 182 of the present text, also runs throughout Florentine anti-Milanese propaganda, and not only in missives of the chancery under Salutati. See the letters of 1390 and 1391 in Langkabel, ep. 114 (the *Epistula Italicis*, fifth in the present volume), ep. 126, and ep. 130 (pp. 261–65, 281–82, 288–89), but also the political poetry of the period. One may point, for example, to three celebrated *canzoni* of Franco Sacchetti, ed. Brambilla Ageno (cited in note 23), 141, v. 38; 149, v. 1; 197, vv. 41–42 (pp. 171, 181, 286, respectively), and Salutati's own verses *Cur tenet infantem coluber crudelis in ore* to Enghiramo Bracci, in *Coluccio Salutati. Index*, ed. C. Zintzen, U. Ecker, P. Riemer (Tübingen: Narr, 1992), p. 243.

145. A reference to the intense diplomatic negotiations between Giangaleazzo and Charles VI in the last decade of the fourteenth century with regard to the kingdom of Adria and control of Genoa; see Bueno de Mesquita, pp. 154–57, 159–60, 187, and Cognasso, *Il ducato*, pp. 3–13. Generally, this part of the text reflects Salutati's official letters at the time of the War of the Eight Saints and the Florentine defense as conveyed in missives as well as embassies; see Peterson, "The War of the Eight Saints" (note 64, above), esp. pp. 191–93.

146. That is, under his own name as the author of the *Invective*, and not in the name of Visconti as his chancellor.

147. That is, the Holy Roman Empire. The popes claimed to have transferred political control of the Roman Empire from the Greeks to the Carolingians in 800, and later to the Ottonians; they continued to claim the power of *translatio imperii* into the fifteenth century and later.

148. Salutati is playing again with the various meanings of *ironia*, which for him, here, is a statement that implies what is true by stating a false-

hood; Loschi probably meant it in its Aristotelian sense of saying less than the full truth. See §79, above, and Dilwyn Knox, *Ironia: Medieval and Renaissance Ideas on Irony* (Leiden: E. J. Brill, 1989).

149. With slight variations, this paragraph corresponds to §102, equivalent to *Invectiva* §13.

150. Giangaleazzo Visconti had been appointed an imperial vicar by the emperor Wencelaus (reigned 1378–1400) in 1380. At the time of the *Reply*, however, the emperor was Robert of Bavaria, who had succeeded the deposed, pro-Visconti Wenceslaus on 21 August 1400; see Bueno de Mesquita, pp. 262–64, and G. Romano, "Giangaleazzo Visconti avvelenatore. Un episodio della spedizione italiana di Ruperto di Baviera," *Archivio Storico Lombardo*, s. III, 21.2 (1894): 309–60.

151. See above, §103.

152. See above, §103, quoting from Loschi. For the historical reference that follows, see Caesar, *Gallic Wars* 7.8.56.

153. Salutati ascribes to divine intervention the sudden death of Giangaleazzo on 3 September 1402, due to an infection of the plague caught the preceding month and not divulged by his inner circle. This was the widespread opinion in Florence once the news arrived, as attested by numerous period sources; see A. Barlucchi in *Coluccio Salutati e Firenze*, pp. 148–49, entry 67.

154. Salutati here makes fun of Loschi's (perfectly classical) use of *licentia*, which Salutati pretends should be restricted to its legal sense.

155. These episodes belong to an attempt, ultimately a failed one, to construct a Franco-Milanese alliance, in which Genoa would have passed under the control of Duke Louis d'Orleans, regent during the illness of Charles VI; see Bueno de Mesquita, pp. 155–58, and Cognasso, *Il ducato*, pp. 3–13.

156. Vergil, *Aeneid* 4.487–89, cited also by Augustine, *City of God* 21.6.2.

157. Psalms 115:11 (115:2).

158. That is, to mean, "The Florentines are unbridled liars and cheats with the exception of other peoples," a grammatically possible but contextually unnatural reading of the sentence.

159. Since Giangaleazzo Visconti came to power in 1387 after imprisoning the reigning duke, his uncle and father-in-law Bernabò, and staging a coup d'état, his title to rule was considered doubtful.

160. For the confines of *Gallia Narbonensis*, Salutati could have drawn upon Pliny, *Natural History* 3.4.31 and 3.4.35; Ptolemy, *Geography* 2.10.1 and 2.10.5; Pomponius Mela 2.5.74–76. For Liguria in general, see Pliny, *Natural History* 3.5.47 and 49–50; Ptolemy, *Geography* 3.1.2; Florus, *Epitome* 1.19.4; Solinus, 2.6; see also Salutati, *De laboribus Herculis* 3.29.5–6 (ed. Ullman, I, p. 332). None of the ancient descriptions mentions the towns of Noli and Ventimiglia. For the tag "duke of Liguria," see §71, above; see also *La vipera e il giglio*, p. 111, for the omission of a verb in this passage of Salutati's text.

161. See Isidore of Seville, *Etymologies* 9.3.21.

162. The familiar biblical phrase of Psalms 84:11 is given in a parodistic vein.

163. Salutati makes fun of Loschi's awkward double negative. In fact, the philological evidence is that the double negative in Salutati's copy of this passage derives from a scribal error in the earliest stages of the textual transmission from multiple sources. See *La vipera e il giglio*, pp. 87–88.

164. See above, §105.

165. Vergil, *Aeneid* 11.425–27 (with slight variations).

166. See Judges 20:21–48.

167. In this passage Salutati distinguishes four Roman battles against Pyrrhus, following Plutarch (*Life of Pyrrhus* 21.9), while Salutati had identified three in his earlier writings (see Langkabel, ep. 23, p. 110, of 1376, and ep. 55, p. 169, of 1379). See also *La vipera e il giglio*, pp. 41 and 48. The king of Epirus was the subject of the never-completed and now-lost poem *De bello Pyrrhi cum Romanis*: see Salutati, *Epistolario*, III, ep. 9.6 (pp. 58–64, esp. 59–60, to Pellegrino Zambeccari, probably of 3 March 1395), and 4/2, pp. 504 and 507 (biographical sketch of Salutati in Domenico di Bandino's unpublished *Fons memorabilium*).

168. For this classical *topos*, see, for example, Caesar, *Gallic Wars* 6.30.2, and Cicero, *Pro Marcello* 2.6.

169. For the conflicting evidence of the sources about the return of the gold of the Capitoline (bought back from the Senones, or perhaps never removed from Rome), see J. Bayet, G. Baillet (eds.), Livy, V (Paris: Belles Lettres, 1964), appendix, pp. 169–70. For the rout by the Senones at Allia (above) see Livy 5.37–38, and Florus, *Epitome* 1.7.7. Concerning the extension of Gallic territory in northern Italy, in large part taken from the Etruscans, Salutati (below) is probably drawing on Livy 5.33.9–10. For the Gallic foundation of cities in the Po valley, see the celebrated passage in Paulus Diaconus, *History of the Longobards* 2.23.

170. See Pliny, *Natural History*, 3.20.138. No doubt due to a corrupt text, the first number given by Salutati is incorrect. Probably for the same reason, *Forovibienses* (residents of Forum Vibii, either Envie or Cavour in modern Piedmont) was erroneously rendered as *Foroiulienses* (residents of Cividale del Friuli): see ibid., 3.14.113 and 3.16.117.

171. That is, Cisalpine and Transalpine Gaul, the lands occupied by Gaulish peoples on either side of the Alps, in Northern Italy and modern France, respectively. Just below, the two Gauls are referred to as Gallia Togata (toga-wearing Gaul, i.e., Roman Gaul), and Gallia Comata (long-haired Gaul, i.e., the Gauls north of the Alps).

172. Here Salutati employs another theological argument. If Rome remained the unique example of a world empire, its universality cannot have been a natural human occurrence but must be a gift of God; this inference in turn removes the events of Roman history from the realm of natural patterns that can be understood and therefore used as a basis for predicting the future. See also Salutati's *De nobilitate* 5 (ed. Garin, p. 32); the argument may be contrasted with that of Dante in Book 2 of *On Monarchy*.

173. The tone of the entire paragraph on the *translatio imperii* reflects Orosius, *Historiae adversus paganos*, esp. 1.4.1–2, 1.19.1, and 2.2.1–3.

174. That is, Asia, Africa, and Europe, the three continents known to late medieval Europeans.

175. See Florus, *Epitome* 1.8.3. See §32, above, for the identification of Florus with Seneca. For Etruscan hegemony, Salutati's source (almost

verbatim) is Livy 5.33.7–10; see also G. Cipriani, *Il mito etrusco nel Rinascimento fiorentino* (Florence: Olschki, 1980), pp. 2–5.

176. See Ptolemy, *Geography* 3.1.43. On this toponym see above, §29. Lucus Feronis or Feroniae has also been identified with a site in northern Latium near Fiano, halfway between Rome and Mount Soracte, but far from the lower Arno valley.

177. See V. Borghini, *Se Firenze fu spianata da Attila, e riedificata da Carlo Magno*, in idem, *Discorsi*, vol. 2 (Florence: Viviani, 1755), pp. 251–306, at 288; R. Davidsohn, *Storia di Firenze*, vol. 1 (Florence: Sansoni, 1956), pp. 117–18; and S. Raveggi, "Tracce carolingie a Firenze," in *Sulle orme di Orlando. Leggende e luoghi carolingi in Italia*, ed. A. I. Galletti and R. Roda (Padua: Interbooks, 1987), pp. 167–77, at 170–71. See also Langkabel, ep. 40 (pp. 146, 28 September 1376), ep. 56 (p. 172, 13 September 1380), ep. 64 (pp. 190–91, 20 October 1384).

178. The chief source followed by Salutati for Charles I's activity in Italy seems to be Villani 8.3. San Germano is the predecessor of the modern Italian town of Cassino. The same incident was later reported by Leonardo Bruni in Book 2.93 of his *History of the Florentine People*, who described the heroism of the Florentines in somewhat more measured terms.

179. Salutati shifts into the historical present, in accordance with classical models, in order to make the scene more vivid.

180. See Villani 8.8, which is, however, used selectively by Salutati.

181. For the events connected with Charles III Durazzo, Louis I of Anjou, and Amedeo VI of Savoy, see Bueno de Mesquita, pp. 19–21, 28–29, and Cognasso, *L'unificazione*, pp. 501–13.

182. A phrase from 1 Kings (= 1 Samuel) 3:18.

183. The Veronese attempt to revolt was suppressed violently by Visconti forces under Ugolotto Biancardo on 26 June 1390: See Galli, pp. 511–18; P. B. Romanelli, *La calata di Giovanni III d'Armagnac in Italia e la disfatta di Alessandria* (Rome: Edizioni Museo, 1936), pp. 17, 22; Bueno de Mesquita, pp. 122, 345–46; Cognasso, *L'unificazione*, p. 555.

184. Nearly a direct quote from Vergil, *Aeneid* 5.230 (games in memory of Anchises); see also ibid. 12.49 (Turnus to Latinus before their combat).

185. §§107–8 above.

186. This theme occurs frequently in Salutati's chancery letters to Giangaleazzo: see, e.g., Langkabel, ep. 134 (pp. 295, 6 September 1396), ep. 152 (p. 320, 26 April 1395) — and also in internal discussions of the Florentine government: see Bueno de Mesquita, pp. 254–55, with references.

187. A common theme of letters of the Florentine chancery in this period, which contrasted that free city's peaceful pursuit of commerce and tyrannies (Milan in the first place) dominated by ambitious notables; see Letter 5 in the present volume, and Langkabel, ep. 126 (p. 281, to the Sienese, 25 January 1391).

188. Here Salutati deals with Loschi's words in the passage quoted above, §107. See Visconti's declaration of war: Langkabel, ep. 109 (pp. 255–56), and Bruni, *Historiae* 9.98, pp. 100–102 (where it is dated 19 April 1390). The claim of Florentine obstructionism made in this passage was rebutted in the official response of the Florentine republic, which further affirms the citizens' rejection of tyranny (*potius eligere mori quam inter suae tyrannidis subditos numerari* — We would rather die than be numbered among the subjects of your tyranny), Langkabel, ep. 110, pp. 256–58, 2 May 1390).

189. This reverses a celebrated dictum of Cicero, *Of Duties*, 1.22.77. For Giangaleazzo's actions regarding Padua and Verona, see further below, §173 and notes.

190. For the agreement signed at Pisa (9 October 1389) by Giangaleazzo and Florence and successive events, see Bueno de Mesquita, pp. 109–11; Cognasso, *L'unificazione*, pp. 548–50 (with references); and Salutati's *Epistula Italicis* (Letter 5 in this volume, and Langkabel, pp. 261–64, esp. p. 262). For the text of the agreement, see L. Osio, *Documenti tratti dagli archivi milanesi* (Milano: Bernardoni, n.d; repr. Milan: Cisalpino-Goliardica, 1970) 1.2: 278–93; Salutati's statement coincides with the first

of the preliminary clauses, preceding the *capitula* themselves. Moreover, in preliminary meetings Giangaleazzo had frequently expressed his intent to form a league with Florence and Bologna (Bueno de Mesquita, pp. 100–101). For the explusion of Florentines and Bolognese from Visconti territories in October 1389, Giangaleazzo's accusation that Florence attempted to poison him, and the latter's response, see De Rosa, pp. 63–67; L. Frati, "La Lega dei Bolognesi e dei Fiorentini contro Giangaleazzo Visconti (1389–90)," *Archivio Storico Lombardo*, s. II, 16 (1889): 5–24, esp. pp. 5–10; Bueno de Mesquita, p. 111; A. Barlucchi in *Coluccio Salutati e Firenze*, p. 147. For Salutati's reply, dated 3 November 1389 (Langkabel, ep. 106, pp. 247–50), see Barlucchi, pp. 146–47. Not surprisingly, §§170–71 recall in style and content both that reply and the official documents (given by De Rosa).

191. For this new set of accusations brought against Florence by Galeazzo and the reply, see Frati (cited in the previous note), pp. 10–13, and Langkabel, ep. 107 (pp. 250–51, a letter of the Milanese dated 13 November 1389), ep. 108 (pp. 252–55, the Signoria's reply of 16 December 1389, previously published by Witt, *Public Letters*, pp. 104–6).

192. A reference to episodes of February 1390, about two months before war was declared: see Bueno de Mesquita, pp. 111–13; Cognasso, *L'unificazione*, pp. 553–54; also Frati (cited in note 190), p. 16. The previous line refers to an accusation made by Giangaleazzo in the letter cited in the preceding note.

193. Here and at §174 Salutati varies Loschi's actual wording as given above, §107, and below, §§167, 169. Below, Salutati alludes once more to Giangaleazzo's capture of Bernabò, his uncle and the father of his second wife (see §57).

194. Salutati here invokes a distinction important to the scholastic theory of the just war, particularly the moral grounds for starting a war (*ius ad bellum*): the distinction between a war that one has to engage in for self-defense and a war that one chooses voluntarily to undertake, which has to meet a higher standard in order to be considered licit. See J. T. Johnson, *The Just War Tradition and the Restraint of War* (Princeton, NJ: Princeton University Press, 1981).

195. Here Salutati ironically overturns Loschi's assertion that the Florentines might have done beneficial actions had they so wished (quoted above, §107).

196. The first part of this paragraph refers to events of 1387–88 in northern Italy. An accord of April 1387 between Giangaleazzo and Francesco da Carrara of Padua assigned Verona to the former and Vicenza to the latter. On 18 October 1387, Milan conquered Verona, and three days later Vicenza was forced to accept the rulership of Caterina Visconti (daughter of Bernabò Visconti by Regina Della Scala of Verona, and wife of Giangaleazzo Visconti). Then in late May 1388 Giangaleazzo and Venice reached an accord by which they would divide the territory controlled by Francesco da Carrara, in June war was declared, and on 24 November Padua capitulated. For all this, see Bueno de Mesquita, pp. 74, 77–82; Cognasso, *L'unificazione*, pp. 531–34, 539–40; and the useful discussion of Galli, pp. 478, 509–10. See also the 20 December 1388 letter of the Venetians to Florence about the conquest of Padua and other cities by the Milan-Venice alliance: Langkabel, ep. 97 (pp. 237–38). It is perhaps significant that the 1387 submission of Vicenza was the occasion for Loschi's return to the north after his studies with Salutati (see *La vipera e il giglio*, pp. 58–59 note 31).

197. See two letters of Salutati: Langkabel ep. 144 (pp. 309–10, 28 January 1394, to the Genoese), and ep. 155 (pp. 323–24, 31 October 1396, to the lords of Padua, Mantua, and Rimini), in which, respectively, the chancellor deplores the endless changes of government in Genoa, and discusses Visconti designs upon that city. The important essay of F. Novati, "Le querele di Genova a Gian Galeazzo Visconti," *Giornale Ligustico di archeologia, storia e letteratura* 13 (1886): 401–13, includes (pp. 407–13) the edition of a text originating in the Visconti ambience around 1396, known as the *Somnium quo Januensis urbis querelae enarrantur* (Dream in which the complaints of the city of Genoa are told). In this propaganda pamphlet a distraught personification of Genoa appeals to Giangaleazzo to control the city and suppress its internal contentions. For stylistic reasons I am inclined to reject the attribution to Loschi advanced by Novati (p. 405); see *La vipera e il giglio*, p. 364, note 278.

198. See Bueno de Mesquita pp. 88–89, 195–96, 233, 241–44; and Cognasso, *Il ducato*, pp. 48 and 59–64, for Visconti involvement in the dispute between the factions in Bologna, Astorre Manfredi (lord of Faenza), and the mercenary Alberico da Barbiano.

199. The references to the earth and the sea constitute a double citation from Vergil, *Aeneid* 4.24, and *Eclogues* 8.58. See also Horace, *Epodes* 5.79–80 and 14.19, and Lucan, *Pharsalia* 4.98–103. While *adynaton* is a common figure in contexts of this kind, especially near to the *peroratio*, it may be relevant that Loschi used it with sharply polemical tones against Florence in a 1396 Latin poem to the lord of Milan (Pastine, p. 848), which depends upon Vergil, *Eclogues* 1.59–60. Salutati eloquently utilizes *adynaton* against Giangaleazzo in a letter to the Venetians (Langkabel, ep. 159, p. 336, 13 April 1397).

200. Salutati seems to have in mind the classical distinction between active and passive justice; see, for instance, Cicero, *Of Duties* 1.7.23. For the traits of Giangaleazzo in the following lines, see the portrait of Clodius in Cicero, *Pro Sestio* 34.

201. Salutati presents here the counterimage of a peaceful hegemon, an image he strove to create for Florence among the cities of Tuscany. The phrase "the land would have grown quiet before his face" alludes to the famous chant of the Easter Vigil, *Exultet*: "Let the heavens rejoice and the earth exult before the face of the Lord."

202. See Salutati, *De fato, Proemium* (ed. Bianca, p. 6), and the closing words in idem, *On Tyranny* 5.8. See also the wording of the conclusion to a disputation on the importance of poetry: *Epistolario*, III, ep. 12.20 (p. 543, 21 September 1401).

203. See Cicero, *In Quintum Caecilium divinatio* 39. The second line of the present paragraph explicates how Salutati has carried out the tasks of the perfect orator as defined in *Rhetorica ad Herennium* 1.10.17.

204. Here Salutati follows Cicero's precept (*De inventione* 1.53.100) regarding the intensification of rhetoric in the *indignatio*. A similar antonomastic list of eleven names is directed against Giangaleazzo in a letter sent by Florence to Count Jean III d'Armagnac on 6 November 1390 (Langkabel, ep. 124, p. 276).

205. This paragraph relies on Valerius Maximus; in this note references are given only for the lesser-known figures. For Lucius Munatius Flaccus, see Valerius Maximus 9.2.4; for Xerxes, see Cicero, *Tusculan Disputations* 5.7.20, and Valerius Maximus 9.1 ext. 3. Clodius appears in numerous major works of Cicero, but the vocabulary indicates that Salutati's source here is *Ad Atticum* 1.16.5. For Publius Mucius, see Valerius Maximus 6.3.2 (reading envy as the cause of an action is discussed in the section *De severitate*); for Aglaurus see Ovid, *Metamorphoses* 2.708–83,5 and Dante, *Purgatorio* 14.139. Fundanus is the protagonist of Plutarch's *Of Anger*; on Salutati's interest in this text see S. U. Baldassarri, *Umanesimo e traduzione* (cited in note 5), pp. 66–70; idem, "Prime ricerche per un'edizione critica della *Invectiva in Antonium Luscum*," *Medioevo e Rinascimento* 22 (2008): 105–29, on p. 128; *La vipera e il giglio*, p. 41, and the entry by D. Speranzi in *Catalogo*, pp. 86–87. For Lucius Settimuleius, see Valerius Maximus 9.4.3, and Cicero, *De oratore* 2.67.269; for Quintus Cassius Longinus, see Valerius Maximus 9.4.2. The first writer to mention (if not invent) the medieval legend of Bladud was Geoffrey of Monmouth, *Historia regum Britanniae*; for the popularity of the story into the early Renaissance, see J. Clark, "Bladud of Bath: The Archaeology of a Legend," *Folklore* 105 (1994): 39–50. "Trinovantum" or "New Troy" corresponds to today's London.

206. Defamation is the subject of Salutati's rhetorical piece known as *Questio est coram decemviris*, for which see the essay of M. Laureys in *Catalogo*, pp. 195–96, with further references.

207. This phrase, typical of formal disputes, also appears in Salutati, *De nobilitate* 1 (ed. Garin, p. 12).

208. Jerome, *Epistles* 68.2, with reference to the celebrated duel in Vergil, *Aeneid* 5.368–484.

209. See Cicero, *De senectute* 55.

210. For the rhetorical figure of *exclamatio*, or apostrophe, see *Rhetorica ad Herrenium* 4.15.22.

211. For this synthesis of the art of rhetoric, see the precepts in Cicero, *De inventione* 1.55.107.

212. See above, §7.

213. Terence, *Eunuch* vv. 102–6.

Bibliography

༺❧༻

EDITIONS AND TRANSLATIONS

SELECTED STATE LETTERS

Langkabel, Heinrich. *Die Staatsbriefe Coluccio Salutatis. Untersuchungen zum Frühhumanismus in der Florentiner Staatskanzlei und Auswahledition.* Cologne-Vienna: Böhlau, 1981.

Salutati, Coluccio. *Epistolae.* Edited by G. Rigacci. 2 vols. Florence: Bruscagli, 1741–42.

ON TYRANNY

Emerton, Ephraim. *Humanism and Tyranny. Studies in the Italian Trecento.* Cambridge, MA: Harvard University Press, 1925. Reprint, Gloucester, MA: Smith, 1964. English translation on pp. 25–116.

Martin, Alfred von. *Traktat vom Tyrannen von C. Salutati: eine kulturgeschichtlichen Untersuchung nebst Textedition.* Berlin-Leipzig: Rothschild, 1913.

Salutati, Coluccio. *Tractatus de Tyranno.* Edited by Francesco Ercole. Berlin-Leipzig: Rothschild, 1914.

———. *Il Trattato "De tyranno" e lettere scelte.* Edited by Francesco Ercole. Bologna: Zanichelli, 1942. Italian translation on pp. 153–84.

INVECTIVA AGAINST THE FLORENTINES

Baldassarri, Stefano Ugo. "La *Invectiva in Florentinos* di Antonio Loschi." *Esperienze Letterarie* 35.1 (2010): 3–28. Italian translation on pp. 18–28.

———. *La vipera e il giglio. Lo scontro tra Milano e Firenze nelle invettive di Antonio Loschi e Coluccio Salutati.* Rome: Aracne, 2012. Italian translation on pp. 135–44.

Fabbri, Renata. "Per l'edizione della *Invectiva in florentinos* di Antonio Loschi." In *Coluccio Salutati cancelliere e politico. Atti del Convegno internazionale del Comitato nazionale delle celebrazioni del VI centenario della morte di Coluccio Salutati. Firenze-Prato, 9–12 dicembre 2008,* edited by Roberto Cardini and Paolo Viti, 307–33. Florence: Polistampa, 2012.

LETTER TO PIETRO TURCHI

Salutati, Coluccio. *Epistolario*. Edited by Francesco Novati, 3:634–40. Rome: Istituto Storico Italiano per il Medio Evo, 1910.

REPLY TO A SLANDEROUS DETRACTOR

Baldassarri. *La vipera e il giglio* (cited above). Italian translation on pp. 237–329.

Invectiva Lini Colucii Salutati Reipublicae Florentinae a secretis in Antonium Luschum Vicentinum de eadem republica male sentientem. Edited by Domenico Moreni, 1–198. Florence: Magheri, 1826.

SELECTED MODERN STUDIES

Baldassarri. "La *Invectiva in Florentinos* di Antonio Loschi" (cited above).
——. *La vipera e il giglio* (cited above).

Baron, Hans. *The Crisis of the Early Italian Renaissance. Civic Humanism and Republican Liberty in an Age of Classicism and Tyranny.* Princeton, NJ: Princeton University Press, 1966.

Bueno de Mesquita, Daniel Meredith. *Giangaleazzo Visconti Duke of Milan (1351–1402). A study in the Political Career of an Italian Despot.* Cambridge: Cambridge University Press, 1941.

Coluccio Salutati e Firenze. Ideologia e formazione dello Stato. Edited by Roberto Cardini and Paolo Viti. Florence: Pagliai, 2008.

Coluccio Salutati e l'invenzione dell'Umanesimo. Atti del Convegno internazionale di studi, Firenze, 29–31 ottobre 2008. Edited by Concetta Bianca. Rome: Edizioni di storia e letteratura, 2010.

Coluccio Salutati e l'invenzione dell'Umanesimo. Catalogo della mostra tenutasi a Firenze, Biblioteca Medicea Laurenziana, 2 novembre 2008–30 gennaio 2009. Edited by Teresa De Robertis, Giuliano Tanturli, and Stefano Zamponi. Florence: Mandragora, 2008.

De Rosa, Daniela. *Coluccio Salutati. Il cancelliere e il pensatore politico.* Florence: La Nuova Italia, 1980.

Faraone, Giovanni. *Antonio Loschi e Antonio da Romagno.* Messina: Centro Interdipartimentale di Studi Umanistici, 2006.

Hankins, James. "Coluccio Salutati e Leonardo Bruni." In *Il contributo italiano alla storia del pensiero. Ottava Appendice: Filosofia*, edited by Michele Ciliberto, 85–94. Rome: Istituto della Enciclopedia Italiana, 2012.

———. "Exclusivist Republicanism and the Non-Monarchical Republic." *Political Theory* 38.4 (2010): 452–82.

Langkabel, Heinrich. *Die Staatsbriefe Coluccio Salutatis* (cited above).

Tanturli, Giuliano. "Un nodo cronologico e tematico: *L'Invectiva in Florentinos* d'Antonio Loschi, la risposta di Coluccio Salutati e la *Laudatio Florentine urbis* di Leonardo Bruni." In *L'Humanisme italien de la Renaissance et l'Europe (Aix-en-Provence, 13–14 mars 2008)*. Edited by Théa Picquet, Lucien Faggion, and Pascal Gandoulphe, 109–19. Aix-en-Provence: Publications de l'Université de Provence, 2010.

Ullman, Berthold Louis. *The Humanism of Coluccio Salutati*. Padua: Antenore, 1963.

Viti, Paolo. "Loschi, Antonio." In *Dizionario biografico degli Italiani*, vol. 66, cols. 154–60. Rome: Istituto della Enciclopedia Italiana, 2006.

Witt, Ronald Gene. *Hercules at the Crossroads. The Life, Works, and Thought of Coluccio Salutati*. Durham, NC: Duke University Press, 1983.

Zaccaria, Vittore. "Antonio Loschi e Coluccio Salutati (con quattro epistole inedite del Loschi)." *Atti dell'Istituto Veneto di Scienze, Lettere ed Arti. Classe di scienze morali, lettere ed arti* 129 (1970–71): 345–87.

———. "Le epistole e i carmi di Antonio Loschi durante il cancellierato visconteo (con tredici inediti)." *Atti della Accademia Nazionale dei Lincei. Memorie. Classe di scienze morali, storiche e filologiche*, s. VIII, 18.5 (1975): 367–443.

Zaggia, Massimo. "Linee per una storia della cultura in Lombardia dall'età di Coluccio Salutati a quella del Valla." In *Le strade di Ercole. Itinerari umanistici e altri percorsi. Seminario internazionale per i centenari di Coluccio Salutati e Lorenzo Valla (Bergamo, 25–26 ottobre 2007)*, edited by Luca Carlo Rossi, 3–125. Florence: SISMEL, 2010.

Index

203; church dedicated to Holy Apostles, 363; Parione area, 203; Piazza della Repubblica, 446n36; Ponte Vecchio, 203; statue of Mars, 203; Temple of Mars, 203, 446n39; via Campidoglio, 446n36; via delle Terme, 446n38; via Torta, 446n37; via Vecchietti, 446n36

Florentia (ancient name of Florence), 209–11, 213, 448n56

Florentine Studium (university), xii

Florentini, 209

Florentinum (Latin name for Ferentino), 213

Florus, 91, 115, 213, 447n54, 448n56; *Epitome*, 115, 213, 431n35, 431n42, 432n46, 434n98, 435n112, 436nn129–30, 436n134, 444n16, 446n41, 447n54, 456n123, 460n160, 461n169, 461n175

Fluentia/Fluentini, 209–11

Forlì, ix

Fortune, xix, 355

Forum Vibii, 461n170

France/French, x, xxii–xxiii, 25, 43, 51, 155–65, 293–309, 323, 325, 333–35, 339, 345, 353, 355, 438n14, 438n18, 440n30, 461n171. *See also* Franks; Gaul/Gauls

Franciscan Order, xxxi n30, 398

Franco-Milanese alliance, 459n155

Franks, 19, 23, 25, 303, 307. *See also* Gaul/Gauls

Frederick I Barbarossa, Holy Roman Emperor, 55, 428n49

Frederick II, Holy Roman Emperor, 11, 55, 289, 425n13, 428n49

Frosinone, 448n55

Fundanus, 389, 467n205

Furies, 165, 187, 197, 303, 373, 440n35

Furius Camillus, Marcus, 119, 357

Galilee, 211

Gallia Comata, 359, 461n171

Gallia/Gallic, 67, 303, 307, 327, 357, 359, 461n169. *See also* Gaul/Gauls

Gallia Narbonensis, 460n160

Gallia Togata, 359, 461n171

Gallican, 339

Galli Senones, 357, 361, 371, 461n169

Gambacorta, Pietro (lord of Pisa), 41, 43, 427n38, 437n8

Gaul, Cisalpine, 163, 265, 301, 321, 371, 373, 461n171

Gaul, Transalpine, 155, 293, 317, 357, 461n171

Gaul/Gauls, 5–7, 17–19, 85–87, 107, 119, 265, 267, 305, 307, 313, 321, 325–35, 341, 353, 357–61, 369–73, 387, 440n30, 458n143, 461n171

Geneva, 341

Genoa/Genoese, 157, 295, 311, 323, 343, 345, 351, 353, 381, 450n79, 458n145, 459n155, 465n197

Geoffrey of Monmouth, *Historia regum Britanniae*, 467n205

Publication of this volume has been made possible by

The Myron and Sheila Gilmore Publication Fund at I Tatti
The Robert Lehman Endowment Fund
The Jean-François Malle Scholarly Programs and Publications Fund
The Andrew W. Mellon Scholarly Publications Fund
The Craig and Barbara Smyth Fund
for Scholarly Programs and Publications
The Lila Wallace–Reader's Digest Endowment Fund
The Malcolm Wiener Fund for Scholarly Programs and Publications